HOW TO BUILD
BUSINESS-WIDE DATABASES

John E. Gessford

John Wiley & Sons, Inc.

New York • Chichester • Brisbane • Toronto • Singapore

Copyright © 1991 by John E. Gessford

Published by John Wiley & Sons, Inc.

ISBN 0-471-53227-4

Printed in the United States of America
10 9 8 7 6 5 4 3 2 1

Preface

There is a problem in the management of the information systems of an organization. The interests of individual functional units within the organization must be balanced against the interests of the organization as a whole. The individual functional unit has an interest in developing computer systems to serve its purposes. The organization as a whole has an interest in developing systems that are integrated and coordinated with respect to hardware, system software, application software, and data. If one or the other of these sometimes conflicting interests is given too much weight, the performance of the organization as a whole suffers.

Since the advent of computer systems, the interests of the individual functional unit in applying the computer to its particular processing needs have dominated the way systems are designed in most organizations. The system development life cycle (SDLC) has long been the only widely understood and accepted paradigm in the field of information systems. It describes how the individual information system—the application—should be planned, developed, installed, and maintained. It is adequate from the viewpoint of the individual functional unit within an organization who wants information systems that will serve the purposes of the unit.

Any assertion of organization-wide interests must interface effectively with the SDLC. The widespread use of the SDLC concept and its suitability for individual application development efforts makes it a useful model upon which to build. The concept of asserting organization-wide interests by building upon the SDLC was advanced by IBM when it introduced business systems planning (BSP) in the early 1970s. BSP added a top-down systems planning methodology to the SDLC which, by contrast, became a bottom-up planning method.

In practice, BSP has proven to be burdensome and ineffective in asserting the interests of the organization as a whole. a well-founded, comprehensive plan for the information systems of the organization is developed but it is ignored or overruled by subsequent development project teams. The business-wide information structuring (BWIS) approach explained in this book is less burdensome because it does not attempt to define all the information systems of the organization. It defines only "information structures"—descriptions of the data of the organization in terms of entity types and relationships. By concentrating only on this description of data needs (at the entity level), the new approach simplifies the plan that must be developed and evolved at a business-wide level.

At the same time, BWIS overcomes the ineffectiveness of BSP by creating a data plan that is more explicit. Data requirements put in terms of entity types and relationships are less ambiguous than the same requirements stated in terms of "subjects." They can more easily be translated within the SDLC into detailed database specifications; there is no ambiguity concerning exactly how the data on a given subject must be organized to be shareable. Nevertheless, a high-level data administration function is needed to make this translation and evolve the business-wide, sharable database.

The distinguishing proposition on which the BWIS approach is based, then, is that it is not necessary to have a comprehensive plan for *all* of the information systems of an organization in order to coordinate their development. The basis for coordination can be a clear definition of the data that should be shared, plus guidelines for computer and communication hardware and systems software acquisitions.

Identifying data as the key to coordinating application software developments leads to an emphasis on the data plan. The data plan, or conceptual database, must be well-founded and not subject to an overhaul with every organizational and personnel change. Thus, a data-planning methodology is needed that produces a plan based on the strategic goals of the enterprise and the fundamental imperatives of the industry in which the firm operates.

The BWIS data planning methodology does this. It is based on three well-known management concepts. They are

1. The leadership role of top management

2. The business functional model

3. The concept of functional information requirements.

The first key concept of BWIS is that top management must play a leadership role in the management of information systems. These systems cannot *support* only strategic goals of the business, they can *be* strategic goals of the business. Information systems can be used to gain a competitive advantage, but only senior management can integrate information systems into the strategies of the business. In *Management Tasks, Responsibilities, Practices* (Harper & Row, 1974), Peter F. Drucker lists as the first task of top management,

> . . . thinking through the mission of the business, that is, of asking the question "What is our business and what should it be?" This leads to the setting of objectives, the development of strategies and plans, and the making of today's decisions for tomorrow's results. This clearly can be done only by an organ of the business that can see the entire business; that can make decisions that affect the entire business; that can balance objectives and the needs of today against the needs of tomorrow; and that can allocate resources of men and money to key results.

The second basic BWIS proposition can be expressed by the Drucker maxim: Objectives must degenerate into work. The functional model defines the path of degeneration from strategic goals to work. As explained in Chapter 4, it defines what has to be done to achieve the purposes of the business.

The third proposition of BWIS is that the data the business should treat as a resource is the data required to effectively and efficiently execute the functions identified in the functional model. An entity-relationship approach is taken to describe these data requirements (Chapters 2, 3, and 5). The approach begins with the information needs of the top-level function. This function requires information about the purposes and goals of the business and resources available to fulfill them. To balance short-term against long-term goals, information is required about the ways in which existing resources constrain what can be accomplished in the short run. This set of information requirements is made the basis of the primary information structure in BWIS as explained in Chapter 5. Through a process of information structure decomposition, the information requirements of lower level functions are derived from the information requirements of top management. When the decomposed structures are integrated (as explained in Chapter 12), the result is a business-wide information structure that describes the information requirements implied by the mission and goals of the enterprise as defined by top management.

This information structure, together with the functional model on which it is based, are intended to serve as guidelines for individual system development projects that are developed according to the SDLC. The incentives for using these guidelines are two-fold. First, it simplifies each step of the SDLC and improves the quality of the result, particularly for the first step, which is system investigation and planning. This is explained in Chapter 14.

Second, the BWIS plan results in information systems that share data. All system development projects that adopt the business-wide information structure build systems that can share data. This means cost savings in data encoding and storage activities. But, more importantly, it means data access flexibility for managerial decision making. A standard information structure for the organization encourages analysts and managers to become familiar with the structure and reach out from their desktop computers for data heretofore unavailable. They are able to correlate data from different functional areas in ways not envisioned when the individual information systems were designed. This opens up new opportunities for managers to see actions that need to be taken today so that they can be in a position to take advantage of future opportunities. For example, the on-time delivery-to-customer performance can be correlated with repeat orders from customers to assess the value of maintaining spare production capacity, or inventory, to enhance on-time delivery capability.

The current method of providing this kind of data access is to set up a secondary database (information center database) that contains a copy of selected data from the operational database. Organizations that can afford the expense of these duplicate databases, and that can tolerate the less than current and complete data in the secondary database, will not be moved by the access advantages of BWIS. For these large organizations, however, the proliferation of microcomputers and the tendency toward distribution of data to departmental computing systems is eroding the utility of the secondary databases and creating another data management problem that requires a business-wide conceptual database for its solution. To share data located on departmental file-servers, standard data definitions and structures are needed.

The characterization of the distributed system planning problem in Chapter 13 shows that it is not merely relational tables of data that need to be distributed, but rather "chunks" of data that may span multiple relations. There is an understandable tendency among the more mathematically inclined to want to overlook the nonlinear, holistic aspects of the system distribution alternatives. This encourages the application of linear programming and other simple algorithms to the problem. The relational data model has encouraged this by hiding relationships between relations in foreign keys where they can be ignored all too easily. The analysis of information requirements by location presented in Chapter 13 shows how requirements defined in terms of information structures identify constraints on the distribution alternatives that should not be overlooked.

The BWIS methodology is built on the entity-relationship (E-R) approach to modeling data. Accordingly, some familiarity with this approach and its diagramming conventions is needed. Chapters 2 and 3 provide an explanation of the E-R approach. The basic concepts and diagramming conventions are contained in Chapter 2. Examples important to business are given in Chapter 3. Unfortunately, space does not permit including a complete tutorial on the E-R model and its normal forms. The correct resolution of the more complex design problems using the E-R approach is usually obtained by applying the normal forms of the relational model. The reader who does not find the explanations of Chapters 2 and 3 adequate is referred to a text on relational database design.

The information structures developed here can be converted to any of the basic data models (network, hierarchical, relational, object-oriented) on which most database management system (DBMS) software is based. The paradigm described here makes no assumptions about the DBMS software used to implement a particular set of applications. It is applicable regardless of the data model used for implementation purposes.

One of the satisfactions in writing a book on an advanced topic is the coherence that can be achieved as compared to that of a collection of journal articles. It allows the reader to penetrate the subject more deeply and to see the subject as a whole rather than as a set of briefly sketched, independent views. Seeing readers master this material and begin to add to it with examples and points of their own has been rewarding.

The support provided by The Claremont Graduate School's Information Science Department and its chairman, Paul Gray, has been vital to this work. It has been a delight to see the Macintosh skills of a graduate student, Jon Wright, transform messy sketches and a draft manuscript into a quality, professional publication for local student use. The editorial assistance of other graduate students, particularly Steve Curl and Jeanne Harris, is gratefully acknowledged. The expression of new views and ideas is inevitably imperfect, but these students have worked tirelessly to identify errors and gaps in the exposition.

The effort put into writing takes time away from other projects. A significant portion of this time loss has consequences for an author's family. The patience of my wife during this time is very much appreciated.

JOHN E. GESSFORD

San Marino, California
July 1991

Contents

PART 1

METHOD OF APPROACH

The notion of database management has been around for several decades now. Many software suppliers offer database management systems and a large number of organizations with computers have one or more of these systems. What approach is being taken to *using* database management systems? Is the same basic approach being taken to application software development as was taken before database management system software was available? Are applications developed more or less independently, using a project by project approach? If so, then methodology has lagged behind technology.

In most organizations, methodology has lagged behind technology because the leadership needed to change the basic approach to information systems development has been lacking. Managers have not understood the opportunity afforded by technology, and the technicians who understand the opportunity have not taken the opportunity to lead.

The objective for Part 1 is to present a way to manage the development of data processing systems that will greatly increase the flexibility and compatibility of these systems while at the same time reducing the cost and time required to build them. This approach requires senior management leadership as well as an investment in database planning, Computer-Aided Software Engineering (CASE) tools and staff training. The payoff is improved organizational effectiveness and a capacity to survive in the fast-paced, computerized world of the twenty-first century.

1

The Information Systems Management Opportunity

Database planning is commonly limited to planning the database for a specific information system, one that serves a specific business function. A DataBase Management System (DBMS) may be used to implement a single-application database while existing Computer-Aided Software Engineering (CASE) tools often only support the definition of a database for a single application.

The purpose of this chapter is to show that database planning *should not* be confined to one information system. It explains why the scope is usually not broader and why it should be. Then some failed attempts to broaden the scope are reviewed and an approach that avoids such failure is described.

Many incompatible databases arise when management fails to lead in the development of information systems. It takes strong leadership to coordinate achieving the goals of the business by using broad-based information systems. Companies in a variety of industries that have gained an advantage by developing uncommon information systems (American Airlines, McKesson, Banc One, Allen-Bradley, for example) have had strong support for their development from top management.* The integrative systems developed by these companies have enabled them to respond more quickly and flexibly to customer needs.

The *approach* taken to database planning and development is key to successfully building systems that make a competitive difference. The way in which a database can serve as a link between information systems is illustrated in Figure 1.1. It requires that the systems be designed to share the same database. The idea of linking systems to the same database simplifies systems development, increases the utility of individual information systems, and makes possible better use of the data resources of the business.

---

* The strategic advantages these and other companies have gained through the development of innovative information systems have been described in a number of publications, including *Information Systems: A Strategic Approach* (Omaha, NB: Mountain Top Publishing, 1990).

3

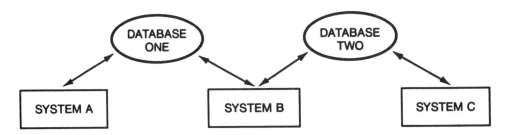

FIGURE 1.1.   Systems sharing databases.

Causing the forces that define systems to accommodate links between systems is the key to managing the development of integrated systems. The intervention must not be so heavy-handed that it forestalls middle management system development initiatives. On the other hand, more than generalities and platitudes are required to avoid the many minor incompatibilities that prevent one system from "talking" to another. Managing this balance should be considered one of the basic top management challenges.

HOW INFORMATION SYSTEMS GET DEFINED

In computer science, defining an information system is often considered to be a technical problem. In the real world, however, defining information systems is more of a managerial problem than a technical one. Organizational power structures have a large influence on information system definitions.

In theory, managing the planning and development of any kind of system, including an information system, is straightforward. A system consists of parts that must work together to achieve a purpose. Managing the creation process is a matter of defining and redefining the parts needed and testing to make sure they work together to produce the desired result.

The managerial aspect of this design and development process lies in the definition of the purpose of the system. This purpose greatly influences the *scope of the system* and its desired results. Defining the scope and objective of a system may be the most significant creative act in the development process. The clock-radio, for example, is a system composed of two older systems. Conceiving the idea of a new *scope* was the key step in creating this new product.

There are compelling reasons to combine information systems and there are compelling reasons not to do so. Evaluating the pros and cons becomes a key managerial imperative. The reasons for combining systems have to do with the advantages of sharing data, programs, support services, and hardware. For example, no one wants to have three terminals because he or she needs to access three different, noncompatible systems.

The reasons for not combining systems are the advantages of simplicity. The manager of an accounts payable group that is paying the same invoice twice if submitted twice by the vender, because records of previous payments to a supplier are not available, does not want to wait a year (or more) for a purchasing management system to be put in place. He wants a simple listing of payments sorted by suppliers that can be developed quickly.

HOW THE ORGANIZATION DEALS WITH SYSTEM DEFINITION

The manager of accounts payable is responsible for a subfunction of the procurement function of the organization. The procurement function is in turn a subfunction of the supply operations (or production) function of the organization. Let us assume that the production function is a subfunction of the Chief Executive Officer (CEO) function that has responsibility for running the entire business.

When it comes to the design of information systems, however, these different levels in the organization want different characteristics and capabilities. The payables function, for example, wants a system that accounts only for what was ordered from suppliers, what was delivered, where payments are to be sent, and what has already been paid for. The supply operations function wants the system to include information on the quality of the product delivered, whether product was delivered on time, and what each supplier potentially could deliver. The CEO wants a system that also identifies, for example, suppliers who are also customers, suppliers who are willing to invest in the business, and suppliers who are willing to be bought out.

In theory, the subject in which the accounts payable, operations, and CEO functions have a common interest is the organization's relations with its suppliers. It should be possible to design a supplier relations database that includes the details of interest to each of these levels in the hierarchy. A single system can then be developed to capture and make available this data to all levels in the hierarchy on a need-to-know basis.

In practice, this seldom happens. Instead, three balkanized systems are created: one for the CEO, one for the Operations Director and one for the Accounts Payable Manager. Two plausible reasons for this outcome can be cited. One is that past experience shows that the time and cost of building information systems increases exponentially with the size of the system. The other reason is the "not-invented-here" syndrome. For these reasons, a tug-of-war over the scope of the system to be used by the manager of accounts payable is likely to be won by that manager. He or she has two advantages in the debate: (1) restricting the scope of the system to the needs of the single function minimizes system development time and cost, and (2) any system provided to support accounts payable needs the resolve of the manager of the function to make it successful.

ROLE OF THE I/S DEPARTMENT IN SYSTEM DEFINITION

As a practical matter, the power of the Information Systems (I/S) department to represent the interests of higher levels of management in the design of systems for lower-level functions is limited. In the first place, I/S analysts usually do not know what data senior managers need. More generally, I/S is often not in a position to dictate to other organizational units.

As an example, consider the advent of the Personal Computer (PC) in the early 1980s. Procurement of microcomputer by individuals and low-level groups in many organizations was met by strong control measures. The veto power granted Information Systems Departments over computer system procurement decisions in the 1960s because of the large cost and complexity of those systems was used in the 1980s to prevent the proliferation of small "user friendly" desktop computers.

But many I/S managers who used that tactic lost political power and some even lost their jobs. They acquired the image of an obstacle to progress in the eyes of the line and other staff departments. They were not providing application development at the rate demanded by the organization and, at the same time, they were denying the more self-reliant managers the right to develop computer applications on their own.

The wiser I/S managers expanded or converted the "information centers" they had developed in the seventies (to make corporate data available on-line) to provide end-user computing support to individuals and departments interested in building their own microcomputer systems. This end-user computing support service enabled the I/S Department to at least keep in touch with the microcomputer and minicomputer systems mushrooming in all parts of the organization. In many cases, this service managed to channel end-user initiatives in prescribed directions in terms of the brands of hardware and software.

The title of a book written in 1987 by Joe Izzo, a leading information systems consultant, nicely describes the viewpoint of many I/S department managers who daily faced an array of grass-roots system development initiatives: *The Embattled Fortress*. The book accepts as a fact of life the power of the end-user to obtain systems that effectively support his or her business function. It argues that this power can be channeled to fit within a "system architecture." The I/S manager is encouraged to think that by deftly putting in place an official system architecture that includes a role for individual and departmental computer systems, a mainframe computer center can be maintained. Regardless of the validity of this thesis, it is evidence that the viewpoint and aims of employees and department managers concerning computer systems are a powerful force that discerning central computing system managers take into account.

LIMITATIONS OF THE APPLICATION PROGRAM VIEWPOINT

The traditional approach to developing software reinforces the tendency of the political forces within an organization to create many independent and incompatible information systems. The traditional approach is to develop software for a particular business function as an independent project. Such software is called *application software.*

We discussed the tendency of people responsible for subfunctions to have unique objectives and priorities. These objectives can be congruent with the organizational goals and yet be distinctive. When an individual responsible for a subfunction finances the development of an information system to support the execution of that subfunction, his or her priorities influence the design of that system, particularly any customized application software included in the system.

Limiting attention to the current needs of a specific functional group results in software that has two shortcomings: (1) The customized software is difficult to revise as the needs of the group change, and (2) the data processed by the programs is usually not easily available to other application programs.

Consider word processing as an example of the first shortcoming. Organizations that acquired word processing software in the early 1980s and later installed electronic mail and FAX machines commonly observed that their word processing software could be better integrated with their electronic mail and FAX systems. Why were the word processing vendors so slow in accommodating their software to the new office environment? The customized, self-sufficient nature of each of the word processing, FAX, and electronic mail application packages made it difficult for any one vendor to integrate the three applications.

The other shortcoming of application systems occurs when one system could use data captured by another system. This often happens between transaction processing and decision support systems. For example, consider a bus route planning application and a bus operations management application. The planning system needs data about bus riders, buses, drivers, traffic conditions, and seasonal variations. The operations management system captures this type of data for use in monitoring operations. But the data in the operations management system is often not accessible to the bus route planning system because the data that the two systems have in common is organized differently in each system. As a result, all the data required for bus route planning must be entered separately into the files of that system.

The concept of an application program as a system exists because groups (departments and other organizational units) see it as suited to their unique objectives. The application program is the type of system for which they are willing to pay. As we argued in a previous section, there are sound management reasons for leaving information systems procurement decisions with local work groups and their managers. Thus, the application view of information systems is a fact of life that is not going to disappear.

OTHER CENTRIFUGAL FORCES

In addition to the tendency of the organizational hierarchy to produce specialized systems, there are other exogenous forces pushing toward balkanization of information systems. The increasing capability and low cost of microcomputers relative to mainframes is one example. As microcomputers become more cost effective, it becomes more difficult to centrally control their use by departments, sections, and small work groups throughout the organization. The result is myriad small, incompatible systems.

The quantum leap in computer sophistication of the new generation of managers in organizations is another force leading to more independent system development initiatives. The generation that used the Apples and PCs sold in the early 1980s is now out of school and moving into the workforce. As this generation moves into managerial positions, we can be sure that they will be far more likely to take on the development of software for applications within their purview than were their predecessors.

The growing attractiveness of automation as a means of direct labor cost reduction broadens the scope of computer usage in business, creating additional application systems. Vendors of automation equipment build their own computer software systems that have data definitions appropriate to the subfunctions automated. The customer buying this equipment may not even have access to some of the data used by the automation equipment.

The development of computer networking systems is eroding the advantages of centralized mainframe transaction processing systems which makes it easier to develop specializations of transaction processing systems in each department. The benefits of the added transaction processing features may justify the specialization, but it tends to further balkanize the information systems of the organization.

At this point, the reality and importance of the forces pushing in the direction of many independent information systems, each optimized to serve the purposes of its users, should be clear. They are the forces that have dominated the design of most of the information systems in use today. Why should we not expect them to continue to dominate? We explore this question in the next section.

WHY PLAN THE DATABASE BUSINESS-WIDE?

The major reason for coordinating the use of data across an organization is the same as the reason for establishing standards for communication between army, navy, and air force units engaged in battle against a common enemy. It is not sufficient that different parts of the organization share a common goal. They must also work from a common base of information or else they will be uncoordinated and will end up blaming one another for failures.

The way in which goals, information, and resources interact to determine what an organization accomplishes needs to be better understood. In one sense, information (data) is a resource because it enables people to effectively execute the functions that need to be performed to achieve the goals of the organization. But, information is different from other resources in the way it shapes goals and guides the use of other resources. Information is not just another resource.

Information shared and communicated is probably the best means for coordinating the daily work of different organizational units in an organization. The goals of the organization determine the organizational units that are needed (in the long run) and they can be used to set up measures of performance and incentives for individual managers as well as for the organization as a whole. However, it takes shared information to really coordinate the work of different parts of an organization on an hour-by-hour and day-by-day basis.

As explained in the last section, the natural tendency of individual managers to develop information systems customized to the needs of their organizational unit leads to a balkanized collection of systems that inhibit the sharing of information. Each unit develops its own version of what is going on and what needs to be done to achieve the goals of the business. The result is misunderstandings and uncoordinated responses to the needs of customers and suppliers.

To obtain fast, coordinated organizational responses to customer requests, data processing systems that transcend organizational boundaries are needed. Interorganizational boundaries as well as intraorganization boundaries may need to be transcended. Such systems can deliver the intelligence each person in the organization(s) needs to work with others in achieving the goals of the organization(s).

The underlying drive to develop information systems clearly should and does come from those who stand to benefit directly from the use of them. But, too often this drive comes from units far down in the organization. As we have seen, such initiatives lead to many separate, narrowly defined systems suited to the needs of the individual department. The manager who is in a position to make an information system profitable and commits to doing so is usually the one who gets the funds and "calls the shots."

The question is, how should upper-level management exert a countervailing force for coordination and integration of information systems? In cases where upper-level management has simply taken over systems development, the result has been "very large systems," which are defined by Dan Appleton, a prominent consultant, as projects that are never completed.[1] A more effective approach is one that creates an environment within which the proactive manager builds his systems. This environment channels the primary creative forces in ways that create systems that transcend organizational boundaries.

A business-wide database plan plays a vital role in creating this environment. It establishes standard ways of organizing and referring to data. It opens the way for systems that can access a common database as illustrated in Figure 1.1. The systems need not be designed and developed as one large system. They can be developed independently and at different times. They only need to conform to the standards set in the business-wide data plan.

When data are viewed as a resource that exists independently of any application system that uses it, the idea of sharing it becomes obvious. As long as it is considered a part of the software of an application, making it available to another application system seems very difficult and not worth the effort.

OTHER REASONS FOR DATABASE PLANNING

A more coordinated and responsive organization is the major reason for business-wide database planning. Other advantages to be gained by managing data on a business-wide basis include:

1. *Access to more data.* In a shared database, all the data are available to each user group that has a valid need to access the data (and the appropriate access codes). This assumes an adequate data communication system is in place.

2. *Shared programs.* Business functions performed at multiple locations can use the same application software if they use the same database design (or the same database). This means that the cost of developing and maintaining the programs can be spread over multiple sites.

3. *Use of compatible purchased software.* Two or more software packages that use the same commands to access a database (SQL commands, for example) and that are designed to access databases that have the same design can share data. Purchased software that does not have these two characteristics results in independent databases that can only be shared by "importing" and "exporting" data, a complex, slow process.

4. *Reduced data capture expense.* Keying in data needs to be done only once when data are shared. Product descriptions, for example, need not be entered separately into the sales, purchasing, manufacturing, inventory, engineering, and other systems. If product descriptions are shared by these systems, they need be entered only once in order to be accessed by all. Independent application systems usually have independent data capture modules and therefore much duplication of both data entry and data storage.

5. *Reduced data expense.* To the extent that two or more applications are using the same physical database, only one copy of the data (instead of two or more) needs to be held in on-line storage (usually disk storage).

6. *Inconsistent data avoided.* When two executives at a meeting present contradictory data on the same subject, a great deal of expensive professional time can be consumed in reconciling the data. The discrepancy is often due to a technical difference in the way updates to the databases are handled in the two application systems.

7. *Improved interface between systems.* The output of one system is often input for another system. For example, the output of a CAD system in engineering is a product definition that must be reviewed by the manufacturing engineers if the product is to be produced in-house. Unless design and manufacturing engineering have integrated databases, a data capture (or data conversion) operation must be performed before production planning analysis can take place.

Information systems departments generally have not been able to develop systems that share a common database, according to a survey conducted by the Sloan School of Management.[2] What they have done is extract data from the files of separate systems and put it into an "information center database" that is accessible to managers and analysts. This provides the first of the seven advantages from data sharing listed, but it fails to provide the other six advantages. If maintaining a duplicate database is worthwhile because of the access it provides, the greater benefits of real systems integration (corporate coordination and the other six minor benefits) must certainly be worthwhile if a workable way to build such systems can be found.

THE VERY LARGE SYSTEM SYNDROME

It is easy to fall into the trap of thinking that the solution to incompatible systems is one large system. In the case of information systems, there is considerable evidence that this apparent solution is a trap. What seems to be a straightforward solution to the problem of balkanized systems turns into a quagmire in many cases. Very large systems lead to an uncontrollable development expense and defective systems. Three reports on this experience follow.

BUSINESS SYSTEMS PLANNING

IBM's version of the very large system approach is called Business Systems Planning (BSP). It was introduced by IBM in the early 1970s, just after the first database management systems were developed. A revised version was published in 1984.[3] It is an elaborate methodology that has been used by many companies. Variations on it are used by many systems consulting organizations today. A careful review of it helps to reveal the scope and complexity of the potential information systems of a business.

To deal with the tendency of the organizational hierarchy to create many incompatible information systems, BSP takes a "top-down" approach. BSP is done as a project that is initiated by the Chief Executive Officer (CEO) of the organization. The project has a team leader and is carried out by a team of upper and middle management people who together have expertise in all the major functional areas of the business. The team leader reports to an "executive sponsor" who reports directly to the CEO.

BSP Methodology

The BSP methodology is summarized in the diagram shown in Figure 1.2. The fact that it is a top-down approach is reflected in the first step of Figure 1.2: to gain the support of the top executives for the project. No lesser person than the chief executive must encourage all senior executives to cooperate with the project team in defining what information the organization needs.

The second and third steps in Figure 1.2 are concerned with various preparations for the project and background briefings on the organization and its existing information systems. The fourth step, "defining business processes," forms the basis for the analysis of data requirements and the definition of a system architecture. Its aim is to explicitly define a functional model of the business. In BSP, the term "process" is often used as a synonym for "business function." We will consider business functional modeling in more detail in Chapter 4.

The next step, "defining business data," identifies the information needed to run the business. It describes this information in terms of "entity types" and "classes of data" for each entity type. Entity types are described in more detail in Chapter 2, but basically, they identify the things about which information is needed. For example, "customer" and "employee" are two common entity types. A data class is a set of facts about an entity type that is captured (and "owned") by a single functional unit of the organization. For each entity type, there can be multiple data classes.

The sixth step, "defining information architecture," is done by identifying groups of business processes (defined in Step 4) that create data about a certain group of data classes (defined in Step 5). The results of this grouping of processes and data classes can be summarized in a table. An example is shown in Figure 1.3. Looking along the diagonal from the upper left of this table to the lower right corner, you will see a series of rectangles. Each rectangle defines a planned "information system." It is defined by the group of business processes supported by the system (listed in the lefthand column) and the data classes "owned" by the system (listed across the top). For example, the third rectangle in Figure 1.3 defines the production planning information system of the business. It includes the following processes:

- Plan Seasonal Production

- Purchase Raw Materials

- Control Raw Material Inventory

- Schedule & Control Production.

It owns the following data classes:

- Seasonal Production Plan

- Supplier Description

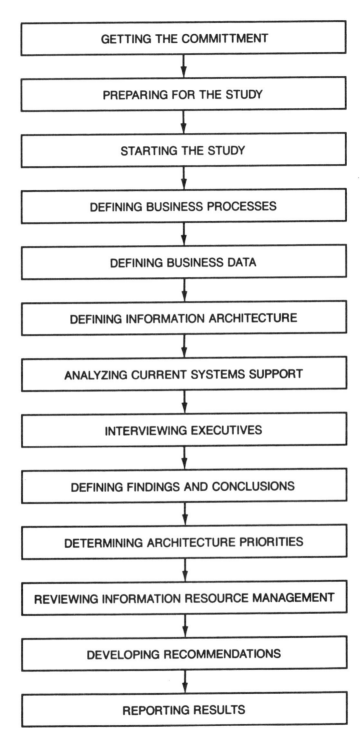

FIGURE 1.2. Steps in BSP study.

- Purchase Order
- Raw Material Inventory
- Production Order.

Figure 1.3 defines five other information systems along the diagonal, in addition to the logistics information system.

The next two steps in the BSP methodology are (1) interviewing executives and (2) defining findings and conclusions. BSP includes an elaborate methodology for conducting, and using the results of, these interviews, which we need not consider for purposes of this discussion. However, it should be noted that the executive input obtained in these two steps is the most valuable part of the whole project in the opinion of most I/S managers who have participated in a BSP study. It ensures that the systems plan reflects top management priorities and it generates top management support for the plan.

The remaining steps in Figure 1.2 are concerned with defining what has to be done to move from the present systems to the ideal defined by the information system architecture. A development schedule is prepared that reflects the priorities and constraints of the organization. Estimates of the resources required to build the new systems are also prepared.

Lessons Learned

BSP studies have been conducted in hundreds of organizations. A survey by Vacca was published in 1983 of organizations that had completed BSP projects.[4] It indicated that the results of BSP have been disappointing in terms of eliminating balkanized systems. However, some positive benefits were noted. The following three conclusions can be drawn from this survey and other evidence.

1. The BSP methodology requires more time and resources than the results justify. The multi-year system development plan is too detailed in view of the uncertainties faced by the organization over the time period encompassed by the plan.

2. The top-down approach is very helpful to the manager of information systems in the organization. One reason for this is that senior management provides a clearer picture of the systems and data needed to effectively run the business than do people at lower levels in the organization.

3. BSP results in a plan for databases that is too vague to assure compatibility between systems.

The first conclusion points to the main reason why the very large system approach fails. The life of a modern organization is too dynamic. The system plans made today are inappropriate for the organization in future years when the resources are available to build the system. A more flexible and results-oriented way of defining systems is needed.

The second conclusion supports the proposition that senior management involvement in systems planning serves to align that planning with the strategic needs of the company. This is one clear benefit of the top-down approach of BSP.

Processes \ Data Classes	Objectives	Policies & Procedures	Organization Unit Desc	Product Forecasts	Bldg & Real Estate Reqt	Equipment Requirements	Organization Unit Budget	G/L Accounts Desc & Budget	Long Term Debt	Employee Requirements	Legal Requirements	Competitor	Marketplace
Establish Business Direction	C	C	C								U	U	U
Forecast Product Requirements	U			C									
Determine Facility & Eqt Reqts	U		U		C	C		U					
Determine & Control Fin Reqts	U		U				C	C	C				
Determine Personnel Reqts		U	U		U	U	U	U		C	U		
Comply With Legal Reqts		U						U			C		
Analyze Marketplace	U											C	C
Design Product	U										U	U	
Buy Finished Goods			U										
Control Product Inventory													
Ship Product													
Advertise & Promote Product													U
Market Product (Wholesale)												U	U
Enter & Cntrl Customer Order													
Plan Seasonal Production				U									
Purchase Raw Materials													
Control Raw Materials Inventory													
Schedule & Control Production													
Acquire & Dispose Fac & Eqt					U	U							
Maintain Equipment													
Manage Facilities													
Manage Cash Receipts													
Deter Product Profitability								U					
Manage Accounts									U				
Manage Cash Disbursements									U				
Hire & Terminate Personnel		U	U					U		U	U		
Manage Personnel		U											

C is create data; U is use data.

FIGURE 1.3. Example BSP information architecture.

Product Description	Raw Material Description	Vendor Description	Buy Order	Product Warehouse Inventory	Shipment	Promotion	Customer Description	Customer Order	Seasonal Production Plan	Supplier Description	Purchase Order	Raw Material Inventory	Production Order	Equipment Description	Bldg & Real Estate Desc	Equipment Status	Accounts Receivable	Product Profitability	G/L Accounts Status	Accounts Payable	Employee Description	Employee Status
																	U	U				
			U					U														
														U	U	U						
																			U			
																						U
U																					U	U
					U																	
C	C													U								
U		C	C															U				
U			U	C	U						U											
				U	C			U							U							
U				U		C												U				
U					U	C	U															
U				U	U		U	C									U					
U									C					U		U					U	U
	U								U	C	C	U						U				
	U									U	C	U										
U	U								U		U	C	U	U		U					U	U
														C	C							
									U					U		C						U
													U									
			U			U												C				
U	U		U								U	U						C	U		U	U
		U									U							U	C	U		U
		U	U	U						U	U									C	U	U
																					C	U
																					U	C

The last conclusion indicates that the methodology needs to be extended to include the establishment of a high level data administration function that can develop data specifications that will assure system compatibility. To assure cooperation, the function must be executed from a high level position.

GOVERNMENT EXPERIENCE

Since 1988, a debate has been going on within the U.S. federal government over what is called the Grand Design Approach to systems procurement.[5] It began when the General Services Administration (GSA) issued a report condemning large contracts that bundle requirements for many different data processing systems into one procurement. The justification for Grand Design contracts is that they avoid the adverse effects of system balkanization. By procuring one very large system for a federal agency, such as the Department of Agriculture or the Federal Aviation Agency (FAA), a set of integrated subsystems is obtained.

The GSA report concludes that there are few examples of success and many examples of failure of the Grand Design Approach. Grand Design procurements for the Internal Revenue Service (IRS), the Navy, and the Patent and Trademark Office are among the examples of failure that are cited. A major author of the GSA report, Francis McDonough, is quoted as saying, "Systems like these are too big. You can't plan them, can't award them and/or can't implement them."

The GSA issued a follow-up report in late 1990 that describes alternatives to the Grand Design Approach. Four alternative strategies are proposed: (1) an incremental investment model that calls for pursuing discrete development projects without a grand scheme when they can be economically justified; (2) a bottom-up model that would let various parts of an agency implement systems within an overall plan that ties them together; (3) the information technology utility model in which various parts of an agency develop their own applications using the hardware and systems software of the utility; and (4) a "bounded Grand Design" Approach that defines restrictive conditions under which the Grand Design Approach is recommended.

The alternatives proposed by the GSA all reflect a mind-set that sees the information system as the primary resource and the data as a secondary resource. For this reason, it is not likely that the proposed four alternatives will really solve the problems of balkanization for the federal government. Nevertheless, the way GSA has persisted in its opposition to Grand Design does indicate that the very large system approach has severe drawbacks. It has not proven to be a sure way to build integrated systems.

PRIVATE SECTOR EXPERIENCE

Finally, from the private sector, a well-known systems consultant, Dan Appleton, reported in 1986 that very large systems can be literally defined as systems that are never finished. In an article entitled "Very Large Systems," he points out that most of the larger organizations have been building computer systems for 30 or 40 years now. This means that any new systems are likely to replace old systems. Obviously, the new systems have to be bigger and better than the old systems replaced, which means each new system will probably replace multiple old systems. This leads to systems that are estimated to cost $5 million at the outset; then this estimate is raised to $10 million after a system planning study identifies the segments and specific functions of the system. Later, the estimate is raise to $20 million after the detail design work identifies 700 system requirements to be met.

The fact that really makes these large systems unfinishable is changing requirements. A system that appears to require 170,000 man-hours, $10 million, and five years to complete is like the moon. As you approach it, it simply moves off into the distance. The 170,000 man-hours is based on a certain system definition. As business requirements change over the five-year period, additional man-hours are required to redo the system to meet the new requirements. It is entirely possible that at the end of the five years 170,000 man-hours are still required to complete the project.

Appleton suggests that the solution to the very large project syndrome is an asset-based lifecycle model. Although he does not define this model in detail, the basic idea is to reduce system customization by using standard "parts" (assets). The parts could be of many types but one is surely computer programs. The most important question is, how can computer programs be defined that can be used in many applications? We explore an answer to that question in Chapter 14.

A STRATEGIC APPROACH TO SYSTEMS DEVELOPMENT

In the preceding sections, the need for leadership in information systems development has been examined from several angles. We have seen that a lack of leadership results in balkanized systems. A business-wide data plan requires senior management sponsorship and can create an environment in which data sharing systems develop. However, if the top-down approach is too sweeping and inflexible, the very large system syndrome is experienced.

In this section, an approach to managing information systems is outlined that provides for senior level management involvement yet avoids very large system commitments. It is a variation on information engineering as defined by James Martin.[6] It provides the context within which the subject of this book fits.

In the approach, different aspects of systems are managed at different organizational levels. Some aspects are managed enterprise-wide, others business-wide, and the others are managed on an application-by-application basis. The enterprise-wide and business-wide management of certain aspects create the environment within which compatible application systems can be developed. The system aspects managed enterprise-wide and business-wide should either determine whether systems are compatible or be vital to the strategic plans of the enterprise. All other aspects are best managed on an application-by-application basis.*

STEPS THAT LINK SYSTEMS TO STRATEGY

The approach is summarized in Table 1.1. The table shows nine steps from strategic goals to functioning information systems. The first four steps have a

---

* The distinction between "enterprise-wide" and "business-wide" is based on the conception of a legal enterprise engaged in more than one line of business. If an enterprise has only one line of business, then the two terms can be considered synonymous.

TABLE 1.1.   Steps from strategy to information systems.

Step	Who/Scope	Data Sources	Software Used
1. Clarify strategy and goals	Top management/business-wide	Investment/policy proposals, industry/enterprise data	Strategic planning support system
2. Define functional model	Top management, DA (data administrator)/business-wide	Business strategy, management discussion	Repository
3. Identify functional experts	HRM, DA/business-wide	Organization chart, job class., employee data	Repository
4. Define the business-wide information structure	Function experts, DA/business-wide	Reports, transactions, existing information structure	Repository
5. Establish the computing environment	I/S management/enterprise-wide	Platform, DBMS, and CASE tool information	Operating system, DBMS, CASE tools
6. Design application	System analyst and users/application-wide	System requirements, prototype screens	CASE design tools
7. Establish physical database	Database administrator/business-wide	Conceptual database, DBMS documentation	Repository, DBMS
8. Generate software	Programmer/application-wide	System design, CASE coding tool requirements	CASE coding tool
9. Implement system	Testers, documentors, trainers, users/application-wide	System design, application software	Application software

business-wide scope. An enterprise-wide scope is recommended for the fifth step. The last four steps are done on an application-by-application basis.

As far as this book is concerned, the first four steps are of particular interest. However, a perspective on the entire systems development process is needed to understand the significance of the first steps. For this reason, each of the nine steps of Table 1.1 is discussed in a following subsection.

Step 1: Clarify Strategy and Goals

Clarifying the strategy and goals of a business is an important first step in aligning the information systems of the business with that business. A clear statement of purpose and explicit strategic plans for achieving the purpose may directly identify some information system needs. They also provide the rationale for the functional model developed in Step 2, which is used to systematically identify information system requirements, and they are needed to set development priorities.

Step 1 can be taken only by the top-management of an organization. Only as the leaders adopt a strategy and specific goals should they be allowed to influence the way resources are used, including resources devoted to information systems. Others in the organization should provide strategic ideas through policy proposals, investment proposals, and suggestions for solving problems. But, it is up to senior management to accept them for the organization.

The procedures and schedule for strategic planning may vary from one organization to another. Pascarella and Frohman describe many variations in their book, *The Purpose-Driven Organization*.[7] Approaches that get a broad cross-section of the organization involved promote a participative style of management. An information system that facilitates the formulation, communication and evaluation of goal suggestions from across the organization (called a "strategic planning support system" in Table 1.1) can be helpful in making such approaches more effective.

Step 2: Define Functional Model

The functional model of a business defines what has to be done to achieve the strategic goals. It is a form of strategic planning that breaks down the overall activity of fulfilling the purposes of the organization into the required actions and decision-making. A more complete description of this type of modeling is given in Chapter 4.

Since it is a part of strategic planning, it is appropriately done by senior managers who understand the organizational purposes and plans to be fulfilled. A data administrator can provide assistance in formulating the model in a way that is compatible with the repository system software used to record and print the functional breakdown.

Once the major functions have been identified, further definition and subdivision of them can be done by experts in each function. This can be done in Step 4. For example, marketing is often a major function required by the strategy of the organization; the definition and subdivision of marketing is best left to marketing experts, or at least done in consultation with such experts.

A type of software package and database that James Martin terms a "system encyclopedia," and which IBM calls a "repository system," can be used to record the functional model and link it to the other plans developed in Steps 3 and 4. It is a system that allows information about the functions and their subfunctions to be entered into a computer system and then displayed or printed out in various formats.

Step 3: Identify Functional Experts

The functional model is not an organization chart. But it can be related to an organization chart, and the jobs and positions in the organization. An analysis of how the functional model relates to the organization needs to be made to determine who should determine the data requirements of each function and subfunction. In most cases, someone who is executing the function is best qualified to serve as the function expert.

This analysis can provide some side benefits to those responsible for Human Resource Management (HRM) that may be as important as the primary reason for conducting the analysis. By comparing job descriptions with the function definitions of the functional model that apply to the job, misalignments of the organization with respect to the strategic goals can be detected. Functions not provided for in the organizational structure (or being done redundantly) are identified.

Ideally, the repository system should provide for the information needed to make this analysis. The fact that the information is useful for both personnel and information systems management points to a need for cooperation and sharing that has not been traditionally recognized by the management of either department.

Step 4: Define the Business-Wide Information Structure

The term "information structure" is used to designate a plan that is not a complete conceptual database but which can serve as the framework of the conceptual database.* It defines the entity types about which the business needs data, but not all the specific types of data required. Relationships between entity types are also defined in an information structure.

The function experts and data administrator work together to characterize data requirements in terms of an information structure. To the extent that reports and transaction forms already exist and are needed, descriptions of these reports and forms as well as the entity types and relationships that they imply should be recorded in the repository system. In addition, any ad hoc query capabilities required for planning purposes should be defined in terms of the entity types and relationships that they involve.

The execution of this step by the data administrator should be business-wide so that data definition standards can be set up to govern all references to data in all software purchased or developed. This is the prerequisite for automatic data sharing, without special "import-export programs." Figure 1.4 illustrates the role played by the results of Step 4 in the development of integrated systems. It provides the database concept, shown in the upper left corner, that guides the development of an integrated set of databases that all information systems of the business can use. The development of the integrated database from the results of Step 4 is the responsibility of the data administration function.

The objective in this fourth step is limited to information structure definition, rather than conceptual database definition, so that the step can be accomplished business-wide within a few months. To obtain a complete database definition would require a far more detailed analysis and could take years. Identifying the entity types gives the data administrator a basis for evolving the conceptual database definition over a period of years as application development projects are undertaken. The business-wide information structure provides an overview of who needs what types of data in the organization.

---

* The term "conceptual database" is used to mean a complete definition of the data that constitutes the information resource which is to be managed as such and made available to all on a "need to know" basis.

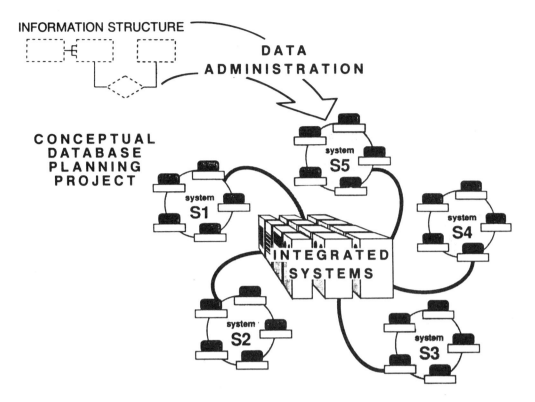

FIGURE 1.4. Data administration uses results of Step 4.

Step 5: Establish the Computing Environment

In this step, the CASE (Computer-Aided Software Engineering) tools, DBMS (Database Management System), operating system standards, data networking standards, security standards, and computer standards are selected. To gain the full benefit of the first four steps, it is imperative that an automated approach be taken to the last four steps. This is what properly designed CASE tools can make possible. They can automate the design of application systems, the creation and testing of application programs, and the preparation of training and reference materials.

The selection of CASE tools and the other aspects of a computing environment should be done by information system professionals, not top management or the board of directors. Hardware standards should be the last issue considered and should be based on what the CASE tools require. To effectively manage training and maintenance expenses, the computing environment decisions should be made on an enterprise-wide basis.

Step 6: Design Application

The definition of an application, its feasibility analysis, and the detailed design of the system are included in this step. The system analyst works with potential system users in this step. The analyst should use prototyping tools (part of

CASE) to work out the details of screen formats and the way users will interact with the system.

This step is greatly simplified if an object-oriented approach is taken and a business-wide information structure is available as described in Step 4. This approach treats entities as objects and organizes the software around object classes. Each computer program is dedicated to simulating objects of a single class (entity type). The entity types and relationships identified in Step 4 can be directly translated into design objects in Step 6. This compatibility is the subject of Chapter 14.

The part of the business-wide information structure that a given application uses needs to be fleshed-out at this time so that it constitutes a conceptual database. This must be done before a physical database can be developed. The process should include taking into account any attributes of the entity types involved in the application that other future applications will require.

Step 7: Establish Databases

The planning and creation of physical database files should be done on a business-wide basis. It may be that every application should have its own physical database. On the other hand, it may be that transaction processing times and data communication costs can be significantly reduced by storing certain data in a separate database close to where it is used intensively.

In managing physical databases, it is also important to satisfy security requirements and to consider the cost of providing adequate technical support to assure that files are not corrupted. A file containing thousands of transactions, or data on thousands of customers, represents a very important asset of the business, even though it is not an asset in the accounting system. These considerations tend to favor a centralized approach to physical database management.

Step 8: Generate Software

This has traditionally been the most expensive and least controllable step. Now, it is where the big payoff is from using a CASE approach. The system designed using CASE tools can be coded automatically using a code generator designed to work from the design specifications created by the CASE design tool. This eliminates the programmer from direct application programming. The time and cost of coding are thereby cut dramatically. Higher quality code is also obtained which means the code testing and debugging cycle is brought under control.

Step 9: Implement System

This final step is commonly underestimated. Failure to properly test and document a new system and train its users can be as fatal to its survival as poor design or an inadequate DBMS. The fact that this last step is the one most likely to suffer from any project budget crunch may contribute to the tendency to underestimate it.

The step should be executed by system user experts, not programmer/analysts. Persons familiar with the business function but not the computer system are most likely to detect operational deficiencies during testing and to provide thorough training and documentation. Programmers tend to take too many details about the system for granted.

SUMMARY

Business management has an opportunity to make better use of computers by exercising more leadership in development of the systems. More technical expertise is not the critical factor. Leadership in creating an environment that fosters systems that share data are the vital factor. Without this leadership, a patchwork of balkanized information systems is inevitable.

Better use of computers can give everyone that is working toward the same goal the same information to use in achieving the goal. It requires that computer systems be set up to capture and provide access to data for all who need it while they are also supporting a particular business function. The prerequisite for this to happen is standards for referring to, storing, and accessing data.

The managerial approach taken to establish systems that share data must avoid the very large system syndrome. Difficulties arise if system development efforts are too centralized. Experience provides ample evidence of the fallacy of trying to centrally plan and manage information resources as one big system. Business is simply too dynamic and multifaceted for that strategy to be practical.

The most promising system development strategy is one in which top management supports the establishment of a business-wide definition of data resources and an enterprise-wide set of standards for the computing environment. The development of individual applications within this environment is then left to individual functional managers and professional staff members.

This book is particularly concerned with Step 4 of Table 1.1 which summarizes the recommended approach to systems development. Chapters 2, 3, and 5 of Part 1, all of Part 2, and Chapter 12 of Part 3 are concerned with Step 4. Chapter 4 discusses Steps 1, 2, and 3. Chapter 13 discusses Step 7 and Chapter 14 discusses the effects of taking Steps 1 thru 4 on the way Steps 6, 8, and 9 should be handled. This book explains the database aspects of the methodology summarized in Table 1.1 and the benefits that a business-wide conceptual database has for other parts of the methodology.

REFERENCES

1. Appleton, Daniel S., "Very Large Projects," *Datamation*, January 1986, pp. 63–70.

2. Goodhue, Dale L., Judith A. Quillard, and John F. Rockart, *Managing the Data Resource: A Contingency Perspective* (Cambridge: Sloan School of Management, M.I.T.), CISR WP No. 150, October 1987.

3. International Business Machines, *Business Systems Planning: Information Systems Planning Guide*, IBM, GE20-0527-4, 145 pages.

4. Vacca, John R., "Survey of BSP Methodology Use," *Systems Development Management*, Auerbach Publishers Inc., Article No. 34-01-03, 1983.

5. Foley, Mary Jo, "Uncle Sam Rethinks Grand Design," *Mini-Micro Systems*, December 1988, pp. 61–67.

6. Martin, James, *Information Engineering, Books I, II, III* (Englewood Cliffs, NJ: Prentice-Hall, Inc., 1989).

7. Pascarella, Perry and Mark A. Frohman, *The Purpose-Driven Organization* (San Francisco: Jossey-Bass Publishers, 1989).

DISCUSSION QUESTIONS

1. Being responsive to customer needs is a characteristic of most successful businesses. Can information systems be used to enhance this characteristic? Can you cite some examples?

2. Why do organizations build balkanized information systems?

3. Compare and contrast the scope of application software that is determined by market forces (word processing software, for example) with that of software developed "in-house" and defined by a certain group of users in a hierarchical organization.

4. What is the best means of coordinating the work of different units in an organization?

5. What difference does it make whether data are viewed as the output of a computer system or as a resource that exists independent of any particular application system that outputs it?

6. Why not create one information system for the whole business?

7. Which aspects of information systems should be managed as though one large system were being developed?

8. Which comes first, the functional model or the functional expert? Does Table 1.1 over-simplify the relationships between Steps 2, 3, and 4?

9. How does this book relate to the methodology summarized in Table 1.1?

10. Suppose Lotech Company has the following characteristics:

    a) The present information systems are not optimal but they work and the organization has adapted to them.

    b) None of the senior managers of the organization is computer literate. They leave computers to the head of data processing.

    c) Introducing a business-wide conceptual database and data administrator would add a new type of overhead to the budget.

    Is it possible for Lotech to successfully implement the methodology of Table 1.1? What are the prerequisites for success?

2

The Entity-Relationship Model

In preparation for managing the way data are defined in a business, we need to learn a language for describing data. The entity-relationship (E-R) model is such a language. It is designed to produce a description that can be easily translated into a definition of data suitable for computer programming. It provides a means of bridging the gap between management's understanding of business information requirements and the data definitions that computer scientists need for programming purposes.

Management's responsibility is to describe the data that is either necessary or desirable in executing the functions of the business. This description will become part of the performance specifications for the information systems. The description needs to be clear, unambiguous, and easily translatable into computer-processing terms.

At the same time, the data requirements description must express the functional experts' understanding of how information can be used to effectively execute each subfunction. Thus, the descriptions need to be in terms that functional experts can easily understand. Descriptions that are understandable only to programmers and systems analysts are unacceptable for this purpose.

The E-R approach to data modeling satisfies these criteria for a data description language. It is both easy to understand and precise. It has more flexibility than other commonly used data models, and it is easier to understand than symbolic logic or a programmer's data definition language (DDL).

In this chapter, the E-R approach is introduced and its basic concepts are defined. In Chapter 3, the approach is applied to various data modeling problems. These two chapters are intended to prepare the reader for Chapter 5 in which the top-down approach to defining data requirements and developing a business-wide information structure (BWIS) is explained.

BACKGROUND

The E-R model was developed in the mid-1970s to provide a more systematic way to deal with the problems faced by database planners. At that time, there were at least 10 different database management system (DBMS) software packages commercially available for a database planner to use. Each offered a different way to model data, although, for the most part, they fell into three categories corresponding to the three data models recognized at the time—the hierarchical, network, and relational models. The hierarchical model was used by IBM in the first commercially available DBMS, which is commonly called IMS. The network model was the basis of a DBMS standard proposed in 1971 by the Database Task Group (DBTG) of the Committee On Data SYstem Languages (CODASYL). It was supported by the other mainframe computer vendors and some independent software producers. The relational model was introduced by Codd in 1970; it has been implemented in IBM's DB2 and in many DBMS designed for personal computers.

The E-R model offered a way to separate the description of business data requirements from implementation issues. It satisfied a need identified by an ad hoc task group of the Standards Planning and Requirements Committee (SPARC) of the American National Standards Institute (ANSI).[1] An interim report issued by this committee in 1975 proposed a database system architecture that consisted of a conceptual schema, a series of external schema, and another series of internal schema. A diagram of this ANSI/SPARC DBMS framework is shown in Figure 2.1. The term "schema" refers to a definition of the data that a system is (or needs to be) capable of handling.

Each of the external schema is a definition of an individual user's data requirements. Each of the internal schema is a description of a data structure

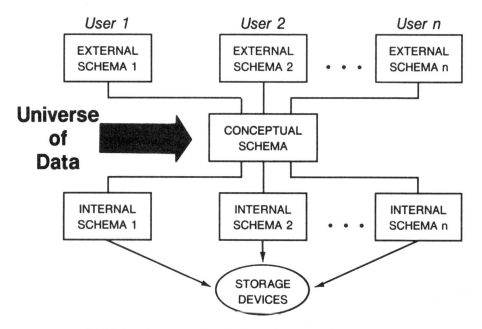

FIGURE 2.1.   ANSI/X3/SPARC DBMS framework.

implemented physically on a computer system. The conceptual schema acts as a translation interface between the user views of data and the way the data are physically stored. It integrates the views of data held by individual users of the database.

Peter Chen's article proposing the entity-relationship model was published in 1976.[2] It described a way to define the conceptual schema of the three-level architecture shown in Figure 2.1. It concentrated on accurately representing the real world data of interest to an enterprise without getting bogged down in the details of a specific DBMS and its data model. Chen carefully contrasted it with the data structure specifications required for an internal database design. He invented a separate diagramming technique and demonstrated how the E-R diagram could be translated into either a data structure diagram or a relational database specification for purposes of internal database design.

E-R modeling has also proven effective as a means of summarizing the data in "end-user views" of data. By "end-user views," we mean not a programmer's view, but a businessperson's view. Businesspeople think in terms of invoices, purchase orders, checks, sales reports, accounting statements, worksheets, tables, and graphs. These views of data can be translated into E-R diagrams that reveal the basic nature of the data contained in a transaction document or report. An E-R diagram of an end-user view of data represents the external schema of that data.

All of the external schema representing different end-user views, can be integrated into a single *conceptual view* of the data resources of the business. (This integration process is the subject of Chapter 12.) The conceptual view of the business-wide data resource provides the basis for developing a set of integrated physical databases that can store the data of a business in a way that is nonredundant, yet makes it accessible to all end users who have a legitimate need for it.

Thus, the E-R model provides a way of linking end-user data needs to the design of actual computer databases. This is illustrated in Figure 2.2. The E-R model is shown in the middle section between the end-user view of data (symbolized by an invoice) and the physical database design (symbolized by a data structure diagram).

Businesspersons need to understand E-R modeling for two reasons. First, it puts them in a position to communicate their data needs more effectively to systems analysts. The person who understands conceptual views of data can check the analyst's translation of his or her end-user view into a conceptual view. Second, an understanding of E-R diagrams is needed to formulate ad hoc database queries. The businessperson familiar with entity types and relationships should be able to understand the conceptual database design of the organization and access corporate databases without the aid of a programmer.

ENTITY TYPE

In the E-R model, an entity is an "object" of interest to the enterprise. In the same way that an object, such as a pencil, is identified by its attributes (length, color, hardness of lead, etc.) so an entity is identified by its attributes.

In the E-R model, an entity is also different from what we commonly think of as an object in the sense that it is not necessarily physical. For example, a role

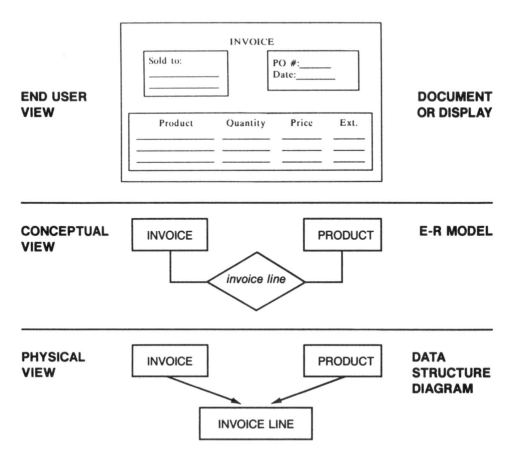

FIGURE 2.2. Role of enterprise schema in database design.

played by a person can be an entity. One person may be both an employee and a stockholder but the employee and stockholder can be modeled as two separate entities. The employee might have the attributes 1134 (employee number), 11 April 1985 (start date), and Margaret Cline (name). The stockholder might have the attributes Margaret Cline (name), 10000 (number of shares), 120 Rose Street, Phoenix (address). Thus, two different entities in the model may refer to the same person.

An entity can be an event, such as the payment of a bill or the birth of a child. Events have attributes, just as objects do. Registering to take a course at school can be described as an entity with the attributes 14 August 1993 (date of registration), 126 Blair Hall (place of registration), and $128 (amount paid).

An entity can also be a concept. The first scene in the second act of a play is an entity with attributes, such as setting, first actor to appear, lines, and special sound effects. In this case, the entity is not an event but a specification for an event or a series of events. An execution of the scene by a group of actors would be another type of entity.

An entity can be anything that has attributes. From the standpoint of database design, an entity is defined by a collection of attribute values. However, an underlying assumption is that the types of attributes of the entity can be predefined so that the database can be set up to store entities of that type.

In E-R analysis, we work in terms of entity types most of the time, rather than with specific instances of an entity type. The real world is reduced to a set of entity types. An entity must fit one of the entity types to be recorded in the database.

Entities are discrete individuals that cannot be blended. The horse can be an entity type and the donkey another entity type but there is no possibility of storing attributes unique to a mule just because it is half horse and half donkey. To store mule attributes, the mule must be included in the model as a separate entity type with attributes peculiar to mules.

Only static attributes can be recognized in an E-R model. The scene in a play can be modeled as a concept or event, but not as a dynamic experience occurring over a period of time. The E-R model is basically a static one and can simulate dynamic events only by making time an attribute of the event and storing a series of discrete versions of the event that can be related to one another by their time sequence.

ENTITY TYPE AS A RELATION

This subsection is for the benefit of the reader who is familiar with relational database systems. Other readers can skip it without missing any vital points.

An entity type can be *implemented* as a relation in the relational model. The entities that are instances of an entity type become rows in the extension set of the relation. There is no ordering among these entity instances just as there can be no ordering of the rows of a relation.

An entity type must have a fixed number of attributes for all instances of it. These entity type attributes become the columns of the relation. As in relations, the ordering of the attributes has no significance; however, the attributes of all instances of an entity type will have the same ordering when stored as rows of a relation.

The attributes of an entity type each have a domain of values that can be assigned to the attribute, as in the case of relations. Two or more attributes may share the same domain and therefore the domains must be identified separately from the attributes to which they apply. The members of a domain must be single values, not lists or arrays or other relations. This means that there can be no nesting of one entity type within another, just as the nesting of one relation within another is not permitted in the relational model.

The set of attributes of an entity type must include at least one candidate key. An attribute (or set of attributes) that has a unique value for each entity instance is necessary to distinguish one entity occurrence from another in the database. Without the capability to uniquely identify an entity, update and delete operations can have unpredictable effects and retrieval operations may have ambiguous results.

There can be good and bad entity types in the same sense that there are good and bad relations (normal and non-normal relations). If an entity type consists of a set of attributes that do not satisfy the Boyce-Codd normal form condition, then contradictions, redundancy and inadvertent deletion can occur whether the database is implemented on a relational, network, or hierarchical DBMS. With respect to the relational model, it should be clear that the translation of entity types to relations would result in a database that does not satisfy the BCNF condition if one or more of the entity types does not satisfy BCNF conditions.

The 4th and 5th normal forms also apply to entity types. An entity type that includes more than one attribute that is a multivalued dependency* of a key attribute(s) will have significant redundancy, contradiction, and deletion problems when implemented on any type of DBMS. Similar problems will occur if three or more attributes of an entity type are involved in interdependent multi-valued dependencies (MVDs) and each has a many-to-many relationship with the others.

The reader who is not familiar with the normal forms should not give up hope at this point. One of the advantages of the E-R approach is that it leads one to naturally define entity types that convert to normal form relations. Any entity type that is meant to model something in the real world that is important in conducting a business has a very high probability of converting to a normal form relation.

RELATIONSHIPS

There are two semantic abstractions used in the upper level of the E-R model. One is the entity type that has been described. The other is the relationship that is a rule of association among entities. (At a lower level there are two more semantic abstractions: the attribute abstraction and the concept of a domain.)

A relationship can be described either as a rule of association or as a mapping. As a rule of association, a relationship defines a way of associating occurrences of one type of entity with those of another (or several others). Take the entity types employee and department, for example. One rule associates each department with the employees that work in that department. This rule defines a relationship between the department and employee entity types. This relationship defines how each department in an organization is associated with certain employees of the organization. It is important that the rule of association be clear; it should be adequate to determine the instances of the relationship in which every entity of each type participates. The "works in rule" is clear and adequate for the example relationship between department and employee.

The relationship between employee and department entity types can also be characterized as a mapping. The employee and department entity types each constitute a set. The members of the employee entity type set are the employee entities and the members of the department set are the departments in an organization. Figure 2.3 depicts these two sets and the way the "works in" relationship defines a mapping of employees onto the department set.

There are 10 employees and three departments in Figure 2.3. Employees 4, 8, and 9 work in department B according to the figure. The mapping of 4, 8, and 9 to B is one instance of the "works in" relationship. The mapping of employees 1 and 3 to department A is another instance of the relationship. This illustrates the fact that in the E-R model, a relationship has instances (also called occurrences). In this case, an "instance" is the application of the relationship rule that identifies all entities of one type that map to a single entity of the other type. Thus, an instance of a relationship is analogous to an instance of an entity type.

---

* See Chapter 3 for a definition of "multivalued dependency."

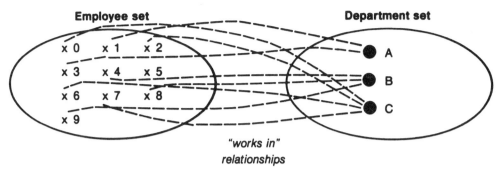

FIGURE 2.3.   Mapping view of a relationship.

For those familiar with symbolic logic it may be helpful to characterize the "works in" relationship between employee and department in terms of symbolic logic. This employee-department relationship could be described as the relation $W(E,D)$, where,

E = employee,

D = department, and

$W(E,D)$ = employee E works in department D.

An instance of this relation* would be a specific sentence, such as "Employee 4 works in department B," which in symbolic terms would be $W(4,B)$.

Note that two different definitions of the concept of an "instance" of a relationship have been given in the preceding two paragraphs. First the mapping of employees 4, 8, and 9 to department B was defined as an "instance." Then, the mapping of employee 4 to department B was defined as an "instance." The first type of "instance" will be called a "CODASYL[†]-instance." The other type will be called a "symbolic logic instance."[††]

---

* "Relation" is used in a different sense here than in the previous section which discussed entity types as relations. The relational data model developed by E.F. Codd is a special case of the concept of a relation as defined in classical symbolic logic. It is the classical symbolic logic concept of a "relation" that is referred to here.

[†] CODASYL is an acronym for Committee On DAta SYstem Languages. This is the committee that defines the COBOL programming language and which has also defined a standard for database management system software.

[††] The CODASYL concept of a relationship "instance" is the same as the concept of an instance of a multivalued dependency (MVD) in the relational data model. In an MVD, a given value of one attribute determines a list of values of another attribute. The only difference between an MVD and a relationship is that a relationship exists between entity types whereas an MVD exists between attributes of one relation. The relationship between employee and department would be called an MVD if employee ID and department number were viewed as attributes of a single relation (which would probably be the Employee Relation).

The fact that a relationship models the same pattern in terms of entity types as does an MVD in terms of attributes means that relationships can be used to include in a database design MVDs (and FDs) that are lost in the decomposition process of normalization, which is necessary in order to have normal form relations. Thus, while normalization considerations cause "department" and "employee," for example, to be treated as two separate relations (entity types) rather than one, an E-R model allows the relationship between "department" and "employee" to be explicitly modeled.

RELATIONSHIP TYPES

The type of a relationship depends on two characteristics. One is the number of entity types that must be involved in a "symbolic logic instance" of the relationship. The other is the number of occurrences of each entity type that can (or must) be in a CODASYL instance of the relationship. We describe the first characteristic by the term binary if two entity types must be involved in the relationship. If only one entity type is involved (a relationship between different occurrences of the same entity type, we call it a "recursive relationship." If n (n > 2) entity types are involved) it is called an n-way relationship.

The second characteristic is called the "cardinality" of the relationship with respect to an entity type that is involved. The minimum cardinality of a relationship is the minimum number of occurrences of an entity type that must be involved in a CODASYL instance of the relationship. The maximum cardinality is the maximum number of occurrences that can be involved. By convention, when neither minimum or maximum is specified, maximum is implied. A one-to-many relationship, for example is a binary relationship in which the maximum cardinality of one entity is one and the maximum cardinality of the other entity type is greater than one (the meaning of many).

Binary Relationships

A binary relationship is one in which two entity types are involved. The relationship just described between employee and department is a binary relationship. Assuming that an employee can be working in only one department at a time, the "works in" relationship is classified as a one-to-many, binary relationship. It involves two entity types and one of the entity types (employee) may have more than one occurrence in an instance of the relationship while the other entity type (department) can have only one occurrence involved in a single instance of the relationship.

Another parameter of this binary relationship (or any relationship) is the minimum number of relationship instances each entity type member must participate in. Does a department have to have employees working in it? If not, then a department occurrence need not participate in any instance of the "works in" relationship. Does an employee have to be in a department? If the answer is "yes" then each employee occurrence of employee type must participate in one instance of the relationship, and membership of the employee entity type in the relationship is said to be "mandatory."

Most DBMS software packages that are based on the network data model require that the type of relationship be specified as far as the entity types participating are concerned. The maximum number of occurrences of each entity type in an instance of the relationship can usually only be specified as one (1) or more than one (n). The minimum number of relationship instances that an entity type must participate in is usually defined in terms of whether or not participation in the relationship is "mandatory."

In a binary one-to-one relationship, only one occurrence of each entity type participates in a single instance of the relationship. An example of a one-to-one relationship between employee and department is the "manages" relationship. A department is related to the employee who manages the department. Assuming there is only one manager for each department, this is a one-to-one relationship.

A many-to-many relationship is one in which many occurrences of each of two entity types may participate in each instance of the relationship. Consider, for example, the "have worked in" relationship between employee and department. Over a period of years, an employee may have worked in many different departments. This means that the "have worked in" relationship links the employee to more than one department. Thus, many departments need to be linked to any one employee in this case, and many employees need to be linked to each department (all that have ever worked in the department).

In the case of many-to-many relationships, the CODASYL concept of an "instance" of a relationship needs special interpretation. Which set of departments should be included in any one "instance"? A CODASYL instance of a many-to-many relationship is all of the occurrences of one of the relationship entity types that are linked to one occurrence of the other entity type. This is in contrast to a "symbolic logic instance" which consists of a set that includes one occurrence of each of the entity types involved. In the case of the "have worked in" relationship, a symbolic logic instance is a specific employee who has worked in a specific department.

N-Way Relationships

An n-way relationship involves three or more entity types. It is based on a rule of association (relation in symbolic logic) that unambiguously relates three or more types of entities. Application of the rule identifies a "symbolic logic instance" of the relationship.

For example, suppose that Project, Part, and Supplier are three entity types in a database. A relationship could be defined by the rule, "order part x from supplier y for project z." For any given part and supplier, presumably many projects could be assigned to get the part from that supplier. For any given supplier and project, many parts could be supplied by that supplier to that project. For any given part and project, however, could more than one supplier be involved? This is a policy decision that could go either way. Suppose that some projects were allowed to split their procurement of a part between suppliers. Then, this n-way relationship is a many-to-many-to-many relationship.

On the other hand, if the policy decision was to restrict a project to one supplier for a given part, then the project-part-supplier relationship just described would be a many-to-one-to-many relationship. For a given part used on a project, there would be only one supplier occurrence in an instance of the relationship. (In this case we use the CODASYL instance, to make the point that there can be at most one supplier involved.)

A many-to-one-to-many relationship is not a valid 3-way relationship. It is not valid in the sense that the relationships among the entity types can be more precisely described by multiple binary (or, in general, smaller n) type relationships. In the case of the relationship described between Project, Part, and Supplier, if there can be only one supplier for a given project and part, then a many-to-many binary relationship between Project and Part (call it *proj-part*) combined with a one-to-many relationship between Supplier and *proj-part* more precisely defines the associations among these three entity types.

The analysis of n-way relationships is discussed in more detail in Chapter 3. However, on the basis of this discussion it should be clear that a simple method to determine the validity of an n-way relationship is the following:

For each possible combination of n-1 entity types in an n-way relationship, does an instance of the combination determine a specific occurrence of the entity type not included in the combination? If the answer is affirmative for any combination, then the n-way relationship is not valid.

The phrase "instance of the combination" means a combination of specific occurrences of each of the n-1 entity types included in the combination of n-1 entity types. The rule over-simplifies the problem of determining relationship validity somewhat but it detects invalid n-way relationships in most practical cases.

Recursive Relationships

It is also possible to define relationships between entity occurrences of a single type in the E-R model. These are called recursive relationships. An example of a one-to-one relationship between employees is "marriage." An example of a one-to-many relationship is "manages." Here manages refers to one employee managing another and it is assumed that an employee has only one other employee as a manager.

An example of a many-to-many recursive relationship defined with respect to employees is "works with." Suppose employee A sometimes works with employees B, C, and D and employee E works with B and C at other times. This means that B and C work with both A and E which makes it a many-to-many relationship.

RELATIONSHIP ATTRIBUTES

Only many-to-many relationships (or valid n-way relationships) can have attributes. In the case of a one-to-many relationship, any attribute that seems to be an attribute of the relationship can be viewed as an attribute of one of the entity types that has many occurrences involved in any one instance of the relationship. In the case of many-to-many relationships (or many-to-many-to-many, etc.), there can be attributes that are functionally dependent on the relationship instance but not on an occurrence of one entity type involved in the relationship. An example is the quantity of an item ordered on a purchase order (in a situation where the item is routinely ordered, either for stock or to fill a customer order). In this situation, the database needs to hold data concerning suppliers, purchase orders, items, and the relationship of an item being on a purchase order. For the purpose of showing that the quantity ordered must be treated as an attribute of a relationship, only the purchase order, item, and the relationship between them need be considered.

The quantity ordered cannot be an attribute of the purchase order unless the number of items on a purchase order is limited to one. As an attribute of purchase order, quantity would be an attribute with multiple values, one for each item on the purchase order.

On the other hand, quantity cannot be made an attribute of item because there is a quantity to be stored every time the item is purchased. If quantity ordered were made an attribute of item then either it would have to be a multivalued attribute or only the last quantity ordered could be stored. Presumably, neither of these alternatives is acceptable.

Consider a relationship between purchase order and item. Each instance of the relationship is between a purchase order and an item on that order. This combination of an item on an order uniquely determines an order quantity that needs to be stored (and retrieved) in the database. Using the symbol → to mean "uniquely determines," we can write,

```
PO, Item → Quantity
```

By treating the relationship between purchase order and item as an entity type, a viable way is created to model the quantity ordered within the constraints imposed by the definitions already given of an entity type and relationship. The fact that a many-to-many relationship can be treated as an entity type in the E-R model is very significant. There are important circumstances in which relationships between relationships are the only way to properly model the information required by management.

DIAGRAMMING

Diagrams provide an easy way to summarize relationships between entity types. Recall that the purpose of the E-R model is to create a conceptual schema that accurately defines the data of likely value to an enterprise and the importance of having a way to effectively communicate conceptual designs is clear. The real experts on "data of likely value" are the enterprise managers and other workers who must turn the information output from the computer system into additional profits that would not have been made without the system. If database system outputs do not have a positive bottom-line impact then the whole system design and development exercise is useless. In most organizations in the developed world, this impact has to amount to more than a substitution of machine costs for clerical expense because the major clerical groups in accounting and production were eliminated decades ago.

The effectiveness of E-R diagrams in communicating with managers and workers is probably the single most important reason for the widespread use of the E-R approach. These diagrams give a high-level overview of a database concept that can be explained to most managers. This communication reduces misunderstandings on the part of computer system developers regarding employee needs and this leads to more effective systems.

LEVELS OF DETAIL

In his writings on the E-R approach, Peter Chen makes a clear distinction between the "upper conceptual domain" and the "lower conceptual domain." The upper domain is concerned with entity types and relationships. The lower domain is concerned with attributes and their domains, as well as relationship sequencing rules, access controls, and other details specified in a database schema.

The diagramming method to be explained in this section deals exclusively with the upper conceptual domain. Entity types and their relationships are all that are shown. Elements in the lower domain, such as attributes and domains are not depicted. The reason for this is to focus on accurately describing the major features of the database before devoting attention to the details.

This top-down approach is important in the strategy of E-R analysis. At the First International Conference on the Entity-Relationship Approach, held at UCLA in 1979, several papers were presented on database projects that had started by identifying all attributes of interest to the enterprise and then proceeded by identifying the entity types that constituted logical groupings of these attributes. By the Third Conference, held in Anaheim in 1983, there were no such papers. It was clear to all (or at least those experienced in E-R analysis) that trying to discover entity types by an analysis of the functional dependencies between attributes was not the best way to model the database structure.

A DIAGRAMMING METHOD

There are many variations on the E-R diagramming method proposed by Peter Chen in his original paper.[3] The method described in this section is one such variant. It uses "crow's feet" in place of "n" to signify one-to-many relationships. Arrowheads are used to identify the entity types involved in a relationship which also functions as an entity type in other relationships. A diamond within a rectangle is used to signify a relationship that is also treated as an entity type.

Entity Type Symbol

An entity type is represented by a rectangle with the name or label of the entity type inside. In this book, entity type names have their initial letter capitalized in the text and the whole name is capitalized in E-R diagrams (Figure 2.4(a)).

Binary One-to-One Relationship

A one-to-one relationship between entity types is represented by a line connecting the rectangles. The name of the relationship may be placed on the line. In this book, relationship names are in lower case italics in the text and in lower case in E-R diagrams (Figure 2.4(b)).

Binary One-to-Many Relationship

A one-to-many relationship is represented by a line with a "crow's foot" at the end that connects to the entity type with many occurrences involved in a single relationship occurrence (Figure 2.4(c)).

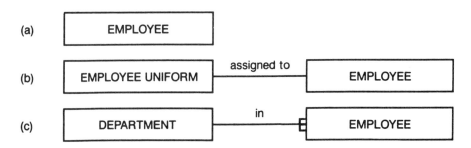

FIGURE 2.4. An entity type and simple relationships: (a) an entity type, (b) one-to-one binary relationship, (c) one-to-many binary relationship.

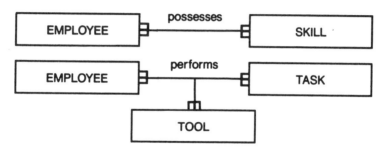

FIGURE 2.5.   Many-to-many relationships without attributes.

Many-to-Many Relationships without Attributes

Many-to-many relationships (either binary or n-way) for which there are no relevant relationship attributes are represented by connecting lines ending in "crow's feet" (Figure 2.5).

Many-to-Many Relationships with Attributes

Many-to-many relationships (either binary or n-way) for which there are relevant relationship attributes are represented by diamonds connected by lines to each entity type involved (Figure 2.6.).

The rule of association in the 4-way relationship of Figure 2.6 is that a commodity is transported between a certain origin and destination by a specific freight carrier (trucker, railroad, etc.). For each commodity moved by a carrier between two points, a rate ($ per cwt) is stored in the database.

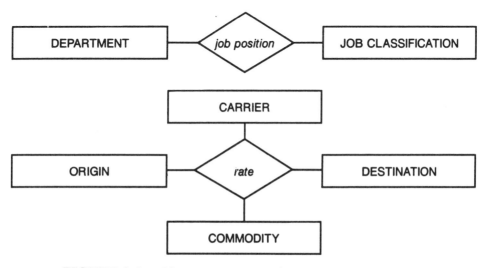

FIGURE 2.6.   Many-to-many relationships with attributes.

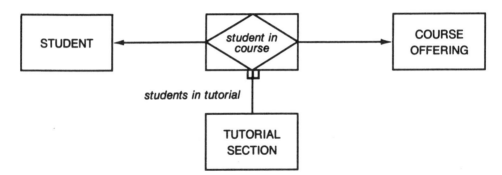

FIGURE 2.7. One-to-many binary relationship involving another relationship.

Relationship between Entity Type and Another Relationship

A relationship between an entity type and another relationship is represented by
putting the diamond of the relationship functioning as an entity type inside a
rectangle. Also, arrows are placed at the "one end" of the lines connecting the
entity types involved in the relationship that is now treated as an entity type
(Figure 2.7). In the figure, the "student in course" relationship is functioning as
an entity type with respect to the "students in tutorial" relationship. The latter
relationship links all students in a tutorial section to that tutorial section record
occurrence.

The tutorial section entity type could have been related to the student entity
type instead of the "student in course" relationship but then either the course
offering would have to be an attribute of the tutorial section or a one-to-many
relationship would have to be set up between the tutorial section and course
offering entity types. The basic FD involved in this situation is,

    Student, Course Offering → Grade, Tutorial Section, etc.

A second example of a relationship functioning as an entity type in another
relationship is shown in Figure 2.8. In this case, the stock relationship is involved

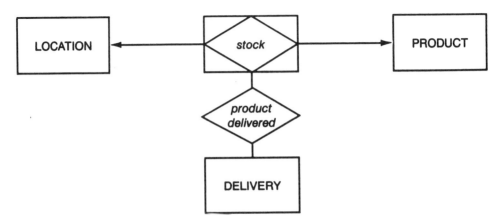

FIGURE 2.8. Many-to-many binary relationship involving another relationship.

in a many-to-many relationship with a customer delivery entity type. The customer delivery entity type models the delivery of products from an inventory to one or more customers.

Recursive Relationships

Recursive relationships are relationships between two or more entities of the same type. Binary recursive relationships are diagrammed in a manner similar to binary relationships between two or more entity types. An example of a one-to-one recursive relationship, marriage, is diagrammed as shown in Figure 2.9(a). A one-to-many recursive employee-manager relationship, is diagrammed in Figure 2.9(b). A many-to-many recursive relationship for which there are no relationship attributes of interest should be depicted as in Figure 2.9(c).

The classic example of a many-to-many recursive relationship for which there are important relationship attributes is the parts list relationship. In this situation, everything from a final product to a raw material is called a "part." The relationship of interest among the parts is which parts go into a higher level "part." For any higher level part, this is a one-to-many relationship; it is simply a list of the parts of which it is composed. But a given part can go into more than one higher level part. This makes it a many-to-many relationship. One important attribute of this relationship is the number of units of the part required to make one unit of the higher level part. Figure 2.9(d) represents this recursive relationship (it is called the product structure relationship in the figure).

The product structure relationship plays a key role in a Materials Requirements Planning (MRP) system—a key application in most manufacturing enterprises.

If a recursive relationship is itself involved in a relationship with one or more other entity types, then a rectangle is placed around the diamond and arrows are added. An example of this is the relationship between the product structure relationship (Figure 2.9(d)) and an operation entity type. An operation is a step in a manufacturing process. One operation in the manufacture of a bicycle, for example, is to attach the handle bar to the "neck piece." This operation has a relationship to the handle bar in the sense that it is the operation at which the

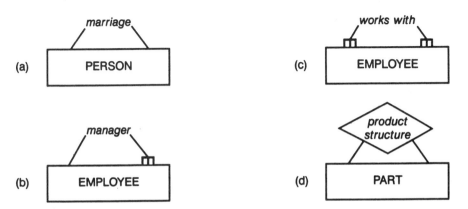

FIGURE 2.9.   Recursive relationships: (a) one-to-one, (b) one-to-many, (c) many-to-many, (d) many-to-many with attributes.

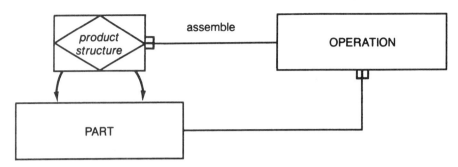

FIGURE 2.10.   Relationship with a recursive relationship.

handle bar is assembled to the bicycle. In Figure 2.10 this "assemble" relationship is shown.

Conditional Relationships

It is occasionally useful to define a relationship that involves two or more specializations rather than involving their generalization in the relationship. For this purpose, a way of symbolizing an "exclusive or" option is needed. We do it by using a straight line to connect the lines that link the specializations to the relationship.

For example, consider a *performance* relationship defined between Review and either Existing Employee or Former Employee. Suppose there is an occurrence of this relationship for each review of the performance of a holder of a job-position. In this case, the relationship can be depicted as shown in Figure 2.11. The review entity type represents a review cycle in which the performance of many employees in their jobs are reviewed. For any given occurrence of the relationship, either a current employee or a former employee is involved.

The fact that either an occurrence of Former Employee or (current) Employee, but not both, participate in each (symbolic logic) occurrence of the *performance* relationship is indicated by the line connecting the two lines just below the *performance* symbol in Figure 2.11.

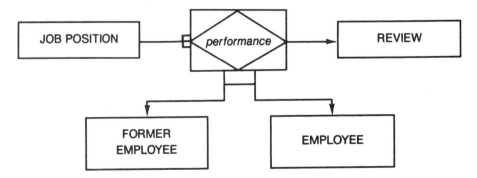

FIGURE 2.11.   Relationship with an exclusive OR.

RELATIONSHIP STORAGE

Understanding how a relationship is physically represented in a computer may help some in understanding the nature of relationships. Some people are comfortable thinking of relationships in the abstract while others prefer a more mechanistic image of a relationship. This section is for the latter.

ONE-TO-MANY RELATIONSHIPS

A one-to-many relationship can be stored in a computer in either of two ways. One way is to make the primary key of the entity type on the "one side" of the relationship an attribute of the other entity type. This is called the "foreign key" technique. In the employee-department relationship example, the foreign key would be a department ID attribute added to the employee entity type.

The other way to store a one-to-many relationship is as a logical list of the related entities. This entails adding pointer fields to the database. Figure 2.12 illustrates the concept. The three rectangles on the left represent three occurrences of the entity type that has a cardinality of one in the relationship. The rectangles on the right represent seven occurrences of the other entity type in the relationship which has a cardinality of "many." The arrows represent pointers. A pointer value is stored in the field of the record occurrence from which the arrow originates and the value is the storage address of the record occurrence to which the arrow points. The middle pointer chain in Figure 2.12, for example, links the 1002 record to the A48, D01, and E20 records.

The foreign key and pointer approaches differ in the access technique required to retrieve the relationship. To obtain the employees in a department using the foreign key approach, the employee and department relations must be "joined" to form an employee-department relation, which can then be printed. To obtain the same listing using the pointer approach, the beginning of the pointer list is

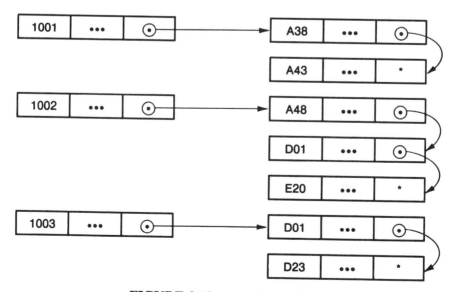

FIGURE 2.12.   A pointer chain.

obtained from the department record. This points to the first employee record. Subsequent employee records are obtained from a pointer in the employee record. Data from each employee record is printed as the record is retrieved.

The second access technique is much faster than the first one. The join operation requires that the employee relation be sorted on the foreign key and then collated with the department relation. On the other hand, the pointer chain only needs to be traversed to obtain the desired information.

The power of the E-R diagramming technique should be noted. The E-R diagram in Figure 2.4(c) represents the same kind of data structure as does the pointer diagram of Figure 2.12. The E-R diagram shows the employee-department relationship at the entity type and relationship type level. The pointer diagram of Figure 2.12 shows the relationship at the entity occurrence and relationship instance level. The E-R diagram is a much more succinct representation of a relationship than is the pointer diagram.

MANY-TO-MANY RELATIONSHIPS

A many-to-many relationship is represented physically by a separate relation that has as attributes the primary keys of the entity types involved in the

Employee

Emp-ID	Name
3254	Howard
6587	Fred
4629	Juan

Possesses

Emp-ID	Skl-ID
3254	SNDBL
3254	CRNOP
4629	WELD-1
4629	SNDBL
4629	DRLL-1
6587	CRNOP

Skill

Skl-ID	Title
WELD-1	level 1 welding
WELD-2	level 2 welding
SNDBL	sandblasting
CRNOP	crane operator
DRLL-1	level 1 drilling

FIGURE 2.13. Employee, possesses, and skill relations.

relationship. The employee-skill relationship of Figure 2.5, for example, would be implemented by establishing a "possesses" relation (record) that has a two-attribute key consisting of employee ID (EMP-ID) and skill ID (SKL-ID). A tuple is entered in this relation table for each skill possessed by each employee (Figure 2.13).

Setting up the possesses relation, in effect, transforms a many-to-many relationship into two one-to-many relationships. We now have a one-to-many relationship between employee and possesses in which a single employee occurrence is related to all possesses occurrences that involve that employee. We also have a one-to-many relationship between skill and possesses. Each skill occurrence is related to all the possesses occurrences that identify that skill. The E-R diagram in Figure 2.14 illustrates the two ways of characterizing the employee-skill relationship.

Each of the two one-to-many relationships in Figure 2.14 can be implemented in either of the two ways previously described for physically representing one-to-many relationships. The foreign key approach requires no changes in the database as depicted in Figure 2.13. The possesses relation has both of the foreign keys required already. Possesses is on the "many side" of both the *has* and *emp-with* one-to-many relationships.

The pointer approach requires that two types of pointer chains be set up. One links certain possesses records to an employee record occurrence. The other links certain possesses records to a skill record. Figure 2.15 shows a pointer diagram of the two pointer chains using the data of Figure 2.13.

The pointer diagram in Figure 2.15 shows one way to implement the many-to-many relationship between employee and skill shown in the E-R diagram of Figure 2.14. The E-R diagram implies all the detail shown in 2.15. It is a high-level view of the relationship that is useful for database planning purposes. The pointer diagram of 2.15 concerns the physical implementation of the relationship. In terms of the three-level ANSI/X3/SPARC architecture shown in Figure 2.1, Figure 2.14 depicts one part of the conceptual schema and Figure 2.15 depicts one part of an internal schema.

NONBINARY RELATIONSHIPS

Implementing a recursive relationship can be done in a manner similar to the pointer implementation of binary relationships. Two pointer fields are added to the record, one for each of the two roles involved in the relationship. Suppose that it is a one-to-many relationship being implemented and that pointer 1 is for role 1 and that only one tuple plays role 1 in any instance of the relationship.

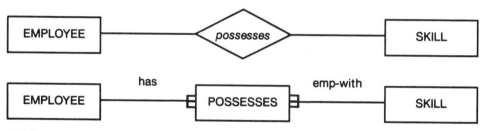

FIGURE 2.14. Alternative E-R diagrams of relationships between relations.

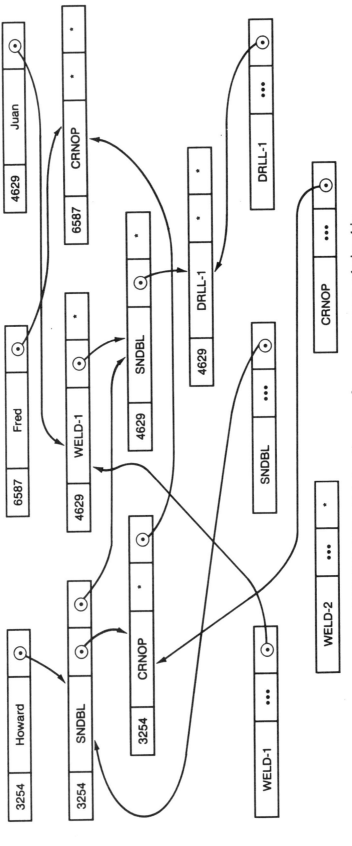

FIGURE 2.15. Pointer diagram of a many-to-many relationship.

44

Pointer 2 is for role 2 and many tuples play role 2 in an instance of the relationship. Then pointer 1 in the tuple playing role 1 points to the first tuple in the list of tuples playing role 2. Pointer 2 in that first tuple playing role 2 points to the next role 2 tuple, and so forth.

The pointer implementation of an n-way relationship is a straightforward extension of the binary implementation illustrated in Figure 2.15. All many-to-many relationships are implemented with a "composite record" which has a key consisting of the keys of the n-entity types involved in the n-way relationship. To this composite record, a pointer field is added for each of the n-entity types. One pointer is also added to each on the n-entity type records. A pointer chain is then started in each of the n-record types; these pointers point to the first composite record occurrence in the list of composite records that are related to the occurrence of the entity type record. Each of the n lists are then continued by pointer values in the composite record pointer fields.

REFERENCES

1. An Interim Report of ANSI/X3/SPARC Group on Data Base Management Systems, ANSI, February, 1975.

2. Peter Chen, "The Entity-Relationship Model—Toward a Unified View of Data," *ACM-TODS*, Vol. 1, No. 1, (1976), pp. 9–35.

3. *Ibid.*

DISCUSSION QUESTIONS

1. Why is the entity-relationship model required for a strategic approach to managing information systems?

2. What was the impetus for the formulation of the entity-relationship approach?

3. An entity is defined as an object, an event, or concept; "anything that has attributes." A product sold by a business can certainly be considered to be either an object (the result of a manufacturing process) or a concept (a product design). Describe the difference between the attributes of these two entity types.

4. What is the difference between a CODASYL instance of a relationship and a symbolic logic instance of a relationship? Does the concept of a CODASYL instance make sense for a many-to-many relationship?

5. Give an example of a valid 3-way relationship not mentioned in the text. Can you think of a valid 4-way relationship?

6. Give an example of a one-to-many recursive relationship not mentioned in the text.

7. The discussion of relationship attributes states that only many-to-many relationships can have attributes. It is suggested that in the case of a one-to-many relationship any "attribute that seems to be an attribute of

the relationship can be seen as an attribute of the entity type that can have many occurrences involved in any given instance of the relationship." Give an example of an attribute that could be associated with either a customer or the relationship between customer and salesman. (Assume many customers relate to one salesman.)

8. The attribute "number of years married" could be an attribute of either the entity types man or woman or of a marriage relationship between them. What would be the meaning of the attribute in each case?

9. In testing the validity of n-way relationships, what is an easily understood criterion to follow?

10. Give an example of a conditional relationship not mentioned in the text.

SUGGESTED READINGS

Hawryszkiewycz, I., *Database Analysis and Design* (Chicago: SRA, 1984), 115–16.

Hull, R. and R. King, "Semantic Database Modeling: Survey, Applications, and Research Issues," *ACM Computing Surveys, 19,* 3 (September 1987), 201–60.

Loomis, M., *Data Management and File Structures* (Englewood Cliffs, NJ: Prentice-Hall, 1989).

Schmidt, J., "Database Models, Where They Are Going Now?" *Lecture Notes in Computer Science,* Vol. 305 (Berlin: Springer Verlag, 1988), 239–40.

3

Entity-Relationship Design Guidelines

We have discussed already the fundamentals of entity-relationship modeling. The concepts of an entity type and a relationship among entity types have been explained in Chapter 2. A system was defined for diagramming information in terms of entity types and relationships. An explanation of how relationships are physically stored in a database file was given as a way to further explain the meaning of a relationship between entity types.

In this chapter we consider how to describe a subject area in terms of entity types and relationships. The subject area is assumed to be limited in scope. In Chapter 5, a general approach is given to defining the data needs of an entire business in terms of entity types and relationships. The focus of this chapter is on the many micro-design problems that arise in the process of executing the general approach of Chapter 5. Characterizing a single management report, accounting transaction, or decision model in terms of entity types and relationships is the concern of this chapter. In Chapter 5, the problem of coordinating the solutions to the many micro-design problems is addressed.

Modeling a specific subject in terms of entity types and relationships—the micro-design problem—can be done in three steps. In the first step, the main entity types are identified. In the second step, many-to-many relationships are defined to accommodate non-key attributes that are "determined" by composite keys. In the third step, other relationships are identified that are needed to provide adequate access to the database and define certain "n-way combinations."

The chapter is organized around this three-step approach. The next section provides guideline for selecting appropriate entity types. This is followed by a section on how to identify and define relationships needed for non-key attributes that cannot be made attributes of any one entity type. The last section discusses other relationships required to fully define the connections between the entities of the database.

47

DEFINING ENTITY TYPES

At each step in developing the description of subject area information requirements, questions arise concerning whether something should be modeled as an attribute or as a separate entity type or as a relationship. It depends on how much detail is required. If only a single-valued "fact" is needed then the data should be modeled as an attribute. If more detail is required then characterizing it as an entity type may be appropriate. If still more detail is required than one entity type allows then one or more relationships may be need to be identified.

The guidelines in this section for selecting entity types are organized into six subsections. The choice between treating something as an attribute and treating it as an entity type is considered in the first subsection. Then, in the next subsection, the question of when to model time as an entity type is considered. This is followed by short subsections on distinguishing between physical and conceptual entity types and on when to model documents as entity types. The fifth subsection deals with a special type of one-to-one relationship, the *isa* relationship. Finally, the sixth subsection introduces the concept of a generalized entity type that is to be later decomposed into other entity types. This concept plays an important role in Chapter 5.

ATTRIBUTE VERSUS ENTITY TYPE

Except for arbitrarily defined entity identifiers (serial numbers, for example), it can be reasonable to treat almost any attribute as an entity type instead. Take, for example, the car as an entity type. As anyone who has looked at specification sheets on the side-window of new cars knows, the list of car attributes can be very long. For purposes of this discussion, let us consider the following abbreviated list of attributes:

1   Price
2. Color
3. Body type
4. Engine type
5. Interior trim package
6. Place of assembly
7. Date of assembly.

Consider why the first attribute, price, might be better modeled as an entity type. If the database is for a car dealer, the need for a history of price changes could dictate that price be treated as an entity type. A history of price changes means, at least, a list of prices and price change dates. This requires that price be modeled as an entity type, with its own attributes, such as price, and effective date. It cannot, in this case, be modeled as an attribute of car because, for any given car, it has multiple values. To model price as an attribute in this case would create as "4NF violation" (Fourth Normal Form violation).*

---

* The normal forms are defined in any of the references at the end of this chapter. It is not necessary to understand normal forms in order to do E-R modeling. This sentence is a comment to those who know the normal forms.

Consider the color attribute. If the database is for a car manufacturer, treating color as an entity type, instead of as an attribute of the car entity type, would allow all of the information about the mixing formula for the color, drying time and temperatures and so forth to be stored once for each color, instead of being stored repeatedly for each car produced. In this case, the reason for modeling color as an entity type instead of as an attribute is different than in the case of the car price.

The reason for treating color as an entity type is to eliminate redundant storage of the same values. For a given color, all the information about that color and how to create it is constant. Therefore, it should only be stored once in the database. By making color an entity type, we provide for storing it once, whereas, if we treat color (and its associated data) as attributes of the car entity type then these values will be stored repeatedly for each car of the same color. Technically, this second reason for making color an entity type is to avoid a BCNF (Boyce-Codd Normal Form) violation.

The third attribute, body type, might be better modeled as an entity type if the database is for a car fleet owner, for example. Data about the cost of repairs for a certain body type could be more significant than total repair costs for any one car. By making body type a separate entity type and creating a relationship between Body Type and Body Repair Charge, we make clear the need to access Body Repair Charges by body type. The information structure that would result from this decision is shown in Figure 3.1. Body Repair Charge must be treated as an entity type rather than as a set of attributes of Car to avoid both BCNF and 4NF violations. Body Type could be legitimately modeled as an attribute; however, treating it as an entity type emphasizes an access requirement.

The reasons for making engine type an entity type could be the same as for color, namely, to avoid redundant storage of details. Or, the reason given for making body type an entity type could apply to engine type.

The reasons for making "interior trim package" an entity type would be the same as for color. The package includes trim details that require further definition. In fact, each of the details could be modeled as an entity with a relationship to trim package. The result would be a structure similar to that in Figure 3.1.

A car manufacturer might want to make place and date of assembly entity types for the same reason as was given for body type—to relate a subset of all cars to facts that apply only to that subset. Considerable data about the supplier (and batch) of parts going into a car is related to the place and date of assembly.

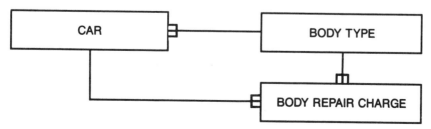

FIGURE 3.1. Body type as an entity type.

The preceding discussion gives examples of three basic reasons for converting an attribute to an entity type:

1. To avoid redundant storage of a series of related attributes, as in the case of color specifications. This is a BCNF requirement.

2. Because the attribute has multiple values for one occurrence of the entity type. In the case of price, the need to keep a history of prices for each car would dictate that price be made an entity type. Making the price attribute an entity type satisfies the 4NF requirement. Multi-valued attributes are common and they constitute good reason to create a separate entity type.

3. To make clear the need for access to subsets of some other entity type that can be classified by the value of the attribute in question. The need for body repair charge information by body type was example given of this reason for using the entity type characterization.

TIME PERIOD INFORMATION

As we intuitively know , the concept of time and time periods is relevant to many business entity types and relationships. The units of measure for time that are used in business vary from seconds for TV time slots to years in finance and long range planning. Figure 3.2 shows the most commonly used measures of time in business as entity types with relationships to one another. This structure suggests that Day is the most basic time period and that all other units of time measure can be viewed in terms of their relationship to the day measure.

The question is whether to model time as an attribute of other entity types and relationships that have a time dimension or to model it as an entity type having relationships with the other entity types and relationships. Consider this question in the light of the three reasons just given for modeling something as an entity rather than an attribute.

The first reason given was to avoid redundant storage. Because time is a one-dimensional continuous variable, its key values tend to be simple scalars that can be very economically stored in the computer. In the case of the names of months and days there is some justification for treating these as attributes of a Month-of-the-Year or Day-of-the-Week entity type to avoid their repetitive storage. But these entity types are not the same as those labeled "Month" and "Day" in Figure 3.2. In general, there seems to be no compelling reason to treat time as an entity type for this first reason.

The second reason given was because the attribute would be multi-valued. Certainly, this applies when we view any type of event, or time-series, as an attribute of another entity type. The marriages that an individual has had, for example, could be viewed as an attribute of the individual. But, in these cases, time is merely an attribute of the event or time series, and should be modeled as an attribute, not as a separate entity time.

The third reason given was to facilitate, or emphasize the need for, access to a subset of occurrences of another entity type. This is a plausible reason for treating time as an entity type in cases where we prefer to view a set of events as attributes of a time period, rather than the time of the event as an attribute of the event. Referring to Figure 3.2, the time periods that are commonly used for grouping events in business are Planning Period, Accounting Period and Fiscal

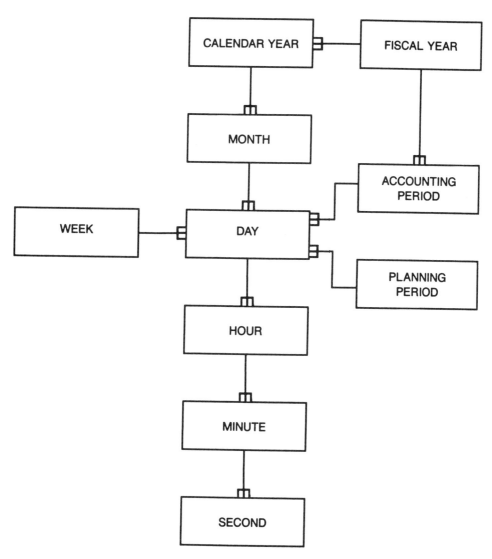

FIGURE 3.2. An E-R diagram of measures of time.

Year. Technically, even in these cases it may be more efficient to physically treat time as an attribute of the event. In most cases, any time interval for which a subset of events is wanted can be calculated more quickly than it can be retrieved from a database.

CONCEPTUAL VERSUS PHYSICAL ENTITY TYPES

The fact that an entity type can be either a concept or a physical object or an event was made clear in Chapter 2. In this section, the need to be clear on exactly what a given entity represents is stressed.

Consider the Car entity type again. What do we mean by an instance of this entity type? Do we mean a specific physical car? Do we mean a certain model of car, with certain options? Do we mean a group of physical cars that are all of the same model and have the same options? These are three quite different entity types. The first is a physical entity type and the second and third are conceptual entity types. The fact that the third is a conceptual entity type is often not understood. The third is a classification of physical objects, which is different from the physical objects per se.

The most important point to understand is that it is necessary to have a separate entity type for each variation on a "subject" that is of importance to the business. This is particularly relevant with respect to the products and services of the business. For some purposes, information about products as design concepts (models) is required. For other purposes, information about products as groups of similar physical products is required. Inventory information is often of this type. For still other purposes, information about specific items sold or purchased by the business needs to be kept. Each of these ways of characterizing product information requires a separate entity type (or relationship).

DOCUMENTS AS ENTITY TYPES

Systems analysts sometimes make the mistake of confusing the concept of a document to be produced by a system with instances of the document. In E-R analysis, a distinction needs to be made between data about a type of document and variable data contained in the document. When a document type is modeled as an entity type, it should be for the purpose of recording information about it, not to define the variable data in it. The variable data in the document should be modeled by other entity types and relationships.

As an example, consider the checks printed and sent to suppliers to pay for products received. Data describing the physical dimensions of the check form and the locations of the payee's name, the amount of the payment, the date, and other variable data are legitimate attributes of a Check Form entity type. But the payee name, amount, date and other variable data should not be treated as attributes of Check Form.

It is conceivable that payee name, and so forth, could be modeled as attributes of a Check entity type. There would be an occurrence of this for each check written. The dimensions of the check and the locations of various items on the check would not be appropriate attributes of the Check entity type. If they were made attributes, this would create considerable redundancy in Check attribute values.

However, if the firm is continually doing business with certain suppliers, even the payee name should probably not be treated as an attribute of Check. The firm is likely to need to know more about its suppliers than just their names. So, Supplier is likely to be another entity type in the database with all the attributes of suppliers of significance to the firm, including the supplier's name. If this is the case, the payee name on a check should be modeled as an attribute on the Supplier entity type and a one-to-many relationship between Check and Supplier can be used to define the payee for each check. This further reduces redundancy in the database.

isa RELATIONSHIPS

An *isa* relationship is a one-to-one binary relationship. It is a relationship between two entity types in which the maximum cardinality for both entity types is one.

In addition, an *isa* relationship has the special property of defining a relation between a generalization and a specific example of that generalization. This relation between a generalization and its specializations has a long history in predicate logic. The relation between turkey and bird is an example of it. It is symbolized in predicate logic as, *isa* (turkey, bird).

When we remember that an entity type is a set of attributes, the *isa* relationship is seen to have an interesting characteristic. The attributes of the entity type that is the generalization are a subset of the attributes of the entity type that is the specialization. A turkey, for example, has all the attributes of a bird. In addition, it has some attributes that not all birds have. This is illustrated by the two attribute sets shown in Figure 3.3. (Neither attribute list is complete.) The point is that the bird attribute list is a subset of the attributes of a turkey list. In an actual database design, one would not include the attributes of the generalization in the list of attributes of the specialization because that would cause duplicate storage. But, the attributes of the generalization do apply to the specialization and are linked to it by the *isa* relationship.

The *isa* relationship can also be used to store information as an entity type definition rather than as an attribute value. This is the effect of using an attribute to define entity subtypes or specializations. A subtype is a subset of all entities of a certain type (or of two or more types). The entities in this subset have the same value for one (or more) attribute(s). As an example, consider dividing all things transported (all shipments) into shipment entity subtypes based on what is being shipped assuming that what is being shipped is an attribute of Shipment. One simple division would be to define as one entity subtype all shipments of "printed matter;" another entity subtype could be for all other shipments (product shipments). It is true that the entity subtype for printed matter may have some attributes not relevant to the product shipment subtype and, in fact, this may be the reason for recognizing the subtype in the database design; however, the basis for the subtype definition is the value of an attribute common to all shipments, namely, "what is being shipped."

It is always possible to divide an entity type into subtypes based on the individual values in the domain of any attribute. The effect of doing this on the database design is to replace the attribute by a series of entity types, one for each value (or set of values) in the domain. These entity subtypes are then related to the parent entity type through an *isa* relationship.

Before considering why it might be advantageous to recognize entity subtypes in a design, we should point out a special connection that may exist between *isa* relationships.

Turkey	Bird
Wing span	Wing span
Weight	Weight
Sex	Sex
Number of wattles	
Length of spurs	

FIGURE 3.3. Attributes of turkeys and birds.

A Special Characteristic of *isa* Relationships

It is not untrue to say that an *isa* relationship is a one-to-one binary relationship; but, neither is it necessarily the whole truth. Unlike other relationships between entity types, an *isa* relationship may not exist independently. All *isa* relationships that derive from declaring subtypes based on the value of some attribute (or set of attributes) in a generalization are related to one another. For any given instance of the generalization, at most one of the *isa* relationships will be used ("instantiated" is the technical term). We call the *isa* relationships that have this type of interconnection a "cluster of relationships."

If there is one generalization and a series of *isa* relationships linking it to specializations, there is an occurrence of the generalization for each instance of a specialization of that generalization. A pointer is added to the record of the generalization which points to the record of the specialization. The record for each specialization has a pointer that points to the generalization record. (See Figure 3.4.)

The three dots in each record of Figure 3.4 indicate additional record fields for the attributes of the generalization or specialization. The only real difference between this pointer scheme and that of Figure 2.12 is that the pointer in the specialization entity type record points back to the generalization record instead of simply being a null (indicated by the *).

In terms of how other relationships are defined, Figure 3.4 depicts how three relationships could be implemented. It shows two occurrences of the BIRD-TURKEY relationship, two of the BIRD-SPARROW relationship and one of the BIRD-CHICKEN relationship. But, in terms of the cluster of *isa* relationships that have BIRD as their generalization, Figure 3.4 depicts one relationship.

To indicate a cluster of interrelated *isa* relationships on an E-R diagram, a special way of symbolizing these relationships is useful. In this text, the technique used is illustrated in Figure 3.5. There are two distinguishing features in this diagram.

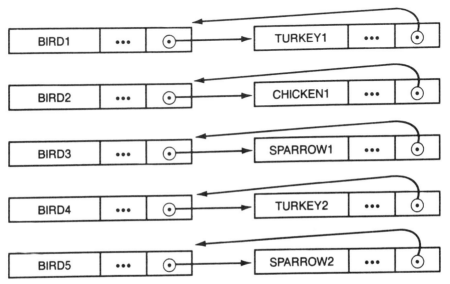

FIGURE 3.4. Pointer diagram for a set of *isa* relationships.

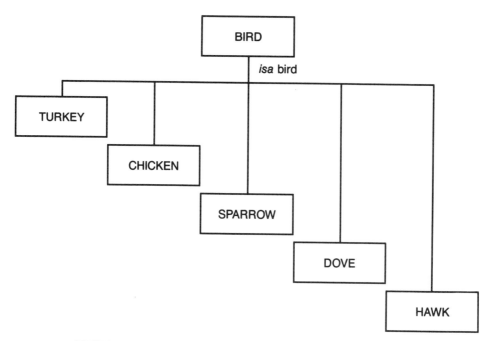

FIGURE 3.5.   E-R diagram of clustered *isa* relationships.

First, all of the specializations are connected by one line to the generalization. Second, these relationships have one name and that is shown just below the point where the connecting line meets the rectangle that symbolizes the generalization. This diagramming method identifies the relationships as a set of *isa* relationships and distinguishes between the generalization and its related specializations.

Multiple Clusters

If an entity type has more than one attribute then it is possible to define multiple clusters of *isa* relationships, one for each attribute. For example, the shipment entity type could have one cluster of subtypes based on the commodity classification attribute, another based on the mode of transport (air, truck, rail, or other), and a third cluster based on the shipment destination (foreign or domestic). The same shipment would then instantiate three *isa* relationships simultaneously. A shipment of documents by air to Chicago would create an instance of the general shipment entity type as well as instances of the Documents, Air, and Domestic entity types. This is illustrated in Figure 3.6. It would also create instances of the Document entity type and *content* relationship, but not of the other entity types and relationships shown in Figure 3.6.

Single *isa* Relationship Clusters

If the domain of an attribute is the binary digits 0 and 1 (which can represent "yes" and "no," "on" and "off," etc.), then a cluster of subtypes (and *isa* relationships) may only contain one member. There may only be a subtype to represent

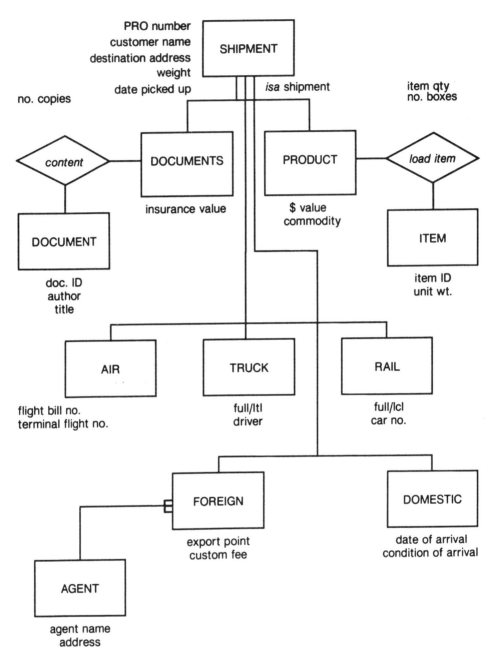

FIGURE 3.6. Example of multiple clusters.

the case in which the entity type has a certain attribute (as opposed to not having it). For example, in manufacturing, a part may either be a purchased part or it may be one that is fabricated in-house by the production organization. If a purchased part has certain attributes that do not apply to parts not purchased, the designer may choose to define a purchased part subtype but not a non-purchased part subtype. In such a case, a part entity type either instantiates a purchased part entity type or it does not.

Specializations of Multiple Generalizations

It is possible to create an entity subtype that is a subtype of more than one generalization (entity type). This simply means that the subtype participates in multiple *isa*
relationships and these *isa* relationships belong to different clusters. To use the
shipment example again, we could treat Documents and Product as generalizations, and the transport modes appropriate for each as specializations. In the case
of Documents, Figure 3.7 shows an *isa* cluster consisting of two specializations, air
and truck shipments. For Product, Figure 3.7 shows an *isa* cluster consisting of
three specializations, air, truck and rail shipments. The result is that the Air and
Truck entity types are each subtypes of two *isa* relationships in Figure 3.7.

Reasons to Use *isa* Relationships

Three of the four reasons given in this section are valid at the conceptual database design stage. The last one given, to avoid a recursive relationship, is only
justified for implementation reasons which need not be considered at the time of
conceptual design.

1. Use of Entity Subtypes to Avoid Nulls

When different occurrences of an *Seperate entity types* ts of relevant
attributes, defining entity subtyp *would solve #1 also* applicable attributes. Depending on how differ w small is the
percentage of occurrences that req *but it introduces redun-* e more or less
worthwhile to declare entity subty *dancy in generalization*

The *isa* cluster in Figure 3.6 for *part. See paper on* s justified by
the null values it avoids. All shipm *Reasons to use classif.* o the right of
the Shipment entity type (PRO n *Reasons to use classif.* tion address,
weight, and date of pick-up). An ᴀ..._..._..._ ᴀ..._ additional attributes of
flight bill number, terminal, and flight number. A truck shipment does not have
these attributes but it does have two other important attributes: full load/less-
than-truckload and driver name. Finally a rail shipment also has some attributes
that air and truck shipments do not have: carload/less-than-car load and car
number. Thus, subtypes are justified for each of the transport modes because
they each have some special attributes. If the Air, Truck, and Rail subtypes did
not exist then their special attributes would have to be added to the attributes of
the Shipment entity type and this would result in null values in shipment record
occurrences for which these special attributes do not apply.

2. Use of Entity Subtypes to Control Participation in Relationships

Another reason to declare subtypes is to better control participation in relationships, and in some cases to make participation mandatory instead of optional.
Consider two examples. In the first, one type of participation is excluded. In the
second example, participation in one relationship is made mandatory and participation in two other relationships is restricted.

The first example is a modification of the shipment database shown in Figure
3.6 to that shown in Figure 3.7. The modification concerns the way shipment
mode subtypes are organized. In Figure 3.6 they are treated as one *isa* cluster; in
Figure 3.7, they are treated as two *isa* clusters. By setting up separate *isa* clusters

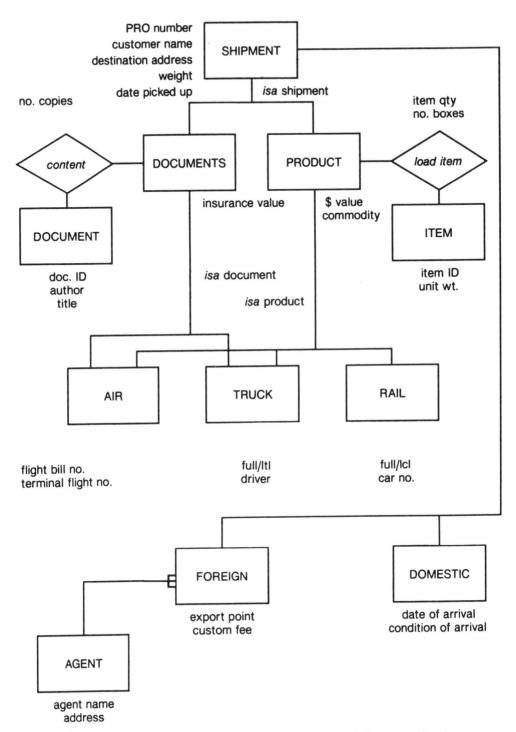

FIGURE 3.7. Example of a specialization of multiple generalizations.

for Documents shipments and Product shipments, we exclude the possibility of shipping documents by rail. If this exclusion is a policy and fact of life for the organization using this database then Figure 3.7 is a better design than 3.6 for that organization.

As a second example, consider identifying labor and materials as specific subtypes of an [Expense ...] r Expense entity type must enter into a relations[hip] e to identify the employee whose time is being [recorded] job or overhead account. The Material Expen[se] relationship with either a *stock* or purchased item material for which the expense is being recorded hown in Figure 3.8.

The advanta[ge] or and material expenses probably includes th[e] ccurrences of the Expense entity type; neverthel[ess] f clarifying the conditions under which the Expense entity type needs to participate in a relationship. If the specializations shown in Figure 3.8 were not included in the design then both the relationship with Employee and the two with Material Expense would have to involve the Expense entity type instead.

[handwritten margin note: Seperate entity-types could do this also except when you discover that you need to control relationships for a specific entity type, then you must create another entity.]

3. Consolidating Similar Relationships

Simplicity is a virtue in database design. For this reason, the designer should consider whether there are two or more relationships in a given design that could be consolidated. If multiple relationships involve entity types that are specializations of the same generalization, then by involving the generalization in the relationships instead of the specializations, the relationships can be consolidated.

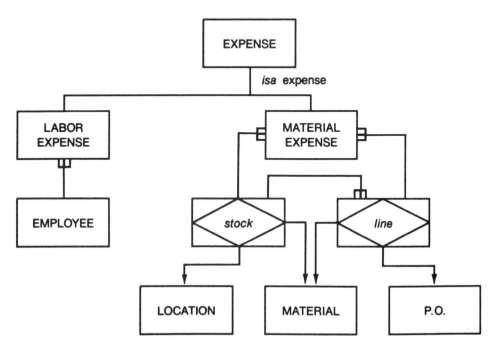

FIGURE 3.8. Example of using *isa* relationships to control participation in relationships.

An example of this is shown in Figure 3.9. The upper E-R diagram involves four entity types and four relationships. The lower diagram of the same information involves six entity types and three relationships, two of them *isa* clusters. By generalizing the Checking and Savings entity types to an Account entity type, we create one entity type to participate in the relationships with the transaction entity types. By creating a generalization of the two transaction types (deposit and withdrawal), called Transaction, we create a single entity type to participate in the relationship with Account. In addition to consolidating the four relationships in the upper diagram of Figure 3.9 into one in the lower diagram, the use of *isa* relationships also shows what the two pairs of entity types (Checking—Savings and Deposit—Withdrawal) have in common.

4. Avoiding Recursive Relationships

A recursive relationship defines different roles that can be played by a single entity type. These roles can be the basis for defining entity subtypes. Thus, *isa* relationships can be used to avoid recursive relationships.

This is useful because all DBMS (Data Base Management Systems) based on the hierarchical data model and almost all commercially available relational DBMS, and many DBMS that are based on the network model, are incapable of handling recursive relationships. Whether this consideration should enter into a conceptual database design or not is debatable. It is more in the nature of an implementation technique. Nevertheless, many people, who are designing a small database and know that it will not be possible to use recursive relationships in implementation, use *isa* relationships to avoid a recursive relationship as a design technique.

As an example of this use of an *isa* relationship, consider the product structure relationship of Figure 2.9(d). This is a many-to-many recursive relationship

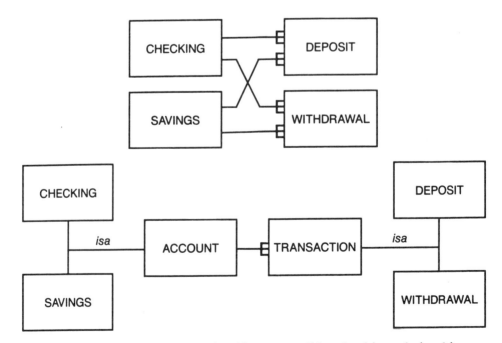

FIGURE 3.9. Use of *isa* relationship to consolidate banking relationships.

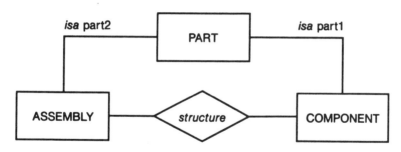

FIGURE 3.10. Nonrecursive version of product structure relationship.

between parts. By making "assembly" and "component" separate entity types, the product structure relationship is converted from a recursive relationship to the binary many-to-many relationship in Figure 3.10. Two *isa* relationships are used to connect the Assembly and Component entity types to the Part entity type. These two *isa* relationships are not part of the same cluster; so, it is possible for one Part occurrence to be both an Assembly and a Component in this design.

The downside of this approach is that at least two records have to be stored in the database for each part. One record is the Part generalization. The other one is either an Assembly specialization or a Component specialization. For parts that are both components and assemblies, three records are required.

In general, creating entity subtypes based on role differentiation for the purpose of avoiding a recursive relationship leads to redundancy and is only justified when the design will be implemented using database management software that cannot handle recursive relationships.

ENTITY DISAGGREGATION VERSUS SPECIALIZATION

In the previous subsection, an entity type was viewed as a generalization and entity types that were specializations of the generalization were related to it by *isa* relationships. In Figure 3.8, for example, Expense is treated as a generalization with two specializations, Labor Expense and Material Expense.

In the top-down method of database design that is explained in Chapter 5, we begin with generalized entity types and later decompose them into more specific entity types. For this purpose, it is useful to have a way of indicating on an E-R diagram which entity types are viewed as generalizations that will eventually be decomposed. The method used in this book is illustrated in Figure 3.11. Double lines, or dark bars, across the top and bottom sides of a rectangle indicate a generalization (or aggregation).

FIGURE 3.11. Symbols for a generalization.

The term "generalization" is used in two ways. First, it can refer to an entity type that is considered a generalization in the strict sense of *isa* relationships. The term "bird" in Figure 3.5 is a generalization in this sense; so is the term "expense" in Figure 3.8. But, the term "expense" can also be viewed as referring to an "aggregation."

When an entity type represents a complex of other entity types and relationships it may be called either an "aggregation," or a "generalization." "Aggregation" is the strict technical term for this view of an entity type; "generalization" is a term used when an entity type may be either a generalization in the strict sense or an aggregation in the strict sense. This ambiguity is useful in the top-down approach because initially the designer may not be sure which type of decomposition will apply. Indeed, it is possible that both types of decomposition will apply.

As an example of an entity type that represents a system composed of other entity types and relationships consider the Expense entity type. An expense is incurred for some purpose, or project. It results in the receipt of some product or service. Furthermore, the product or service is obtained from a supplier. Therefore, Expense can be considered a relationship between project, product/service and supplier, as shown in Figure 3.12.

When the Expense entity type is viewed from this perspective, it can be called an aggregation. The disaggregated, or decomposed, view of the entity type replaces the aggregation. The original term for the aggregation may, or may not, appear in the disaggregated version. In Figure 3.12, the term "expense" does appear as the name of the relationship between the three entity types, but not as an entity type.

A comparison of Figures 3.8 and 3.12 should make clear the difference between specializing a generalization and disaggregating an aggregation. When an entity type is specialized, attributes are added to it that restrict the entities to which it applies. This is the case in Figure 3.8. On the other hand, when an entity type is disaggregated, attributes are taken from it and made into new entity types which are then related to one another in some way. Although not explicitly shown, we can assume that project, product/service and supplier were attributes of Expense before it was decomposed into the system shown in Figure 3.12. So, specializing and disaggregating are quite different.

The term "decompose" will be used to refer to either specializing or disaggregating a generalized entity type. A generalized entity type, such as, Shipment, is decomposed into Documents and Product shipment entity types. An aggregate entity type, such as, Expense, is said to be decomposed when it is transformed

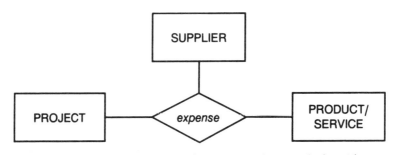

FIGURE 3.12. Expense disaggregated to a relationship.

into a complex of other entity types and relationships, as is the case in both Figures 3.8 and 3.12.

DEFINING RELATIONSHIPS WITH NON-KEY ATTRIBUTES

The first step in modeling a subject in terms of entity types and relationships is to identify the entity types. The second is to define relationships needed to accommodate facts that are "determined" by two or more key attributes of the entity types already identified. This second step is the subject of this section. In the next section, relationships needed for other reasons are considered.

Experience has shown that E-R diagrams developed by taking this second step are often less complex than those developed by adding relationships in a random manner for a variety of reasons. There are usually alternative E-R designs for a subject area that are all fully normalized* and capable of accommodating all of the data and access requirements of system users. But, they differ in the number of relationship and in the use of n-way relationships. The designs that result from the three-step approach described in this chapter tend to have fewer relationships and fewer n-way relationships. They tend to have more relationships between relationships.

The discussion of the second step is organized into four subsections. First, we define the special meaning of "determine" that is used in identifying composite keys and explain the importance of composite key analysis in database design. In the second subsection, examples of binary relationships that have non-key attributes are considered. In the third subsection, examples of recursive relationships that have non-key attributes are given. The last subsection considers n-way relationships needed to accommodate non-key attributes.

DEPENDENCIES IN RELATIONSHIP ATTRIBUTES

The concepts of functional dependency and multi-valued functional dependency are needed to explain in general terms how to identify key attributes (and analyze the validity of an n-way relationship). Understanding key attributes also gives an understanding of non-key attributes and their relationship to key attributes and this is needed to take this second step.

The concepts of functional dependency and multi-valued functional dependency come from the mathematical concept of a function. When we say y is a function of x in mathematics, we mean that the value of y is determined, through a formula, by the value of x. The area of a square, for example, is determine by the length of a side of the square, through the formula: Area = Side.^{2}

Functional Dependency

The value of one attribute of an entity (or many-to-many relationship) is said to be functionally dependent on another attribute (or a group of attributes) if the value of the second attribute (or group) is sufficient to determine the value of the first attribute. For

---

* Normalized databases are composed of entity types and relationships that satisfy the normal forms of relational mathematics. For a definition of normal form requirements, see any of the references at the end of the chapter.

example, assume that name and social security number are two attributes of every American citizen. Social security number is sufficient to determine the name of an American. It is sufficient in the sense that if one knows the social security number, there is only [ ] ciated with that number. The social security num[ ] . If one has access to a database of social securit[ ] n be found if the number is known. Therefore, the [ ] nally dependent on the social security number o[ ] t true. Social security number is not functionally [ ] e name of an American does not mean that the[ ] ber for that name.

$A \rightarrow B$

"A" determines "B".

"A" is the determinant.

The attribu[ ] alue of another attribute is called the *determinan[ ]* [ ] the determinant in the functional dependency that exists between social security number and name. Symbolically, we can express this functional dependency (FD) as,

    Social Security Number $\rightarrow$ Name

Notice that we are using the term "determine" in a theoretical sense. It is not necessary that the analyst be able to immediately respond with a name when given a social security number in order for social security number to qualify as a determinant. It is only necessary that if a database contains a file of Americans with their social security numbers and names, it is possible to get the name of an American if his or her social security number can be located in the file. In other words, a functional dependency is inherent in the meaning of the attributes and does not depend on which example values of the attributes are considered.

Multi-Valued Dependency

A multi-valued dependency (MVD) is an extension of the concept of an FD. All FDs are also MVDs. *In an MVD, the value of one attribute (or group of attributes) determines a series of values of another attribute of the same entity type (or many-to-many relationship).* Whereas an FD determines a single value of an attribute, an MVD can determine multiple values of the attribute. But, notice that values are determined for only one attribute.

As an example, consider author name and article title, which are two attributes of an author. We can say that two MVDs exists between these attributes. Given an author name (now we assume that name uniquely identifies an author), a list of articles written by that author is "determined." And, given an article title, a list of the authors of that article is "determined." Each of these lists constitutes a "series of values" that are determined by the value of the determinant.

The symbolic representation of an MVD is as follows:

    author name $-\!\!->>$ article title

This expresses the idea that the name of an author determines a list of articles written by that author.

Two MVDs between the same two attributes can be expressed as,

    author name $<<\!\!-\!\!-\!\!->>$ article title

Significance of Dependencies in Relationships

Good database designs have a minimum of redundant data. Bad database designs have excessive redundant storage of same data. Data redundancy is bad, not only because it is wasteful, but because it leads to data inconsistencies and the inadvertent loss of valuable data.

FDs and MVDs define the associations between data items that are used to construct databases that have minimum redundancy. For individual entity types, they define valid key and non-key attributes of the entity type. A valid entity key consists of one or more attributes that together form a determinant of every other attribute of the entity type. The key of a well defined entity type will have MVDs between only two key attributes, at most.

Relationships in an E-R model define associations between entity types. The link between FDs and MVDs on the one hand and relationships on the other is the dependencies between the key attributes of the entity types involved in the relationships. In the case of one-to-many relationships, there is one FD and one MVD between the keys attributes of the two entity types involved. This is because the rule of association that defines the relationship is essentially the same as the rule that makes the key of one entity type the determinant of the value of the key of the other entity type involved in the relationship. To say that an author name, for example, determines a list of titles of articles written by the author is equivalent to saying that there is a relationship between the Author and Article entity types.

The key attributes of the entity types involved in a many-to-many (or n-way) relationship are also the key attributes of that relationship. Many-to-many relationships must have their own keys and may also have non-key attributes. They are essentially the same as entity types. By definition, the key attributes of a many-to-many relationship must be the determinant of every non-key attribute of that relationship.

In the following subsections, these facts about the FDs and MVDs that should exist in a well designed database will be used to explain how to develop good database designs. In the process, a number of examples are given which illustrate the FDs and MVDs that can be discovered in a subject area as the entity types and relationships involved in the subject are identified.

MANY-TO-MANY BINARY RELATIONSHIPS

In taking the second step in E-R design, one should first look for binary many-to-many relationships required to accommodate facts that are determined by composite keys. Only after the binary relationship possibilities are exhausted should the n-way (n > 2) relationship possibilities be considered.

One way to survey the possibilities is to take each pair of entity types identified in Step 1 and ask whether there are any facts (attributes) to be included in the database that depend on these two entity types. Consider, for example the subject of magazine publishing. Suppose two entity types are Author and Article. Some facts that one might want in a publishing database that depend on the combination of these two entity type are (1) the amount the author was paid for the article, (2) copyrights retained by the author, and (3) the date by which the author has promised to complete his or her part of the work. If any of these potential, non-key attributes of the relationship between Author and Article must be in the database then the relationship should be added to the E-R diagram, using a diamond to symbolize the relationship. The key of this relationship is a composite key consisting of the keys for Author and Article, author name and article title, for example.

Instead of taking the combinations of entity types in a random order, it may be preferable to first consider cases in which one entity type could have been treated as an attribute of the other if one of the three reasons given in the first section had not force [_Forth paragraph_] [separat]e entity type. These entity type pairs often hav[e] [_reason for entity with_] [w]ith important non-key attributes. Three exam[ple] [_two parents vs n:n_] One concerns the line items on an order. The sec[ond] [concerns the recordi]ng of the salary changes of an employee. A third [_relationship. "In Case 2..._] [concerns] inventory data.

Consider the orde[r] [_Consider the reverse too._] [entity types] identified in Step 1 include Order and Order Li[ne] [but not Item (where an Item is] either a product or service) then there can be no [relationship bet]ween Order and Order Line because an order lin[e] [belongs] [to one order]. In this case, Diagram 1(a) in Figure 3.13 is appropriate and the one-to-many relationship would be identified in Step 3 which is described in the next section. However, if there is a need to keep information about the products and services of the business and Item (or a specialization of it) is an entity type identified in Step 1 then a binary relationship as shown in Diagram 1(b) is appropriate. One important fact that depends on the combination of Order and Item is the quantity of the item on the order.

In case 2, we suppose that employees are given a salary within a range allowed for the job they are doing. They may receive increases (or decreases) within that salary range but their salary can only go outside the range when they change jobs. Assuming that it is important to record salary changes by salary range, some type of relationship between Employee and Salary Range is required. Figure 3.13 shows two ways of relating Employee to Salary Range. According to the guidelines so far given, Diagram 2(b) would seem appropriate if we think of salary change as dependent on employee and salary range. But, the key of a *salary change* relationship must be the combination of the Employee and Salary Range keys (employee ID and salary range code) and salary change is not functionally dependent on this key. There can be many salary changes for a single combination of employee and salary range. There is an MVD but not an FD between salary change and the key of *salary change*:

```
employee, salary range -->> salary change
```

In a case such as this, a new entity type, Salary Change, must be added to the database instead of a many-to-many relationship. Diagram 2(a) is the correct solution. The key of Salary Change could be employee and date-of-change or any other combination of attributes that has a unique value for each salary change.

As a third case, consider the subject of inventory in multiple warehouses. Suppose Step 1 has identified four entity types: Product, Location, Delivery and Shipment. A delivery is a load of product taken out of a warehouse. A shipment is a load of product delivered to a warehouse. A load may be either a truckload or a railcar load; it can consists of more than one type of product. Diagrams 3(a) and 3(b) in Figure 3.13 show alternate designs for the information structure. In both

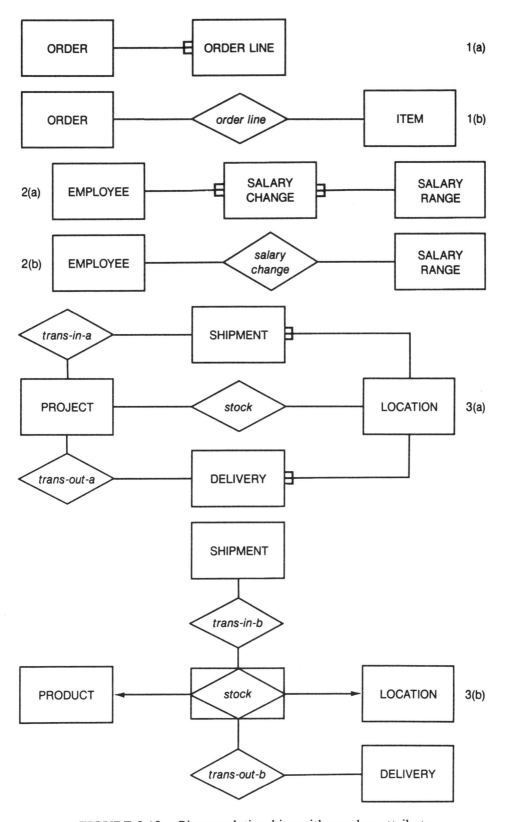

FIGURE 3.13. Binary relationships with non-key attributes.

designs, a many-to-many relationship, called *stock,* is shown between Location and Product. Data about the inventory of a product at a warehouse, such as the stock balance, stock value, and stock location within the warehouse, would depend on the combined Product and Location keys and thus be appropriate attributes of *stock.*

In Diagram 3(a), Shipment and Delivery each have a many-to-many relationship with Product. The quantity of each product on a shipment is an important fact that is dependent on the composite key of the *trans-in-a* relationship and thus this relationship is fully justified in Diagram 3(a). The quantity of a product on a delivery is an important fact that is dependent on the composite key of the *trans-out-a* relationship and so this relationship is also fully justified. However, the three many-to-many relationships of Diagram 3(a) do not make it clear which warehouse a Shipment or Delivery occurrence is concerned with. To rectify this in Step 3, it is necessary to add the two one-to-many relationships shown in 3(a) that involve Location.

In Diagram 3(b), the alternative of defining two binary relationship that involve *stock* as one of the entity types in the relationship is shown. *Trans-in-b* and *trans-out-b* are both relationships between an entity type and another many-to-many relationship, *stock.* Because *stock* functions both as a relationship and an entity type, it is shown as a diamond within a rectangle. The keys of *trans-in-a* and *trans-in-b* are different; the key of Location is part of the key for *trans-in-b* but it is not part of the *trans-in-a* key. Nevertheless, making the quantity of a product on a shipment a non-key attribute of *trans-in-b* will not cause any redundancy in the storage of this quantity because the number of occurrences of *trans-in-b* is the same as that for *trans-in-a,* namely one for each product on a shipment. The same is true for *trans-out-b* vis à vis *trans-out-a.*

Diagram 3(b) shows that in Step 2 binary relationships involving other binary relationships should be considered. The design of Diagram 3(b) has no major advantage over Diagram 3(a) from a technical standpoint but many business people would find 3(a) to be an indirect way of relating shipments and deliveries to inventory.

MANY-TO-MANY RECURSIVE RELATIONSHIPS

In the previous chapter, it is shown that recursive relationships define associations between different occurrences of the same entity type. These associations can be of any cardinality including many-to-many relationships. In some very common cases, these many-to-many recursive relationships have important non-key attributes. For this reason, recursive relationships with important non-key attributes should also be detected in Step 2.

One of the most common recursive relationships with important non-key attributes is the *is-part* relationship. One example of it is shown in Figure 2.9(d). The parts of a physical object are related to the composite object which is itself another occurrence of the Part entity type. One important non-key attribute of this relationship is the number of units of the part per unit of the composite item. Another is the way in which the part is attached to the composite item.

N-WAY RELATIONSHIPS WITH NON-KEY ATTRIBUTES

In Step 2, the possibility should also be considered that an n-way (n > 2) relationship is required to accommodate non-key attributes that depend on three or more

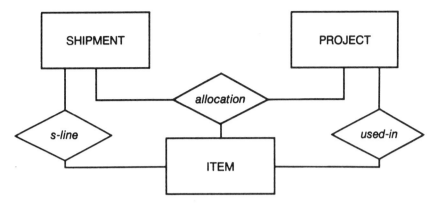

FIGURE 3.14. A three-way relationship with non-key attributes.

other attributes. The freight rates of Figure 2.6, for example, depend on (1) shipment point of origin, (2) shipment destination, (3) commodity classification, and (4) the carrier.

As another example, consider the procurement management activity in which items are ordered from suppliers by a central purchasing department and allocated internally among projects of the organization by the receiving department when shipments of items ordered are received. Two concept entity types relevant to this situation are Item and Project; an event entity type involved is Shipment Received (from a supplier).* For purposes of this example, only these three entity types need be considered.

The *S-line* relationship in Figure 3.14 is needed for information about an item on a shipment received from a supplier. How much was received? How many units were damaged in shipment? What was done with damaged units? Storage of the answers to these questions as attributes of the *allocation* relationship is inappropriate because they do not relate to a specific allocation instance.

The *used-in* relationship of Figure 3.14 defines the Items required by a Project. One plausible non-key attribute of this relationship is the estimated total quantity of the item that will be required during the life of a certain project. This is not the same as the units of an item allocated to a project from a particular shipment. The estimated cost of the item for the project is another plausible non-key attribute of *used-in*.

Another important non-key attribute of this procurement management subject is the units of an item on a shipment that are sent to a certain project. A specific instance of this fact "depends" on three other facts: (1) the shipment, (2) the item and (3) the project. Thus, the units allocated is a natural non-key attribute of a 3-way relationship between Shipment, Item and Project. This relationship is shown in Figure 3.14 as the *allocation* relationship. An instance of the *allocation* relationship involves one shipment of one item and the amount of item on the shipment allocated to one project.

The *allocation* relationship is needed because of its important non-key attribute; however, it need not be modeled as a 3-way relationship. Figure 3.15

---

* Further analysis would show that Supplier and Purchase Order should also be modeled as entity types but they are not recognized as such here because they are irrelevant to the points being made in this subsection.

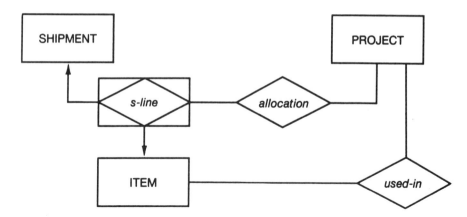

FIGURE 3.15.   An alternative to the three-way allocation relationship.

shows an alternative design for the same database as is shown in Figure 3.14. In 3.15, the 3-way relationship is replaced by a binary relationship. It can be replaced by the binary relationship because the binary relationship labeled *allocation* in 3.15 involves the s-*line relationship.* The key of the *s-line* relationship is composed of the keys of Item and Shipment, say I-NO and S-NO. This means that the key of *allocation* as defined in 3.15 is the same as it is in 3.14, namely, the three part key, I-NO, S-NO and P-NO. Thus, *allocation* in 3.15 is capable of having the units of an item on a shipment allocated to a project as a non-key attribute.

DEFINING OTHER RELATIONSHIPS

This third and last step in the E-R design process adds other relationships to the design that are needed for one or more of three reasons. The most common reason is to provide access to a subset of the occurrences of an entity type. A second reason is to avoid duplicate storage of attribute values. The third reason is to define valid combinations of values for three or more key attributes.

The first two of these reasons apply to one-to-one and one-to-many relationships. The third reason applies to all-key, n-way relationships only. Each of the three reasons is further described in one of the following subsections.

ACCESS TO PARTS OF THE DATABASE

In the first section of this chapter, conditions that justify converting an attribute to an entity type are discussed. The first and third reasons given at the end of that section basically are variations on the theme of providing access. A one-to-many relationship between Car and Price is required to implement the idea of treating the price of a car as a separate entity type. This relationship provides access to the list of prices for a given car. Figure 3.1 shows two examples of using one-to-many relationships to give access to body repair charges by body type and by car.

There are examples of using relationships to provide access to data subsets in almost every example in this chapter. The one-to-many relationship between Agent and Foreign in Figures 3.6 and 3.7 provides access to foreign shipments by agent. The one-to-many relationship between *stock* and *line* in Figure 3.8 provides access to purchases made to replenish stock. The relationship between Account and Transaction in Figure 3.9 links transactions to the account to which they have been debited of credited.

Case 3 in Figure 3.13 can be used to illustrate the use of a one-to-one relationships to provide access. One-to-one relationships between Shipment and Delivery could be added to both 3(a) and 3(b) to link deliveries that are actually just transfers to another warehouse to the appropriate shipment occurrence linked to the stock that is being replenished by the delivery.

AVOID DUPLICATE STORAGE

In terms of the discussion of car attributes in the first section, this reason for a one-to-many relationship applies to the color attribute. If color is converted to an entity type to avoid duplicate storage of a lot of color data that applies to many cars then that entity type needs to be linked to Car by a one-to-many relationship so that all the color data are linked to each car to which it applies.

The one-to-many relationship between Agent and Foreign in Figures 3.6 and 3.7 can be viewed as avoiding the need to store all the information about an agent with every shipment to that agent. Thus, this relationship is justified by two reasons for using one-to-many relationships.

The relationship between Employee and Labor Expense in Figure 3.8 is another example of the use of a one-to-many relationship to avoid storing data redundantly. A given employee could generate many labor charges every day which means that much duplication would occur if the employee name and other data were to be stored as part of each charge record.

DEFINE VALID COMBINATIONS

When an n-way relationship without non-key attributes (or an entity type with a key composed of three or more attributes and no non-key attributes) is being considered for possible addition to a database design, the question should be considered of using some combination of binary relationships instead. There are three conditions in which a combination of binary relationships should be used instead. The first condition is discussed in the next part of this subsection. This is followed by a part on the difference between independent and interdependent MVDs which is the basis for the distinction between the second and third conditions for using binary instead of n-way relationships. Then the other two conditions are discussed.

Decomposition in the Case of a Functional Dependency

If an FD exists between the key attributes of an n-way relationship (n > 2), the attribute(s) that is determined can be removed from the relationship and linked to the entity type of the determinant (the entity type for which the determinant attribute is the key) in a one-to-many relationship. This will leave the remaining

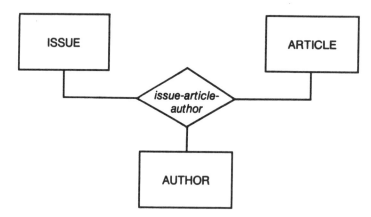

FIGURE 3.16.   Three-way relationship.

entity types in an (n-1)-way relationship and remove the attribute of the removed entity type from the relationship key.

As an example, suppose an n-way relationship is being considered among (1) Magazine Issue, (2) Article (in the magazine) and (3) Author (of article). Figure 3.16 shows a diagram of the relationship. An instance of the relationship involves an issue of the magazine, an article in it and an author of the article.

If this issue-article-author relationship is a valid three-way relationship then it is necessary to know the values of the key attributes for all three entity types in order to identify a specific (symbolic logic) instance of the relationship. Let us suppose the key attributes are: issue number, article title, and author name. Is it necessary to know all three of these to identify an instance of the relationship? No, we only need to know author name and the article title, assuming that an article is never published in more than one issue.

This means that the three way relationship of Figure 3.16 can be replaced by the two binary relationships. According to the rule stated above, the Issue entity type is pulled out of the *issue-article-author* relationship of Figure 3.16, leaving the *article-author* relationship as shown in Figure 3.17. Also, according

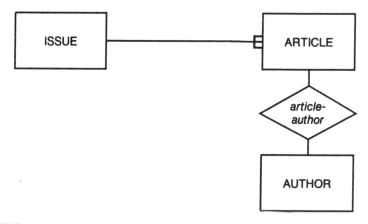

FIGURE 3.17.   Two binary relationships, one is one-to-many.

to the rule, a one-to-many relationship is established between the Issue and Article entity types because article title is the attribute that determines the issue number.

The Figure 3.17 design avoids redundancy in the storage of the magazine issue numbers that the Figure 3.16 design will cause. For any article with more than one author, the Figure 3.16 design will store the same issue number for each author, whereas the Figure 3.17 design will store the issue number only once and link it to all articles in that issue.

It is possible that the determinant of an FD consists of more than one attribute. In such cases the rule needs to be modified. The attribute (or attributes) determined are still removed from the relationship. However, the one-to-many relationship would be with a relationship among the attributes of the determinant rather than with the entity type of the attribute that is the determinant.

Independent and Interdependent MVDs

When there are three or more attributes in an all key relationship, there can be MVDs that have the same determinant but determine a series of values for a different attribute. These MVDs may or may not be independent of one another. If they are independent then the relationship violates what is called the fourth normal form condition and can be decomposed into two relationships each having fewer attributes without losing any information. If they are interdependent then a fifth normal form condition is violated and the relationship can be decomposed into three or more binary relationships without loss of information.

For the case of a 3-way relationship, the difference between MVD independence and interdependence can be defined abstractly as follows: If A, B, and C are the three key attributes of the relationship and A -->> B and A -->> C then these two MVDs are interdependent if B -->> C. Otherwise, the two MVDs are independent.

The most common error in applying these rules is to assume an MVD between two attributes that is not really valid. It is important that the dependencies between two attributes be as definite and fixed as a functional relation between variables in mathematics. To illustrated this, consider some examples.

Suppose a relationship between Employee, Skill, and Job (with key attributes E, S and J, respectively) is being considered. Let us assume that each employee has a definite set of skills. This is the basis for one MVD: E -->> S. If an employee is assigned a series of jobs over time then a second MVD is E -->> J. If it is assumed that employees are never assigned jobs they lack the skills to do and that there is a definite set of skills required for each job then a third MVD is S -->> J. In this case, the first two MVDs are interdependent.

As a second example, consider the keys of a relationship shown in Figure 3.18 between Article (in a periodical), Author, and Subject (as in a subject index). Let their key attributes be R, U and S, respectively. One MVD already discussed between the keys of these entity types is R -->> U. For each article there is a definite list of authors. Each article can be assumed to cover a certain number of subjects as the subjects are defined in a subject index. Therefore, an MVD between article and subject needs to be recognized: R -->> S. But, no MVD should be assumed between author and subject. One could be defined, based on history: a given author has written articles on certain subjects. But an author is not

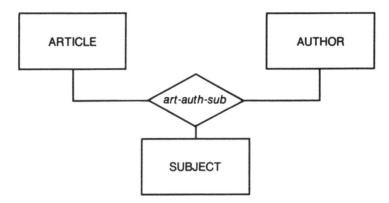

FIGURE 3.18.   Author-article-subject relationship.

limited to that fixed list of subjects. In the future, the author may write on new subjects. So, there is no MVD between subject and author. Therefore, in this case the two MVDs are independent.

As a third case, consider the *allocation* relationship of Figure 3.14. The key attributes of this relationship are shipment number, item number, and project number (S-NO, I-NO and P-NO). One definite MVD among these attributes is that between S-NO and I-NO. A given shipment has a specific set of items included in it. However, there are no other MVDs with single attribute keys. An item is not linked to a fixed set of projects. The set of projects to which an item is allocated can vary from one shipment to the next. The MVD (S-NO, I-NO) -->> P-NO is valid but I-NO -->> P-NO is invalid.

Notice that the multiple MVDs must involve more than two attributes and have single key determinants. The example previously given of the two MVDs between article and author would not meet the requirement that more than two attributes be involved.

Decomposition in the Case of Multiple Independent MVDs

If there are multiple MVDs between more than two attributes in an n-way relationship and one of them is independent of the other(s) then the entity type corresponding to an attribute whose values are determined by an independent MVD should be removed from the relationship. A many-to-many relationship should then be established between the entity removed and the entity having the attribute that is the determinant of the independent MVD.

This leaves the remaining entity types in an (n-1)-way relationship which includes the entity type of the determinant of the independent MVD. But, it does not include the entity type of the attribute determined by the independent MVD.

We can apply this decomposition algorithm to article-author-subject relationship of Figure 3.18. This relationship was shown to have two independent MVDs in the previous subsection. If we take the key of Author (U in the previous discussion) as the attribute whose values are determined by the MVD R -->> U, then according to the rule, Author should be removed from the relationship shown in Figure 3.18 and linked to Article in a separate many-to-many relationship. This leaves Article and Subject in the original relationship. The net result is

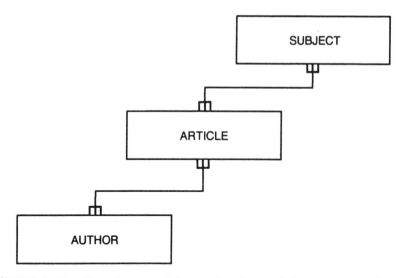

FIGURE 3.19. Fourth normal form of author-article-subject relationship.

the structure shown in Figure 3.19. The two binary relationships in 3.19 will store everything that 3.18 would store but with less redundancy.

Decomposition in the Case of Interdependent MVDs

If there are multiple MVDs between more than two attributes in an n-way relationship and they are all interdependent then the relationship should be decomposed to n relationships that are each (n-1)-way relationships. In the case of three-way relationships, this means that three binary relationships should be formed to replace the three way relationship.*

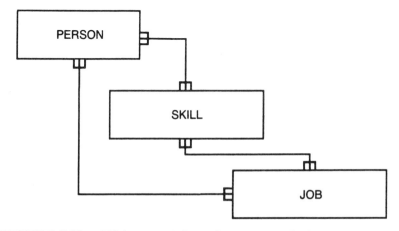

FIGURE 3.20. Fifth normal form for person-skill-job relationship.

* This rule is based on the fifth normal form in relational mathematics.

As an example of this rule, consider the *employee-skill-job* relationship discussed in the previous subsection on independent and interdependent MVDs. It was shown there to have two interdependent MVDs, E -->> S and E -->> J. According to the rule, the 3-way relationship between Employee, Skill, and Job should be decomposed into three binary relationships as shown in Figure 3.20. These three binary relationships will store the same information as would a 3-way relationship between the three entity types but with less redundancy.

SUMMARY

A three step approach to modeling a subject in terms of entity types and relationships is explained. In the first step, the entity types are identified. A number of considerations that bear on the selection of entity types are discussed, including converting attributes to entity types, modeling time, distinguishing between conceptual and physical versions of an entity, and the use of specializations and generalizations.

The second step is to identify many-to-many relationships needed to accommodate attributes that are determined by composite keys. Functional dependency is defined. Examples of binary, recursive and n-way relationships that should be identified in the second step are given.

In the third and last step, other relationships are added for one or more of three reasons. The three reasons are discussed, namely, (1) provide access to parts of the database, (2) avoid duplicate storage, and (3) define an n-way or multiple binary relationships so that important entity combinations can be recorded. With respect to n-way relationships, three conditions under which an n-way relationship should be decomposed are given.

REFERENCES

1. Date, C. J., *An Introduction to Database Systems,* 3rd ed. (Reading, MA: Addison-Wesley, 1982).
2. Kent, Williams, "A Simple Guide to Five Normal Forms in Relational Database Theory," *Communications of the ACM, 26,* No.2, (Feb. 1983), pp. 120–125.
3. Loomis, Mary, *The Database Book* (New York: Macmillan, 1987).

DISCUSSION

1. Under what conditions should a subject be treated as an entity type rather than as an attribute?

2. Under what conditions should time be modeled as an entity type?

3. When is an *isa* relationship appropriate?

4. Explain the fundamental difference between specializing a generalization and decomposing an aggregation.

5. When should an apparent relationship between two entity types be modeled as a separate entity type with one-to-many relationships with each of the other two entity types?

6. Consider a 3-way relationship between the entity types Customer, Invoice and Shipment. Is this a valid 3-way relationship?

PROBLEMS

1. In wholesaling and in the "just-in-time" supply arrangements that a manufacturer makes with a parts supplier, blanket purchase orders are commonly issued for one or more products. Simultaneously and subsequently, shipment release orders are given to the supplier to ship under a blanket purchase order specific quantities of various products to a specific location on a certain date. Define the relationships that need to be recognized among the three entity types: PO (Purchase Order), REL (shipment release order), and PROD (product) in this situation. What about any relationships between the relationships?

2. The systems engineering department of an aerospace firm needs information about the documents in its possession. Describe the information needed in terms of an E-R diagram. The department receives documents from its customers (mainly from a few government agencies, but not always), its employees (project reports and test results), conferences and seminars, and purchased technical periodicals, monographs and books. In addition to basic bibliographic data on each document, the department needs to know when each document was received, who has custody of it, and who actually has it at the moment. In the case of multiple copies of a document, this latter data may be different for each copy. The managers would also like to be able to locate the documents in the department by a topical index which they will define. This set of topics, subtopics, sub-subtopics, etc. is to be tailored to the needs of the engineers and is expected to evolve as the work of the department changes. Each document may deal with multiple subtopics. In the case of some documents, such as periodicals, the engineers want to be able to record the pages that deal with a specific subtopic.

3. The administrator of the health insurance provided for employees in a large corporation needs access to certain information on the subject of employee health insurance services. Develop an E-R diagram of this subject. The organization has the following relevant characteristics.

   a) The organization is divided into departments. Each department is characterized by a unique department number and name.

   b) Each employee is assigned to a department. Information maintained about each employee is employee name, address, age, and name of spouse. Each employee can also have a number of children that also may be included in the insurance plan.

   c) Each employee can belong to only one health insurance plan.

d) Each insurance plan is identified by an insurance company name, address, and contact and a series of three deductible amounts per year: (1) deductible amount per employee, (2) deductible amount per dependent, and (3) deductible amount per family.

e) Claims filed by employees and their dependents are stored as well as payments made either to a hospital, doctor, or employee.

f) Claims are paid when the amounts claimed exceed the relevant deductible amounts of the plan.

g) The amount allowed for a claim may depend on the medical procedure(s) carried out for the case. There is a maximum amount paid per medical procedure. Each claim lists the medical procedures for which payment is requested.

4

Functional Modeling

Chapter 1 contains an overview of the opportunity to use information systems as a competitive weapon. The opportunity requires that senior management avoid both too much and too little control of information systems development. The recommended steps in managing development of these systems are summarized in Table 1.1.

The second step in the recommended approach is to define the functional model implied by the goals of the business. The main subject of this chapter is taking that step. The top-level function is described. Guidelines for subdividing a function into subfunctions are given. The question of when not to subdivide a function is answered. The likelihood that two or more functions may share the same subfunction is considered. Also, the difference between this form of functional modeling and various structured systems analysis methods is made clear.

The step of constructing a functional model follows the first step in Table 1.1 which is to clarify the purpose, strategy, and goals of the business. Functional modeling naturally follows this first step because the whole purpose of the model is to describe what has to be done (the functions) to execute the strategy and achieve the goals. To make clear how functions relate to strategy and goals, this chapter begins with a discussion of strategic planning and its relation to functional modeling.

The step of defining functions also needs to be related to the step of identifying functional experts, step 3 of Table 1.1. These experts are the managers and staff members who subdivide the functions and create the detailed functional model. Identifying these experts is tantamount to relating functions to organizational units and job classifications. This is discussed in the last section of the chapter.

ORGANIZATIONAL PURPOSE

Clarifying and developing the purpose and strategy of an organization is of central importance. Functional modeling is only one among many aspects of an enterprise that should be strongly influenced by the shared sense of purpose in an organization. Worthy goals and a credible plan to achieve them are behind every successful human endeavor.

The purpose of this section is to show how strategic planning relates to functional modeling and database planning. It is not to present a methodology for strategic planning. Managing the sense of purpose and goals that prevails in an organization is central to the subject of management itself and is beyond the scope of this book.

PURPOSE SHAPES AND ENERGIZES

Every new business plan and prospectus for a new stock issue promotes the purposes of the enterprise. The goals may be described as exploiting market opportunities, advancing technology, improving justice, or developing resources. The plan may include financial, operational, and technological aspects. In any case, an opportunity is described to motivate prospective participants and mobilize the necessary resources.

Within an established organization, worthy and reasonable goals are the basis for all project initiatives. Market research, new product development, production process development, personnel policy review, and information systems development are all projects beginning with goals believed to be worthy by an organization. Personal relations and persuasive abilities can help to launch or sustain a project, but a project with a purpose that is not congruent with the goals of the organization has very little chance of ever getting funded, let alone surviving, in a well-run enterprise.

Shared Purpose Upholds Authority

A common purpose is the ultimate basis for managerial authority. It is the worthiness and feasibility of the objectives that attract and hold investor or governmental support for an enterprise. It is respect for purposes that makes the difference between a devoted worker and "organizational deadwood." The manager who fails to give priority to the goals of the organization, and instead substitutes his or her own goals, is misusing the position and failing as a manager.

The role of objectives in establishing authority can be seen in discussions of the relationship between the chief executive and board of directors of an organization. In one case reported in *Executive Speeches,* [1] Ross Van Ness observes that "a positive relationship between library board members and the library director depends on mutual trust, mutual expectations, a clear understanding of lines of authority, and a shared mission." Legally, a library board can employ a library chief executive either "at will" or under a contract. The contract gives the executive more apparent authority. However, if a shared sense of the mission of the library is missing, the authority provided by the contract is rather quickly eroded by events. Thus, the real basis for both the contract and the authority is seen to be the shared sense of mission.

Management by Results

The basis for all measures of managerial performance is the objectives and goals of the organization. If objectives are unclear, performance evaluations become highly subjective and erratic. Evaluations of the performance of overhead functions, such as data processing, are particularly prone to this deficiency, because the goals of data processing are often not clearly linked to the objectives of the organization. Consequently, the overhead function evaluations are often based on anecdotal evidence and subjective opinions.

The fact that objectives and goals are the basis for both managerial authority and sound performance evaluation is illustrated by the experience of Security Pacific Bank as reported in the *MIS Quarterly*.[2] In the 1970s, the bank's data processing department developed a reputation for high costs and low productivity. Its budget grew at an annual rate in excess of 20 percent, and its systems development projects were typically behind schedule and over budget. In 1982, two steps were taken: (1) the data processing department was made a separate corporation (Security Pacific Automation Company or SPAC) and (2) a Management by Results (MBR) program was introduced. MBR is a variation on MBO (Management by Objectives). The MBR program has four components. One is strategic planning which is aimed at defining the objectives and goals of the organization (in this case, SPAC and the bank). The second is service level agreements; these are agreements with the bank units that buy SPAC services that translate the strategic goals into SPAC performance measures. The third component is commitment planning which sets up objectives for individual SPAC managers, including the objective of meeting service level agreements for which the manager is responsible. The fourth component is performance appraisal and compensation which determines the manager's pay and advancement opportunities.

It took SPAC nearly three years to fully implement MBR; but the beneficial effects began to show up in aggregate statistics and financial performance even before full implementation. By 1985, SPAC had slowed the growth of its budget significantly and in 1986 the budget actually decreased, while the volume of services being provided continued to increase. To quote from a banking industry survey, "Security Pacific's performance has improved two to three hundred percent. In operating volume, they moved from 19th to 8th place nationally and are the top rated wholesale bank in California."[3] MBR is credited with playing a significant role in this performance improvement.

CLARIFYING PURPOSES

Clarifying the purposes of an enterprise has several facets. Agreeing on a statement of purpose or mission is one aspect. Building an awareness and common understanding of corporate objectives and values in the minds of the stakeholders is another. Identifying what has to be done to achieve a purpose is a third facet.

These facets are not unrelated. Agreeing on a statement of purpose involves building a common understanding and analyzing action and policy implications. Building awareness of objectives and values is aided by a statement of purpose and the linking of actions to purposes. Identifying the actions implied by a purpose is only possible if the purpose is clear and understood by those who can identify what has to be done to achieve it.

It is the third facet, identifying what has to be done, that connects strategic planning to functional modeling. Developing a functional model appropriate for information systems planning is inextricably connected to strategic planning because the functional model should describe what has to be done to achieve the objectives of the enterprise. Only those familiar with the objectives can do this modeling with some sense of authority. At the same time, doing it helps the strategic planners to evaluate and refine proposed objectives in the light of available resources.

Getting Specific

Many systems have been devised to manage the development and implementation of a corporate strategy. It is not necessary to consider them in detail here. Note, however, that in one way or another, a *result* is the linking of general purposes to specific actions or activities. In the MBR system used at Security Pacific Bank, for example, strategic planning is linked to service level agreements which are linked to individual manager commitment planning which is linked to managerial compensation and advancement actions.

Somewhere along this chain that links purposes to actions the focus shifts from ends to means. In the case of MBR, the shift occurs at the service level agreement step. At this step, the primary focus is on what is going to be done, not on why it should be done. The why question is presumed to have been answered in the first step—strategic planning.

Functional modeling starts at that point where the primary focus shifts from ends to means. It is an analysis of what has to be done to accomplish an end result. The end result is taken as given. The concern is with spelling out the details of what has to be done.

Critical Success Factors

Even though the primary focus shifts from ends to means at a point in the chain from purpose to actions, the need for strategy, goals, and ethical values does not stop at that point. At the lower functional levels, strategy becomes tactics and goals become subgoals but some sense of purpose and plan should and will govern actions at every level.

One method of defining tactics and goals at any functional level is to identify the critical success factors. The basic concept of critical success factors is that the success of a business, or of a subfunction of the business, depends on only a few factors. If those few factors are well managed, then the business, or subfunction, will be successfully managed. If one or more of these critical factors is not well managed, the business will not flourish.

The critical success factors for a function help to prioritize the steps to be taken in executing the function. Consider, for example, the function of running a supermarket. The originator of the critical success factor concept, John Rockart, reports finding four critical success factors for this function:[4]

Product mix

Inventory

Sales promotion

Pricing.

A supermarket manager who considers these four factors to be the key to success will focus attention on managing these aspects of the business well and devote less attention to other responsibilities, such as employee relations, store appearance, and the length of checkout lines.

The subdividing of a function into subfunctions is naturally influenced by the critical success factors found for the function. The breakdown often closely parallels these critical factors. There should never be more than seven critical success factors, and the breakdown of a function should be limited to seven or fewer subfunctions.

Long- and Short-Term Planning

Strategic planning can result in both long- and short-term goals and plans. Long-term planning clarifies objectives, strategy, and goals for the next five years or so. Short-term planning defines goals for the next year and resource allocation plans for achieving the goals. Budgeting is a common form of short-range planning.

Functional modeling for information systems planning purposes should attempt to define what has to be done to execute a long-term strategy and achieve the goals set under that strategy. The data definitions and system requirements derived from an analysis of the functions should be as stable as possible. Any differences between the functions required for the short and long terms would be important for system implementation planning but not for defining database standards.

Existing Business Operations versus a Major Innovation

Two kinds of strategic plans need to be distinguished. One is financial, marketing, and other goals for the existing product lines of the business. The other is plans for a radical innovation in the business.

The functional model should take into account what has to be done to achieve both kinds of goals. The approach, however, can begin with a determination of the functional activity required to achieve the goals for the existing business. Then, additional functions, and changes in existing functions, required for the radical innovation can be identified. A major innovation, such as a merger or sale of a product line, can require both additional subfunctions and changes in existing functions.

Plans to develop new information systems that will radically change the way customers are served, or other aspects of the business, are a type of major innovation of particular importance to functional modeling for database planning purposes. Information systems that cross enterprise boundaries may need to work with the data used in functions performed by customers, suppliers or other stakeholders in the business. In such cases, the functional model should be extended to include these functions performed externally.

DERIVING FUNCTIONS FROM STRATEGY

A function is something that is done to achieve one or more goals. To illustrate, suppose the goal of a student is to get an A grade in a course. The functions the student performs to earn the grade include attending class meetings, studying assigned materials, and taking examinations. Carrying out these functions does not guarantee that the goal will be achieved, but it does make achievement of the goal possible.

A business or other organization carries out the functions that it sees as necessary to achieve its goals. If a goal is to achieve certain volumes in certain markets then the business is likely to include the execution of marketing and sales functions, procurement functions, and customer service functions. All of these functions, and others, are seen as necessary to achieving the sales goal.

Carrying out a necessary function becomes a subgoal of the business. To those carrying it out, the subgoal may seem to be The Goal. If it is a difficult function to do well, and if there is competition, successfully performing it can be all-consuming. In moments of rationality, however, it should be possible to see that achievement of a subgoal is not the same as achieving the ultimate goals of the organization.

The major functions required by the goals of a company that manufactures products and then markets them through various channels may well be those in List 4.1. Performing each of these functions well becomes a subgoal of the organization.

List 4.1.   First-level breakdown for consumer products manufacturer.

Marketing	Personnel
Materials management	Financial/accounting
Production	Information systems
Engineering	

Each of the functions just listed can be broken into subfunctions. Marketing, for example, includes advertising, direct sales, pricing, and customer service. Each of these subfunctions can be considered a function to be performed to achieve the goals of the company.

Each of these subfunctions can be further divided into components. This subdividing of functions can continue until we arrive at elemental activities that must be performed as one activity. The result is a network (directed graph) of subfunctions all of which need to be performed to achieve the goals of the company.

GOALS DEFINE THE INFORMATION RESOURCE

Data relates to the goals of an organization via the functional breakdown. The information used to carry out the functions and subfunctions has value because it enables them to be carried out more effectively, which causes the organization to better achieve its goals.

Thus, goals make data valuable. They turn it into information. The value of data depends on how it affects the receiver of it. If it makes no difference in how the receiver acts or thinks (other than to recognize the data), then it is of no value. If it causes the receiver to make a million dollars, then it can be said to have the value of a million dollars.

Information systems are built with the expectation that they will deliver data that has value. Thus, the value of an information system depends on the value of the data it delivers. If the data it delivers is not used then the system is valueless, or has a negative value. Information has no value; it is merely data, unless it causes someone to behave more intelligently than he otherwise would in working to achieve the goals of the organization. The system that produces a listing of all of the sales of a company each month actually has a negative value equal to the operating costs of the system unless someone plows through the listing each month and bases some marketing actions on the data.

The fact that the value of an information system is zero or negative, unless someone acts on the information it produces, has important management implications. It makes assigning responsibility for system development decisions to the manager or workers who will use the system appropriate and natural. Why allow a computer scientist to impose his idea of a new information system on a group of workers if the value of the system depends on the workers' acceptance and use of the information provided by the system?

THE TOP-LEVEL FUNCTION

A functional model of a business is similar to an outline for an article or book. (It can be clearly represented by an action diagram.) In an outline, each topical point in the outline can have subtopics under it, and any subtopic can itself have its own subtopics. In a functional model, each function can be divided into subfunctions, and each subfunction can be further subdivided.

The title of the book or article is analogous to the top-level function of the functional model. The title is intended to encompass everything included in the book or article. Similarly, the top-level function is unique and includes all the other functions in the model.

Given this characterization of a top-level function, we can conclude that it must encompass what the functional model as a whole defines. As previously stated, the functional model as a whole should describe what has to be done to achieve the purposes, strategy, and goals of the business. Thus, the top-level function is to take the actions and decisions necessary to achieve the goals of the business.

Several points need to be made about the top-level function. One is that it needs to include defining of business purpose, strategy, and business-wide goals. A second is the difference between the function and who executes it. The third point concerns the relation between the top-level function and the scope of the functional model. These points are explained next.

STRATEGIC PLANNING

The general purpose and strategy of the business are set by the top-level function. This function also sets strategic goals for the business that are consistent with the resources available. In fact, the top-level function can be described as setting the goals of the business and seeing that the available resources are used to achieve them in the most effective way.

The top-level function is a dynamic and continuing activity, not a static, one-time formulation of a "mission statement." The opportunities available to the organization need to be continually assessed. When a major new opportunity appears that is attractive and reasonable from the standpoint of resource requirements, the top-level function redefines the strategy and goals, and lower level functions of the organization as necessary, to take advantage of the opportunity, whether it be a new market channel, a new product, a new production technique, or a change in the regulatory environment.

FUNCTION VERSUS ORGANIZATION

In a private business, the top-level function of setting goals may be performed by either the owners of the business or the senior managers or both. For example, the owners may define the purpose and senior management may formulate the strategy and goals. In a publicly owned corporation, a board of directors represents the owners and is expected to play a role in defining purpose, strategy, and goals. In a governmental agency, the purpose is usually defined by the legislature in the laws that establish and govern the agency; the executive branch may define strategy and set goals for the agency.

There is certainly a role for senior management in execution of the top-level function. Managing the resources of the organization gives familiarity with what the enterprise can potentially do. This familiarity should influence the choice of strategy and the way goals are expressed and evolved. Managing resources includes the leadership functions of articulating goals and relating resource allocations to the goal statements. In most organizations, the managers of the organization conform short-term goals to the resources of the organization.

CONSTRAINT ON SCOPE OF MODEL

The scope of a functional model is determined both by the definition of its top level, and by the subfunctions that are identified. If the top-level function is to define the goals of a company and to lead the organization toward their achievement, then the scope of the functional model will be company-wide if all possible subfunctions are identified in the model. On the other hand, if the top-level function in the model is to set the objectives of the food services department of the company and lead the department towards their achievement, for example, then the maximum possible scope of the model is the functions performed by the food services department. This means that the top level of a functional model does not necessarily have to be the function performed by the top level of authority in a legal entity, such as a corporation.

In the previous discussion of the top level, it was assumed that the top functional level could be mapped to the top level of authority in the organization, whether this is the owner, the board of directors, or the chief executive officer. This gives the broadest scope but is not necessarily the most appropriate for conceptual database modeling purposes. It may be that the information requirements of a subunit of an organization are completely separable from those of other parts of the organization. In this case, it is best to develop and use a functional model of that subunit in defining the database for the subunit. This is particularly true in the initial stages of introducing a business-wide approach to information systems management.

Theoretically, the scope of a functional model used for conceptual database planning purposes should be determined by the set of subfunctions that need to access the same data. That set should include only those subfunctions that need to share data. Applying this rule to the subfunctions in Figure 4.1 would result in two functional models, one for subfunctions f1, f2, f3, f4 and the other model for subfunctions f5 through f11. The first group of subfunctions creates and uses data about entity types E1, E2, and E3. The second group of subfunctions creates and uses data about entity types E4 through E7.

Notice that the scope of the functional models appropriate for the subfunctions listed in the columns of Figure 4.1 is defined in terms of subfunctions, not in terms of the top-level function. This should make it clear that the top-level function does not necessarily define the scope of a model. It only sets a limit on what that scope can be. The scope of the model is set by the subfunctions of the top-level function that have some common data requirements.

Most organizations are dedicated to providing certain types of products and/or services in certain markets. In such cases, it is appropriate for the functional breakdown to be based on what must be done to supply the products and services of a product division to the markets. The subfunctions usually require data about the products and services being supplied. In this case, one functional model for a division is developed because all of the subfunctions use data about the product and service entity types.

If the enterprise is organized along product lines and each "product division" has its own marketing, staffing, purchasing, and production functions then separate functional models for each product division are likely to make sense. The only reason for defining the top-level function at a higher level than the product division in this case would be if the divisions could benefit by sharing other types of data besides data about products and services.

Subfunctions

	f1	f2	f3	f4	f5	f6	f7	f8	f9	f10	f11
E1	U	U	C	U							
E2	C	U									
E3	C		U								
E4					U		U			U	C
E5					U	C		U		U	
E6						U	U	C			U
E7					C	C			U		U

U = used by subfunction

C = created or changed by subfunction

FIGURE 4.1. Entity types created and used by subfunctions.

FIRST BREAKDOWN

The top-level function can usually be subdivided into a set of subfunctions such that, if performance of all the subfunctions is properly coordinated by the top-level function, then the top-level function will be performed. One approach to identifying major subfunctions is to answer the question, What are the critical success factors for the top-level function? For an existing business, the way responsibilities are divided among the senior managers should also be considered in defining the first-level breakdown of the top-level function.

These subfunctions will not be the same for all organizations. They will be quite different for car manufacturing and movie making enterprises, for example. Within a given industry, however, the first-level subfunctions are usually similar.

HOW MANY SUBFUNCTIONS?

The analysis of what must be done to define and achieve the goals should first identify major subfunctions rather than small steps within a subfunction. This results in a model that reveals more of the relationships between subfunctions. It also facilitates the decomposition of data requirements as explained in Chapter 5.

As an example of the possibilities in subdividing a top-level function, consider the simplest of enterprises, a lemonade stand. Assuming the resources for lemonade

Alternative 1	Alternative 2	Alternative 3
Produce	Get ingredients	Get lemons Get sugar Get ice Get water
	Prepare lemonade	Get pitcher Squeeze lemons Mix ingredients Taste the results
	Prepare booth	Get box Get chair Make sign Get cups Get money for change
Sell	Advertise	Call to passers-by Phone relatives
	Fill orders	Pour cup Give to customer Take money Make change

FIGURE 4.2. Alternative first-level subfunctions.

and a booth are available, how would you define the subfunctions of the top-level function that is to sell lemonade from a stand? Three alternatives are shown in Figure 4.2.

Alternative 1 in Figure 4.2 defines two subfunctions. In alternative 2, five subfunctions are identified. In alternative 3, there are 19 subfunctions. Other alternatives could no doubt be defined either by combining the subfunctions in alternative 3 in a different way or by further subdividing the subfunctions of alternative 3.

Which alternative results in the most useful functional model of the enterprise? Alternative 1 has the advantage of minimizing the effort required to identify the data requirements of the enterprise. As will be explained in more detail in Chapter 5, the entity types involved in the producing and selling subfunctions are also likely to be the ones relevant to any subfunction of their subfunctions. In addition, alternative 1 gives information about the way subfunctions relate to one another which would be missing if alternatives 2 or 3 were used as the first-level breakdown of the top-level function.

FIRST-LEVEL BREAKDOWN EXAMPLES

Although it is not possible to define the best first-level breakdown for a business without knowing its purpose, goals, and resources, it is possible to approximate it from a general knowledge of businesses in an industry. There are norms of performance in each industry that imply certain priority relationships among the goals of businesses in the industry and these priorities lead to a pattern of subfunctions.

Manufacturer of Low-Cost Engineered Product

A manufacturer of relatively inexpensive engineered products, such as toys, appliances, or hand tools, could be expected to have the first-level subfunctions shown in List 4.1. These represent essential functions for a manufacturing business. There may be others that are essential in certain cases (for example, public relations) but these seven are basic.

Should the first-level breakdown combine the three support functions: personnel, finance/accounting, and information systems? A first-level breakdown that combined them all under a heading such as administration could be construed as conforming to the guideline just given in discussing the lemonade stand case. The reason for not combining them is that they do not have any significant data requirements in common that are not shared by the other functions as well. Budgeting, personnel, and computer/communication system usage data, for example, are required by all of the functions in List 4.1, not just by the three administrative functions. The fact that there are no data requirements unique to the three functions means that nothing is gained by developing a definition of their combined data requirement (as described in Chapter 5).

It should be noted that the enterprise may have organizational units dedicated to performing each of these subfunctions, or it may contract with outside suppliers to perform them. Instances could be cited in which any or all of these functions are contracted out. The fact that a function is performed by a separate organization does not mean that its information requirements should not be included in the scope of the business-wide information structuring project. The information requirements that separate, cooperating organizations have in common should be identified to facilitate the identification of systems that should be jointly developed and shared by the organizations.

Manufacturer of Capital Goods

In the case of expensive capital goods, more resources are put into direct selling to prospects and less into general advertising and indirect marketing channels. There is also a need to install the product at the customer site, and in some cases to provide a maintenance service on a continuing basis. This accounts for the difference between the lists of subfunctions in Lists 4.1 and 4.2. The latter is suited to the capital good manufacturer.

List 4.2.   First-level breakdown for capital goods manufacturer.

Sales	Personnel
Installation	Financial/accounting
Production	Information systems
Engineering	

Publisher

The first-level functional breakdown for a publisher might be as shown in List 4.3. Marketing is again important because the organization must sell to a mass market, and it is not cost-effective to communicate directly with individual prospects.

List 4.3.   First-level breakdown for a publisher.

Marketing	Personnel
Circulation	Financial/accounting
Editorial	Information systems
Production	

Depending upon whether books, periodicals, newspapers, video tapes, or television shows are being published, the first two subfunctions in List 4.3 will vary somewhat. In the case of newspapers, the advertising function may be deemed too important not to be a first-level subfunction. The circulation function concerns the delivery of the published material to customers or retailers and will vary greatly in both its importance and nature depending on the type of publishing.

Additional examples of top-level functional breakdowns are contained in Appendix D of the *IBM BSP Planning Guide*.[5] These examples show both the first- and second-level breakdowns.

SECOND AND SUBSEQUENT BREAKDOWNS

If the first level breakdown has the character of alternative 1 in Figure 4.2, then each of the subfunctions must be broken down further. Each is too complex to easily and clearly identify all the data required, or useful, in executing it. The objective of the second and subsequent breakdowns of the functional model is to define a set of subfunctions that are sufficiently detailed so that their data requirements are clear.

One basic question that this concept of successive breakdowns of subfunctions raises is when to stop. According to the criterion just given, the breakdown process should stop when all the data requirements of a subfunction are "clear." A subfunction at this lowest level breakdown is called an "activity."[6] Using this term, the problem is how to recognize an activity?

To explore the problem of recognizing activities, we consider two functional modeling problems. The first is the lemonade enterprise previously referred to in the discussion of the first breakdown. The second is the functional model for the personnel administration (or human resource management) function.

BREAKDOWNS FOR A LEMONADE ENTERPRISE

Is the breakdown of the lemonade enterprise represented by alternative 2 in Figure 4.2 sufficient for information requirements definitions purposes? Consider the first subfunction, "Get ingredients." The data requirements for this subfunction are a list of ingredients and instructions about how to obtain each one. By the rule that the breakdown process should stop when the information requirements are obvious, the "get ingredients" subfunction is an activity and the breakdown process can stop at alternative 2. However, if the model were being developed to define what a robot needs to do to get each ingredient, then the alternative 3 breakdown would be appropriate because getting each ingredient is a significant subfunction in that case.

Consider next the second subfunction in alternative 2, "Prepare lemonade." The data requirement for this subfunction is a lemonade recipe. The alternative 3 breakdown of this subfunction is essentially the recipe. Therefore the subfunction in alternative 2 need not be broken down. Again, the only reason for breaking down this subfunction would be to automate it, which would require very detailed data on how to perform each step.

The third subfunction in alternative 2, "Prepare booth," is similar to the first one; it consists of a series of four "gets" and one "make." As far as the four "gets" are concerned, the same reasoning applies as is appropriate for the "Get ingredients" subfunction. The "Make sign" subfunction, however, has some information requirements embedded within it that are more easily seen if the "Make sign" subfunction is made explicit. For this reason, "Prepare booth" is subdivided into two subfunctions. One would be "Make sign" and the other "Get materials."

The fourth subfunction of alternative 2, "Advertise," should be broken down to the alternative 3 level. One of its subfunctions, "Phone relatives" has an information requirement (phone numbers) that is not evident until the subfunction is made explicit. The other subfunction, "Call to passers-by," might benefit from some instructions on acceptable protocols for hailing neighbors and strangers.

The last alternative 2 subfunction, "Fill orders," is similar to the "Prepare lemonade" subfunction. It requires information on how to do it. In this case, the information could be referred to as a script rather than a recipe; nevertheless, the information required is essentially the same as the alternative 3 breakdown.

The result of this functional analysis is a functional model for the lemonade stand enterprise (Figure 4.3). Some of the branch tips are at the second-level breakdown and some at the third.

Conclusions

What can be learned from this simple exercise in functional analysis for the purpose of determining data requirements? One observation is that in order to conclusively identify an activity, it is helpful to break down the "activity" to ascertain that the breakdown does not contain a subfunction that itself has information requirements.

A second observation is that an information requirement of a function should itself be treated as a subfunction only if obtaining the information is a function that needs to be defined. There can be several circumstances that make a definition of how data are to be obtained worthwhile. One is that the data are to be obtained by a computer system and we want to specify how the computer system will do it. Another is that the data are to be obtained by sensors and the operation of the sensor systems needs to be specified. Still another circumstance is that obtaining the data is a complex human activity, such as conducting a survey, that needs to be defined.

In the simple functions considered, the subdivisions consisted of lists of things to do. For some of these lists, there is a definite sequence in which the items on the list should be done. For other lists, there is not. The list for "Prepare lemonade" has a definite sequence. The list for "Get ingredients" or "Prepare booth"

First Level	Second Level	Third Level
Produce	Get ingredients	
	Prepare lemonade	
	Prepare booth	Get materials Make sign
Sell	Advertise	Call to passers-by Phone relatives
	Fill orders	

FIGURE 4.3. Functional model for lemonade enterprise.

does not. The functional model does not require that there be a sequential relationship between subfunctions.

The concept of a business as a series of sequential processes is closely related to the functional model of business. Both are event-oriented views of an enterprise. When the breakdown of a function in a functional model is a list of sequential steps that must be taken to accomplish the function, then a process flow approach is being taken in the development of that functional model. However, functional modeling should not be confused with the flowcharting and data flow diagramming techniques of information systems analysis and design. Flowcharting and data flow diagramming are useful techniques of analysis for system design purposes but not for conceptual database design. The extra detail they require about the sequence in which things are done is burdensome and useless for conceptual database planning purposes. This is a point of crucial importance to the approach described in this book.

The aim in business-wide conceptual database planning is to create a framework within which the database requirements of individual system development projects can be coordinated. To succeed in spanning the entire range of potential applications that can share data, it is vital that the analysis techniques that are used do not gather unnecessary information. Doing any kind of planning for an entire enterprise can easily bog down in a quagmire of details. This is the reason it is important to use the functional modeling approach rather than a flowcharting approach in conceptual database planning.

SECOND EXAMPLE: PERSONNEL FUNCTION

The lemonade stand modeling problem is small enough to analyze and depict in a few paragraphs and with one figure. Modeling the functions of a real business is a much larger task. To handle the details, a computerized system encyclopedia, or repository, is required. This is a database designed to hold data about the functions of a business, their data requirements, and many other aspects of the information systems of a business. The system encyclopedia is discussed in Chapter 11.

Depth First Approach

To keep the discussion of the functional analysis process within bounds and yet show how the analysis process leads to the identification of activities, we focus on only one subfunction at each stage in the breakdown process. This can be termed a "depth first" approach to functional analysis, to borrow a term from artificial intelligence. The alternative is to breakdown each subfunction at a given level before analyzing any subfunctions at a lower level in the hierarchy. This would be a "breadth first" approach.

The difference between the two approaches is made clearer by referring to the example of a functional breakdown in Figure 4.4. A depth first approach to developing this model would start with the top-level function in the model, labeled 0 (zero) in the figure. It would subdivide this function into subfunctions 1, 2, and 3 as shown. Next, it would take one of these, say 1, and subdivide it into 1.1 and 1.2. In the depth first approach, one of these subfunctions, say 1.1, would then be selected for further subdivision, into 1.1.1, 1.1.2, 1.1.3, and 1.1.4.

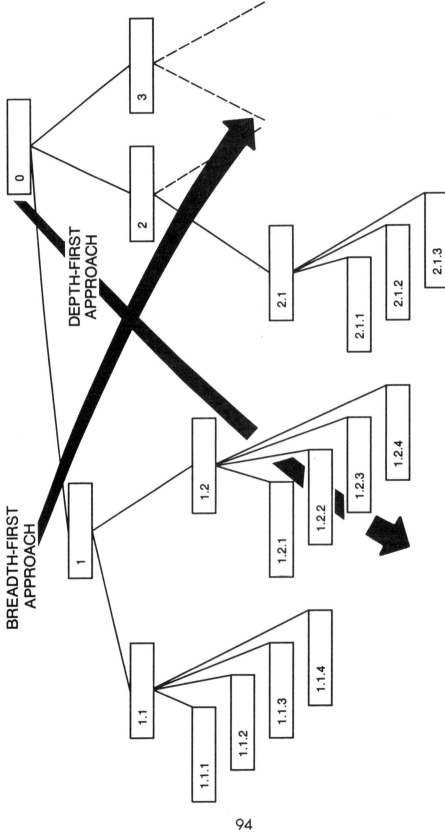

FIGURE 4.4. Ways to traverse a functional breakdown.

In contrast, the breadth first approach subdivides 1 and 2, as well as 3, before subdividing 1.1.

The first-level breakdown of the functional model can be any of those discussed in the previous section and shown in Lists 4.1, 4.2, and 4.3. It could also be any other first-level breakdown that includes personnel (which may be called employee relations or human resources) as a subfunction.

Second-Level Breakdown

In this discussion, we begin with the breakdown of the personnel subfunction shown in Lists 4.1, 4.2, and 4.3. The personnel function usually has several aspects. One is to assist in filling all positions in the organization with the most qualified people available. Another is to formulate the human resource management policies of the enterprise and to see that they are implemented. The personnel function may also be concerned with negotiating contracts with labor unions and seeing that the compensation given employees is competitive with prevailing rates in the area.

In defining this second-level breakdown, we face the same granularity issue that we faced in choosing a first-level breakdown. Should we aim to minimize or maximize the number of subfunctions in the breakdown? In the case of the first level, it was recommended that the number be minimized for two reasons: first, because it groups more detailed subfunctions that share the same data requirements; second, because it reveals relationships between subfunctions in the model that are otherwise hidden. These same reasons apply to the second and subsequent breakdowns. Therefore, the number of subfunctions in a breakdown should be made as small as possible while still being complete.

The subfunctions of the personnel function will vary somewhat from one organization to another. The list of subfunctions in List 4.4 represents a basic set of concerns that are commonly considered part of the personnel function.

List 4.4. Subfunctions of the personnel function.

Employment	Benefit administration
Compensation	Health and safety
Labor relations	Training

It should be noted that the personnel department may have responsibilities that are not part of the personnel function. For example, the personnel department may be responsible for building security, visitor management, or public relations. But in the functional model, these should not be subfunctions of the personnel function. They require data that have nothing to do with the employees of the organization. These extraneous functions should be modeled as subfunctions of the function of which they are a part.

The second-level breakdown reveals some entity types about which information will definitely be required in the database. Information about employees and job applicants is certainly needed for the employment function which is concerned with filling open positions with the most qualified people. But we cannot be sure that these are the only two entity types with which the employment subfunction is concerned. The employment subfunction needs to be subdivided to be sure all of its data requirements are clear.

The same can be said for the other second-level subfunctions. The information requirements of compensation, labor relations, benefit administration, and health and safety are all more or less unclear at this stage. We need more details about these subfunctions.

Third-Level Breakdown

As an example of a third-level breakdown, consider the employment subfunction. What is involved in filling openings with the most qualified people available? First, the available openings are identified and defined. Then, a pool of applicants qualified to fill an opening is created. Once the pool exists, a selection process is conducted to find the best person. Finally, there is an induction and orientation process that can be considered part of the employment subfunction.

This series of steps composes the employment subfunction. The breakdown of this function is simply a matter of listing these steps. They are shown in List 4.5.

List 4.5.   Subfunctions of the employment function.

Personnel requisition approval	Selection
Recruitment	Induction

The data requirements of the employment function are made clearer by this breakdown. The personnel requisition approval process involves job descriptions and staffing budget data. Recruitment involves data about (1) which existing qualified employees should be notified of it, (2) sources of outside applicants that should be notified, (3) application procedures and deadlines, and (4) initial screening procedures to be followed. The selection subfunction involves data about references and a number of other subjects. Finally, the induction process will require schedule data and a list of people to be introduced, places to visit, and points to be covered.

The data requirements are becoming clearer but they are still not absolutely clear for any of these subfunctions. A further level of breakdowns is needed. For purposes of this discussion, we will concentrate on only one of the subfunctions, selection.

Fourth-Level Breakdown

The selection of an application from the pool is a matter of investigating the applicants in the pool in more detail to discover who is really qualified for the job and, if more than one applicant is qualified, who is the best qualified. The manager to whom the person filling the position will report and others in the organization who will have to work with the selected applicant become involved in the selection processes and make the decision about whether to offer the position to an applicant. In the selection process, there is interaction between the personnel staff and the managers of the position being filled.

The breakdown of the selection subfunction is shown in List 4.6. The four subfunctions listed should be self-explanatory. It should be noted that the selection function will not always consist of exactly these four subfunctions. Different steps in the selection process may be appropriate in certain circumstances.

List 4.6.   Subfunctions of the selection function.

Screening tests	Interviewing
Reference checking	Negotiating offers

Have we arrived at a set of subfunctions that have clear data requirements, or do we have just a list of things to be done, none of which require data? No. Each of these subfunctions is a process that needs to be defined before its data requirements are absolutely clear.

The breakdown in List 4.6 reveals some new entity types of interest. One is screening tests; another is references. The interview and the offer are two additional entity types important to the selection subfunction.

Fifth-Level Breakdown

As an example of a fifth-level breakdown, we consider the interview subfunction. This is the process of scheduling an interview with an applicant, conducting the interview, and evaluating the applicant after the interview. The applicant's post-interview evaluation of the organization and position may also be an important consideration.

The subfunctions of the interview process are the three steps just described. They are shown in List 4.7. The term "follow-up evaluation" is meant to cover both the manager evaluations of the applicant and the applicant's evaluation of the position.

List 4.7.   Subfunctions of the interview function.

Schedule interview

Conduct interview

Follow-up evaluation

The data requirements of these subfunctions are not difficult to discern. Take, for example, the first subfunction. To schedule an interview, information is needed about who will do the interviewing and the times when they are available to interview. Information is also required concerning the applicant and his availability for an interview. Finally, the scheduling process will result in an interview time and plan which needs to be stored in the database. So, the interview itself becomes an entity type required by the scheduling subfunction.

If this first subfunction were to be subdivided, it would result in a series of simple "gets" and "puts." A breakdown to show this is given in List 4.8. The fourth step, setting the interview date, requires no data other than that assembled by the first three steps.

List 4.8.   Subfunctions of schedule interview.

Get list of interviewers	Set interview date
Get future availability of interviewers	Notify all parties
Get future availability of applicant	

The conclusion is that the interview scheduling subfunction is an activity. It is a branch tip in the functional model of the enterprise. The steps in List 4.8 are steps that a computer can be programmed to perform.

In general an activity is simple enough to be automated, or else it is a function so complex that it is not worth the effort required to analyze it. The fourth item in List 4.8 may be an example of a function too complex to be worth analyzing. The suggested criterion of "first time when all can meet" may be too simplistic. Many considerations could conceivably enter into setting a meeting date for a job interview.

The other two interview subfunctions shown in List 4.7 can be analyzed in a manner similar to "schedule interview." The conduct interview subfunction has few mandatory data requirements but many types of data that may be very useful. All sorts of information about the organization and the position may be useful in an interview, but none of it is absolutely mandatory in order for the interview to take place. This data requirements specification problem is treated in the next chapter.

Cross Section of Functional Model

The portion of the functional model developed in this analysis of the personnel function is summarized in Figure 4.5. The portion shown is a cross section of the total model in the sense that is shows one path from the top level to three branch tips at the bottom. There are many other paths to many other branch tips in the complete functional model.

This same cross section is shown in outline in Figure 4.6. The outline format places the portion of the functional model that has been developed in clearer perspective than does the depiction in Figure 4.5. However, the view shown in Figure 4.5 emphasizes the particular path we just described through the hierarchy.

REDUNDANT SUBFUNCTIONS

A functional model will not necessarily have a strict hierarchical form. There is a top-level function that is the starting point for the functional breakdown process. When two different subfunctions are broken down, however, the breakdowns may have subfunctions in common.

Common office functions, such as typing a letter or scheduling a meeting, can occur as subfunctions of many functions in a model. Within the personnel function, for example, it not difficult to see that scheduling a meeting will be a subfunction of many functions in addition to interviewing. It will be a subfunction of (1) labor relations, which includes handling employee grievances, (2) compensation, which includes wage negotiations, (3) benefits administration, which

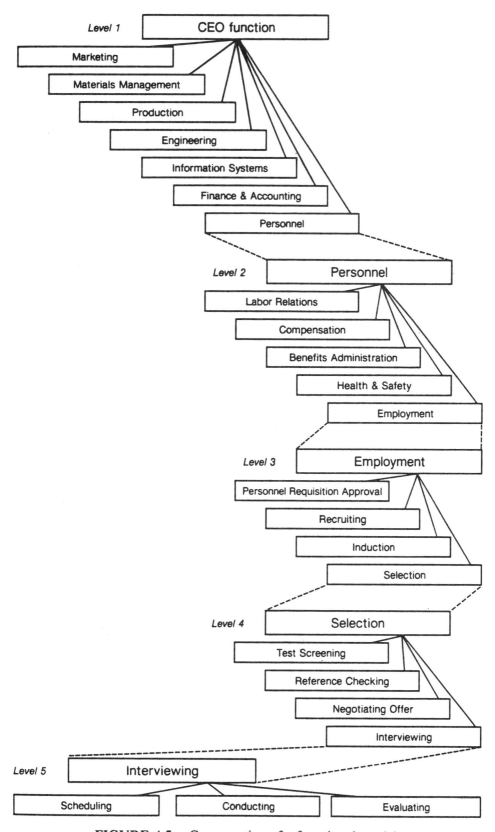

FIGURE 4.5. Cross section of a functional model.

```
I. CEO
    A. Marketing
    B. Materials Management
    C. Production
    D. Engineering
    E. Personnel
        1. Labor Relations
        2. Employment
            a. Personnel Requisition Approval
            b. Recruitment
            c. Selection
                (1) Test Screening
                (2) Reference Checking
                (3) Interviewing
                    (a) Scheduling Interview
                    (b) Conducting Interview
                    (c) Follow-up Evaluation
                (4) Negotiating Offer
            d. Inducting
        3. Compensation
        4. Benefits Administration
        5. Health and Safety
    F. Information Systems
    G. Finance and Accounting
```

FIGURE 4.6.   Functional model in outline form.

includes meeting with employees on pension benefit issues, and (4) health and safety, which includes scheduling safety education meetings with employees.

A function such as "scheduling a meeting" that is common to many functions in an organization should only be shown once in the functional model. All other places in the functional model where it occurs should reference the one occurrence of it. This minimizes redundancy in information requirements specification and shows clearly where in an organization a given subfunction needs to be executed.

An example that uses references to the meeting scheduling subfunction at various points in the functional breakdown for personnel is shown in Figure 4.7. Meeting scheduling subfunctions are only shown for those subfunctions mentioned in the previous discussion of this example. There are probably others within the personnel function which would be revealed in a complete analysis.

The fact that two or more functions may share the same subfunction is the reason for describing functional models as "directed graphs" rather than hierarchies. From a mathematical standpoint, the structure of a functional model is not a pure hierarchy. It is a directed graph.

Care must be taken to distinguish subfunctions that appear to be the same, and have the same subfunctions, but which require different data. For example,

---

EXAMPLE OF REFERENCES TO A COMMON SUBFUNCTION

I. CEO
   A. Marketing
   B. Materials Management
   C. Production
   D. Engineering
   E. Personnel
      1. Labor Relations
         a. Grievance Processing
            (1) Schedule Grievance Meeting
                (see I.E.2.c(3)(a))
      2. Employment
         a. Personnel Requisition Approval
         b. Recruitment
         c. Selection
            (1) Test Screening
            (2) Reference Checking
            (3) Interviewing
                (a) Scheduling Interview
                (b) Conducting Interview
                (c) Follow-up Evaluation
            (4) Negotiating Offer
         d. Inducting
      3. Compensation
         a. Wage Negotiation
            (1) Schedule Meeting with Labor Negotiator
                (see I.E.2.c(3)(a))
      4. Benefits Administration
         a. Pension Plan Administration
            (1) Schedule Meeting with Retiring Employee
                (see I.E.2.c(3)(a))
      5. Health and Safety
         a. Safety Education
            (1) Schedule Meeting
                (see I.E.2.c(3)(a))
   F. Information Systems
   G. Finance and Accounting

FIGURE 4.7. Functional model with references.

consider typing a letter. This is a subfunction that appears to be the same whether it is a letter sent by a salesman to a new prospect or a letter sent by the pension plan administrator to someone receiving pension benefits. However, a letter to a new prospect is likely to require information about the products of the company while a letter to a retired employee requires information on the status of the former employee and pension plan provisions. If these two instances of letter typing are treated as identical, important information requirements will be overlooked.

So, for two subfunctions to be identical they must have the same data requirements as well as the same procedural characteristics. Does the "scheduling a meeting" subfunction satisfy this condition? It does as long as it is reasonable to assume that the future schedules of the meeting participants are in the database. This would not be the case for officers who represent the organization in meetings with people outside the organization. Thus, not all meeting scheduling subfunctions should be treated as identical; however, there are categories of meeting scheduling subfunctions that are identical.

IDENTIFYING FUNCTIONAL EXPERTS

The difference between functions and people who execute functions was pointed out in the discussion of the top-level function. Execution of this function is often done jointly by a board of directors and the senior management of the business.

Subfunctions may also be performed by one or more persons who are either employees or contractors of the business. Companies and government agencies commonly contract with firms that specialize in computer technology to develop and operate the computer systems used in the business. This is an example of a contractor performing a business function for a company.

It is also common for one person to perform more than one subfunction. An example of this is the personnel director who handles public relations as well as employee relations. The administrator who manages the finance, accounting, and personnel functions of an organization is another example.

Normally, the people who perform a function should be considered the experts in it. This is because the information system that supports, or executes, the function should provide the data that those responsible for the function find useful. Why provide data that is not used by those performing a function?

Identifying functional experts, then, is a matter of relating functions to those responsible for performing them. Traditionally, functional responsibilities have been defined in job descriptions. For the system encyclopedia, or repository, we need a database design that links a function to the job-positions that include responsibility for its execution. In other words, we need an index to the traditional job descriptions of an organization.

To define this part of the system encyclopedia database design, an entity-relationship model of an organization can be integrated with an entity-relationship characterization of the functional model. This is done in the remainder of this section.

ORGANIZATIONAL MODEL

The organizational model defines organizational units and relationships between them. The simplest type of organizational model is a hierarchical model with one reporting relationship defined within each unit and another reporting relationship defined between units. Each unit reports to one other unit and may have any number of units reporting to it. A unit has a number of authorized employee positions and each position represents a type of job defined by a job description.

XYZ, INC. ORGANIZATION

I. Chief Executive's Office—President K. Dempsey (4)
  A. Marketing—VP H. Manning (5)
    1. Advertizing and public relations—Director B. Gao (4)
    2. Direct Sales—Director C. Smith (4)
      a. USA/East Sales Office—Manager F. Goetz (5)
      b. USA/Midwest Sales Office—Manager Z. Ali (3)
      c. USA/West Sales Office—Manager P. Sorrensen (4)
      d. Asian Sales Office—Manager W. Chen (5)
      e. European Sales Office—Manager A. Lientz (2)
    3. Market Research and Pricing—Director M. Case (3)
    4. Customer Service and Technical Support—E. Ben (3)
  B. Materials Management—VP B. Cooper (4)
    1. Production Planning & Forecasting—Director C. Lu (4)
    2. Purchasing—Director V. Macais (5)
    3. Shipping, Receiving & Warehousing—Director H. Cane (12)
  C. Production—VP R. Bork (5)
    1. Plant Operations—Director X. Garcia (7)
      a. Department A—Manager B. Grace (16)
      b. Department B—Manager B. Carlson (11)
      c. Department C—Manager G. Bally (23)
    2. Production Control—Director V. Mains (4)
    3. Operations Planning—Director L. Collins (2)
    4. Plant Maintenance—Director E. Bains (4)
  D. Engineering—VP C. Cutting (3)
    1. Product Design—Director P. Smith (5)
    2. Product Testing—Director D. Vine (4)
    3. Specification Preparation—Director M. Mu (6)
    4. Special Projects—Director L. Gains (3)
  E. Administration—VP W. Beacon (3)
    1. Personnel—Director S. Said (2)
      a. Employment and Compensation—Manager I. Lang (3)
      b. Payroll—Manager S. Nam (1)
      c. Benefit Administration—Manager L. Wang (1)
      d. Health and Safety—Manager G. Pool (1)
    2. Finance—Director U. Gale (3)
    3. Controller—Director M. Munger (3)
      a. Receivables—Manager D. Doll (2)
      b. General Ledger and Payables—Manager E. Lang (2)
    4. Information Systems—Director J. Frank (2)
      a. Operations—Manager R. Vince (3)
      b. Technical Support and Training—Y. Lu (2)
      c. Applications Development—F. Carlson (3)
    5. Internal Audit—Director W. Webster (2)
    6. Office Facilities—Director D. Dryer (2)

FIGURE 4.8. Organizational model of XYZ, Inc.

Figure 4.8 shows an example of an organizational model for a manufacturer with a single plant and world-wide sales. Each line identifies an organizational unit. The position of the manager of the unit is shown along with the name of the person filling the position. The number in parentheses on the line is the number of authorized positions in the unit. The indentations signify reporting relationships between units.

One aspect of an organizational model that is not completely shown in Figure 4.8 is the types of positions authorized for each unit. This could be done by listing the job title for each position in each unit rather than the job title of the manager only. Examples of job titles that would appear on such a listing are: secretary, salesman, invoicing clerk, shipping clerk, and electronics technician.

An organization model can be depicted as an Entity-Relationship (E-R) diagram. The entity types in the model are Organizational Unit and Job. The job entity type refers to all jobs that have a distinct job description. The number of positions that have the same job description in a unit is an attribute of the relationship between Organizational Unit and Job. These entity types and the relationship between them are shown in Figure 4.9. There is an occurrence of the many-to-many relationship between Organizational Unit and Job, which is called *job-position,* for each organizational unit that has a given job description.

The relationship between occurrences of Organizational Unit, called *hierarchy* in Figure 4.9, records the reporting relationships between organizational units. In terms of Figure 4.8, it records the indentations shown in that figure. It is a one-to-many relationship because it is assumed that an organizational unit can report to only one other unit.

The database for the simple hierarchical model shown in Figure 4.9 can be made more elaborate to accommodate more complex organizational structures. For example, a distinction between technical reporting relationships and administrative reporting relationships can be incorporated by creating two recursive relationships instead of the one relationship labeled "hierarchy" in Figure 4.9. Liaison relationships between units or job-positions can be modeled by adding relationships to the E-R model. Also, a matrix form of organization can be represented by adding project and employee entity types to the database and adding relationships between:

1.   Project and Employee

2.   Employee and *job-position*

3.   Project and Organizational Unit.

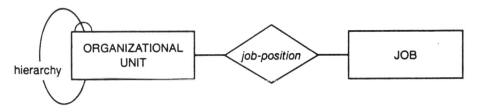

FIGURE 4.9.   E-R diagram of organizational model.

RELATIONSHIP TO FUNCTIONAL MODEL

A subfunction of the functional model is performed by one or more positions in the organizational model. This is the basis for the relationship between these two models of an enterprise. It is depicted as an E-R diagram in Figure 4.10.

The relationship between Function (which represents subfunctions at all levels) and *job-position* is a many-to-many relationship (called *perform* in Figure 4.10) because a given subfunction can be performed by more than one job-position and a job-position can perform more than one subfunction.

The recursive relationship in Figure 4.10 labeled *functional hierarchy* relates a function to its subfunctions. In terms of the functional model shown in Figure 4.7, it records the indentation shown there. There is an occurrence of this one-to-many relationship for each breakdown in the functional model.

The recursive relationship, *reference,* represents the references in redundant subfunctions to the first occurrence of the subfunction in the model. Referring to Figure 4.7, there would one occurrence of this relationship that links the "schedule meeting" subfunction to each subfunction that includes the reference (see I.E.2.c.(3).(a)). The functional hierarchy and reference relationships could be combined into one many-to-many relationship.

The attributes of the job entity type would traditionally include "duties" and "responsibilities," in addition to job title, experience qualifications, educational qualifications, and wage or salary range classification. However, this would lead to some redundancy in a database defined by Figure 4.10 because a subfunction essentially defines certain "duties" or "responsibilities." To avoid this, the Job attributes should not include "duties" or "responsibilities."

ADDING LOCATIONAL INFORMATION

A locational model describes the spatial distribution of a business. It is needed to evaluate alternatives to the existing distribution and for several more detailed types of planning. Our interest in it stems from its applicability to the planning of distributed database systems.

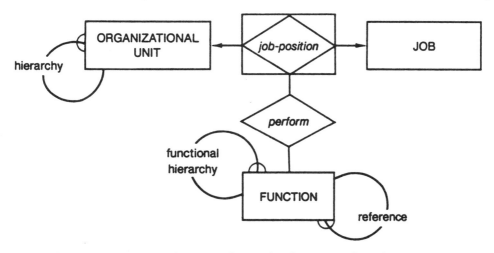

FIGURE 4.10. E-R diagram of organizational and functional models.

In this book, we focus on the database aspects of locational models. A locational model may also be used by search algorithms designed to find superior locational arrangements for the operations of the organization. Algorithms are needed to manage the location of databases, but first a database must be developed to hold an accurate picture of the facts with which the algorithm works. A description of that database is the concern of this subsection.

By expanding the database defined in Figure 4.10 to include the location at which functions are executed, a capability is created to store and analyze data requirements by location. The purpose of the functional model is to identify data requirements by function. If the locations where each function is performed are known, the locations where the data are required can be determined.

Basic to the locational model is the concept of a location. Location becomes an entity type in the E-R representation of the locational model. It is modeled as an entity type rather than as an attribute of Function because it may be multivalued for a given function, and there is a need to list all functions performed at a location along with their data requirements.

The appropriate relationship between the location entity type and the information structure of Figure 4.10 is not obvious. Can we assume that an organizational unit is at a location? Is the organizational unit wherever the manager of the unit is? This would be an over-simplification. Is a job-position at a location? Even airline stewardess positions have a home-base, although the home-base can change. But, even if all positions have a home-base, it does not follow that all functions performed by the job-position are performed at the same location.

The atomic fact in the structure of Figure 4.10 is the performance of a function by a job-position. It is not clear that an occurrence of this relationship will necessarily be at one location. The performed relationship could be associated with different locations at different times. Thus, the appropriate relationship is many-to-many; it defines that set of locations where an occurrence of *performed* can take place. This relationship is shown in Figure 4.11.

The relationship between the location entity type and *performed* in Figure 4.11 is a worst-case arrangement. For many businesses, the assumption that an

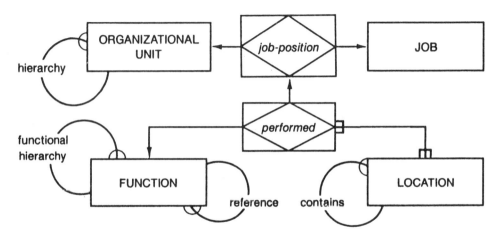

FIGURE 4.11.   E-R diagram of functions by location.

organizational unit is at a location may be completely viable. In this case, Location should be related to Organization Unit, not *performed*.

The granularity of locational measurement is an important consideration. For purposes of database distribution planning, the location of demand for data may need to identify the room, or floor in a multistory building. A file server, or database processor, can potentially be placed in any room where sufficient demand exists. If a fine grain approach to locational definition is taken, there is a need to group locations by building and by city for communication system planning purposes. The *contains* relationship shown in Figure 4.11 serves this purpose.

A database that stores information on organizational functions by location is useful in planning the locations where operations should be conducted, as opposed to where they are currently conducted. For this analysis, the database probably also needs to include the locations of customers and suppliers. If access to certain parts of the database by customers and suppliers would be a valuable service to offer, then their location is important for planning database locations as well as for planning the location of warehouses, branch sales offices, and so forth. One way to add customer and supplier functions by location to the model shown in Figure 4.11 is to redefine Organizational Unit to be either a customer, supplier, or one of our own organizational units. When the range of functions to be served by the database is expanded to include functions of customers and/or suppliers, then the concept of the organization for which the database exists has expanded and the model should reflect this broader viewpoint.

OTHER BENEFITS OF FUNCTIONAL MODELING

The development of a functional model of a business requires a considerable effort. The personnel example summarized in Figure 4.5 gives some idea of the magnitude of the project. When considering a commitment to create a functional model, all of the uses for it should be taken into account. The fact that it is vital to achieving integration of the data used by information systems may be sufficient justification. However, there are other benefits, and the project will be conducted differently if the objective is to achieve all of them.

The functional model can provide a basis for analyzing the organizational structure. In addition, there are a number of planning problems, concerning technical support and hardware and software configurations, to which a functional model can be applied. These additional benefits are described in the following subsections.

Organizational Realignment

Functional analysis can have at least two impacts on the way a business is organized. It can reveal redundant, counterproductive and incomplete practices caused by the way existing functions are handled in the current organization. Also, if during the analysis process the way functions should be structured in an on-line integrated database environment is considered, the need for radical changes in business practices may be detected.

Rationally, it should be possible to derive the organization structure from the functional breakdown. Each major function should be represented by an organizational unit. In cases where one function has subfunctions that are also subfunctions of other functions , it is usually not difficult to distinguish between cases where the subfunction should be replicated and cases where one function should serve another one via the subfunction. The scheduling subfunction discussed previously, for example, is a simple function that should be replicated wherever it is needed in the organization. On the other hand, a facilities management or accounting subfunction, for example, is likely to be a service provided to several other functions, such as marketing and engineering. In this case, it may be better not to replicate the subfunction; rather, a service agreement or administrative/technical reporting arrangement can be used to coordinate the work of the two functions.

But an organization has a history, and it consists of people that have their strengths, weaknesses, and biases. As a result, there are wide discrepancies between the way the enterprise should be organized and the way it is. Some of these discrepancies may be costly enough to warrant taking actions to resolve them. A functional analysis project can be the event that causes long-standing inefficiencies to be recognized and eliminated.

The way a function is performed can be affected by the information systems available to support its execution. If purchasing, receiving purchases, and paying for purchases are supported by three separate information systems, for example, then functions such as checking on the status of a purchase will be more complicated than if one integrated system supports all three functions. When a functional analysis is performed in anticipation of later creating more integrated systems, it is important that the functions are broken down into the subfunctions that will be necessary when the integrated systems are in place, as well as being broken down to reflect current conditions. In this way organizational realignments that integrated systems make possible can be foreseen.

Both of these effects of functional analysis should be of prime concern to the top management of the enterprise. Any significant change in the organizational structure requires a top management initiative. And if a system opportunity that gives a strategic advantage may be identified by the functional modeling project, top management will want to make sure the idea is not smothered by bureaucratic thinking. Thus, awareness that functional analysis can lead to fundamental improvements in business practices causes the project to be conducted at a much higher level.

Office Automation Opportunity Assessment

One major investment in office automation is the terminal or workstation and its application software. There are many alternative hardware-software configurations to choose among and some advantages to minimizing the variety of configurations used by the organization. The advantages of restricting variety concern the costs of training and maintenance as well as avoiding problems of data communication between workstations and to printers and other peripheral devices.

In one approach to this planning problem,[7] nine alternative workstation configurations were defined in terms of functional capabilities. The nine alternatives were:

1. Word processing

2. Spreadsheet processing

3. Personal database processing

4. A combination of 1, 2, and 3

5. Graphics processing, desktop publishing, and 4

6. E-mail, "calendaring," and word processing

7. Graphics processing, 2, and 6

8. Corporate database accessing, and 7

9. Desktop publishing and 8.

The functional model was used to show the functions performed by each job-position at each location. Based on this information one of the nine work-station configurations was picked for the job-position at the location. By adding these selections across all job-positions in the enterprise, a forecast of the demand for each type of workstation was obtained.

Software Package Selection

When selecting word processing, spreadsheet, and other software packages as standards in a business, one important consideration is the differences in the features of each package. How important is each feature to the firm? One way to evaluate a feature is to count the subfunctions (and job-positions) that can use it. Would the capability of a certain word processing package to produce two and three column print formats be used, for example? The functional model could be used to identify the job-positions that include word processing activities and to assess whether a two or three column output formatting capability would be useful.

REFERENCES

1. Van Ness, Ross, "Replacing Employment-at-Will with Effectiveness-at-Will," *Executive Speeches*, Vol. 3, No. 1 (Aug. 1988), ISSN 0888-4110, pp. 18–21.

2. Singleton, John P., Ephriam R. McLean, and Edward N. Altman, "Measuring Information Systems Performance: Experience with Management by Results at Security Pacific Bank," *MIS Quarterly*, University of Minnesota, June 1988.

3. Baroudi, Jack J., "The Impact of Role Variables on IS Personnel Work Attitiudes and Intentions," *MIS Quarterly*, University of Minnesota, December 1985.

4. Rockart, John F., "Chief Executives Define their Data Needs," *Harvard Business Review*, March–April 1979.

5. IBM, *Business Systems Planning: Information Systems Planning Guide*, IBM No. GE20-0527-4, 1984.

6. Martin, James, *Strategic Data-Planning Methodologies* (Englewood Cliffs, NJ: Prentice-Hall, 1982).

7. Bier, K., W. Liem, J. Miketta, and J. Wall, "Los Angeles Times Practicum Report," Information Science Application Center at The Claremont Graduate School, 1987.

DISCUSSION QUESTIONS

1. How should the strategy and goal clarification work of top management be approached? How long range should the goals be for information systems planning purposes?

2. Is the scope of a functional model totally determined by the definition of the top-level function?

3. What would be an appropriate first-level functional breakdown for a university?

4. What is the difference between a breath first and a depth first approach to constructing a functional model of an enterprise?

5. Under what conditions is it possible for two or more functions to have a subfunction in common?

6. Under what conditions should a subfunction be considered an "activity?"

7. How common is it for two different functions to have the same subfunction?

8. Modify Figure 4.9 to accommodate information about projects undertaken using a matrix form of organization to manage the projects.

9. In some matrix organizations, long term functions are distinguished from temporary project functions in the organizational structure. Should the subfunctions of projects be treated as subfunctions in this case?

10. What are the basic attributes of the entity types and relationships of Figure 4.10 (there may be additional attributes in specific cases)?

11. What attributes would be needed, in addition to those identified in the answer to Question 10, for the entity types and attributes of Figure 4.11 if the database is to be used in Electronic Data Interchange (EDI) systems with suppliers and customers, as well as for internal information systems purposes?

12. What information does a data flow diagram contain that a functional model does not?

13. Suppose a functional modeling project gathered data on the personal computer (or workstation) performance requirements of each subfunction in an organization. What uses could be made of this data?

14. Give examples of how information systems can affect the subfunctions of a business. Should the functional model depict the subfunctions required with the existing information systems or with planned new information systems?

15. If top management realizes that a functional modeling project will identify situations in which a function is being split between two organizational units or a function is being duplicated by multiple units or a vital function is not being done by any unit, how will this realization affect the conduct of the project?

5

Top-Down Database Planning

In this chapter, we develop the idea of combining the functional model with the concept of decomposing generalized entity types and relationships. The strategy of Business-Wide Information Structuring (BWIS) is to use the functional model of an organization to guide the decomposition of a general characterization of the organization's information requirements. The decomposition leads to a characterization that is sufficiently specific to serve as a conceptual database framework that can be used to guide individual system development projects toward the gradual development of integrated systems.

The BWIS decomposition methodology is explained and illustrated in this chapter. Then, in Part 2, it is applied to some of the most common business functions, such as marketing, materials management, and financial management. To the extent that the logic by which these information structures are derived is accepted, the structures become potential standards.

Standard information structures for common business functions would be very significant to the packaged application software industry. An application program with embedded Data Management Language (DML) commands (such as SQL commands) can function in an environment that has two characteristics: (1) a DBMS that processes the DML commands, and (2) a database with a design that is compatible with the one the application program was designed to access. A BWIS standard database design used by both the application program developer and the user organizations is needed to satisfy the second condition.

TOP-LEVEL DATA REQUIREMENTS

In Chapter 4, a top-level function was described that is essentially the same for all organizations: To define the goals of the organization and to see that the available resources are effectively applied toward reaching those goals. What information is required to perform this top-level function?

111

Information about two generalized entity types is required by the top-level function. One is Goal and the other is Resource. These information requirements are derived directly from the definition of the top-level function already given. In *Leadership in Administration* (Evanston, IL: Row, Peterson, 1957), Philip Selznick writes of the top-level function, "Leadership sets goals, but in doing so takes account of the conditions that have already determined what the organization can do and to some extent what it must do."

THE GOAL ENTITY TYPE

The information about goals that the chief executive needs includes the following:

1. Goal definitions.

2. The relative priorities of the different goals (priorities, however, are not usually made explicit and can be seen only indirectly in resource allocation decisions).

3. The sources of support for each goal from the coalition that keeps the organization in business (some goals are supported by the owners, others by the employees, or suppliers, customers, or communities where the organization is located).

4. The strategy that links the goal to a purpose of the organization.

The Goal entity type is shown in Figure 5.1 with a dark band on the top and bottom sides of a rectangle signifying that further decomposition is expected to arrive at a description of the goal that is sufficiently explicit for implementation purposes.* While items 1 and 2 in the above list may be representable as attributes, items 3 and 4 seem likely to involve other entity types. Other reasons for viewing Goal as a generalization (and aggregation) will become clear as we consider the information about goals required by subfunctions.

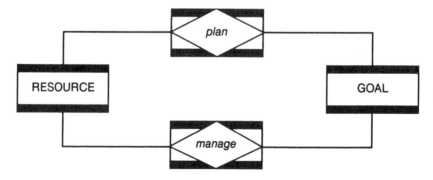

FIGURE 5.1.   Top-level information structure.

* The dark band at the top and bottom of a rectangle indicates that the entity type represented is considered a generalization.

THE RESOURCE ENTITY TYPE

The Resource entity type includes all types of resources important to the business. The assets recognized in the accounts; the human resources; the patents and copyrights; and the goodwill of customers, suppliers, and governments are all important resources of the organization. It encompasses more than the conventional accounting concept of "assets."

For all resources, a description is important. Not all resources are quantitatively measurable, but for those that are, a measure of the resource is often useful information. Ownership of resources may be significant in some cases; an enterprise need not own all the resources it utilizes.

Resource, like Goal, is shown in Figure 5.1 as a generalization because there are many versions of resource, each with its own important attributes.

THE TWO RELATIONSHIPS

One basic relationship between the Goal and Resource generalizations is that resources are used to achieve goals. This relationship will be called the *manage* relationship because management orders and actions cause resources to be dedicated to certain purposes. An order to a supplier to deliver goods to a plant or customer is an example of a management order that allocates resources to meet a delivery commitment. The event of the delivery actually occurring is an example of a "management action." Both orders and actions that cause resources to be committed are examples of the *manage* relationship.

A second basic relationship between Goal and Resource is the way in which goals are planned to fit the available resources. The customers of a business, for example, are a resource whose expectations shape the products and services offered by the business. The capabilities of the facilities, workforce, and suppliers likewise are taken into consideration in formulating business goals, at least in the short term. The requirements and capabilities of resources with respect to specific goals are examples of the *plan* relationship between the Goal and Resource entity types.

The distinction between the *manage* and *plan* relationship is that *manage* relationships involve resource commitments whereas *plan* relationships are plans and policies that show how the resources may be related to a set of goals under certain conditions. The distinction, then, can be characterized as the difference between a *real* and a *hypothetical* commitment of resources. In many business situations, plans are hypothetical commitments and orders are real commitments. Certainly, actions are real commitments. Budgets and engineering designs are real commitments in one sense; however, in the overall scheme, they are still plans.

Figure 5.1 depicts the information structure required to support the top level function. The relationship that defines how resources are used to achieve goals is labeled *manage*. The relationship concerned with the influence that resources have on goals is labeled *plan*. The fact that these entity types and relationships are very general and are subject to decomposition into much more detailed data specifications is indicated by the dark bands. The rectangles signify entity types and the diamonds signify relationships. (For a complete description of the E-R diagramming technique used in Figure 5.1 and in subsequent figures see Chapters 2 and 3.)

SIGNIFICANCE

The significance of this characterization of top level information requirements lies in the proposition that *all* of the information requirements of the organization can be derived from it. The functional model defines what has to be done to effectively apply the available resources to achieve the goals. By decomposing the information structure of Figure 5.1, it should be possible to define the information requirements of each subfunction in the functional model. This should lead to formulation of lower level requirements in a way that is modular with respect to higher level requirements. The information required by high level functions should be obtainable as aggregations of data required to support the subfunctions of the high level function. Or, in the case of a need for details, the higher level function should be able to get the components of an aggregate via a clearly defined "drill-down path."

In addition to modularity, the decomposition approach to defining data requirements promotes standardized database designs, because all database designers who use it start with the same general design, namely, that shown in Figure 5.1. Assuming they are working with the same functional model for a given organization, designers should create database designs that are comparable. The main reason for design differences will be the failure of one analyst to identify a data requirement of a subfunction that is recognized and included by another analyst.

DECOMPOSING DATA REQUIREMENTS

The information required to manage the entire business is summarized in Figure 5.1. To uncover the implications of this general depiction of requirements, we turn to the first-level breakdown of the top-level function. By analyzing the data requirements of these subfunctions, a more specific definition of requirements can be obtained.

The first-level breakdown depends on the industry in which the business functions. Several variations were described in Chapter 4. Lists 4.1, 4.2, and 4.3 summarize generic breakdowns for a consumer goods manufacturer, capital goods manufacturer, and publisher, respectively. In this discussion, we will use the consumer goods breakdown in List 4.1 as the example. In an actual case, the database designer should make sure that the first-level breakdown is both suitable and complete for the organization before proceeding with the analysis.

According to List 4.1, the top-level function subdivides into seven functions: marketing, materials management, production, engineering, personnel, finance/ accounting, and information systems. The information structure of Figure 5.1 can be decomposed to describe the information requirements of each of these seven functions. As examples, we will apply the decomposition analysis to two of these functions: marketing and personnel. The decompositions of the top-level function appropriate for the other subfunctions are given in Part 2.

MARKETING INFORMATION REQUIREMENTS

The information requirements of those who do the marketing for the organization is what should be described, not the data that information systems analysts think marketers should want. Nor should the specification include what marketing experts say a marketing or sales manager should take into account. Only data that will actually get used by those doing the marketing for the company is relevant and the experts on this data are the people in the marketing function and subfunctions.

To explain the simple two-step methodology that can be used to develop an information structure that describes the information requirements of marketing (or any other subfunction), we will make plausible assertions about the type of data required by a function. But it should be understood that these assertions are only for purposes of illustrating the method of information structure development. The real expert on information requirements is always the system users.

First Step

The first step is to develop a clear and concise concept of the function for which data requirements are to be specified. It should be a concept of the function as a whole, its objectives, scope, and methods. In an actual case, the characterization should be that of the person responsible for the function.

Suppose the marketing function is defined by its manager as having two basic aspects. One is to let prospective customers know what the business can do for them. The other is to analyze market demand and work with other functions to devise product and service offerings that are viable and contribute to achieving the goals of the business. These two aspects indicate the objectives and scope of marketing in a general way. These two aspects are described further in Chapter 6.

A specific definition of marketing objectives, scope, and methods is contained in the marketing plan of the organization. The marketing plan defines the objectives of the marketing function and the steps to be taken in reaching them. It defines the marketing channels to be used, the advertising program, promotion plans, salesforce deployment, pricing and credit policy, and new product introductions. A forecast of the sales that will result in future periods from execution of the plan is also considered a part of the plan.

Second Step

The second step in decomposing the information requirements of the top-level function to fit the needs of marketing is to decide what information about Goals and Resources (and the two relationships between them in Figure 5.1) is needed by the marketing function. In other words, the entity types and relationships about which information is needed for marketing are identified in this second step. The specific items of data about these entities and relationships need not be identified at this stage.

Marketing Goals
The Goal entity type of Figure 5.1 can be specialized to the particular group of goals that concern the marketing function. This specialization is labeled Marketing

Goal in Figure 5.2. It is intended to represent all the goals included in the marketing plan for the business. It will eventually be decomposed into more specific goals that concern such things as sales, gross margins, advertising, quotations, and credit granted.

The Marketing Goal entity type is depicted as a generalization in Figure 5.2. It is not intended to be implemented in a real database as a single entity type. In subsequent cycles of this decomposition procedure, it will be transformed into more specific entity types and relationships. (This is done in Chapter 6.) The fact that these, and other generalizations, do not stand for a finite set of single-valued attributes, does not mean they are invalid. They represent a high-level view of the information requirement.

Resources Used by Marketing

What are the resources used in marketing? One type of resource is the markets open to the business. Although in classical macroeconomics, demand may not be considered a resource, from the standpoint of the individual firm, it plays the role of a resource. The market opportunities open to a firm are vital to the achievement of its goals. The good reputation that a firm is able to develop in a market segment is a definite asset that needs to be developed and used in the same way as any other asset of the business. A market opportunity may not be as tangible as a building but it can be at least as significant in the eyes of an investment banker.

Another resource of concern in marketing is the products and services that the business has to offer. It is the function of marketing to broadcast information about these offerings to prospects. Marketing also has a responsibility to work with other functions in the development of product and service improvements. Thus, marketing requires information about existing and planned products and services of the business.

There is another category of resources that the marketing function is responsible for managing. This is the marketing staff and the facilities and equipment used by that staff. Also to be included in the category are various suppliers employed to execute marketing plans, such as advertising agencies and designers. We refer to

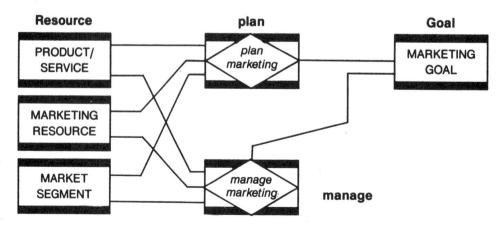

FIGURE 5.2.   Information structure for marketing function.

the entity type that represents this category of resources as the Marketing Resource entity type.

The Resource entity type of Figure 5.1, then, decomposes into three specializations for the marketing function. These are shown in Figure 5.2 as the Market Segment, Product/Service, and Marketing Resource entity types. It is conceivable that there could be meaningful relationships between the three entity types; however, none seem of sufficient general applicability to warrant showing them in the figure.

The Manage Relationship

The *manage* relationship of Figure 5.1 defines how resources are used to achieve goals. In the case of marketing, information about product/service entities is communicated to market segments using marketing resources according to a marketing plan. The resulting marketing actions are instances of *manage marketing* that is shown in Figure 5.2 as a four-way relationship.

It should be noted that although a verb is used in the label for this relationship, Figures 5.1 and 5.2 are not flow diagrams or action diagrams. Manage marketing represents a management decision that results in certain marketing actions. Figures 5.1 and 5.2 are E-R diagrams that show how data are to be organized around the management decision, the actions that result, and the resources and plans involved.

The Plan Relationship

The *plan* relationship of Figure 5.1 diagrams how goals are shaped by resources. In the case of marketing, the marketing plan must take into account the market segments, product/services, and marketing resources that are available. The *plan* relationship, then, becomes the event of formulating marketing plans that take the resource constraints into consideration. This version of the *plan* relationship is called *plan marketing* (Figure 5.2).

An occurrence of the *plan marketing* relationship is a marketing plan decision. To the extent that the three types of resources in Figure 5.2 are taken into account by the decision, the four-way relationship would involve all four entity types.

SUMMARY: THE DECOMPOSITION METHOD

The first example of the decomposition method is now complete. In this example, each of the entity types and relationships in the information structure for a function (Figure 5.1) was decomposed (or specialized) to describe the information requirements of one of its subfunctions (marketing). The entity types of Figure 5.1 were decomposed first. Then the relationships between them were specialized to describe the relationships between the marketing entity types.

In decomposing each entity type, we redefined it to apply specifically to the subfunction, marketing. Goal was decomposed by considering how information about the objectives of the marketing function is normally organized. Resource was decomposed by identifying the resources about which information is required for marketing.

In decomposing each of the two relationships of Figure 5.1, the basic rule of association of the relationship was adapted to marketing. In the case of the *manage* relationship, resources are to be associated with the goals they are used to achieve.

In the case of the *plan* relationship, goals are to be associated with the resource constraints that influence their formulation.

PERSONNEL INFORMATION REQUIREMENTS

We now consider a second example of defining information requirements for a subfunction. Again we use as a guideline the information structure required for the function of which it is a subfunction. This time we take the personnel subfunction from the list of subfunctions in List 4.1. In this example, we will not stop after one decomposition but will continue the decomposition process following the path charted in Chapter 4 down to the interview subfunction.

Information Structure for Personnel Function

The first step toward defining the information requirements of the personnel function is to clearly define the function as a whole. The second step is to define the information about goals and resources and the two relationships between them (see Figure 5.1).

Personnel Function Definition

The personnel function should be defined by the manager of the function. Each personnel manager will have a somewhat different sense of the function. The manager's point of view probably reflects the expectations of top management and the talents of the manager and staff.

In this example, we will assume that the personnel function assists management in formulating and executing policies concerning employees. Personnel assists in recruiting new employees; arranging transfers and promotions within the organization; maintaining current information on the status of each employee; maintaining pay equity; and managing employee relations and all programs designed to protect, upgrade, and benefit employees.

This assistance in executing these policies includes dealing with external agencies regarding employee matters, including tax collection, insurance, and judicial agencies. Responsibility for managing the data required in payroll processing is considered a personnel function, including the supervision of employee time reporting by each organizational unit. However, paying employees is considered an accounting function.

Goal Information Requirements

Given this concept of the function, what information about goals is required? The personnel function needs to know (and is involved in defining) how the goals of the organization relate to employees. What does the organization expect of an employee? Job descriptions, the organizational structure, and policies on a wide range of issues express these expectations. What commitments does the organization make to the employee? In addition to salary, most benefit programs, such as sick leave, vacation, insurance, training, and education, represent both an investment in employees and compensation to the employee for services provided.

These questions suggest that the Goal entity type be decomposed to identify two aspects of the organization's goals that concern employees. One is the goals that the organization expects the employee to adopt. These are commonly part of the job description, but they may also be defined in general policies that the employee is expected to follow. A specific job description applies to all positions in the organization that have essentially the same duties, responsibilities, and qualifications. This means that the information structure of the "goals for employee" data must involve organizational units (groups, sections, departments, divisions, etc.) and job descriptions and a relationship between them that may be called *job-position*. This decomposition of Goal is part of the E-R diagram shown in Figure 5.3. In this decomposed view of Goal, an instance of Job Description defines goals for all employees holding a certain type of job. This job may occur in many organizational units, and a *job-position* occurrence represents all instances of the job in a single organizational unit.

The Company Policy entity type, which may also define a goal for employees, is shown linked to the *job-position* relationship occurrences in Figure 5.3 to which it applies This is another part of the "goals for employee" information.

The other aspect of Goal that concerns the personnel function encompasses the commitments that the organization makes to its employees. These may take the form of benefit programs, sections in a labor contract, or a general employee policy. This type of information is represented in Figure 5.3 by the Benefit, Labor Contract, Company Policy, and Employee entity types. The Employee entity type is needed to define these commitments in cases where the commitment is not the same for all employees. Two relationships, *grievance* and *participate*, connect Employee to the two types of commitments. The relationship in Figure 5.3 between *job-position* and Employee defines the employees who hold a certain job in each organizational unit.

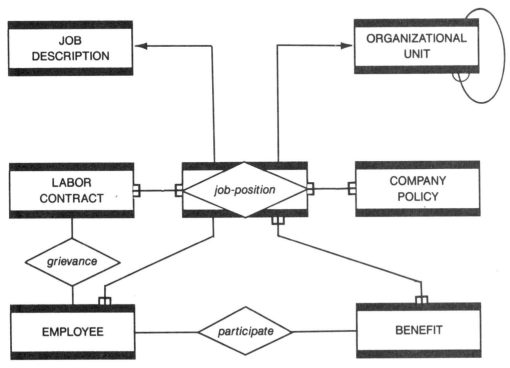

FIGURE 5.3. Decomposition of goal entity type for personnel function.

The *grievance* relationship records data about disputes over whether an employer commitment is being fulfilled. An instance of this relationship occurs each time an employee claims that a "commitment" is not being fulfilled that was made by the employer to employees in a labor contract.

The *participate* relationship defines an employee's benefits under general benefit programs supported by the employer. Pension benefits, sick leave, accrued vacation time, and so forth each have their own set of attributes. For some of these attributes in each set, there will be different data values for each employee.

Resource Information Requirements

The resource information needed in personnel work is information about people. For employees and job applicants this includes information about their capabilities and performance as well as identification and status information. Information must be retained on former employees for many reasons, including unemployment insurance charges and pension fund obligations.

All three of these people roles are included in the Person entity type shown in Figure 5.4 which summarizes the personnel function information requirements. The Person entity type represents all the ways in which a person serves as a resource of the enterprise. Figure 5.4 also shows an *isa* relationship between Person and Employee, where Employee is an entity type involved in defining the goals of the business. The Employee entity type could be consolidated into the Person entity type in Figure 5.4 but in our example this has not been done to clarify how the goal information structure of Figure 5.3 has been incorporated into Figure 5.4.

Information about a number of outside resources is important to personnel. It is necessary to know about sources of job applicants. Personnel also needs information on insurance providers, educational programs, child-care facilities, and health care services. These outside resources are characterized by the Provider entity type in Figure 5.4.

A third category of resource information consists of the company resources dedicated to the personnel function. These can include office, testing, training, recreational facilities, safety equipment, food service or child-care operations. This entity type is shown in Figure 5.4 as Facility.

The Manage Relationship

The *manage* relationship between Goal and Resource in Figure 5.1 defines how resources are allocated to achieving the goals of the organization. Since both Goal and Resource decompose into several specialities that relate to the personnel function, the general *manage* relationship takes several forms for the personnel function. In the case of Person, the allocation of resources is the assignment of employees to positions, which is indicated in Figure 5.4 by the *assign* relationship. In the case of a vacancy, the *assign* relationship is between the job-position and the applicants for it and might be more aptly called an *apply* relationship. Nevertheless, in Figure 5.4, *assign* stands for both the filling and applying for a job-position.

A commitment to employees may involve a contract with a provider to supply a benefit to employees. This is another allocation of resources that is of concern to the personnel function. It is designated as a *contract service* relationship in Figure 5.4. An alternate version of this relationship occurs when a firm contracts with an agency to provide either temporary workers or job applicants; in this case, *contract service* is a relationship between *job-position* and Provider.

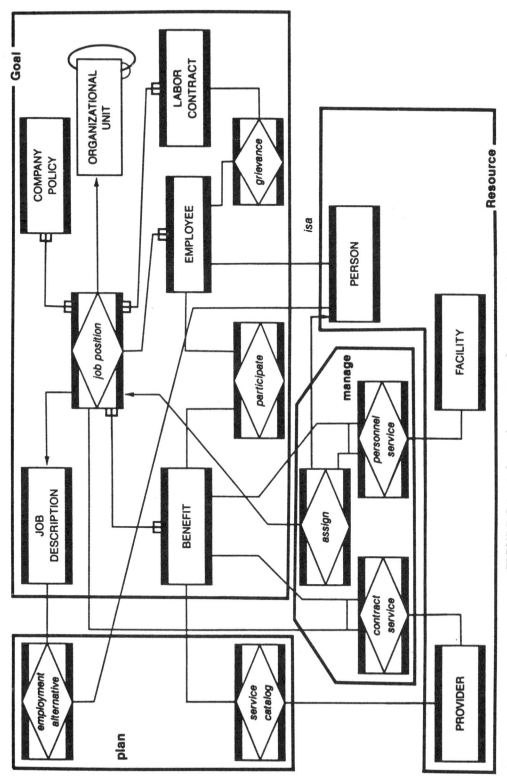

FIGURE 5.4. Information structure for personnel function.

A third version of the *manage* relationship is for the use of facilities to achieve goals. Facilities may be used to provide benefits or they may be used to fill vacant positions. Both of these possibilities are modeled as one relationship in Figure 5.4, called *personnel service*. An example of the use of a facility to meet a benefit commitment is a training facility used to train employees. An example of a facility used to fill positions is a test given to job applicants. The fact that the *personnel service* relationship for filling a vacancy involves *assign* rather than *job-position* is noteworthy. For the example of testing applicants, it more directly relates the test results to the applicant than would a relationship with *job-position*. However, for other examples, such as a videotape shown to certain new employees, the *personnel service* relationship should be between Facility and *job-position*.

The Plan Relationship

The *plan* relationship of Figure 5.1 has two specializations in Figure 5.4. One defines the options an employee or applicant has in the job market. In Figure 5.4, this specialization is called *employment alternative*, another specialization is called *service catalog*.

The *employment alternative* relationship supports the personnel function of watching the alternative employment opportunities people have and adjusting the commitments made to employees so that the company is competitive and attracts qualified persons. The Person entity in this case should be considered a type of person, with certain qualifications, rather than a specific person.

The other specialization of the *plan* relationship defines a catalog of services available from a provider. It covers such services as group insurance, banking, and child care. The availability of services can affect the commitments made to employees.

Information Requirements for a Subfunction of Personnel

Having established the information requirements for the personnel function, we are in a position to derive the requirements for subfunctions of personnel work. These subfunctions were defined in Chapter 4 in List 4.4. The information requirements for each of the six subfunctions listed there (employment, compensation, labor relations, benefit administration, health and safety, and training) can be obtained by the same type of decomposition analysis used to develop Figure 5.4. As an example of decomposition at this level, the data requirements of the employment subfunction will be derived.

Employment Function Definition

The employment function assists managers in locating the best qualified, available person for each vacant position. This means that the function is concerned with identifying vacancies, clarifying the qualifications required for each vacancy, using sources of job applicants to create an applicant pool, selecting the best qualified applicant from the pool, negotiating an offer with that applicant, and inducting the applicant who accepts the offer into the position.

The manager of the position being filled is likely to play a role in each phase of the employment process. In the selection phase, the manager is particularly active in evaluating the candidates and making the selection decision. The personnel function, however, monitors the selection process and ensures that applicable company policies are followed.

The data requirements of the employment subfunction are determined by decomposing the information structure for the personnel function to fit the needs of this subfunction. This could be done either by identifying the parts of Figure 5.4 needed for each aspect of the employment subfunction as given in the previous description, or by taking the entity types and relationships in Figure 5.4 one at a time and defining the specific version of each (or no version) appropriate to the employment subfunction. The latter approach will be taken.

Decomposition of Goal Entities and Relationships

The E-R diagram for the employment subfunction is shown in Figure 5.5. The reasons for the changes in the goals section of this diagram from that in Figure 5.4 are as follows:

Company Policy: The employment subfunction requires company policy data for preparation of vacancy announcements and explanations to job applicants.

Organizational Unit: The employment subfunction works with managers throughout the organization in filling vacancies and thus requires organizational unit data.

Job Description: The employment subfunction must prepare vacancy announcements for job openings that include a description of the duties, experience, and educational qualifications for the position. This data cannot be modeled as simple attributes of a Job Description entity type. Therefore, Job Description needs to be decomposed into four entity types and three relationships, as shown in Figure 5.5. In this decomposition, it is assumed that educational qualifications can be standardized so that they apply to many jobs, whereas, experience requirements and duties are assumed to be unique to each job. Duty is shown as a generalization in anticipation of its replacement by an aggregate involving Function as discussed in Chapter 4.

Job-Position: The employment subfunction is concerned with vacant positions. It requires authorization to take actions to find an employee for the position. This authorization is a decision regarding the job-position that can be characterized as "job requisition." It is modeled in Figure 5.5 as a decomposition of *job-position* into, *job-position* and Job Requisition, linked by a one-to-many relationship. The employment subfunction includes preparing announcements of the opening. Because the announcement can take more than one form, it is necessary to create a separate Opening Announcement entity type linked to Job Requisition to provide for this information requirement.

Labor Contract: In Figure 5.5, it is assumed that the employment subfunction does not require any information about labor contracts. This may not always be true, and if it is an inappropriate assumption, it should be added to Figure 5.5

Benefit: The employment subfunction requires information about the benefits associated with a position for a number of purposes. Therefore, this entity type is retained in its generalized form. The analysis of information requirements for the benefit administration subfunction will provide a breakdown of this generalization that the employment subfunction will want to make use of.

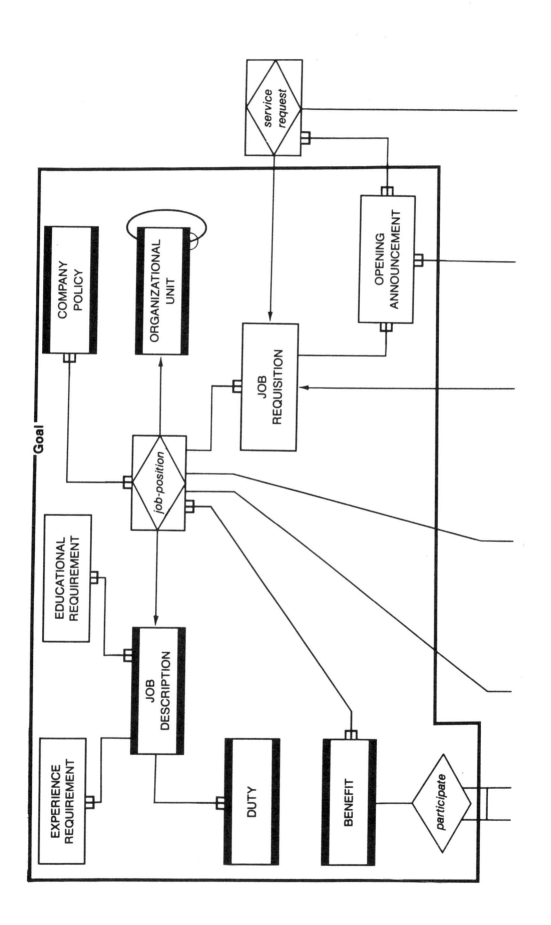

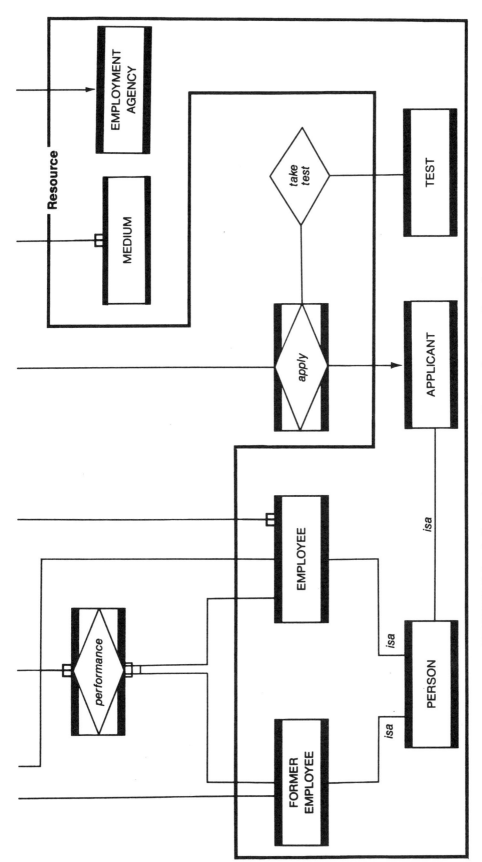

FIGURE 5.5. Information structure for employment function.

Employee: This entity type is shown only once in Figure 5.5 as a Resource entity type.

Grievance: The employment subfunction is assumed not to require information about grievances in Figure 5.5.

Participate: Information about the benefits of existing and former employees is assumed to be required by the employment subfunction when these employees are applicants (or potential applicants) for an opening.

Decomposition of Resource Entities for the Employment Subfunction

The E-R diagram for the employment subfunction is shown in Figure 5.5. The reasons for the changes in the resources section of this diagram from that in Figure 5.4 are as follows:

Person: The employment function requires information about applicants. It needs access to information on existing employees because they may be interested in moving to a vacant position and because managers are employees who are involved in the recruitment and selection processes. It is conceivable that information about former employees could also be important to the employment function if such a person applies for another position. These three specializations of Person have certain attributes in common and some that are peculiar to each specialization. Therefore, an *isa*-type relationship is appropriate between them. However, it should not be considered a cluster since it is possible for either an employee or former employee to also be an applicant. The decomposition of Person for purposes of the employment function is shown in Figure 5.6. Three one-to-one relationships link the three specializations of Person to the Person entity type. All entity types in Figure 5.6 are shown as generalized entity types, that is, further decomposition of each is anticipated.

Provider: The employment subfunction requires information about two specializations of Provider. One is the employment agency. This outside source of job applicants can be notified of vacancies and be paid a commission for each qualified applicant sent to the firm. An Employment Agency entity is shown in Figure 5.5.

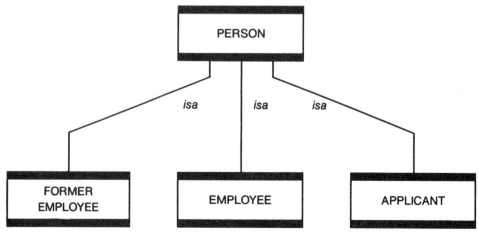

FIGURE 5.6. Decomposition of person entity type.

The second specialization is the broadcast media used to announce the opening to the general public. The Medium entity type, shown in Figure 5.5 linked to Opening Announcement, represents this information requirement.

Facility: The Facility entity type of Figure 5.4 includes screening tests given to applicants as part of the employment function. Therefore, this entity type is specialized to Test in Figure 5.5. If other specializations of Facility are relevant to the employment subfunction, they should be added to Figure 5.5.

Decomposition of the Manage Relationships

The *assign, contract service,* and *personnel service* relationships of Figure 5.4 become the *performance, apply, service request,* and *take test* relationships of Figure 5.5, plus two other unnamed relationships in Figure 5.5. The rationale for these specializations are as follows:

Assign: The differentiation between applicants and employees in the resource section of Figure 5.5 and the breakout of Job Requisition in the goals section allows the *assign* relationship for Figure 5.4 to be made more explicit. For current and former employees, it becomes a *performance* relationship as shown in Figure 5.5. Performance on current and past assignments is the purpose of the *performance* relationship. This information is relevant to the employment function for several reasons. Employees may also be applicants for another job and, in this case, their current position and past performance is of interest. For applicants the *assign* relationship becomes the *apply* relationship of Figure 5.5. Job Requisition, rather than *job-position,* is used in this relationship because it concerns only those job-positions for which there is a job requisition.

It should be noted that the simple one-to-many relationship between *job-position* and Employee in Figure 5.5 can be considered a decomposition of *assign* because it defines the current assignment of an employee. However, because it is shown in Figure 5.4 as part of the goals information requirements, it can also be viewed as deriving from that part of the information structure. One use for it by the employment subfunction is to identify the managers who should interview applicants.

Contract Service: The *contract service* relationship of Figure 5.4 becomes the *service request* relationship of Figure 5.5 and the unnamed many-to-many relationships between Medium and Opening Announcement. A service request is a job vacancy announcement sent to an employment agency. The unnamed many-to-many relationship between Opening Announcement and *service request* can be considered another part of the *service request* relationship that defines specifically which versions of the announcement were sent to the agency. If a vacancy announcement may also be sent to qualified or former employees, then additional relationships should be added to Figure 5.5.

Personnel Service: The employment subfunction requires information about the performance of each applicant on any screening test given. The *take test* relationship of Figure 5.5 serves this purpose.

Decomposition of Plan Relationships

Neither of the two plan-type relationships in Figure 5.4 (*service catalog* and *employment alternative*) is shown in Figure 5.5. Neither is considered relevant to the employment subfunction. It could be argued that the *employment alternative* relationship is relevant to the preparation of a job announcement because it provides information about the benefits that other employers are offering for the job in question. We assume that this information is taken into account by the job classification subfunction.

Information Requirements for a Subfunction of Employment

Having established the information requirements for the employment function, we are in a position to derive the requirements for its subfunctions. These subfunctions were defined in the previous chapter and are summarized in List 4.5. The information requirements for each of the four subfunctions listed there (personnel requisition approval, recruitment, selection, and induction) can be obtained by the same type of decomposition analysis used to develop Figures 5.4 and 5.5. In this example, the analysis is performed for only one of them—the selection subfunction.

Selection Function Definition

As stated in Chapter 4, the selection subfunction involves investigating applicants in the pool created by the recruitment function and selecting one to fill the vacant position. Any investigation is an information gathering process, and the activities of a thorough investigation are necessarily somewhat open-ended. Nevertheless, there are some basic steps that are commonly taken to investigate job applicants. One is to test the applicant with respect to skills and other job-related characteristics. Those who pass these screening tests may then be asked for character and professional references, people who know of the applicant and can attest to his or her character or performance. A discussion with, or letter from, the references reveals more information about each applicant remaining in the pool. Applicants who appear the most qualified and promising after the reference check information are invited for a personal interview. The interview gives the manager and others interested in who should fill the position an opportunity to carefully assess the qualifications of each applicant remaining in the pool.

The other part of the selection function involves selecting an applicant for the position. This may be as simple as picking the applicant who appears most qualified, offering the position to the applicant, and having the applicant accept the offer; or it may become an involved negotiating process. The position may have to be offered to more than one candidate before the position is filled.

Information Requirements for Selection

The data requirements of the selection subfunction are determined by decomposing the information structure for the employment function (Figure 5.5) to fit the needs of this subfunction.

This could be done either by identifying the parts of Figure 5.5 needed for each aspect of the selection subfunction, as given in the above description of the selection subfunction, or it could be done by taking the entity types and relationships in Figure 5.5 one at a time and defining the specific version of each (or no version) appropriate to the employment subfunction. We use the former approach in this case.

According to the above description of selection, it consists of four parts: applicant testing, reference checking, interviewing, and negotiating an offer. The information requirements of each of the four parts include:

1. *Applicant Testing*: The investigation part of the selection function concerns gathering information about applicants. This means that it will use those parts of Figure 5.5 that contain information about applicants. Screening tests are defined by the Test entity-type and the test results are attributes of the *take test* relationship between Apply and Test. Therefore, *apply, take test,* and Test are included in Figure 5.7 from Figure 5.5.

2. *Reference Checking*: The identification of references and their assessments requires that Applicant be decomposed to show the references of an applicant as a separate entity type. This new entity type is linked to Applicant in a one-to-many relationship in Figure 5.7.

3. *Interviewing Applicants*: The interview process includes selecting applicants to interview, interviewing them, and evaluating them based on the interview. The information requirements of each of these subprocesses will be considered.

Choosing applicants to interview should cause the manager to carefully evaluate how well the qualifications of each applicant satisfy the requirements of the job description. To make this evaluation, details about both the job description and the applicant are required. In Figure 5.5, education, experience, and duty requirements of the job are shown as separate entity types. To evaluate applicants with respect to education and experience, we need data on these characteristics of each applicant. Because an applicant can have multiple educational and experience qualifications, separate entity types need to be defined for this data, and linked to the Person entity type and the corresponding job requirement by relationships. The Prior Job and Educational Achievement entity types shown in Figure 5.7 represent these new entity types. Note that each is shown to be involved in two relationships. In contrast to the way Reference was modeled, experience and education are derived by decomposing the Person entity type of Figure 5.5 because it is assumed that they are multivalued attributes of significance for Employee regardless of whether an employee is an applicant for another job or not. If this assumption is unwarranted the relationships should be with Applicant rather than Person.

The Experience Requirement entity type of Figure 5.5 is not quite the same as a skill requirement for a job. Suppose that this distinction is made at the Selection level of the requirements analysis. It requires that the previous decomposition of Job Description be revised to identify a set of skill requirements for the job, as well as experience requirements. This decomposition is shown in Figure 5.7. The skills of applicants also need to be made explicit information requirements of the selection function. In Figure 5.7, Skill is treated as a set of categories that apply to many persons, whereas Prior Job and Educational Achievement are modeled as personal attributes of Person.

For existing and former employee, past performance on jobs in the enterprise is relevant to the decision on whether to interview them for the open position. Hence, the Performance entity type of Figure 5.5 is retained in Figure 5.7. The participation of existing and former employees in various benefit plans may also

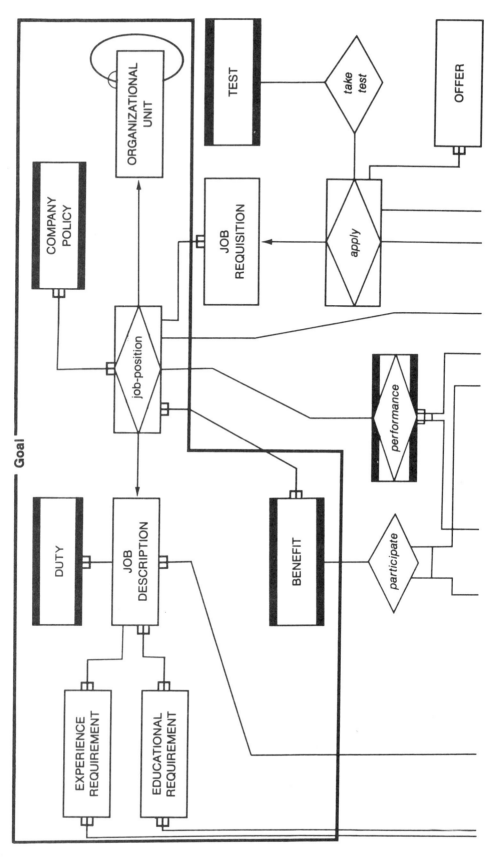

130

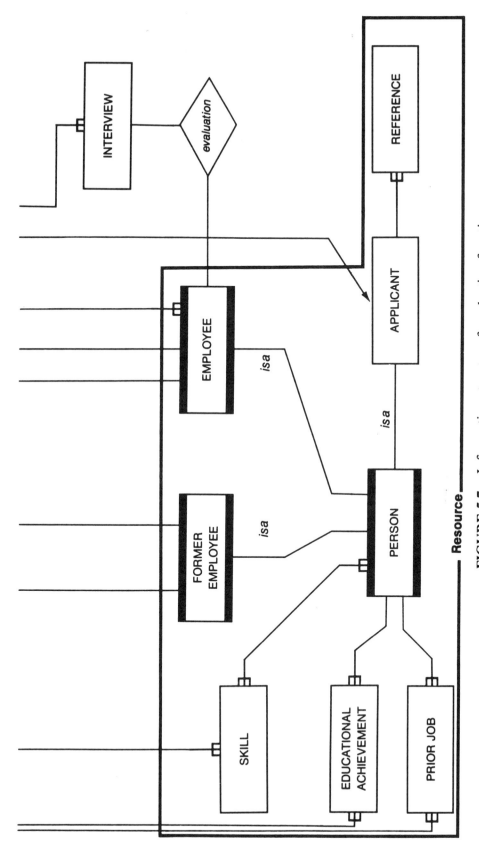

FIGURE 5.7. Information structure for selection function.

131

be relevant to considering them for an opening, therefore the *participate* relationship is retained in Figure 5.7.

Arranging the interviews involves defining who will be interviewing the applicant. The one-to-many relationship between *job-position* and Employee can be used to identify the organizational unit manager and others who are responsible for the interviews.

The interview process requires that information about each interview be available. This is derived as a decomposition of the *apply* relationship; an Interview entity type is recognized in Figure 5.7 and is related to Apply in a one-to-many relationship.

The interview process includes telling the applicant about the opening, as well as gathering more information about the applicant. The information about the open position is represented as attributes of several entity types in Figure 5.5, including Job Description, *job-position*, Benefit, Company Policy, and Organizational Unit. Therefore, they should all be included in the information structure for the selection function (Figure 5.7).

The interviewers evaluate the interviewee after the interview. Provision should be made to record these evaluations in the database. The relationship between Interview and Employee in Figure 5.7 serves this purpose.

4. *Negotiate Offer*: The process of offering the position to an applicant creates another event that should be captured in the database. This is derived in the same manner as the Interview entity type, by decomposing the *apply* relationship. It is shown in a one-to-many relationship with Apply to accommodate the possible need to record revised offers and counter-offers.

This completes the definition of information requirements for the selection subfunction. The entity types and relationships in Figure 5.5 that concern announcing the opening and working with employment agencies have been left out of Figure 5.7 because they are irrelevant to the selection function. (This may not be valid as far as the Opening Announcement is concerned because it could be relevant to the questions considered during an interview.) Otherwise, Figure 5.7 resembles Figure 5.5 except for the addition of the entities and relationships added to Figure 5.7 to provide more detail in support of the interview subfunction.

Information Requirements for a Subfunction of Selection

Having established the information requirements for the selection function, we are in a position to derive the requirements for its subfunctions. These subfunctions were defined in Chapter 4 and are summarized in List 4.6. The information requirements for each of the four subfunctions listed there (test screening, reference checking, interviewing, and negotiating an offer) can be obtained by the same type of decomposition analysis used to develop Figures 5.4, 5.5, and 5.7. In this example, the analysis is performed for only one of them, namely the interview subfunction.

Interview Function Definition
As already stated, the interview subfunction arranges and conducts personal interviews with the most promising applicants so that as much information as possible is available when the decision is made to offer the job to one of the

applicants. The interview gives the manager and others interested in who should fill the position an opportunity to carefully assess the qualifications of each remaining applicant.

Sound business practice, as well as Equal Employment Opportunity law in the United States, requires that the evaluation of applicants who are interviewed be in written form. The interview subfunction includes preparation of these evaluations.

Information Requirements for Interview Function

The data requirements of the interview subfunction are determined by decomposing the information structure for the selection function (Figure 5.7) to fit the needs of this subfunction. Two approaches to this decomposition analysis have already been identified and illustrated. One, which can be called the "data approach," is to consider the entity types and relationships in the "parent function" information requirements structure (E-R diagram) one at a time and define the specific version, if any, that is needed for the subfunction. The other approach, which can be called the "process approach," is to consider each aspect of the subfunction whose data requirements are being defined and define for that aspect the parts of the parent function information requirements that are relevant to accomplishing the aspect. For very general subfunctions, the data approach seems to work well. For more specialized subfunctions, the process approach is more efficient. In view of this, we take the process approach to defining the information requirements for Interviewing.

1. *Scheduling Interviews*: Scheduling an interview requires information on when the applicant and interviewers are available. In terms of Figure 5.7, this is information about Persons. To make the requirement explicit, we need to decompose the Person entity so that the time schedule of the individual is depicted. The decomposition is shown in Figure 5.8 as a relationship between Time and Person called "calendar item."

Scheduling the interview could involve reserving facilities for the interview, such as meeting room, restaurant table, and hotel room. This is additional information about the interview that cannot be treated as attributes of interview because it may be multivalued and because it may be necessary to link the reservation to the entity that is being reserved. In Figure 5.8, Interview is decomposed to show Reservation as a separate entity type linked to Interview in a one-to-many relationship. This treatment assumes that what is being reserved can be adequately modeled as an attribute of Reservation.

2. *Conduct Interview*: In the interview, a wide variety of data may be useful. Information about the opening and about the organization, as well as information about the applicant may be helpful. For this reason, all of the information structure of Figure 5.7 can be included in Figure 5.8 except for the Offer entity type and its relationship with the *apply* relationship.

3. *Evaluate the Applicant*: Evaluations by interviewers after the interview are another information requirement of the interview function. This need is met by the *evaluation* relationship between the Interview and Employee entity types. The attributes of this relationship would include the evaluation given by the interviewer.

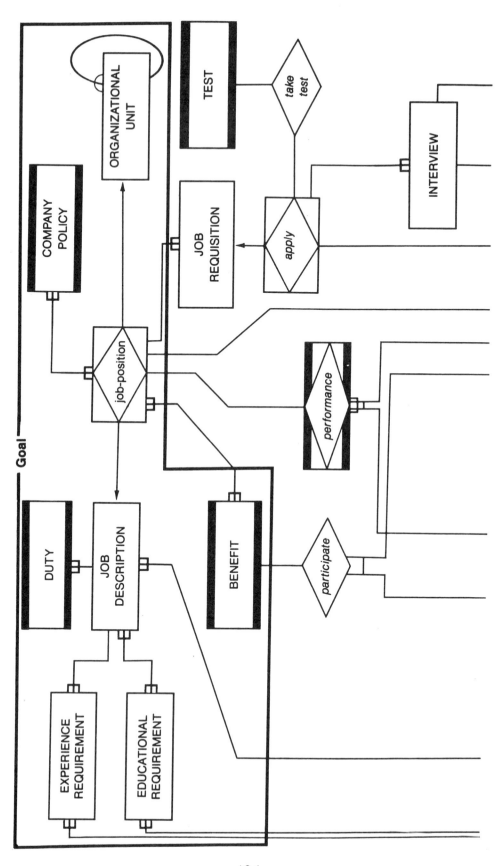

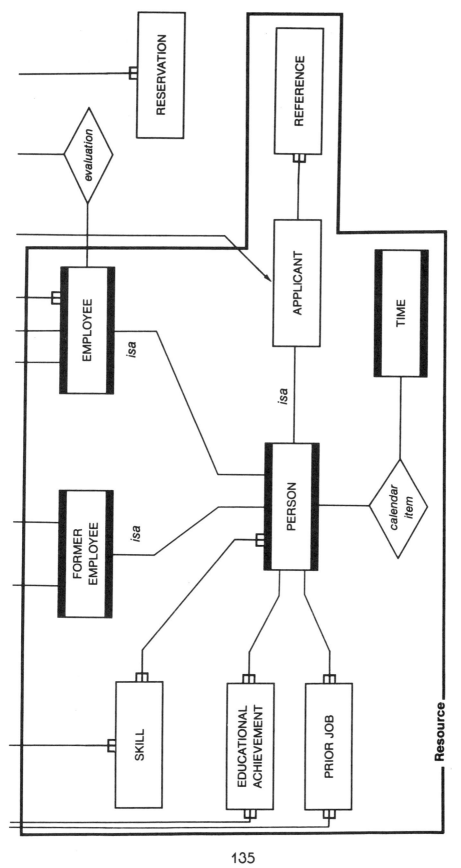

FIGURE 5.8. Information structure for interview function.

Information Structure for a Branch Tip

The analysis of the interview subfunction in Chapter 4 concluded that it is a branch tip subfunction or activity that need not be further broken down. This means that the information structure for it represents a final result, at least in the sense that it will not serve as the basis for further breakdowns.

Yet, looking at the structure as shown in Figure 5.8, there are still a number of entity types and relationships that have the double lines on the top and bottom sides of the rectangle which means further decomposition is anticipated. This further decomposition will take place when we come to the view integration stage of database planning (see Chapter 12).

In this chapter, we focused on developing a view of the conceptual database that is appropriate for a particular function. The approach is to develop a view that is consistent with the views developed for functions that encompass this function. The view in Figure 5.8 is for the interview function which is a subfunction of the selection function which is a subfunction of the employment function and so forth.

There are certain entity types in Figure 5.8 that are clearly important to other functions but have little to do with interviewing applicants. For example, Benefit is an entity type of central importance to the benefit administration subfunction of the personnel function. We can anticipate that the analysis of the information requirements of benefit administration will reveal aspects of the Benefit entity type that require decomposition in order to clearly state information requirements. This is the reason for the double lines on the rectangle for Benefit in Figure 5.8.

Eventually, the information structure developed for benefit administration must be integrated with that of Figure 5.8 to create a conceptual database for the business. When that occurs we can anticipate that the rectangles with double lines in Figure 5.8 will be replaced with more complex structures that represent the information requirements of other functions. After view integration, the structure of Figure 5.8 must be reconsidered again to determine exactly how those involved in interviewing want to think about the data resources they have available. They will definitely want more detail concerning general entity types such as Time. But, for other entity types, such as Employee, they may not be concerned with all of the subcategories of Employee that are important to other functions. In this case, the definition of the database used for interviewing purposes should retain Employee as a single entity type.

Further consideration of view integration is contained in Part 3. After the examples of Part 2 have been studied, the problem of integrating diverse views is more easily explained and dealt with.

METHOD OF APPROACH TO TOP-DOWN ANALYSIS

In Chapter 4, the development of a functional model was discussed. In this chapter, we have taken that model for the personnel function and concentrated on the derivation of information structures from higher level structures. In practice, these two modeling activities need to be combined, unless a functional model already exists for the organization.

It has been noted at several points in the discussion that the authority and expert on a function and its information requirements is the manager or performer of the function. This means that the mode of this top-down method of data planning must be one that involves these user experts. In the absence of an expert system to act as the analyst, two alternative modes are feasible. One is an interview mode in which a database analyst obtains the functional breakdowns and function information requirements through an interview process. The other is a training mode in which a database analyst trains the function experts in functional and entity-relationship modeling and the function experts then do the analysis for the functions with which they are familiar.

Assuming there is more than one function expert, some coordination between function experts is advisable, both with respect to subfunction breakdowns and entity type and relationship definitions. If there is only one database analyst who takes the interview approach then the coordination problem is automatically taken care of. This is feasible for a small organization. If more than one database analyst is involved, or the training mode is used, then explicit provisions are required for coordination. A meta-database that can store information about the functional model and the information structures as they are developed by the analysts is useful for this purpose. James Martin calls it a system encyclopedia[1] and IBM calls it a Repository. This special type of database is described in Chapter 11.

There are two precedence constraints that the method of approach should take into account. Subfunctions of a function cannot be defined until the function has been included in the model. Also, the information structure for a subfunction should not be derived until the structure for the function is established. Within these constraints, there is considerable flexibility as to who does which part of the analysis and when, especially at the lower levels of the functional model.

This discussion of method of approach is supplemental to that given in the last section of Chapter 1. After the exposure provided by this chapter to the method of defining information requirements, the reader is in a better position to appreciate the problems involved in designing a method of approach. It may be worthwhile to review the discussion of the method of approach in Chapter 1.

SUMMARY AND CONCLUSION

The starting point for developing a description of information requirements in terms of information structures is the structure shown in Figure 5.1 which is for the top-level function. Even if the scope of a functional model is not business-wide and the top level of the model is a function within the business, marketing for example, Figure 5.1 is still an appropriate starting point. If marketing is the top-level function then the information structure for marketing as a whole can be derived as described in the second section and the decomposition can proceed from that point (Figure 5.2).

In addition to this top-level structure (and all the basic rules of entity-relationship analysis), two other guidelines have been described by example in this chapter. One is the entity types and relationships of the "parent information structure." The parent structure describes the requirements for the function of the subfunction for which information requirements are to be defined. This set of the entity types and relationships in the parent structure can serve as a checklist of types of information to look for that may be required by the subfunction. All of the items on this checklist may not apply to a particular subfunction but some will. Some may apply directly without any specialization or decomposition. Others will have to be made more specific or detailed to accurately depict the information requirements of the subfunction.

Two ways of working with this checklist have been explained: (1) the data approach and (2) the process approach. If the data approach is taken, the entity types on the list should be considered before the relationships. When an item is found on the list that does apply, however, then other entity types or relationships to which it is related can be analyzed to see if they also have relevance to the subfunction. The list does not guarantee that all the information required by the subfunction will be identified. Nor does it guarantee that two analysts will create the same information structure for the subfunction. It does in some sense define the scope of the relevant information if the subfunction is truly a component of the parent function.

The second guideline is the functional model. It serves to organize the analysis. It controls the perspective and focus of the analyst so that he or she systematically reviews the information requirements of each part of the organization. It causes higher level functions to be analyzed before lower level functions. This allows higher level management to influence the designs developed at lower levels. Thus, the perspective of top management on what is important to include in the database can be allowed to dominate the design.

The starting point and two guidelines do not lead deterministically to the best conceptual database design for each of the functional areas. The important question is whether, if the analysis is carefully done, they lead to "satisficing designs." By this we mean that if all the designs the method can yield are compared, the differences between any two of them are insignificant from the user's standpoint. If the method produces satisficing designs then it is safe to use it and over time standard designs for each functional area will emerge. If it does not produce satisficing designs then it will not be used when a better methodology is available.

The emergence of standard designs that can be used as a starting point and guideline in the analysis of the information requirements of an organization in a certain industry seems very likely. If you had the task of developing a conceptual database for a personnel function, would you start with the structures in this chapter? It is natural to use whatever has been done rather than starting from scratch unless one sees it to be totally misleading. The fact that the design is based on a certain functional breakdown provides a way to quickly detect parts of the design that need to be reworked because the functional breakdown is inappropriate. In the same way that experienced programmers rarely write a new program completely from scratch, we can expect database analysts to modify existing designs rather than start with a clean sheet, once some business-wide designs are available.

REFERENCES

1. Martin, James, *Information Engineering*, Vol. 1 (Englewood Cliffs, NJ: Prentice-Hall, 1989).

DISCUSSION QUESTIONS

1. What is required to use a purchased application software package with a business-wide database?

2. Will two database planners who start with the same functional model develop the same information structure (E-R diagram) for an organization if they start with the structure shown in Figure 5.1 and use the decomposition approach described in the chapter?

3. In decomposing the information structure that describes the information requirements of a function to derive a structure that describes the information requirements of one of its subfunctions, should the entities or relationships of the structure be decomposed first?

4. The terms "job," "position," and "job-position" each have a precise meaning in Figure 5.3. Define and contrast the meanings of the three terms.

5. Compare and contrast the *assign* and *participate* relationships of Figure 5.4. Are they both examples of the *manage* relationship?

6. A specialization of an entity type is another entity type that has an *isa* relationship with the original entity type. What is a specialization of a relationship?

7. In Figure 5.7, an Interview entity type is shown. It is derived from the *apply* relationship of Figure 5.5 by decomposition. Is this a specialization or disaggregation of the *apply* relationship?

8. Define how you would organize and manage the development of a business-wide information structure for a medium size manufacturer of consumer hard goods. Assume you have the support of top management and that no one in the company knows anything about data planning or entity-relationship analysis or business-wide information structuring. Assume the company does have an Information Systems department and that they have a mainframe computer which presently handles the usual business transaction processing.

9. Derive the information structure that defines the requirements of the compensation subfunction of the personnel function. Assume that the compensation subfunction takes care of wage and salary administration. This would include the development and maintenance of job descriptions and a job evaluation system, the preparation of comparisons of the wage and salary rates (and benefits) of the business with those of other employers in the area, and the planning of blanket, special and merit pay increases within the firm.

PART 2

APPLICATION OF THE
METHODOLOGY

The methodology explained in Part 1 is applied in Part 2. A top-down approach is taken to describe the information requirements of six major functions in a manufacturing business. The marketing function is analyzed in Chapter 6 and the materials management function in Chapter 7. The information requirements of a production function are characterized in Chapter 8, and those for engineering in Chapter 9. The Information needs of two administrative functions, finance and information systems, are covered in Chapters 10 and 11.

Throughout Part 2, assertions are made about the information required to execute particular business functions. These assertions should be seen as surrogates for the information requirements that the manager of the function, or the worker performing the function, would specify if asked. In all cases, system users should be considered the real experts on both the functional breakdown and entity types and relationships about which information is required.

The functional breakdowns and entity-relationship diagrams developed in Part 2 are intended to serve as general models for any organization. They can be used as a starting point for defining the business-wide information needs of any business, particularly a manufacturing business. Each business will have peculiar needs that make it necessary to modify the functional model and diagrams of Part 2 to accommodate them. It will also be necessary to further subdivide some of the functions to identify all of the information requirements. Nevertheless, much time and confusion can be avoided by starting with the structures in Part 2 and modifying and developing them as necessary, rather than starting from scratch.

6

Marketing

THE PURPOSE OF MARKETING

The general goal of marketing is to create sales of a product by presenting information to sway potential customers. "Getting the word out" is the primary objective of marketing, but to do that requires some homework. The marketer needs to know product features and benefits, customer needs, and how his product fits customer needs. Mastery of this marketing information is the key to marketing effectiveness.

The customer has a valuable resource, namely money, and the marketer represents the enterprise that creates the product desired by the customer. To bring these two interested parties together, the right "message" must be delivered to the customer. "Message" can stand for any means of translating meaning from marketer to customers in a market segment.

However, all potential customers are not created equal, and since the enterprise must sell to many customers, it is the marketing function's (or department's) job to translate what it knows best (the product or service) into terms the customer knows best (his or her needs) so that all interested customers feel inclined to enter into mutual exchange with the enterprise. The marketer has a multiplicity of tools he must use to send the right message to each potential customer. They are all needed because the assemblages of customers collectively known as market segments (a generalization of customers) do not all perceive alike. Think for a minute about how many messages affect your senses, and you will get an idea of the vast array of sensory impacts your mind receives. Spoken or written words make up only a part of the mechanisms advertisers and other marketers employ to persuade you to do something. The usage of sounds, colors, hues, styles, associations, and even the timing and delivery of messages affect how a message is finally perceived.

Marketing can be viewed in terms of providing the proper information to the proper people in the proper way so as to achieve the aims of the enterprise. This is the information management problem. The management of marketing efforts

143

involves the planning of many "deliveries" of informational messages. Marketers often find themselves trying to create messages in various mediums such as television ads and radio announcements that appeal to certain characteristics in customers they think are close to making a purchase. Important details such as what the message says, how it is said, and to whom it is said require that these informational tidbits be orchestrated from a database of potential customers with propensities for spending. These facts shape a scenario incorporating perhaps a thirty second spiel during half time at the Super Bowl or breaks at the Stanley Cup play-offs, etc., followed by free product evaluations at participating dealers involving numerous factory representatives and Bobo the Clown. As you can see, the potential for informational chaos is tremendous, but the enterprise that leverages its marketing power to formulate all these interconnected facts into events gains an important edge over the competition, whose product incidentally represents another factor to consider when marketing.

From the decision above it might be inferred that the flow of information is only from enterprise to market, but transfers actually occur in both directions. The enterprise probes and pokes the marketplace to gather information about its constituents, exhaustively reassembling and reviewing the data to glean valuable associations that give meaning to the public's observed buying behaviors. Much money is spent hoping to unearth what drives buyers, and the deployment of information systems not only to store data, but also to allow creative and powerful retrievals can prove to be advantageous. Information about communication media and the audience they reach is therefore central to marketing.

Information about customers and marketing plans is needed in forecasting sales, coordinating deliveries of products, and even in the design of a product. The management of accounts receivable and customer credit should include marketing decisions. The pricing and packaging of products also convey messages, and therefore must be closely managed by marketers for optimum effect.

GENERALIZED INFORMATION STRUCTURE

The information structure required to support the marketing function is shown in Figure 6.1. It is a copy of Figure 5.2 which is reproduced here for the reader's convenience. The analysis that leads to this characterization is given in Chapter 5. Each of the entity types and relationships in Figure 6.1 is described below in preparation for the next cycle of information structure decomposition.

PRODUCT/SERVICE

The product/service entity type of Figure 6.1 is a generalization that includes everything the enterprise sells in any market. For a chemical manufacturer, this might include both household products sold through supermarkets and bulk chemicals sold to other manufacturers or farmers. For a computer manufacturer, it would include the software and technical support provided as well as the computers. Clearly, the attributes of interest will be different for products or services that have a different nature. For this reason it is shown as a generalization.

In some cases, it is not the product or service per se that is of primary interest in Marketing. Rather it is the capacity to produce certain products or services. This is true for professional services and for some capital goods, such as buildings, nuclear

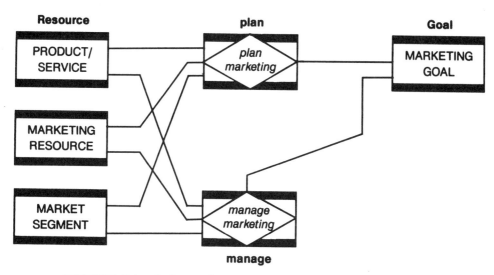

FIGURE 6.1. Information structure for marketing function.

reactors, and commercial aircraft. In such cases, the Product/Service entity type should be replaced by a Productive Capacity entity type.

In cases where a product is being marketed, the availability of the product is usually important. This means information about delivery times is required, and often this depends on the existence of inventories of the product at certain locations. This information can be obtained by decomposing the Product/Service entity type.

MARKETING RESOURCE

A marketing resource is any talent, contract, facility or system that is dedicated to the marketing function. This includes the direct sales force and its management and facilities, the inside sales force, the advertising staff, ad agencies, exhibit booth facilities, and mailing lists. It can also include the marketing budget since this represents resources placed at the disposal of marketing management.

MARKET SEGMENT

The term "market segment" in Figure 6.1 can be interpreted in many ways. For a manufacturer, there are usually at least two levels of customers in the distribution chain. First, there are the distributors and wholesalers to whom the manufacturer sells directly. Next, there are dealers and retailers to whom the distributors and wholesalers sell. Finally, there is the consumer who buys from the dealer and retail outlet. The marketer must know about customers at each of these levels in the distribution chain. If the product and services offered do not meet customer requirements at any of these levels, sales will suffer.

A market segment can also refer to a geographical area. A region, state, city, or part of a city can be a market segment. There is normally a parallel between the levels in the distribution chain and the geographical breakdown. A distributor supplies all of the dealers in a certain area. However, if a distributor or dealer

operates a mail order or television sales program, then the correspondence between distributor and geographical area is more complex.

It may also be useful to define market segments in terms of socioeconomic
classes. Age groups, income brackets, sex, and home ownership are examples of
distinguishing characteristics that can be used for purposes of marketing planning. The use of scanners at store checkout stations combined with data gathered
in the process of handling customer payments can make a detailed analysis of
customer characteristics possible.

Information about competitors in each market segment can be of value. The
goals of an enterprise may include market-share targets which imply that the
sales of competitors can be obtained, at least in the aggregate. Information on
competitor promotions and advertising may play a role in defining short-term
marketing plans.

MARKETING GOAL AND PLAN MARKETING RELATIONSHIP

The Marketing Goal* entity type represents the objectives of Marketing. It is an
internally consistent combination of sales goals, prices, direct sales activities,
advertising plans and other marketing variables. To the extent that marketing
goals for different classes of products are separable, there can be a series of
marketing goals that each address a different class of products.

A marketing goal may also be linked to a market segment or market resource.
This involves the plan marketing relationship which defines how a marketing goal
relates to the resources available. The marketing goal, for example, could include a
planned total number of prospect visits per month by the direct sales force; the
plan marketing relationship could then include the number of calls planned for
each salesperson in the sales force, a marketing resource. The plan marketing
relationship associates a marketing goal with the resources that it involves. It may
include the products and services, marketing resources, and market segments.

The Marketing Goal can be viewed as something that evolves through a series
of decisions made at different times by various combinations of managers. Credit
policy and pricing plans may be made in cooperation with financial executives.
Product design and packaging plans are made in cooperation with the engineers.
The circumstances of each of these decisions are another possible type of attribute of marketing goal entity types.

THE MANAGE RELATIONSHIP

A major objective of marketing is to communicate to market segments what
the organization has to offer. The "manage marketing" relationship defines how
the marketing resources available to the enterprise are mobilized to communicate
messages about the products and services offered to market segments. Presumably, the orders and actions that accomplish this allocation of marketing resources relate to the marketing goals. Communicating messages that cause sales is
certainly a goal. Organizing resources to do that relates the goal to the resources.

---

* The term "marketing goal" is used to emphasize the relation of this subject to the Goal entity type of
Figure 5.1. However, the term "marketing plan" is commonly used to identify the subject and will be
used as a synonym in this chapter.

Marketing actions can include all forms of communication with prospective customers. Media advertising, brochures, and quotations are obvious messages. The messages delivered by salesperson making direct sales calls, the interactions that inside salespeople have with customers and the treatment given customers by the customer service and accounts receivable staff also send messages that influence sales.

Marketing orders and actions also include arrangements made with service suppliers and internal functions to carry out the marketing plan. A contract with an advertising agency or an agreement on terms of credit for certain customers are examples of this kind of marketing activity.

FIRST-LEVEL BREAKDOWN OF MARKETING

The next step in the development of information structures for marketing is to divide the marketing function into subfunctions. The information requirements of these more specific marketing activities can then be analyzed to develop more specific marketing information structures.

The marketing function can be divided in several ways. One way is to differentiate between external and internal marketing activities (Figure 6.2). The external activity concerns formulating and broadcasting messages to market segments. The internal activity concerns analyzing market intelligence information and representing the marketing viewpoint internally. The marketing plan is formulated by the internal marketing function and executed by the external function.

In other words, marketing can be viewed as consisting of two types of functions:

External marketing: Developing and delivering messages to market segments about the products and services of the enterprise, and gathering marketing intelligence.

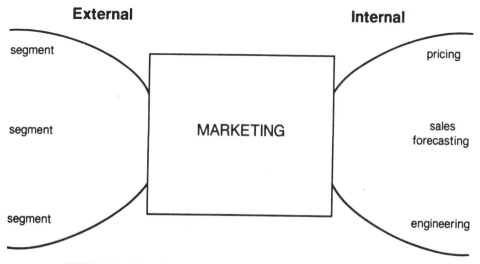

FIGURE 6.2.   External and internal aspects of marketing.

Internal marketing: Market research and the formulation of market-
                         ing strategy and policy, including pricing, pack-
                         aging design, sales forecasting, and receivables
                         collection.

Another useful marketing dichotomy distinguishes between "sales" and "marketing." Sales is concerned with negotiating specific sales with customers whereas "marketing" is concerned with broadcasting messages to the market, market
research, marketing intelligence, and marketing planning. Thus, the term
"marketing" has two meanings. In the remainder of this chapter we will refer to
the broad meaning (used up to this point) as Marketing, with a capital M; and the
term marketing (with a small m) for the narrow meaning of marketing as a
function that does not include "sales."

The internal/external and sales/marketing dichotomies can be combined to
create four groups of marketing functions as shown in Table 6.1. The body of
Table 6.1 contains examples of Marketing subfunctions that fit into each of the
four functional groupings. The examples are intended to clarify the meaning of
each subcategory and to illustrate how specific sales and marketing functions
have both internal and external components. The list of examples in each quad-
rant is suggestive, not exhaustive.

"Direct sales" as an organizational unit is a staff that carries out both sales and
marketing functions. Messages are conveyed to potential customers as well as
current customers by direct sales. Direct sales is also a "broadcast channel" in
marketing. Salespersons making calls on prospects deliver messages about the
products and services the company has to offer, while at the same time performing sales functions.

Notice the different effect that the internal/external dichotomy has on sales
compared to marketing. It divides sales into an early and late stage in the handling of a sale. On the other hand, it divides marketing into long-range planning
and execution activities.

In the case of sales, the information involved in both stages concerns individual prospects and customers and specific product sale possibilities. In the case of
marketing, the information involved in internal marketing is less detailed than
that required for external marketing. Internal marketing requires marketing intelligence data, marketing plan data and budgetary information. The information

TABLE 6.1.   Two-way breakdown of marketing function.

	Internal	External
Sales	• Receive orders • Acknowledge order • Provide customer service	• Send quotation and follow-up • Negotiate terms of payment
Marketing	• Plan price changes • Conduct market research • Prepare budget	• Prepare advertising • Advertise • Make cold calls • Announce new pricing

for the execution of a marketing plan concerns all of this plus more detailed information on the products and services of the firm, broadcast media, and market segments.

In the discussion of subdividing functions in Chapter 4, it was recommended that the number of subfunctions be minimized. Two reasons were given. One was to identify relations between subfunctions. The other was to simplify the information requirement definition task by identifying at an early stage entity types and relationships that apply to large groups of subfunctions.

In the case at hand, both reasons can be used to justify not distinguishing between internal and external sales at this second level. The internal and external sales functions are definitely related, with respect to both the sequence in which they handle a sale and the information required. Most of the information required for both internal and external sales is about the same entity types and relationships. This is not as clearly the case for internal and external marketing.

Consequently, Marketing is divided into three subfunctions for BWIS (Business-Wide Information Structuring) purposes. They are sales, external marketing, and internal marketing. Definitions of each of these subfunctions are as follows:

Sales: Negotiate sales with customers

External marketing: Manage the short-term formulation and execution of marketing plans, including advertising, promotions and direct sales activities

Internal marketing: Manage long-term marketing planning; collect and analyze marketing data and present the marketing viewpoint in all internal business deliberations and planning activities.

SECOND-LEVEL INFORMATION REQUIREMENTS

In this subsection, we characterize the information requirements for the sales, external marketing, and internal marketing subfunctions. The information structures derived are based on the framework established by Figure 6.1 which describes the information requirements for the Marketing function as a whole. They are also based on assumptions about the data required by each of the three subfunctions. As has been said before, these data requirements should actually come from those doing the sales, external marketing or internal marketing for the organization.

INFORMATION STRUCTURE FOR SALES

The information requirements of the sales function encompass all of the information required to "negotiate sales with customers and provide customer services." Sales negotiations typically begin with a request from the prospect for information about products or services that the enterprise has to offer. The response to this request can take many forms, but one standard response is to give the prospective customer a "quotation" which defines the product and services of interest, a schedule of prices, terms and conditions of sale, and delivery services.

The next stage in negotiations after information exchange is for the prospect to become a customer by issuing a purchase order. This is an order for certain products and services and a commitment to pay for them. Sales has the responsibility to determine whether the terms and conditions of the purchase order are acceptable and to let the customer know whether the order is accepted.

Provided that the purchase order is accepted, the third stage is to deliver products and services as ordered. This may be a single delivery which may be a simple matter of transportation, or it may involve a complex production, site erection and testing procedure, or it may involve multiple deliveries over a period of time. In the latter case, the deliveries may be controlled by "shipment release orders" issued by the customer. The involvement of the sales function in this third stage will vary depending on how much clarification of the agreement with the customer is needed as delivery proceeds. To the extent that misunderstandings arise, sales may be involved in straightening out the confusion.

The final stage involves invoicing the customer for products and services provided and receiving payment from the customer. Sales may be involved in this stage to the extent that disputes arise over invoices issued and payments due.

This four-stage sales process involves six types of actions that can be modeled as *manage marketing* relationships. They are:

1. Prospect inquiry

2. Quotation

3. Purchase order

4. Order acknowledgement

5. Ship and invoice

6. Receive payment.

In this analysis, only the first four types will be considered. They are the primary concern of the sales function. At times, sales may require information on the latter two, but this is the exception.

The decomposition of the information structure for Marketing as a whole (shown in Figure 6.1) to fit the information requirements of the sales subfunction can be based on an analysis of the information involved in defining the four specializations of the *manage marketing* relationship. In each case, we ask what entity types are required to describe the action type and what relationships between them are needed? This approach does not systematically cover all the information required to manage the sales staff so that requirement is discussed in a subsequent subsection.

Prospect Inquiry

A prospect inquiry involves information about the inquiry and the prospect making it. It is assumed that the inquiry is given to a salesperson to answer, and that answering it will require information about the products and services of the organization.

Prospect can be viewed as a specialization of the Market Segment entity type of Figure 6.1. Since information about it is required in handling inquiries, it is made an entity type in Figure 6.3 which shows the complete information structure for the sales subfunction.

Prospect Inquiry is, of course, also made an entity type in Figure 6.3. It can be considered a part of the decomposition of the *manage marketing* relationship. A one-to-many relationship between Prospect and Prospect Inquiry links the two entity types in Figure 6.3.

Information about the salesperson that handles an inquiry could be modeled as attributes of Prospect. However, this would lead to considerable data redundancy because one salesperson can be assumed to handle many inquiries. In addition, we can anticipate that information about salespersons will be required by the marketing function for many purposes. Therefore, Salesperson is identified in Figure 6.3 as a specialization of Marketing Resource. A one-to-many relationship between Prospect Inquiry and Salesperson allows the salesperson assigned to answer an inquiry to be recorded.

As the salesperson identifies the products and services relevant to the inquiry, the many-to-many relationship between Prospect Inquiry and Product/Service in Figure 6.3 can be used to define the inquiry more specifically, as understood by the salesperson. To this extent the Product/Service entity type of Figure 6.1 is relevant to prospect inquiries.

Finally, the marketing plan may have a goal for prospect inquiries. This is shown in Figure 6.3 as Forecast Inquiries, a specialization of the Marketing Goal entity type of Figure 6.1. This goal might simply be the total number of inquiries expected during a month or year. Or, it could be in terms of inquiries from a certain market segment for a certain group of products. The many-to-many relationship between Prospect Inquiry and Forecast Inquiries links this forecast, or goal, to the actual inquiries received.

Quotation

A quotation is one possible answer to a prospect inquiry. For inquiries that warrant this type of response, the entity types that are directly involved in a description of the quotation would be: (1) the quotation itself, (2) the prospect to whom it is sent, (3) the products and services for which quotes are provided, (4) the inquiry or inquiries for which this is the response, and (5) the salesperson who prepared the quotation.

The quotation itself is shown as an entity type in Figure 6.3. This entity type is then linked by a relationship to each of the other four entity types listed in the preceding paragraph. Thus, Figure 6.3 should provide for all information required to describe quotations.

Preparation of a quotation requires information about pricing policy, and possibly other company policies. Pricing policy is represented in Figure 6.3 by the Pricing Category entity type, another specialization of Marketing Goal. In the simple case, pricing categories are based on purchasing volumes. Individual units are sold at "list price," which is one category. Multiple units may be sold at some percentage of list price, which creates other categories.

The relationship between Pricing Category and Product/Service, called *pricing schedule* in Figure 6.3, contains the specific price guidelines. It defines the

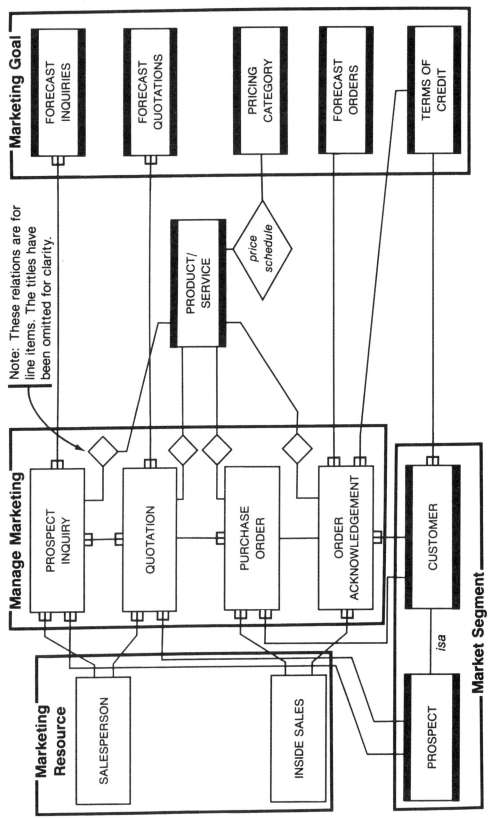

FIGURE 6.3. Information structure for sales.

prices (perhaps, a minimum and normal price) for each product or service and for each price category. The price schedule relationship is a specialization of the *plan marketing* relationship of Figure 6.1.

Another aspect of the marketing plan that can relate to quotations is a goal for quotation activities. In Figure 6.3, this is represented by the Forecast Quotation entity type. The one-to-many relationship that it has with Quotation is part of the decomposition of the *manage marketing* relationship.

Purchase Order

The event of receiving a purchase order from a customer is of basic importance to the sales subfunction. It can be treated as an entity type obtained by disaggregating the *manage marketing* relationship because it represents a resource allocation decision on the part of the prospect who now becomes a customer.

The Purchase Order entity type is shown in Figure 6.3 related to the occurrence of the Quotation sent to the prospect and, also, related to the Product/Service occurrences that are on the order. The quantity of each product ordered would be an attribute of the relationship between Product/Service and Purchase Order.

The event of receiving a purchase order from a prospect creates a need for more information about the prospect, such as shipping and billing addresses. This is the reason for creating the Customer entity type in Figure 6.3 and considering it to be a specialization of prospect.

We assume that purchase orders are handled by the inside sales staff, rather than the salesperson. This is the reason for identifying Inside Sales as another specialization of Marketing Resource in Figure 6.3. The relationship between Inside Sales and Purchase Order should identify which inside sales staff member is responsible for approving an order.

Order Acknowledgement

After the inside sales staff determines the acceptability of the customer's purchase order, an order acknowledgement is sent to the customer. This entails information about the purchase order, inside sales, customer, and products and services. Accordingly, relationships are shown in Figure 6.3 linking the Order Acknowledgement to each of these entity types.

In checking the order, the inside sales staff would also need access to the quotation on which the order is based, including the prices quoted which would be an attribute of the relationship between Quotation and Product/Service. The relationship between Purchase Order and Quotation makes that quotation information readily available.

Checking the order and acknowledging it should also include determining the terms of credit under which the sale will be made. The purchase order may specify terms; it is the responsibility of inside sales to either grant the requested terms or specify other terms in the acknowledgement. The marketing goals can be expected to include a policy on terms of credit. This is represented in Figure 6.3 by the Terms of Credit entity type. The relationship between Terms of Credit and Order Acknowledgement provides for recording the terms that inside sales grants to the customer in the acknowledgement. On the other hand, the relationship between

Terms of Credit and Customer is not part of the *manage marketing* decomposition. Instead, it defines the default terms of credit that can be granted to the customer as a matter of policy. More liberal terms of credit are granted only on an exception basis. As in the case of the *price schedule* relationship, this relationship is a specialization of the *plan marketing* relationship.

Management of the Sales Function

The supervision of any function requires information not required to simply perform the function. In general, supervision requires information about:

1. Operating expenses (budgeted and actual)

2. Staff performance (planned and actual)

3. Facilities (required and provided).

These information requirements are not considered in this chapter. The operating expense information requirements are modeled in Chapter 10. The staff performance information requirements are derivable from Figure 5.4 in Chapter 5. The management of facilities and fixed assets is partially handled in Chapter 10.

INFORMATION STRUCTURE FOR EXTERNAL MARKETING

The information structure required for the external marketing subfunction can be obtained by decomposing the structure shown in Figure 6.1, which is a guideline appropriate for all Marketing subfunctions. The explanation of this decomposition is organized by the Figure 6.1 entity types and relationships. In other words, each of these entity types and relationships is decomposed to fit the needs to external marketing.

The decomposition of Figure 6.1 to suit the needs of external marketing is shown in Figure 6.4. The Product/Service entity type is decomposed to show marketing information prepared about one or more products and services. The marketing information is called a Formatted Message entity type. It could be a brochure, a picture, an audio taped message, or advertising copy for printed media, or a TV commercial.

The Marketing Resource entity type of Figure 6.1 is decomposed in 6.4 to show two kinds of resources and their generalization. Direct Sales and Advertising Resources are both specializations of Medium, that is broadcast media. The Direct Sales entity type is intended to include the facilities and managers as well as the salesperson that do direct sales work. Direct Sales is not normally characterized as a broadcast medium; however, it does serve as a channel for distributing advertising while at the same time serving other purposes. The Advertising Resources entity type includes advertising agencies as well as broadcast media available for advertising.

The Broadcast Plan entity type is a specialization of Marketing Goal. It defines the external marketing objectives in terms of both general policies and specific types of actions.

The *external marketing budget* is a specialization of the *plan marketing* relationship of Figure 6.1. It defines constraints on broadcasting activities in terms of specific formatted messages delivered via a certain medium to satisfy a broadcast

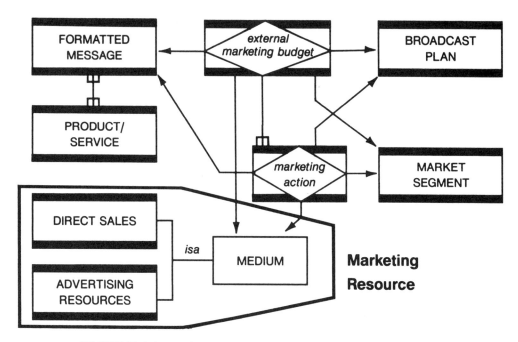

FIGURE 6.4. Information structure for external marketing.

objective. The relationship between *external marketing budget* and *marketing action* provides for linking actions to their budgetary authorization. This characterization of a budget as a plan type of relationship rather than as a manage relationship is somewhat arbitrary as was explained in the discussion of these two relationships in Chapter 5. However, in this case, the budget is used mainly as a means of control, rather than as a resource allocation mechanism.

The "manage marketing" relationship of 6.1 is specialized to *marketing action* in 6.4. It represents a specific commitment to use certain resources to deliver a message. The generalization symbol is superimposed on the diamond to show that any one action may be part of a larger commitment to a series of marketing actions. The lines that link Medium, Formatted Message, Market Segment and Broadcast Plan in this relationship indicate that all four participate in a given instance of the relationship.

INFORMATION STRUCTURE FOR INTERNAL MARKETING

The information structure for internal marketing must support both the information gathering and analysis aspects of the subfunction. The information gathering aspect relates to the *manage marketing* relationship in 6.1 in the sense that gathering information involves the use of resources. In view of the fact that a variety of marketing resources are used to gather information about market segments, including the sales force, it should not be considered a distortion of the *manage marketing* relationship in 6.1 to decompose it into an information gathering activity.

The proposed decomposition of the general marketing information structure tailored to the needs of internal marketing is shown in Figure 6.5. The *manage marketing* relationship is shown as specialized to a *market research activity*

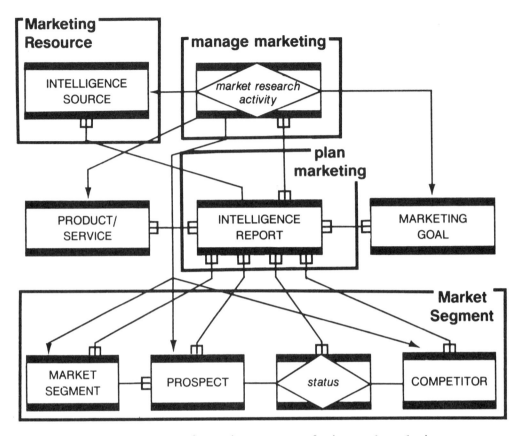

FIGURE 6.5. Information structure for internal marketing.

relationship that involves the Marketing Goal, Product/Service, Intelligence Source and either a Market Segment, Prospect, or Competitor entity types. This relationship is intended to include both small and large intelligence gathering efforts, everything from a salesperson's visit with a prospect to a formal questionnaire survey or product test marketing program.

The Marketing Resource entity type of Figure 6.1 is specialized to Intelligence Source in Figure 6.5. This Source entity type is meant to represent any source of marketing intelligence, including salespersons, publications, trade shows and conferences, and other resources used in budgeted market research projects.

The analysis and planning aspect of the internal marketing subfunction are reflected in the *intelligence report* relationship and decomposition of Market Segment shown in Figure 6.5. These marketing intelligence reports provide information about the prospects for products and services in market segments that should be taken into account in formulating the marketing plan. An instance of the intelligence report relationship could be any kind of report that concerns one or more market segments and the products and services of interest to the enterprise. Salesperson's call reports, reports from publications, and formal market research reports are examples of this relationship.

The Market Segment entity type of 6.1 is decomposed in 6.5 to show individual prospects in a market segment and the relationships of prospects with competitors. This relationship is called "status" in Figure 6.5. The figure also shows Market Segment to be part of the decomposition of Market Segment. This is because some intelligence information will not relate to specific prospects, but to a class of prospects.

SECOND-LEVEL MARKETING FUNCTION BREAKDOWNS

The next step in the information requirements analysis process is to break down the subfunctions of marketing already identified. These subfunctions are sales and external and internal marketing. The process of breaking down these subfunctions is the subject of this section.

The proposed breakdown is shown in Figure 6.6. It is a breakdown designed to suit the marketing function of a manufacturer of consumer hard goods whose customers are distributors, retail chains, and very large customer organizations. It is appropriate for a maker of appliances or personal computers. It is not intended to represent marketing functions in capital goods or consumable goods and services businesses.

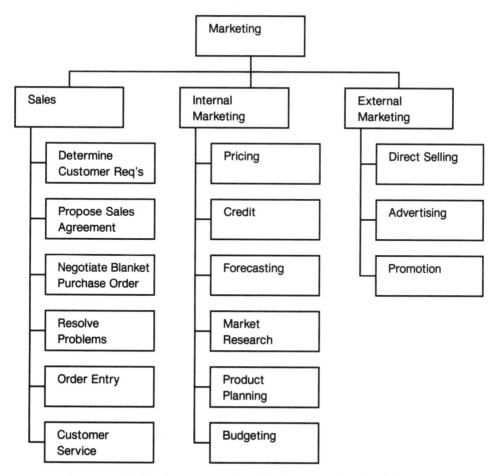

FIGURE 6.6.   Second-level marketing function breakdown.

The initial steps in the sales function concern negotiating blanket sales orders, or distributor agreements, with customers. These agreements cover everything ordered by the customer during a period of time, usually six months or a year. They contain a price schedule covering all of the products that may be ordered and a definition of the duties and responsibilities of each party with regard to the agreement. The development and administration of these blanket purchase agreements is divided into four subfunctions in Figure 6.6. The first is to meet with the customer and determine the type of supplier relationship that can be established. The second subfunction is to prepare and send to the customer a proposed sales agreement. The third subfunction is to obtain from the customer a blanket purchase order that incorporates the proposed sales agreement, or a negotiated modified version of it. Finally, there is the subfunction of resolving problems that arise during the life of the agreement, and monitoring conformance with the terms of the agreement.

The inside sales function is divided into two subfunctions, order entry and customer service. The orders received are shipment orders issued under the blanket purchase agreements negotiated with customers by the outside sales force. The order entry function includes verifying the items and prices on the order, checking the customer's credit and determining when the items can be delivered. Assuming the order passes the tests, it is acknowledged and given to the materials management function to be fulfilled. The customer service aspects of the function include answering customer inquiries concerning orders being processed and handling changes in orders made by customers.

The external marketing function is divided into three subfunctions in Figure 6.6. They represent three ways of influencing the procurement decisions of potential customers. There may be other ways, and they should be added to the breakdown if they are used. Direct selling is done by having salespersons call on potential customers to present the products and services of the manufacturer. Advertising is preparing and broadcasting information about the manufacturer and its products using media other than the direct sales force. Television, radio, newspapers, trade publications and billboards are examples of these other media. Promoting products refers to techniques used to cause purchase decisions to be made now rather than later. Price discounts and chances to win a prize are examples of promotional techniques. Planning and successfully managing a promotion is made challenging by the fact that the advertising of the promotion must be coordinated with the steps taken to ensure that the supply of product is adequate.

The internal marketing function is broken into the six subfunctions shown in Figure 6.6. The market research subfunction is an information gathering and analysis function that can serve any of the other five subfunctions plus a number of other purposes. The other five subfunctions concern interfaces with other functions in the firm; pricing policy must be worked out in cooperation with the finance and cost accounting functions; sales forecasting is worked out in cooperation with materials management; product planning represents a marketing-engineering interface. Credit policy and budgeting involves working with the finance function in defining the resources to be devoted to marketing activities.

There are a number of linkages between and among the internal and external marketing functions that do not appear in Figure 6.6. They become evident as these subfunctions are broken down further. For example, market research can include the analysis of "call reports" prepared by a salesperson after each sales call. Preparing the call report is a subfunction of direct selling. Analyzing call reports can be a subfunction of market research.

It should be noted that the functional breakdown of Figure 6.6 is not likely to be the same as the organizational breakdown of the marketing function. Some likely differences are as follows:

1. The outside sales function and the direct selling subfunction may be performed by the same sales force. The sales force is often organized by territories. In each territory there is a branch office that serves as a point of coordination for salespersons working in that territory.

2. The inside sales function may be centralized and in some organizations it may be considered part of the materials management organization, rather than part of marketing.

3. The sales forecasting subfunction may involve the sales force in preparing forecasts; the sales force can often improve on the forecast obtained from historical sales statistics. Sales forecasting may also take into account the advertising and promotion plans as well as changes in pricing and credit policies.

The breakdown of Figure 6.6 should be judged on how well it defines what has to be done to carry out the marketing function, not on whether it is practical to organize people so that they perform only one subfunction.

THIRD-LEVEL MARKETING INFORMATION REQUIREMENTS

The next step in this approach to defining the information requirements of marketing is to define the data requirements of each of the 15 subfunctions shown in Figure 6.6. Each of these subfunctions can be analyzed to determine the entity types about which information is needed and to determine the relationships between these entities that provide the kinds of lists and database access capabilities useful to the subfunction.

The purpose of this chapter is to show how the proposed top-down approach to conceptual database design applies to the marketing function. However, an exhaustive analysis of these 15 subfunctions would require more space than is justified. Hopefully, an analysis of a select subset of subfunctions will illustrate how the methodology could be applied to the remainder. The information requirements of five of the subfunctions are determined in the remainder of this chapter. They are the three subfunctions of external marketing and the pricing and sales forecasting subfunctions of internal marketing.

DIRECT SELLING

The information requirements for direct selling can be obtained from the information structure in Figure 6.4, which describes the information required for all external marketing subfunctions. To see how Figure 6.4 applies to direct selling, however, it is necessary to first specify the information that is useful in direct selling and then consider how that information is contained in the structure in Figure 6.4.

Two aspects of direct sales are the making of sales calls and the planning and managing of a direct sales force. The information requirements of each of these aspects are considered in the two subsections that follow.

Making Sales Calls

Direct selling is personally calling on prospective customers (distributors and large retailers, in the case of a consumer hard goods manufacturer) for the purpose of providing information about products and services available from the manufacturer. The information may be conveyed verbally, in written and graphical form, and by a demonstration or sample. Because the information is conveyed in a two-way conversation, it is important that the salesperson know as much as possible about the prospect so that the conversation can be managed in the most effective way.

Information that can help to make a sales call as productive as possible is indicated by the first of the three lists shown in Table 6.2. The first item on this list is a prospect visit schedule, which shows where and when the meeting with the prospect is to take place. It should also give a telephone number in case the salesperson is unable to keep the appointment.

TABLE 6.2.   Information requirements for direct sales.

Information to Support Salesman
- Prospect visit schedule and basic prospect data
- Information mailed to prospect
- Past calls on prospect
- Past quotes given to prospect
- Past orders from prospect
- Invoiced sales
- Credit status of prospect
- Product information available, promised or given

Information to Aid in Managing Direct Sales
- Information about organization of direct sales
- Information about salesman
- Data on prospects per territory or sales office
- Statistics on activity per salesman
- Direct sales budget data
- Data on total sales and market share per territory

Marketing Intelligence Data That Could Be Gathered
- Competitor contacts with prospect
- Competitor business with prospect
- Prospect opinion of competitors
- Prospect opinions of products and practice
- Prospect's future needs and plans

This list can be analyzed to identify the entity types and relationships that it implies. In other words, this list of information needs of a salesperson making direct sales calls can be converted into a set of entity types and relationships that constitute a description of what the salesperson needs to know. In arriving at these entity types and relationships, the information structure of Figure 6.4 should be consulted. It should be possible to identify specializations and decompositions of parts of Figure 6.4 that are the entity types and relationships appropriate for defining direct selling information requirements. To support this proposition, the items on the first list in Table 6.2 are analyzed one by one in the following subsections. The result of this analysis is the decomposed information structure shown in Figure 6.7.

Prospect Visit Schedule

A visit is a specialization of what is called a *marketing action* in Figure 6.4. It is an occasion on which one or more "formatted messages" are delivered to a "market segment." In Figure 6.7, the *call* relationship stands for a visit or call made by a salesperson. The relationship between *call* and Formatted Message is shown as many-to-many because more than one message could be delivered during a single visit.

The Market Segment entity type of Figure 6.4 is disaggregated in Figure 6.7. As far as information about a sales call is concerned, information about the prospect to be visited is the level of detail required. Prospect is one of the entity types shown in the disaggregation of Market Segment in Figure 6.7.

The word "schedule" in the definition of the information requirement indicates that it is a list of visits that is required, not just one visit. For this reason, the Call entity type is linked to the *schedule* of the Salesperson which is shown in the Market Resource section of Figure 6.7. The Salesperson, *schedule*, Time Period relationship of 6.7 is a decomposition of the Direct Sales entity type in Figure 6.4.

The *call* relationship is also shown to involve the Broadcast Plan entity type. Presumably, the sales call is required, or at least permitted, by the plan.

Basic Prospect Data

The entity type in this case is the Prospect. This is a specialization of what is called Market Segment in Figure 6.4. At this stage, it can be assumed that the data about a prospect can be modeled as attributes of Prospect.

Information Mailed to Prospect

Prior to the visit, information may have been mailed to the prospect. In terms of Figure 6.4, a mailed letter is another specialization of *marketing action*. It is an instance of a message being delivered to a market segment. Thus, it is modeled in Figure 6.7 as a relationship between Broadcast Plan and Prospect. The relationship between *mail* and Formatted Message is shown as many-to-many because multiple messages could go in one mailing. The relationship between *mail* and *call* permits mail to be associated with a call that it precedes or follows. This relationship is the result of a disaggregation of the *marketing action* relationship.

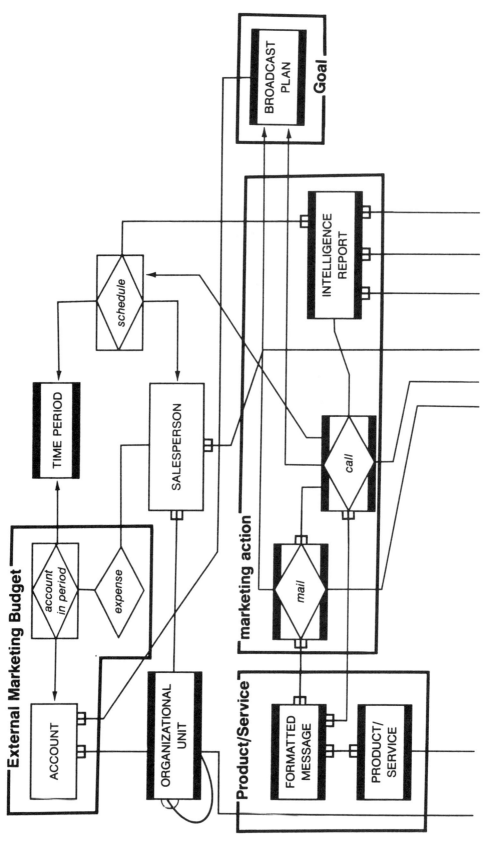

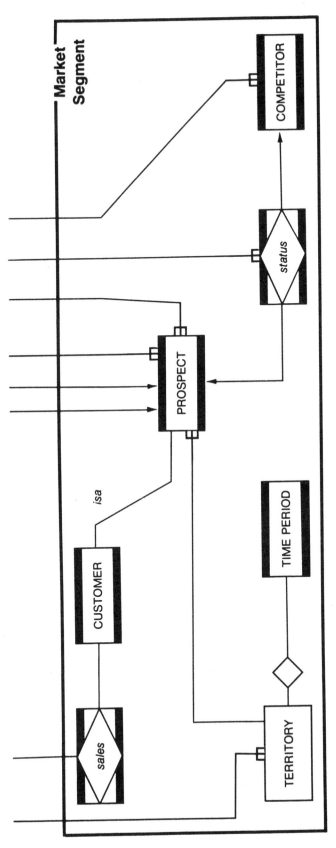

FIGURE 6.7. Information structure for direct sales.

163

Past Calls

The "past calls on prospect" item refers to information about any past calls that have been made to the prospect. The *call* relationship in this case is clearly the entity type about which the salesperson needs information. But this information requirement of Table 6.2 points to the value of more data on the call than simply its time and place. It points to the call report prepared after the call.

The fact that this data constitutes a form of what is called *intelligence report* in Figure 6.5 means that the guideline provided by 6.5 should be considered when defining the information structure to represent this data. This guideline suggests that a Competitor entity type should be recognized and that the relationship between Competitor and Prospect should be made explicit. In Table 6.2 there is a third list labeled "Marketing Intelligence Data that Could Be Gathered." This list indicates the kinds of data about Prospects that could be gathered in the process of making direct sales calls.

In Figure 6.7, the information on past calls is provided for by the relationship between *call* and Prospect and by the one between Call and Intelligence Report. This requirement for information on past calls is an interesting case as far as the theory of the methodology is concerned. In one sense, it is a case of a function requiring historical data about itself. It is certainly not surprising that such data could be useful. Ordinarily, such a requirement would simply result in the function also being treated as an entity type. However, in this case the call function is associated with a rich assortment of tidbits about a market segment some of which have value beyond their relevance to subsequent "calls." It is this additional utility of the information that justified invoking Figure 6.5.

Past Quotes, Orders, and Invoices

If the prospect has been a customer in the past, the salesperson should be aware of this and should have access to information about past exchanges. This is information about a former customer and the products and services provided to that customer. To provide this information the Market Segment entity type of Figure 6.4 is decomposed to Customer and Prospect entity types and a one-to-one relationship between them as shown in Figure 6.7.

The relationships between customer and the products and services of the business were defined in a previous section where the sales functions are considered. They are summarized in Figure 6.3. In Figure 6.7, this information about past sales is summarized by the *sales* relationship in the Market Segment section. If warranted, this relationship could be decomposed to the four entity types in Figure 6.3, namely, the inquiry, quote, purchase order, and order acknowledgement entity types, and an invoice entity type could be added.

Credit Status of Prospect

If the prospect is a past or current customer then credit status information should be available either as an attribute of the Customer or as a relationship with the terms of credit policy defined in the Marketing Plan. For reasons of simplicity, we will assume the former alternative in Figure 6.7.

If the prospect has not been a customer, information concerning credit worthiness may still be available from an external database of corporate financial information. If so, this information can be modeled as attributes of Prospect.

Product Information

Last but not least, information about products and services that can be shared with the prospect during a visit should be accessible by the salesperson. This data is modeled as attributes of the Formatted Message entity type of Figure 6.7. The material given to the prospect, or promised, could be defined by the relationship between Formatted Message and call.

Managing Direct Sales

In addition to direct selling itself, we should consider the information that is useful in planning and managing a direct sales force. A list of types of information that can be useful in this function is shown in Table 6.2 under the heading, Information to Aid in Managing Direct Sales. The entity types about which information is required according to this list need to be identified. Then these entity types need to be related to one another and to the other entity types of Figure 6.7 to give a complete picture of the information structure required to support the direct marketing function.

To clarify how the information requirements as stated in Table 6.2 are converted to the information structure shown in Figure 6.7, each of the items on the list concerned with managing direct sales is discussed below.

Information about Organization of Direct Sales Force

If we assume a traditional hierarchical organization of the sales force, then the organization of the sales force can be modeled as a series of Organizational Units with a reporting relationship between them. The entity type labeled Organizational Unit in Figure 6.7 is intended to represent this way of defining the sales force organization and can be considered a decomposition of the Direct Sales entity type of Figure 6.4.

Each individual salesperson belongs to an Organizational Unit. This is represented in Figure 6.7 by the relationship between Salesperson and Organizational Unit. The Salesperson entity type is another decomposition of Direct Sales.

Information about Salespeople

This requirement is satisfied by the Salesperson entity type and its attributes and relationships. Presumably, the prospects serviced by the sales person are defined by the organizational unit to which the salesperson belongs and the Prospect occurrences to which the Salesperson entity type is related.

To define how the sales force is allocated to market segments, the concept of sales territories is useful. Market Segment can be decomposed to Territory and a relationship between Territory and Prospect. Territory can also be related to the Organizational Units responsible for the territory.

Statistics on Activity per Salespeople

The actual calls made by a salesperson can be seen from the relationship between the Salesperson's schedule and *call* shown in Figure 6.7. Using the attributes of *call* and its relationships, other statistics can be derived.

The *expense* relationship between Salesperson and Account can also contain information relating to the activity of a salesperson. This relationship is explained below in the subsection on the direct sales budget. It might be useful to define a relationship between the expense and schedule relationships, although this is not included in Figure 6.7.

Data on Prospects per Territory

The information about prospects that is useful for direct sales planning purposes should be defined as attributes of Prospect. The relationship between Prospect and Territory enables the planner to aggregate data for each territory.

Direct Sales Budget

The budget information requires a decomposition of the *external marketing budget* relationship of Figure 6.4. It is decomposed into a relationship between Account and Time Period entity types, and another relationship called *expense* in Figure 6.7. The *account-in-period* relationship can be used to define the budget for each marketing account in each period. The *expense* relationship allows individual expenses to be identified by salesperson for each account and accounting period. A more complete derivation of this structure is given in Chapter 10.

Total Sales and Market Share Data

Total industry sales by territory can be treated as an attribute of the relationship between Territory and Time Period. To obtain market share per territory, the invoiced sales are needed. The sales relationship should include sales amounts as an attribute. This could be used to calculate the period sales of the business by Customer and by Territory. Thus, the market share per Territory can be obtained. It might be useful to have this sales information broken down by Product/Service. This would necessitate expanding the relationship between Territory and Time Period in Figure 6.7, to one between Time Period, Territory, and Product/Service.

Conclusion

It is possible to derive a description of the information required to manage a direct sales activity by decomposing the information structure appropriate for all external marketing activities. The information structure shown in Figure 6.7 represents the information required by the direct sales function. It describes information requirements for both direct selling and the management of a direct sales force.

ADVERTISING

Advertising is planning and preparing information about the organization and its products and services. It also involves selecting broadcast media and broadcasting the material prepared.

The objective of this discussion is to identify the entity types and relationships about which information is needed in order to prepare advertising materials and manage broadcasting activities. Also, there is information that this subfunction should collect; we want to define that responsibility. The lists of information shown in Table 6.3 are intended to provide a basis for achieving these objectives.

The information listed in Table 6.3 can be analyzed to determine with which entity types and relationships each item of data is associated. Some entity types that seem relatively obvious are: Product/Service, Competitor, Competitor Ad, Print Media, Direct Mail, Radio, Television, and Special Event Advertising.

Maintaining information about every possible indirect customer is not likely to be cost-effective. Even maintaining data on all potential direct customers (retailers and wholesalers) is of questionable value. For advertising planning, statistics about direct and indirect customers by type and geographic area (the demographics) are necessary. An example of a direct customer type is a regional appliance distributor with sales between fifty and one hundred million dollars. An example of an indirect customer type is a low-income household in a metropolitan area.

The generalization that applies in this case is clearly Figure 6.4. Advertising uses media to convey messages and this is the essence of that generalization. The relationships in Figure 6.4 are needed to define a useful advertising management database.

The decomposition of Figure 6.4 tailored to the needs of advertising is shown in Figure 6.8. For the most part, the decomposition of Figure 6.4 entity types in

TABLE 6.3. Information requirements to manage advertising.

Information to Support Planning of Advertising
- Product and service information
- Marketing intelligence on direct customers, end users, and competitors
- Competitor advertising to direct and indirect customers
- Information about media and advertising techniques
- Advertising budget

Information to Manage Media Usage
- Print media reaching direct customer prospects
- Print media reaching retail customers
- Direct mailing services
- Radio and television media
- Seasonal and special event advertising opportunities
- Past advertising
- Advertising budget

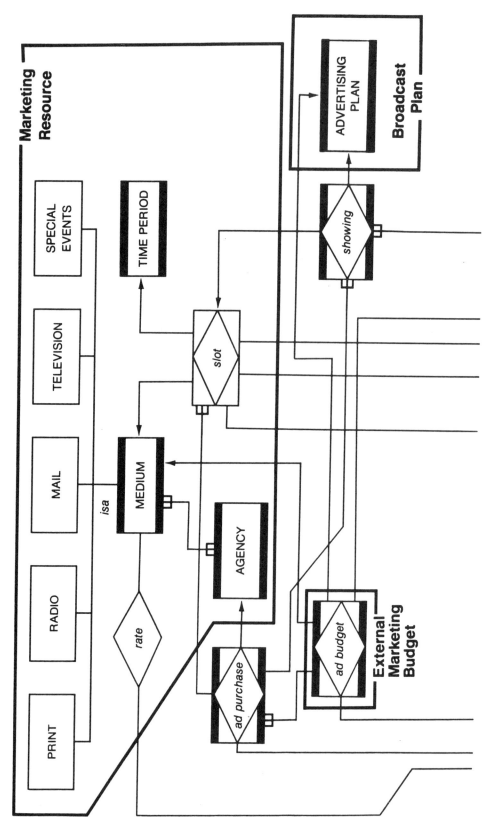

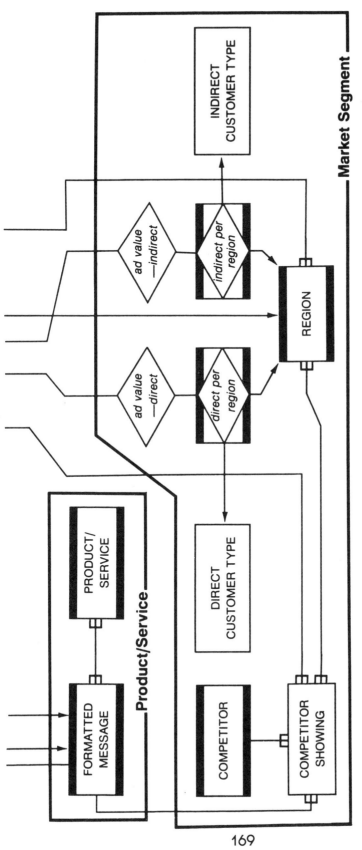

FIGURE 6.8. Information structure for advertising.

Figure 6.8 is shown by areas defined by heavy black lines. Therefore, this discussion concentrates on explaining how Figure 6.8 satisfies the requirements of Table 6.3.

Information to Support the Planning of Advertising

The first item on the list in Table 6.3, information about products and services, is obviously satisfied by the Product/Service entity type of 6.8. The second requirement, information about direct and indirect customer prospects and competitors, is satisfied by the decomposition of the Market Segment entity type as shown in Figure 6.8.

The third item on the list, competitor advertising, is satisfied by the inclusion of Competitor Showing as an entity type in the Market Segment decomposition and the relationship between Competitor Showing and Region. The fact that the Direct and Indirect Customer entity types are linked to Region by relationships means that competitor's advertising (or previous advertising by the enterprise) in these market segments can be analyzed. The two relationships labeled "ad value—direct" and "ad value—indirect" are for any available data on the effectiveness of using a certain medium in a time slot to reach a direct or an indirect customer.

Much information about media and advertising techniques is treated as attributes of the Medium, Agency and Formatted Messages entity types. The Rate relationship between Medium and Formatted Message is to store advertising rates.

The advertising budget is represented by *ad budget* which is a specialization of *external marketing budget*, shown in Figure 6.4. It is a relationship between Medium, Advertising Plan, Region, and Formatted Message. Thus, the budget for advertising can be specified by medium, region, message, and advertising plan. Not shown explicitly in Figure 6.8 is the fact that both the advertising plan and budget could be defined by time period.

Information to Manage Media Usage

The information about print media reaching direct and indirect customers is provided for in Figure 6.8 by the "ad value—direct" and "ad value—indirect" relationships. Information on whether or not a certain media will reach a certain class of customers can be stored as an attribute of these two relationships.

Information on the next three items in the second list of Table 6.3 should be modeled as attributes of one of the five specializations of Medium shown in an ISA cluster in Figure 6.8. Each of these specializations can have its own set of attributes.

Information on past advertising is found in the *ad purchase* relationship which is part of the decomposition of the *marketing action* relationship of Figure 6.4. There can be an occurrence of this relationship for each past advertising expenditure. The other part of the decomposition of *marketing action* is the *showing* relationship which represents an actual message broadcast.

The final item on the list in Table 6.3 is advertising budget. This is represented in Figure 6.8 by the *ad budget* relationship, which has already been described.

PROMOTION

A promotion is a special advertising focus and "deal" related to one or a limited number of products for a limited period of time. The deal may be a simple price reduction or it may be some more complicated scheme involving volume discounts, coupons, or a chance for a trip to Hawaii.

The planning and management of promotions is a matter of coordinating advertising and supply. It is important that the supply of the items being promoted is adequate and is located in the right place. Special advertising is needed. Timing is critical to the success of a promotion. The information useful to promotion management includes a definition of the promotion, an estimate of its effect on gross margin, a schedule of promotion preparatory steps, an advertising plan, and a product supply plan.

The fact that promotion involves both advertising and supply information implies that it is not appropriate to derive the information requirements solely from the information structure for external marketing (Figure 6.5). The characterization of the supply information should be based on goals, resources and their two types of relationships other than those shown in Figure 6.5. Because this subject of supply management is considered in depth in Chapter 7, an extensive development of it at this point would be redundant. In describing the information structure for the promotion function here, reference will be made to the relevant part of Chapter 7.

The information requirements in the five areas just described are summarized in Table 6.4. This set of lists can serve as a basis for developing a decomposition of Figure 6.4 that reflects the needs of Promotion Management.

The promotion itself should be modeled as a marketing action based on a promotion plan. It is something about which information is required. In Figure 6.9, *promotion* is shown as a part of the decomposition of *marketing action*. It is a relationship between Promotion Plan, Market Segment, and Product/Service because a promotion can be aimed at a certain market segment and product or service.

The estimated effects on gross margin of a promotion could be treated as attributes of the relationship between *promotion* and *forecast sales* called *promotion effect* in Figure 6.9. A promotion is usually considered successful if the increase in gross margin exceeds the costs of the promotion. The advertising costs would be attributes of *ad purchase*. Other costs could be attributes of either *promotion* or *promotion step*.

The schedule of promotion preparatory steps, which a promotion manager might wish to create and use to monitor progress, is another part of the decomposition of *marketing action*. It is modeled in Figure 6.9 as a relationship between *promotion* and Time. This type of information is concerned with planning how messages will be broadcast to market segments as well as making sure product supplies are adequate.

Information about the promotion advertising program would be stored in the *ad purchase* relationship of Figure 6.9. For a more detailed definition of this part of the database refer to Figure 6.8.

The information structure for the product supply plan should be congruent with that developed to support the materials management function. Major

TABLE 6.4.   Information requirements to manage promotion.

Information for Defining Promotion

- Product/services included
- Market segments included
- Timing and duration
- Pricing reduction
- Other expenses

Information for Estimating Effect on Gross Margin

- Effect on marginal income
- Fixed costs

Information for Scheduling Preparatory Steps

- Advertising preparations
- Supply preparations
- Other preparations

Information for Creating Advertising Plan

- Advertising materials
- Media
- Timing
- Advertising budget

Information for Creating Product Supply Plan

- Initial stock levels per week
- Production
- Purchases
- Demand forecast

responsibility for preparing this plan usually lies with the organizational units assigned to carry out the materials management function. Information about the forecast sales (including promotion effects) is modeled as a relationship between Time Period and *item-in-market* in Figure 6.9. This is based on the design for materials management developed in the next chapter and summarized in Figure 7.3. The relationship called *demand schedule* in Figure 7.3 is called *forecast sales* in Figure 6.9. The *promotion effect* relationship in 6.9 is for data on the sales effects of a single promotion.

PRICING

We turn now to a subfunction of internal marketing, namely, setting prices on the products and services of the business. This is a function that requires both marketing and cost accounting expertise. In this discussion, we focus on the marketing aspects of the information requirements. The information structure of Figure 6.5 is taken as the framework from which to derive a description of pricing information requirements. However, provision is made for the basic results of cost accounting which are the product cost estimates.

Pricing of products and services is usually done on an incremental basis. That is, existing prices are adjusted in response to evolving market conditions,

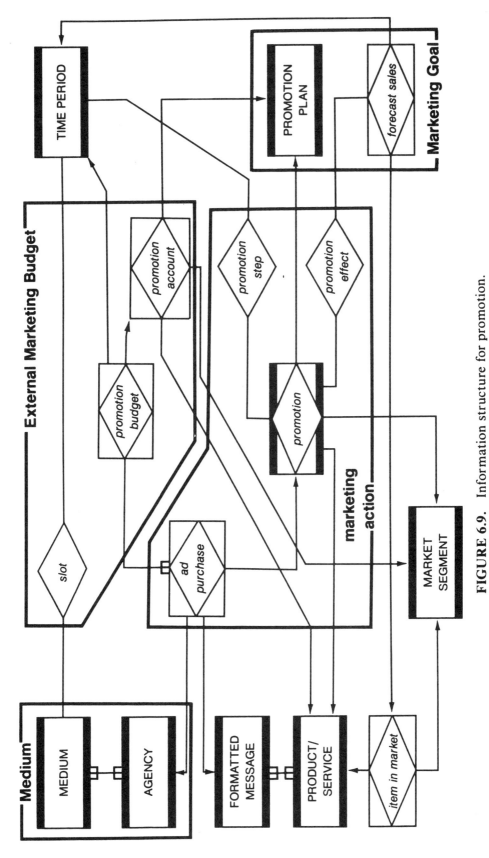

FIGURE 6.9. Information structure for promotion.

corporate strategy, and supply conditions. A hard goods manufacturer usually issues a new price list only a few times a year.

Two aspects of pricing in consumer hard goods should be distinguished. One is the general price level and the other is consistency between prices for variations on the same basic product. The information requirements for these aspects are different. Both are considered in the following analysis of price management information requirements.

General Price Level Management

Decisions to change the general price level in a market segment benefit from information about the likely effect the change will have on unit sales in the future. The factors that are commonly considered when the level of prices is reviewed include some that vary with the product or service, some that vary with the market segment, some that vary with the competitor, some that vary with the customer, and some that depend upon combinations of these basic entity types. Examples of factors in each of these categories are shown in Table 6.5.

The way in which this information is used to estimate the effect of a price level change is not relevant to this discussion. From a conceptual database planning viewpoint, the important point is that the database should be capable of storing

TABLE 6.5.   Information requirements to manage pricing.

Information about Product/Service-Related Factors
- Our existing prices
- Our change-in-price history
- Changes in our costs
- Sales volumes
- Price changes being considered

Information about Market Segment-Related Factors
- Inflation trend
- Forecast of disposable income

Information about Competitor-Related Factors
- Competitor management personnel
- Competitor financing

Information about Customer-Related Factors
- Customer loyalty
- Customer purchase commitments

Information about Competitor–Product-Related Factors
- Competitor prices
- Competitor price changes

Information about Customer–Product-Related Factors
- Sales rate
- Average price

the information for price management purposes. To store the information, the information structure designed to support the internal marketing function (Figure 6.5) needs to be decomposed to make explicit the entity types and relationships identified in Table 6.5. This decomposition to fit price management needs is shown in Figure 6.10.

In Figure 6.10, the Product/Service, Market Segment, Competitor, Customer, *competitor price,* and *sales* entity types and relationships provide for the six types of variables identified in Table 6.5. The decomposition of Market Segment in Figure 6.10 differs from that of Figure 6.5 in only two respects. The Prospect entity type of 6.5 has been specialized to Customer, and a *competitor price* relationship has been added.

Price Variation Management

Volume discounts are an important aspect of pricing. Discounts may be offered based on the quantity of an item that is ordered, on the total value of an order, or

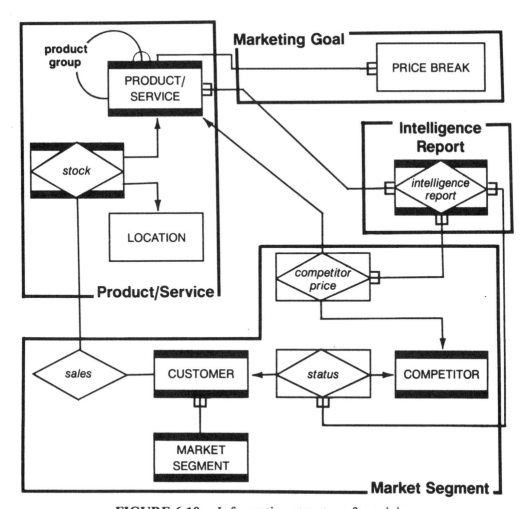

FIGURE 6.10. Information structure for pricing.

on total purchases during a year. Price breaks that are based on the volume of a product or service purchased can be incorporated in the database defining a relationship between the Product/Service and a Price Break entity type as shown in Figure 6.10. Basically, this is a decomposition of the Marketing Goal entity type of Figure 6.5 It is decomposed to focus on prices that are set as a function of the volume purchased. The reduced price and minimum volume required to qualify for it are attributes of Price Break.

Discounts that are independent of the product or service purchased can be modeled as attributes of Market Segment. If certain customers have signed contracts to buy at certain volume levels, this information should be characterized as attributes of the Customer entity type.

Another important aspect of price variation management is controlling the price difference between variations on the same basic product. A group of products that differ only in color or in their options needs to be priced so that demand substitution is controlled. Cost differentials may be used to set the price differences in this case. In any case, it is useful to be able to segregate products and services into subgroups and this is the reason for the recursive relationship shown for the Product/Service entity type in Figure 6.10.

Finally, there may be price variations based on the location from which stock is delivered to the customer. These variations should reflect transportation and warehousing cost differences. To manage these variations, Figure 6.10 contains a decomposition of the Product/Service entity type that shows the locations where a product is stored or produced. Transportation and storage cost differences can be made attributes of the Location entity type and the *stock* relationship.

SALES FORECASTING

In this subsection, the information requirements of another internal marketing subfunction are considered. This subfunction is sales forecasting. Forecasts of sales are needed for many planning activities. Perhaps, the most demanding is the forecast for supply planning purposes. Material management must base its purchase commitments, production schedules, and product movements on anticipated sales in the hard goods business. A sales forecast broken down geographically as well as by product group and planning period is required.

The exact way information is used to arrive at a forecast will vary. It is common, however, to begin by forecasting industry sales and then forecast the share of total industry sales that the organization will obtain. Once total sales for the organization is forecast, it can be broken down by product, planning period, and geographical area using past sales patterns and break downs of any of the other factors listed above.

Another factor to be taken into account is inventory swings at the retail and wholesale level. The forecast just described is based on macro-economic considerations and is likely to be for retail sales. To anticipate orders from retailers and wholesalers to the manufacturer, inventory swings must be forecast. This forecast should take into account surveys of retailer attitudes about the future in general and about the product lines being forecast.

Either the retail or wholesale forecasts, based on the above mentioned factors, can be calculated using formulas. However, there are many other factors that affect sales that cannot easily be quantified. Changes in the advertising budget, price level, sales force, and promotional budget can all have an effect on sales in a market segment. To estimate the effects of these and other factors, a forecast based only on quantitative factors is usually reviewed and adjusted by marketing experts.

Information Required

The information needed to make a sales forecast is fundamentally information about the market segments. But to provide a detailed forecast by product and by time period, it must also be based on information about these entities as well. Of course, some of the information will depend on some combination of product, market region, and time period.

In Table 6.6, examples of information useful in sales forecasting that depend on a certain entity type, or combination of entity types are shown. These examples indicate that information is required that concerns three entity types and two relationships. The analysis of these requirements in the following subsections will identify two additional entity types and four additional relationships that are involved in this information requirements structure.

TABLE 6.6.   Information requirements for sales forecasting.

Information about Product/Service

- Total product inventories of customers
- Supply limit

Information about Market Territory

- Boundaries
- Distribution channels

Information about Time Period

- Start date
- Total days
- Working days

Information about Sales

- Past company sales to customers
- Forecast industry sales
- Forecast market share
- Forecast sales
- Sales forecast adjustments

Information about Time Series

- Industry sales and estimates
- Interest rate
- Disposable income
- Advertising budget
- Sales force
- Price level

Information Structure

The information structure that reflects these sales forecasting requirements can be obtained by decomposing Figure 6.5. The first requirement in Table 6.6 is for information about products and services. Therefore, Product/Service is included in Figure 6.11 as an entity type.

The total product inventories of customers should be an attribute of a relationship between Product/Service, Customer, and Time Period. Data on past company sales to customers (listed in Table 6.6 under "Information about Sales") would also have these same three determinants. Both of these data types can be considered the data of an intelligence report on customers. Thus, we should create a specialization of the *intelligence report* relationship of Figure 6.5 for this

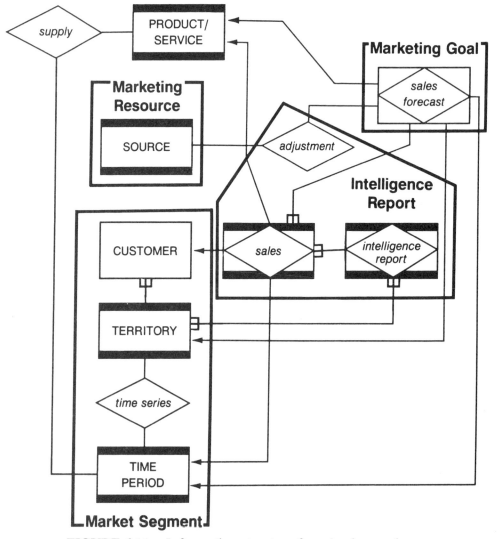

FIGURE 6.11.   Information structure for sales forecasting.

data. This specialization is called *sales* in Figure 6.11. To create it, Market Segment was decomposed to make the Customer and Time Period aspects of Market Segment explicit.

The supply limit information needed for sales forecasting is the total amount of a product that can be made available during a period. This depends on the product and time period. It should therefore be an attribute of a relationship between Product/Service and Time Period. This relationship is called *supply* in Figure 6.11.

The information about market territories listed in Table 6.6 is basic territory descriptive data. For this we need to specialize the Market Segment entity type of Figure 6.5 to Territory. This entity type is shown in Figure 6.11 linked to the Customer entities in the territory.

The information required about time periods in Table 6.6 can be treated as attributes of the Time Period entity type in Figure 6.11. For the information about time series listed in Table 6.6, a relationship between Time Period and Territory is needed because all of these items of information should be accessible by Territory as well as by Time Period. This relationship is labeled *time series* in Figure 6.11.

It is assumed that the information about sales needs to be at both the customer and territory level and for each product or service and time period. As already explained, the information at the customer level can be treated as attributes of the *sales* relationship in Figure 6.11, which has already been discussed. The information at the territory level is modeled as attributes of the *sales forecast* relationship in Figure 6.11. This relationship is viewed as a decomposition of the Marketing Goal entity type of Figure 6.5. The sales forecast does represent the company goal as well as the objective of this subfunction.

There are some other items of information suggested by Figure 6.5 and the previous discussion of forecasting. One is intelligence reports other than those represented by the *sales* relationship. This additional information could suggest adjustments to the sales forecast obtained by projection of historical sales patterns. For this reason, the *intelligence report* relationship of Figure 6.5 is shown in Figure 6.11, linked to *sales* and Territory.

The Source entity type of Figure 6.5 is shown in Figure 6.11 in a relationship with Sales Forecast that is labeled "Adjustment." The main attributes of this relationship are adjustments to the sales forecast recommended by experts and the reasons for the recommendations.

SUMMARY

The conceptual database planning technique explained in Part 1 is applied to the Marketing function of a consumer goods manufacturer in this chapter. Two levels of the functional model and information structure are developed, although the lower level of the information structure is incomplete. The information requirements of only five of the fifteen subfunctions at the lower level were defined.

In Chapter 5, the "data approach" and "process approach" to developing an information structure were introduced. Both approaches are used in Chapter 6. The data approach is used for Figures 6.4 and 6.5. The process approach is used in all the other cases. This suggests that the data approach is best for high level functions and the process approach for lower level, more process-oriented functions.

The proposition that the information requirements of a subfunction can be characterized as a decomposition of the information structure of the higher level function is demonstrated in this chapter. Probably the greatest challenge to this proposition was the decomposition of Market Segment in Figure 6.4 to the complex of market segment entity types and relationships shown in Figure 6.7. Information about past sales to customers is provided in Figure 6.7 and the higher level Sales information structure of Figure 6.3 was referenced in explaining the characterization of this sales information in Figure 6.7.

In considering the information requirements for the sales forecasting subfunction, a different approach was taken in deriving sales information. It was derived as a specialization of the *intelligence report* relationship of Figure 6.5. Is the method used in deriving Figure 6.7 wrong? No, past (and current) sales to customers can legitimately be viewed as information about market segments, and therefore a decomposition of the Market Segment entity type may include details concerning actual sales in market segments. The methodology simply does not provide a unique way to derive an information requirement.

In general, the methodology appears to provide a more systematic approach to business-wide conceptual database design than the tradition entity relationship approach. It incorporates all the "micro-modeling" guidelines of the traditional E-R approach, which are derived from the normal forms of the relational model, while adding the "macro-modeling" guidelines of functional modeling and decomposition.

DISCUSSION QUESTIONS

1. Describe the objectives of marketing.

2. Describe three or more different bases for decomposing the Market Segment entity type.

3. What is the difference between the Marketing Goal entity type and the *plan marketing* relationship?

4. Describe the range of events that the *manage marketing* relationship includes.

5. Why are the internal and external sales functions not distinguished in the first level breakdown of Marketing?

6. Describe the approach taken to defining the information requirements of the sales subfunction. Is it a data approach or a process approach?

7. What types of information about the marketing plan may be required in preparing quotations for prospect?

8. Identify the entity types and relationships in Figure 6.3 that derive from decomposition of the plan relationship in of Figure 5.1.

9. Contrast the approach taken to deriving Figure 6.3 with that taken to derive Figure 6.4.

10. Discuss the appropriateness and adequacy of the specialization of the *plan marketing* relationship of Figure 6.1 to the *external marketing budget* relationship of Figure 6.4.

11. Discuss the difference between the *intelligence report* and *market research activity* relationships of Figure 6.5.

12. Discuss the subfunctions of external marketing shown in Figure 6.6. How does the "direct selling subfunction differ from the "determine customer requirements" subfunction of the sales function? Are there other subfunctions of external marketing that should be executed by a hard goods manufacturer?

13. Table 6.2 shows a need for information on past calls made on a prospect. How is this provided for in Figure 6.7 and which higher level information structure(s) are involved in its derivation?

14. Explain how market share data could be stored and obtained from a database defined by Figure 6.7.

15. Describe the kind of data that could be modeled as attributes of the *ad value—indirect* relationship of Figure 6.8.

16. Table 6.3 calls for information on "print media reaching direct customer prospects." How can this be stored and retrieved from a database described by Figure 6.8?

17. Describe the difference between the *ad purchase, slot,* and *showing* relationships of Figure 6.8.

18. Should the *promotion effect* relationship in Figure 6.9 be considered a part of the decomposition of Marketing Plan or *marketing action*?

19. How would competitor price changes be accommodated in Figure 6.10?

20. Where would data on customer inventories be stored in the database defined by Figure 6.11?

7

Materials Management

OBJECTIVES OF MATERIALS MANAGEMENT

Materials management has the task of supplying the right materials to the right place on time. (The term "materials" is intended to include raw materials, purchased and semi-finished parts, operating materials, and finished goods.) In a retail or wholesale business, this would include the functions of purchasing, warehousing, and delivery to customers (and stores). In a manufacturing business, it also includes managing the supply of materials to production, scheduling production, and managing plant inventories and shipments.

The objective is not only to provide the material needed, but to do so efficiently. Cost is a consideration. Material of satisfactory quality should be provided at a low cost. The percentage of late deliveries and the degree of lateness should be held to a minimum. Transportation and material handling costs must be controlled. Working capital should not be wasted; inventories should be created only when justified as the most cost-effective way to meet supply requirements.

Foreseeing supply requirements is a key to achieving the objectives of materials management. The more clearly supply requirements are foreseen, the more efficiently and effectively they can be met. Foreseeing supply requirements begins with forecasting finished product sales. This forecast function is described in the chapter on marketing. For materials management, the forecast defines an objective: Be prepared to deliver the sales that are forecast.

Materials management plans supply actions that will make it possible to deliver the sales that are forecast. If there are multiple sources of supply, the role each source is to play in fulfilling demand needs to be clarified. If the sources are geographically distributed, the forecast demand is often allocated to sources in a way that minimizes total delivered cost of goods sold. Other considerations that might be allowed to influence the allocation (of forecast total demand) to supply sources are commitments to use a certain amount of production capacity at a source, delivery time constraints, and government regulations.

Materials management includes planning resupply actions at each supply source, as well as planning the allocation of forecast sales to supply sources. The acronym MRP is used differently by various people and organizations. In this book, we use it to stand for Material Requirements Planning and to refer to a system for allocating forecast demand to sources and scheduling procurement actions and production work orders at each supply source in a way that minimizes inventories yet maximizes on-time delivery of sales orders and warehouse resupply orders allocated to the source. The MRP system operates at both a total system level and at a supply source level, whether the source is a manufacturing plant or a warehouse.

Materials management also includes executing the orders recommended by the MRP system. Key objectives in the process of converting these recommendations into orders and managing the fulfillment of those orders are meeting quality and delivery time requirements while at the same time minimizing costs.

Materials management is also responsible for transporting product from a supply point to the customer or another supplier. The objectives in this activity are to have competitive customer delivery times and to minimize high cost, expedited shipments.

GENERALIZED INFORMATION STRUCTURE

The materials manager handles a part of the CEO function. In Chapter 1, the CEO function was defined as managing the resources of the enterprise to achieve the goals of the stakeholders. The materials manager manages the material (and material producing) resources of the enterprise in meeting its commitments to customers, suppliers, and production units. The information structure required to carry out this part of the CEO function is shown in Figure 7.1 as a specialization of the CEO information structure of Figure 5.1.

The generalized entity type labeled "Goal" in Figure 5.1 is specialized to "Supply Commitment" in Figure 7.1. Materials management is normally committed to supplying a certain quantity of each material used in the business at appropriate locations in each time period. This commitment has two aspects. First, there is a

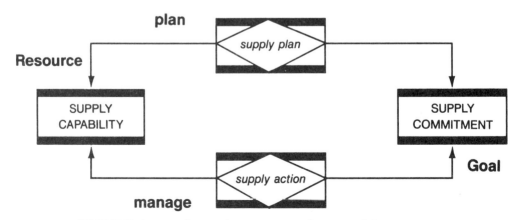

FIGURE 7.1. Information structure for materials management.

general commitment based on sales forecasts, production capacities, supplier agreements, and other factors that affect supply capabilities. Second, there is the commitment to supply specific sales orders and work orders. The dynamics of sales and various supply activities may render the general commitment obsolete within a short time. Nevertheless, there remains some sense of obligation to use supply capabilities in ways that best support marketing operations and the long-term profitability of the enterprise.

The "Resource" generalization of Figure 5.1 is specialized to "Supply Capability" in Figure 7.1. Materials management is responsible for directing the use of resources dedicated to supplying the materials and products of the business. This includes the warehousing and transport of materials, parts, and products. It includes the function that schedules the use of production facilities and the purchasing function. But, it does not include the production function itself. In some organizations, materials management is considered a subfunction of the production function. In others, it is considered a subfunction of marketing. In this book, we consider it to be a separate function at the same level as marketing and production.

The *plan* relationship of Figure 5.1 is specialized to a *supply plan* relationship in 7.1. This plan relates the supply commitments to the use of supply capabilities. It shapes supply commitments in the sense that it shows how they can be satisfied with the supply capabilities expected to be available. A supply commitment that could not be satisfied is detected by the MRP system which maintains the short-term *supply plan* relationship.

The *manage* relationship of 5.1 becomes the *supply action* relationship of 7.1. The *supply plan* is implemented by issuing orders to use supply capabilities in certain ways to meet specific supply commitments. The *supply action* generalization includes purchase and shipment orders, production orders, deliver from stock orders, and transport service orders. It also includes the events that mark the execution of orders. The shipment of product to a customer is an example of an event that is included in the *supply action* generalization.

A sales order (or customer's purchase order), on the other hand, is not to be considered a specialization of the *supply action* relationship. A sales order, when accepted, defines a supply commitment from the viewpoint of materials management. From the customer's viewpoint, it is a resource commitment, but as far as materials management is concerned, the sales order defines one or more delivery commitments.

FIRST-LEVEL FUNCTION BREAKDOWN

Managing the material resources of an enterprise consists of managing a number of related operational and planning functions. This suggests a breakdown between the planning and execution subfunctions. The information requirements of material supply planning are less specific and broader than are those of executing supply activities. Certainly, this first-level breakdown would create the minimum number of subfunctions at the second level, as recommended in Chapter 4.

However, the subject of materials management planning is broader than need be considered at this level. A distinction can be made between planning the capacities required to supply materials and planning specifically how the capacities can best be used on an on-going basis. Using this distinction, we will identify three first-level materials management subfunctions:

Materials transaction processing

Materials requirements planning

Capacity planning.

Materials transaction processing refers to the execution of materials management activities. It includes both the issuing of orders that will cause material supply actions and the actions themselves. The term "transaction" is used here in the same sense as it is used in accounting, except that it is meant to include a broader range of resource commitments than is included in traditional accounting. It includes, for example, purchase orders issued to suppliers and shipment release orders issued under blanket purchase agreements. This is in addition to traditional accounting transactions, such as the receipt of a shipment from a supplier and the delivery of goods and services to a customer.

Material requirements planning (MRP) refers to the allocation of forecast demand and the planning of specific materials resupply transactions. The planning of supply activities includes obtaining parts and materials from suppliers and producing parts and products in the plants of the enterprise. In the case of internally produced items, the MRP function can include the scheduling of production activities to produce what is needed to meet customer delivery requirements.

The capacity planning subfunction concerns planning production capacities required to meet forecast sales. This may include both internal production capacities and supplier capacities for which commitments should be made. Actually making the commitments to suppliers is a material management executive function and, thus, is part of the transaction processing subfunction. However, planning the commitments to suppliers that should be made is a capacity planning function.

The distinctions made here between materials transaction processing, MRP, and capacity planning are not universally recognized. Many MRP software packages include transaction processing and capacity planning modules. All three have certain common data requirements and should share the same database. They each also have unique data requirements. Analyzing their data requirements separately simplifies the requirements specification process.

In addition to the three subfunctions already noted, material management could include the other administrative subfunctions of staff and facilities management, budgeting, and information systems management. As explained in the previous chapter, we recommend treating the information requirements of these administrative subfunctions separately. The personnel function is considered in Chapter 5, budgeting is considered in Chapter 10, and the management of information systems is discussed in Chapter 11.

INFORMATION STRUCTURES FOR SECOND-LEVEL FUNCTIONS

The functional area of materials management has been described as consisting of three functional groupings: materials transaction processing, material requirements planning (MRP), and capacity planning. These are the second-level functions of materials management.

In this section we characterize, in terms of information structures, the information useful in executing these second-level functions. These information structures are derived by considering how the first-level structure shown in Figure 7.1 can be specialized and disaggregated to focus on the information needs of a specific second-level function.

MATERIALS TRANSACTION PROCESSING

The information needed for materials transaction processing certainly includes information about specific supply orders and actions. Orders to deliver product to customers, orders sent to suppliers for materials and services, and production work orders are examples of specific supply orders. Reports of customer deliveries made, supplier shipments received, and production work orders completed are examples of events that materials managers need to know about.

These orders and actions have the effect of allocating the supply capabilities to meet specific product delivery commitments. Thus, they should be treated as specializations of the *supply action* relationship of Figure 7.1. At this level, however, only two types of supply actions need to be distinguished. One is called *delivery* in Figure 7.2 and the other is termed *resupply*. More detailed versions of the supply actions in each of these two categories are given for lower level subfunctions. This serves to keep the individual information structure diagrams as simple as possible.

The *delivery* relationship in Figure 7.2 refers to specific customer orders and the actions taken to fulfill them. This includes receipt and acknowledgment of the customer's order, the issuing of orders to deliver, the deliveries actually made, and any returns of product delivered.

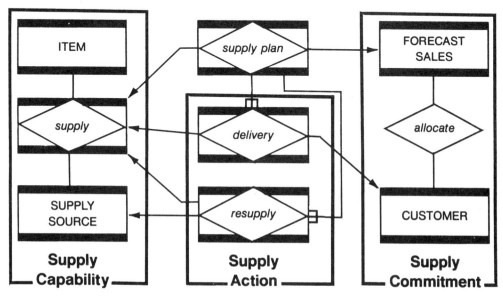

FIGURE 7.2. Information structure for transaction processing.

The *resupply* relationship of Figure 7.2 represents actions taken to obtain from suppliers (which could include other plants and warehouses in the organization) the materials, parts, finished products, and services required to produce and deliver the goods ordered by customers. It is a relationship between two levels in the supply system. One level (the primary level) is the plants and warehouses from which customer orders are delivered. The other (the secondary level) is the internal and external plants and warehouses that supply the primary level. Although useful, Figure 7.1 is an oversimplification. For example, all *supply action* instances do not directly address a customer delivery commitment. Many, in fact, address organizing the Supply Capability entities so that other supply actions can be taken in a timely manner to meet customer delivery requirements.

In materials transaction processing, information is needed about supply capabilities in terms of the items of product that can be supplied from each available source. A source may be a warehouse, a company plant, or a supplier. Figure 7.2 shows the Supply Capability entity type of Figure 7.1 decomposed into a relationship between Supply Source and Item. An instance of this *supply* relationship provides information about the availability of a specific product type (an item) from a particular source.

The Supply Commitment of Figure 7.1 is decomposed in Figure 7.2 to two entity types linked by a relationship. One is Forecast Sales which is a generalization of the *sales forecast* relationship of Figure 6.11. It is relevant to materials transaction processing because it represents the commitment made by materials management to the marketing function to supply a certain amount of product to the marketplace within a time period. As specific commitments are made to deliver to customers, they need to be allocated to specific forecast totals so that the performance of materials management can be measured against its commitment to deliver product. The relationship between Forecast Sales and the Customer defines this allocation.

The *supply plan* relationship of Figure 7.1 is used in materials transaction processing to decide which supply capability to use to fulfill a customer order (or warehouse resupply order). It is shown in Figure 7.2 in the same form as it appears in Figure 7.1. A more detailed version of this generalization is deferred until the information needs of material requirements planning are considered in the next subsection. The one-to-many relationship between *supply plan* and *supply action* in Figure 7.2 defines how the supply actions conform to the supply plan.

MATERIAL REQUIREMENTS PLANNING

This subfunction is not concerned with supplying specific orders. Rather, it is responsible for planning the resupply of warehouses and plants so that the forecast demand for end-products can be satisfied. The information used in doing this centers around the *supply plan* relationship in Figure 7.1. With respect to the MRP subfunction, Supply Commitment represents the forecast of sales that materials management is committed to supply. The Supply Capability generalization represents the production capacities and inventories than can be used to meet future supply commitments. The *supply plan* itself is a definition of how supply capabilities can be used to satisfy supply commitments.

In formulating and updating the plan and outputting recommendations based on it, MRP must work with information about items of material, or simply "items" as we will henceforth call them. An item can be any type of material: raw material, part, operating material, or finished product. Item is one of the basic entity types used in MRP.

The task in MRP is to figure out how much of an item to have, and where and when to have it. This means that MRP must work with information about an item at a location at a point in time. Therefore, Item, Location, and Time are three entity types that MRP is concerned with. In addition, relationships between Item, Location, and Time have important attributes for MRP.

Figure 7.3 shows decompositions of the two entity types in Figure 7.1 that reveal the roles played by item, location, and time in these generalizations. The *supply plan* relationship of Figure 7.1 becomes the *allocation* relationship in Figure 7.3. There is a relationship between Item and Supply Location labeled *item at location* and another relationship between *item at location* and Time labeled *supply schedule*. This *supply schedule* can be either a production schedule or an MRP plan for an inventory.

The Supply Commitment entity type of Figure 7.1 is decomposed into three entity types and two relationships in Figure 7.3. Market Segment is assumed to have a location attribute and therefore to represent a market location. The *item in market* relationship represents information about items in particular market segments. The relationship between *item in market* and Time is labeled *demand schedule*. This could just as well be called the *sales forecast* relationship since the

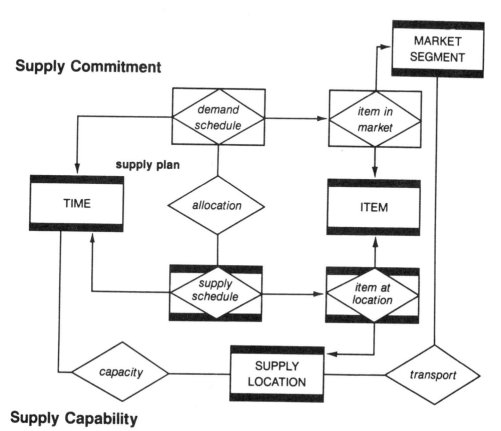

FIGURE 7.3. Information structure for MRP.

forecasted quantity to be sold in a market segment during a time period is a natural attribute of this relationship.

The relationship between Supply Location and Time, labeled *capacity*, is important for factory (and some supplier) locations. The available production capacity of a factory during a time period is an attribute of this relationship. Exactly how this capacity should be measured is not always clear but, to the extent that a "most limited resource" can be identified, a measure of that resource is the appropriate measure to use. The discussion of capacity planning in the following subsection should clarify this point.

The Item entity type is an aggregation that contains a recursive relationship (not shown in Figure 7.3) often called *product structure*. It represents the bill of materials for each manufactured part and product. This information is required in MRP to calculate the raw material and parts requirements of a forecast demand for end products.

It should be noted that the *supply schedule* relationship may also contain a recursive relationship (which could be called *replenishment*). It defines the plan for allocating production output to warehouse locations, which is important for the global planning tasks of MRP discussed later in the chapter.

Finally, transport cost information is needed to plan the least costly way to use supply capacities to meet demand. The *transport* relationship between Market Segment and Supply Location in Figure 7.3 represents this information. This is part of the decomposition of the Supply Capability entity type of Figure 7.1.

CAPACITY PLANNING

In the long run, everything is variable, and capacity planning is concerned with setting the determinants of supply capabilities that are fixed in the short run (of MRP) but can be expanded or contracted in the long run. The long-term changes that should be made in supply capability are the focus of capacity planning.

Capacity planning works from a forecast of long-term demand for the products of the enterprise that have been allocated to supply locations. The allocation of the long-term forecast of demand to supply sources could be based on different criteria and constraints than is this same allocation in the MRP system. However, it is likely that the data involved in making the allocation can be modeled as attributes of the same entity types and relationships as are used in the MRP allocation. Thus, the information requirements of the capacity planning function are shown in Figure 7.4 with the same information structure as MRP as far as the decomposition of Supply Commitment is concerned.

The *supply requirement* relationship of Figure 7.4 is virtually the same as the *supply schedule* relationship of Figure 7.3. Capacity planning seeks to find the best way of setting supply capabilities to meet the supply requirements of each location. A projected supply performance in MRP is viewed as a requirement to be met in capacity planning, by setting capacity limits at the right levels.

With respect to Supply Capability, capacity planning needs information about the same entities and relationships as does MRP plus more detail about production facilities. In Figure 7.4, this additional detail is shown as a decomposition of what is called Supply Location in Figure 7.3. In this decomposition, Supply Location is a generalization and Work Center, Resource, Operation, and *amount* are a disaggregation of Supply Location.

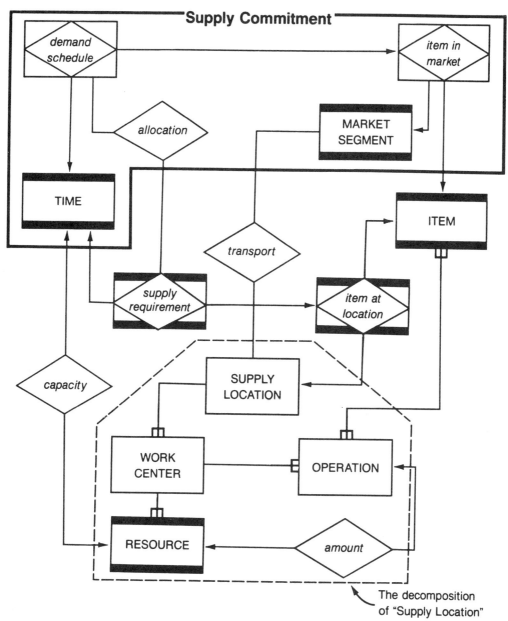

FIGURE 7.4.   Information structure for capacity planning.

Resource represents a type of capacity to be planned. Instances of Resource could be a certain type of skilled labor or a type of equipment or an operating material (such as steam). The *capacity* relationship between resource and time in Figure 7.4 would have as one of its attributes the amount of the resource planned for the time period. Capacity planning assigns values to this attribute.

Resource is shown in a one-to-many relationship with Work Center in Figure 7.4. This relationship indicates where the resource is located in the production organization. Work centers are tied to the Supply Location entity that designates which plant they are in.

Another important entity type for capacity planning is Operation. An operation is a specific step taken when producing a specific item. The resources required to take that step are identified by the relationship between Operation and Resource. The amount of a resource required to perform an operation, which is an attribute of this relationship, is a fundamental factor used in capacity planning. The work center in which each operation may be performed is indicated by the relationship between operation and work center. Where a cellular organization of production is in effect and a work center performs all the operations on a group of items, the *item-at-location* relationship should involve Work Center instead of Supply Location.

The supply locations considered in capacity planning need not be limited to production facilities owned by the company. Long-term commitments with outside suppliers can be planned as well. Each outside supplier becomes one or more occurrences of Supply Location in the database of Figure 7.4. If local job shops are used to execute certain operations for a company-owned plant, it may be that the Work Center entity type can be extended to include the local shop that is relied on to handle certain operations.

BREAKDOWN OF SELECTED SECOND-LEVEL FUNCTIONS

In this section, two of the second-level functions, transaction processing and MRP, are further analyzed. The descriptions of subfunctions given in this section are brief and incomplete. The objective is to present an overview of a proposed breakdown of the higher level functions, not to exhaustively explain each subfunction. The reader wanting additional clarification of a subfunction is encouraged to skip to that part of the next section that deals with the information requirements of the subfunction.

The subfunctions for both transaction processing and MRP are identified in this subsection. Then, in the next subsection, all of the information requirements for both sets of subfunctions are derived.

TRANSACTION PROCESSING SUBFUNCTIONS

Managing the fulfillment of customer orders and resupply activities which make competitive delivery times possible can include many subfunctions. We consider only the most basic ones here. The four considered are:

Purchasing

Receiving

Processing customer orders

Delivering customer orders.

An important set of transactions omitted from this list concerns factory materials transactions. The withdrawal of raw material and parts from stock is one such transaction. The addition of items to factory inventories is another. The movement of work-in-process from one department to another is a third example. This set of transactions is considered in the chapter on production.

Purchasing

Suppliers must be found for each product and service the organization decides to procure. These suppliers should be evaluated; first, using published materials and references and, after they have been given some orders, by their performance and the quality of the product supplied. This points to one set of supplier information requirements.

Building good relations with suppliers is an important part of purchasing. Negotiating long-term contracts with suppliers helps them plan the most cost effective way to provide good service. However, relying too heavily on one supplier creates an undesirable vulnerability. There is much more to purchasing management than arranging one-time purchase orders.

Purchasing procedures can vary substantially. In cases where a blanket purchase contract exists, a buyer can order a delivery by simply issuing a "shipment release" to the supplier. In other cases where the item is expensive or not covered by an existing contract, the purchasing process normally requires that quotes be obtained from two or more suppliers; these quotes are evaluated and after a supplier is chosen, a formal purchase order is sent to the winning bidder. Between these extremes are many variations in procurement procedures.

Receiving

When goods ordered from suppliers are delivered, they must be received. The fact that they have been delivered must be entered into the database. Goods received are commonly inspected to determine the quantity received and to detect shipping damage. Inspection results must be recorded. Finally, received goods must be sent to the appropriate warehouse or factory location; the disposition of all units processed by receiving should be recorded.

In addition, there is at least one activity in receiving that requires information from the purchasing database. It is determining whether delivered goods were in fact ordered. If goods are delivered that were not ordered, this should be detected by the receiving operation so that a decision can be made explicitly to accept or refuse the delivery.

Processing Customer Orders

We assume this subfunction begins when the sales order is entered into the database. If orders are received by materials management in machine readable form, then this first phase of customer order processing can be dispensed with.

Once entered, sales orders can be filled in one of four ways:

1. From inventory

2. By purchasing

3. By standardized production

4. By customized design and production (or purchase).

The order-processing subfunction determines which of these means of supply is appropriate and ensures that the order is filled by that means. If an order cannot be filled from stock at the closest warehouse location, then the order must be held either for the next resupply shipment to the closest warehouse or delivered from a location further away. If an item is out of stock and there is reason to think that demand is exceeding the forecast, then this subfunction may be responsible for adjusting the forecast (which will trigger the MRP order release planning subfunction). If an item on an order is purchased after a sale is made as a matter of policy, then sales order processing should create a purchase requisition for the item which is then processed by the purchasing function. A purchase requisition is a request that one or more items be purchased.

If the item ordered is produced to order as a matter of policy, then the order release plans for the item (created in MRP) must be consulted and the fulfillment of this order must be provided for by an allocation of scheduled output to the order.

In the case of customized items, engineering work as well as production (or purchase) should be scheduled and monitored by the order processing subfunction.

Another aspect of processing customer orders is keeping the customer informed. Once it has been determined that an order can be supplied in a certain way, an acknowledgment of the order should be sent to the customer. It should indicate how and when the ordered items will be supplied.

Delivering Customer Orders

Warehouse order picking, packing, transportation scheduling, and preparation of shipping and invoicing records constitute this subfunction. For purposes of this analysis, it is assumed that common carriers provide all transportation services required to deliver products to customers. The management of a fleet of delivery vehicles would introduce a number of additional entity types and relationships to the database.

MRP SUBFUNCTIONS

MRP is a computer-based system that coordinates responses to an order and a sales forecast. It can reduce the "bloat" in inventory that an overly optimistic sales forecast produces. To some extent, it avoids the shortages that an overly pessimistic forecast produces. If the forecast is on target, MRP will supply what is needed with minimum inventory investment, given the level of just-in-time production technology that is in effect.

The subfunctions of the MRP portion of materials management that we will consider in this analysis are as follows:

Sales forecast allocation

Order release planning

Explosion

Requisitioning

Reporting.

Sales Forecast Allocation

The sales forecasting subfunction in marketing should result in a forecast of sales by planning period, item and market location (region). If the forecast is by product group rather than by item, it can be broken down to items using past item sales data. The sales allocation subfunction allocates the sales forecast to supply points.

Allocation of anticipated sales is necessary only if there are alternative sources (either warehouses or factories) from which items can be delivered to customers. If all deliveries to customers are made from a single source, then the sales forecast allocation function is unnecessary.

Order Release Planning

This subfunction is repeated for each supply point (warehouse or factory). It determines the timing and quantity for each planned replenishment order release required to satisfy a projected item requirement defined by the sales forecast allocation function (or by the explosion function explained next). The planning procedure is executed for each change in the projected item requirements. It covers both the product to be purchased and the product to be manufactured in a job shop or on a production line. It handles stock, standard and custom items, for parts and finished products. If there is a master production schedule or a supplier contract that calls for a certain pattern of deliveries, this subfunction plans orders that conform to the limitations imposed by that plan. If the only limitations are general production capacity limits, the subfunction should include the planning of a production schedule within those limits.

Explosion

In the case of manufactured products, an order release creates a requirement for the component parts used to make the item. Whenever the order release scheduling process creates or revises a planned order release, it calls the explosion program unless the item is a purchased part, a raw material, or a stock item at a warehouse. The explosion program retrieves the list of component parts and the quantity of each per unit of product being ordered. For each component, it retrieves the item requirements schedule and increases the appropriate requirement figure by the quantity of the component required to meet this new planned order release. Any such change in a requirement figure immediately invokes the order release planning subfunction for that component part. Thus, the explosion subfunction is involved in a recursive relationship with order release planning.

Requisitioning

Order release action takes place when a planned order "matures." That is, when the time planned for the release of an order arrives, it is released, or at least recommended for release. Release takes the form of a requisition. For purchased items, it is a purchase requisition. For manufactured items, it is a work order requisition.

The subfunction for handling purchase requisitions is purchasing which is described in a previous subsection. The subfunction for handling work order requisitions is work order preparation which is discussed in Chapter 8.

Reporting

The reporting subfunction generates reports, especially exception reports on past-due actions in the material management plan. The discrepancies reported might include late supplier deliveries, production output delays, unreleased requisitions, and differences between actual and calculated inventories.

THIRD-LEVEL FUNCTION INFORMATION STRUCTURES

The information relevant to each of the subfunctions described above will be somewhat more specific than the information shown in Figures 7.2 and 7.3. The concepts of information requirements in these figures are based on overviews of the entire functions of transaction processing and materials requirements planning. This time we consider the requirements of the subfunctions. For subfunctions of material transaction processing, Figure 7.2 provides the main guideline for designing information structure. For subfunctions of MRP, Figure 7.3 provides the guideline.

PURCHASING

Let us first consider the information involved in the basic transaction sequence of purchasing. Once the information structure for this transaction processing is clear, we can consider other information requirements of purchasing.

First, there is a purchase requisition. This is a supply action that can be taken by any unit in the organization (or by a system, such as the MRP system). It is a request that something be purchased. It comes to the purchasing function and initiates the steps required to make the purchase.

A purchase requisition is an order from a "requesting department" to the purchasing department. It is an internal order that the purchasing department is obligated to fill and the requesting department is obligated to pay. Payment capability is usually indicated by a cost or expense account number and the signature of someone authorized to make charges to the account. For production materials, the purchase requisition can be created by the MRP system.

The steps required to make a purchase may include:

1. Obtaining information from potential suppliers about the items that need to be purchased. Supplier catalogs, quotes, and phone conversations are possible sources for this information.

2. Issuing a purchase order to the supplier(s) of choice for the items on one or more purchase requisitions. This is an authorization for the supplier to supply the items on the order. (Exactly when they are to be supplied may or may not be specified on this order.) It represents a commitment to pay for the items when delivered.

3. Issuing shipment release instructions to the supplier, describing exactly what to deliver, where, and when.

4. Monitoring supplier performance; if items are not delivered as ordered, follow up with the supplier.

It should be noted that the definitions of purchase order and shipment release used in this discussion are not universally accepted. Other names may be used for the same types of commitments in various sectors of business and in different countries. In this discussion, a purchase order is considered a relatively long-term commitment with a supplier. It is often called a blanket agreement covering a series of shipments over a period of time. Information about a supplier's performance under this contract is important. The volume of purchases under the agreement is usually monitored and controlled to conform to contract terms. A shipment release, on the other hand, is an order to make a single shipment. A purchase order is normally cited on the release and the terms of that purchase order presumably apply to the shipment release.

The information required for the steps in purchasing is shown in Figure 7.5. Each step constitutes a supply action and therefore is shown as an entity type in a disaggregation of the *resupply* relationship of Figure 7.2. Purchase Requisition, Quote, Purchase Order, Shipment Release, and Shipment are entity types representing steps in the purchasing process. The Quote entity type is shown as a generalization because it represents all forms of data about potential suppliers, including supplier catalogs and phone conversations with potential suppliers as well as formal quotations. It also includes the request for a quotation which can be viewed as a separate event.

Each of the five specializations of *resupply* in Figure 7.5 (requisition, quote, purchase order, release, and shipment) involves information about an indefinite number of items. This means each must be decomposed to make the item information explicit. This is the reason for the relationships between Item or *item-of-stock* and the five specializations. Possible attributes of each of these five relationships in Figure 7.5 (*requisition item, item quote, order line, release line,* and *shipment item*) are supplier's item name or code, unit of measure, quantity of item, and (only in the case of quote and order line) price.

The *resupply* relationship (Figure 7.2) is between two levels in the supply system. In Figure 7.5, these two levels are designated the primary supply source and the secondary supply source. In the case of primary supply source, a specialization of the *supply* relationship of Figure 7.2 is shown (*item of stock* relationship). For the secondary supply source, Supply Source is decomposed to Supplier, Supplier Location, and a relationship between them. This is sufficient for purposes of managing purchasing transactions.

The relationship between Receiving Location and Item in figure 7.5, labeled *item of stock,* is based on the concept of the item in stock at the warehouse. The item is related to the location in the sense that the type of item is either stocked or used at that location. If the receiving location is a plant where the item is used as a part, the relationship should be called *item of production.*

The Buyer entity type is included in Figure 7.5 as a further decomposition of Supply Capability. The primary and secondary supply Source information structures, together with Buyer, constitute the decomposition of Supply Capability.

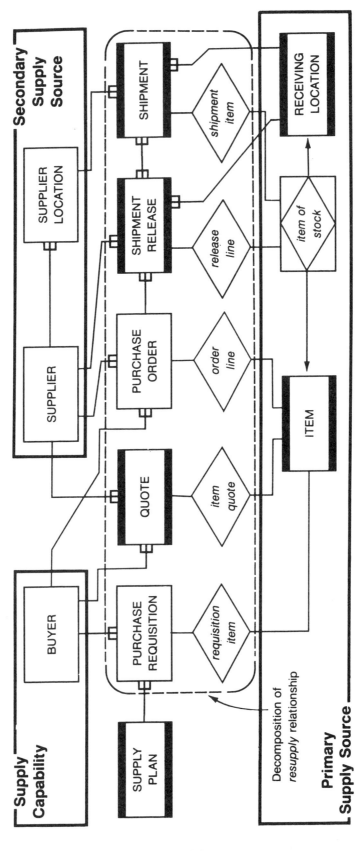

FIGURE 7.5. Information structure for purchasing.

198

Supply Plan is shown as a generalized entity type in Figure 7.5 whereas it appears in Figure 7.2 as a relationship. It is included in 7.5 to show how the relationship between *supply plan* and *resupply* in Figure 7.2 is specialized to a relationship between Supply Plan and Purchase Requisition in 7.5. There could be cases in which Supply Plan information is needed by the purchasing function.

Some of the relationships between entity types in Figure 7.5 have not been discussed. In most cases, the rule of association for the relationship should be clear from a consideration of the meaning of the entities involved. The reason for showing a given relationship as one-to-many or as many-to-many may not be clear and in fact may not even be appropriate for a specific business situation. Thus, these minor relationships should be taken only as possibilities that may be useful in some situations.

Let us now consider the information requirements of purchasing for purposes other than transaction processing. Information about orders that have been placed with a supplier in the past, information about existing orders not yet delivered, and information about things that can be ordered are needed for a number of purchasing management purposes. Quality of performance on these orders, in terms of good quality product and on-time delivery, is especially important in planning long-term supplier relationships.

The monitoring of supplier performance in real time requires access to shipment release, and shipment data by delivery due date, and by quality problems. Access to information about due dates can be provided by decomposing the Shipment Release and Shipment entity types of Figure 7.5 to make the shipment timing information more explicit. This decomposition is shown in Figure 7.6.

Quality problem information can be identified by decomposing the *shipment item* relationship to show which shipments have a particular quality problem. This also is shown in Figure 7.6.

Finally, the management of a purchasing function could require information about entities not included in either Figures 7.5 or 7.6. In addition to the standard personnel and budgeting information, there could be a need for special information about the people doing the buying in the purchasing organization. In Figure 7.5, Buyer is shown as a specialization of Supply Capability, and it is related to the supply actions in which the buyers are typically involved.

RECEIVING

From the standpoint of information systems, receiving is often a key data capture function. All material coming into the enterprise should pass through a receiving process. In this process, the material is identified and its disposition recorded.

The event of receiving a shipment from a supplier can be considered an aspect of the Shipment entity type shown in Figure 7.5 in most cases. After all, the shipment is not recognized by most firms until it has been received. As such, details about the receiving actions can be modeled either as attributes of Shipment or as a separate entity type developed as a decomposition of the Shipment entity type. Unless there is a possibility of receiving things for which there is no shipment, it should be sufficient to model information about the receipt of a shipment in terms of shipment attributes.

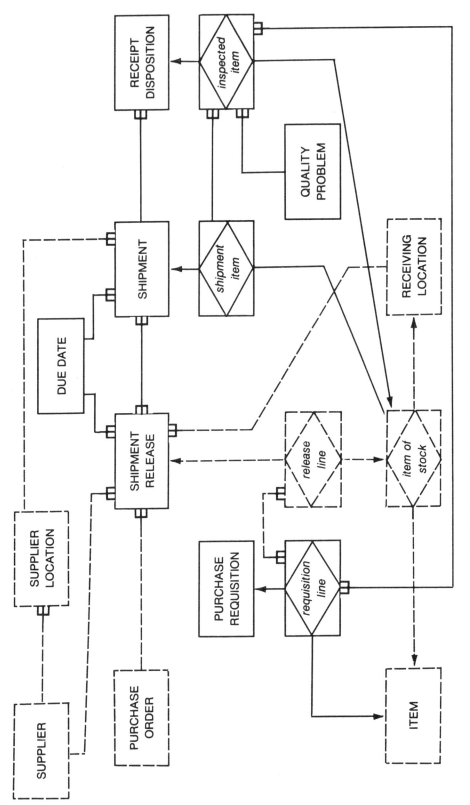

FIGURE 7.6. Information structure for receiving.

Certainly, general information, such as the date the shipment was received can be modeled as attributes of the Shipment entity type. Details such as the number of an item received and the number that pass inspection would be attributes of the *shipment item* relationship.

However, the disposition of a shipment after the receiving inspection is complete may need to be treated as a separate entity type. This is because different parts of the shipment may be disposed of in different ways by the receiving function. For this purpose, a Receipt Disposition entity type is established in Figure 7.6. This can be considered a decomposition of the Shipment entity type of Figure 7.5. The attributes of this entity are the department or warehouse or supplier or other entity to which part of the shipment is sent and the transport service used.

An *inspected item* relationship is also shown in Figure 7.6. This is for information about a subset of the items on a shipment that were disposed of in the manner defined by the occurrence of Receipt Disposition to which they are linked. In the case of items that have a quality problem, it is important that the nature of the problem be recorded. This could be done by treating the quality problem as an attribute of *inspected item*, but a better alternative is to treat a quality problem as an entity type and link *inspected item* occurrences to it when appropriate. This avoids assigning an attribute to *inspected item* that is not always relevant and it facilitates the analysis of quality problems.

In some cases, a supplier is ordered to ship directly to a customer. If this occurs, the data about the shipment that is normally captured in receiving must be obtained in another way. One alternative is to expand the supplier invoice data entry subfunction of accounts payable to include the capture of details about the shipment.

PROCESSING CUSTOMER ORDERS

The sales subfunction of marketing begins the processing of a customer order. As discussed in Chapter 6, it records the customer's purchase order as a sale and acknowledges receipt of the order. The acknowledgment indicates whether or not the order is accepted or not.

The materials management responsibility for customer order processing (also called sales order processing) may, or may not, include what is called inside sales in Chapter 6 on marketing. In this chapter, we will assume that it does, even though this contradicts the definition of inside sales previously given. In any case, processing customer orders also involves determining what has to be done to supply what has been ordered, issuing the orders necessary to initiate supply actions, and making sure those orders are carried out.

Of the four phases of customer order processing just mentioned, all but one are exclusively concerned with supply actions. The one that involves more than supply actions is the second phase, "determining what has to be done to supply what has been ordered." This second phase requires information about the supply plan because this should influence how order fulfillment is accomplished.

We will first consider the information requirements for Phases 1, 3, and 4. Then the information structure for Phase 2 of order processing will be defined. The guideline for these phases that deal with orders and actions is Figure 7.2, the basic information structure for all materials transaction processing.

Phases 1, 3, and 4

The discussion of purchasing in the previous subsection pointed out gradations in the degree of commitment included in the concept of the *resupply* relationship of Figure 7.2. The five entity types in the middle of Figure 7.5 (beginning with Purchase Requisition and ending with Shipment) summarize the gradations. The same is true for customer orders and the *delivery* relationship of Figure 7.2. The supplier's customer order is the customer's purchase order. Therefore, we can go immediately to a decomposition of Figure 7.2 that is analogous to the decomposition represented in 7.5. This decomposition is shown in Figure 7.7.

The two differences in structure between Figures 7.5 and 7.7 are the Purchase Requisition and Supply Order entity types. There is no requisition involved in processing a customer order; in the case of sales, we must order the delivery whereas in the case of purchasing, we only have to receive it.

The reason for including the Quote entity type in an information structure for order processing may not be self-evident. Quotation data can be used to simplify order entry. Order entry can begin with the quotation information and merely change and add to it as necessary to enter the sales order into the system.

Phase 2

Order processing may have to consider several supply options. It may deliver from one or another warehouse; or it may choose to ship directly from a factory or a supplier. Thus, information about supply options is required for this function.

Determining how a given order will be supplied requires information about the *allocation* relationship in Figure 7.3. Each item on the shipment release for a sales order is a demand from a specific market segment in a certain time period. This means that there is a single occurrence of the *demand schedule* relationship that applies to supplying the item on the given order; it is the one linked to the appropriate *item in market* occurrence and the time period in which the order is to be delivered. This particular *demand schedule* occurrence is also linked to one or more *allocation* relationship occurrences that define the amount of the item available for shipment from a source to the market segment in the time period. The amount of a specific allocation already used in filling other orders can also be an attribute of the *allocation* relationship. Thus, if an unused allocation of supply suitable for an order exists, it can be found and used to plan a delivery in response to the shipment release being processed.

Processing sales orders then requires a combination of the information represented by Figures 7.3 and 7.7. The integration of the two structures that fulfill the needs of order processing is shown in Figure 7.8. This is the first example of view integration, which is the subject of Chapter 12.

In some cases, there is not enough supply of an item allocated to a market segment to fill a shipment release. Then the *supply schedule* linked to the relevant *demand schedule* should be examined for possible re-allocations of supply currently allocated to other market segments. If this does not provide the supply needed, then the possibility of increasing one or more supply schedule amounts should be investigated. This is done by changing the supply requirement of a supply location in a certain time period. This causes the MRP system to attempt to re-schedule planned order releases to provide the additional supply. If it is not

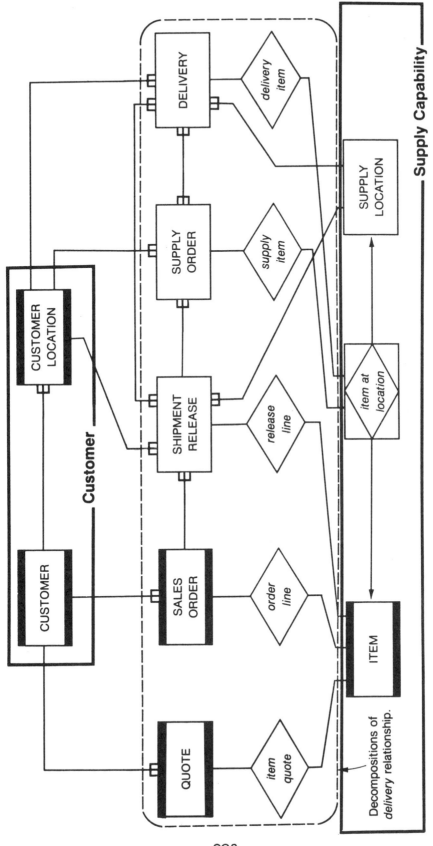

FIGURE 7.7. Customer order information structure.

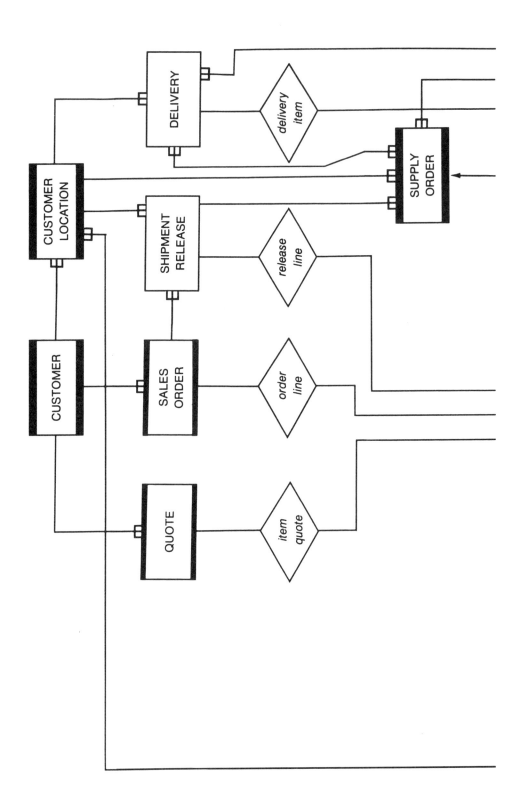

204

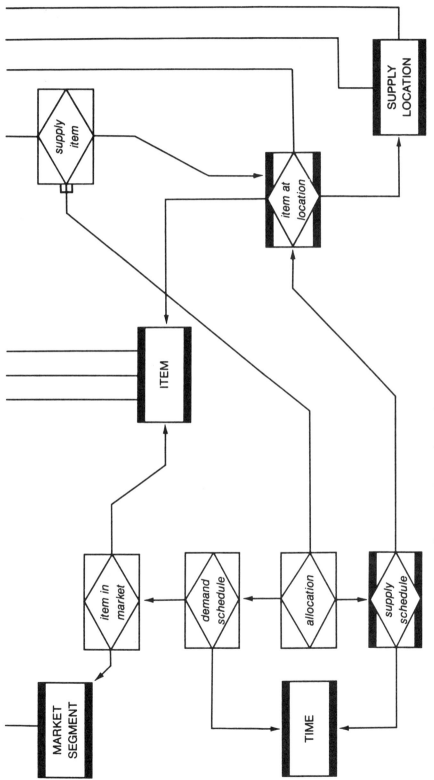

FIGURE 7.8. Information structure for order processing.

feasible to re-schedule the planned order releases, MRP issues a report saying that the proposed supply adjustment is not feasible.

Once the allocation of an order (or portion thereof) to a supply location has been decided, an order to supply from the location must be issued. The attributes of this order vary slightly depending on the nature of the supply source. If the source is a warehouse of the business, then a delivery order is issued which gives information needed to find and pack the items and to get them shipped. If the source is factory production, then a shipment order is issued identifying a portion of future production to be shipped to a particular customer. If the source is a supplier with whom we have a purchase contract, then a shipment release order is issued which includes the information required to ship directly to the customer, but bill us. Supply Order is the generalization used in Figure 7.8 to represent these types of orders.

The relationship in Figure 7.8 between the *supply item* and *allocation* relationships can be used to record the assignment of an ordered item to a supply allocation. If the item is standard but not stocked then the assignment amounts to reserving a portion of the next production run of the item for the fulfillment of the order. In any case, it is a way to record the portion of a planned allocation that has been used in filling specific orders.

DELIVERING CUSTOMER ORDERS

Delivering product to customers, either from a warehouse or directly from factory production is analogous to the receiving function in that it is an important data capturing activity. Receiving captures information about materials coming into the enterprise and delivery captures information about material leaving the enterprise. It is appropriate, and not unusual, to have a single department responsible for both functions.

To determine the information required for the delivery of products (and in some cases services), which is both a subfunction and an entity type, consider what this subfunction involves. It can be said to consist of two subfunctions and to trigger the execution of an accounting subfunction. One subfunction concerns getting the material ready for shipment and the other concerns transporting the shipment. The two delivery subfunctions are serially related in the sense that one must be done before the other. But, they have separate information requirements. In the following subsections, the information requirements of the picking/packing, transporting, and invoicing subfunctions are defined.

Picking and Packing

The information needed for warehouse picking and packing operations concerns (1) delivery orders, (2) items on an order, (3) the inventory from which the items will be withdrawn (which is the relationship between Item and Supply Location in Figure 7.7), and (4) the mode of transport. The first three of these four types of information are included in Figure 7.7. An important attribute of the *item at location* relationship for the picking operation is the location of the item in the warehouse.

A characterization of the mode of transport information is shown in Figure 7.9 which is explained in the next subsection. The mode of transport for a specific shipment could be an attribute of the Carrier Order of Figure 7.9.

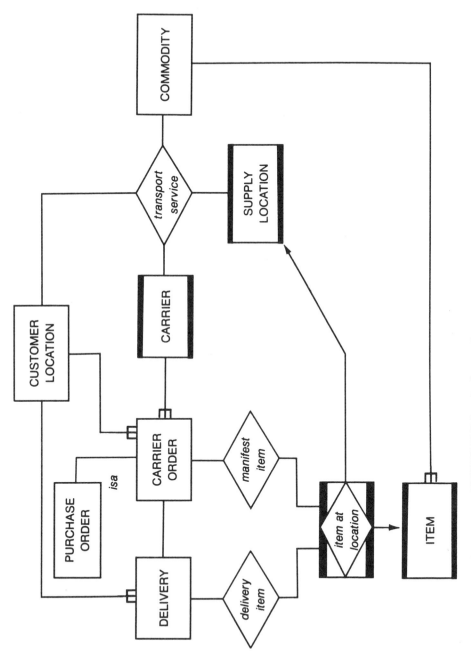

FIGURE 7.9. Information structure for shipping.

The Transport Subfunction

Transporting the shipment can be done in several ways. The enterprise may have a fleet of trucks that are used to make deliveries. Customers may send their own trucks to pick up a delivery. The delivery service of a common freight carrier can be used. The information required to manage the transport varies somewhat, depending on which of these alternatives is used.

If we assume the use of common freight carrier services, then two types of information become important. One is information about transport service alternatives, if any, that are available. The other is information about the order issued for transport service and the transport service provided in response.

In theory, transport service alternatives are determined by four major factors. Two are the origin and destination of the transport desired. A third is the nature of the material to be transported. The fourth is the mode (or modes) of transportation used. In the case at hand, the origin is defined by Supply Location occurrences that have already been introduced in Figure 7.8. The destination is defined by the Customer Location entity type which also may have many occurrences. The nature of the material to be hauled is defined by common carriers using what can be called a commodity classification system. A commodity classification can be treated as an entity type (called Commodity). Finally, the mode of transport can be modeled in terms of a Carrier entity type. This entity type has attributes that identify a particular way of moving product between two points, not only in terms of a mode or modes of transport but also in terms of a certain pick up schedule and specific conditions imposed by the individual carrier.

This information about transport service alternatives is shown in Figure 7.9 as a four-way relationship labeled *transport service*. Attributes of the relationship would include the service price and any weight or volume limitations. Each occurrence of this relationship is for a different combination of the four entity types that it involves. If all the items shipped by the firm fall into the same commodity classification, then that entity type is not needed.

The other type of information required for transport service management is the facts on requests for carrier services and the service provided. What entity types is the information about? One entity type is the request, or order, for a carrier service. The other entity type is the delivery service provided. The Delivery entity type, which has already been introduced in Figure 7.8, stands for this event. These two entity types are shown in Figure 7.9 with a one-to-one relationship between them. (It may be that this should be a one-to-many relationship to accommodate those cases in which the first carrier service ordered does not work out for some reason and a second order must be placed for the delivery.)

An *isa* relationship is shown in Figure 7.9 between Carrier Order and Purchase Order. This is to point out that a carrier order is actually a purchase of a service. The accounting subfunction that deals with paying bills from freight carriers needs to access the carrier orders to verify that the service for which a payment is demanded was in fact ordered and provided.

The Invoicing Subfunction

The invoicing subfunction is triggered by the delivery subfunction. For each delivery, an invoice is sent to the customer showing the amount to be paid for the products and services delivered. If there is a one-to-one relationship between

Delivery and Customer Invoice then it is reasonable to ask why not treat them as one event and entity type? One answer is that for services there may be no delivery, only an invoice. The set of attributes required for a delivery is somewhat different from that required for an invoice, and thus treating the two as one would result in null attributes for occurrences that did not involve a delivery.

The relationships between invoicing data and the data required for customer delivery management are shown in Figure 7.10. The one-to-one relationship between Delivery and Customer Invoice can be considered optional as far as customer invoices are concerned but mandatory for occurrences of the Delivery entity type. All Customer Invoice occurrences need not link to a Delivery occurrence. On the other hand, it is reasonable to assume that all Delivery occurrences will link to an invoice.

It should also be noted that Customer Invoice is related to Customer, not Customer Location. This is based on the assumption that the invoice goes to the accounts payable subfunction of accounting, not to the location where the product is delivered.

The customer invoice plays a role in the accounts receivable function of accounting and in cash management. It is also of fundamental importance to sales

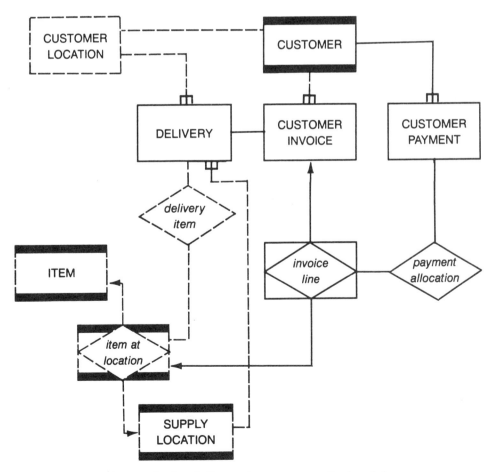

FIGURE 7.10.   Information structure for invoicing.

and marketing management. These needs for information about customer invoices are discussed in the chapters dealing with marketing and accounting data requirements. The point to note here is that this important data should be captured as part of the delivery to customer function.

SALES FORECAST ALLOCATION

Finding the best plan for supplying customers from a given set of supply points is the task of sales forecast allocation. Normally, the best plan is the least cost plan. Transportation costs may be a major consideration in this analysis, but supply capacities of various locations and the marginal product cost at alternate locations are also important factors.

The forecast of sales in each market area is assumed to be the volume of product that should be delivered to each market if demanded. This forecast is broken down by planning period and product item. The creation of this forecast is described in the chapter on marketing.

The analysis of the information used in MRP as a whole yielded the information structure shown in Figure 7.3. Two aspects of this information structure must be defined in more detail for purposes of allocating the sales forecast. One is to differentiate between various types of supply locations. The other is to define transportation costs more explicitly.

In the simplest case, there is only one kind of supply location. It may be a series of warehouses, or it may be a series of factories, or it may be that everything is purchased from suppliers after it is sold. In the last case, whether to deliver from a warehouse or factory is the supplier's problem, and we ignore it (which leaves the sales function vulnerable to variability in lead time). In any event, Figure 7.3 is sufficient for this simplest case. Change supply location to warehouse location or factory location or supplier in Figure 7.3 and it becomes the appropriate information structure for the situation.

In a more complex situation, the enterprise delivers to customers from both warehouses and factories, or alternatively, from both warehouses and directly from suppliers. In these cases, replenishment shipments to the warehouses from the factories or suppliers usually must be taken into account. The capacity limitations of factories and suppliers make it necessary to take into account the destination of the total amount produced.

Figure 7.11 shows the information structure for the complex case in which Supply Location is specialized to both Warehouse Location and Factory Location. This change requires corresponding changes in the meaning of the relationships in which Supply Location is involved in Figure 7.3. *Item at location* becomes *production item* and *stock item* in Figure 7.11. The *capacity* relationship in Figure 7.3 is carried over to 7.11 for factory location but not warehouse location. (It could be added for warehouse location if needed.)

The change in *item at location* causes changes in what is called *supply schedule* in Figure 7.3. It becomes *production schedule* in the case of production item and *stock plan* in the case of stock item. In decomposing *supply schedule*, a relationship between *production schedule* and *stock plan* is added which defines plans for replenishing the warehouse supply of each item. This relationship is called *replenishment* in Figure 7.11.

Finally, the decomposition of *supply schedule* leads to a specialization of the *allocation* relationship in Figure 7.3. It specializes to two relationships, *production allocation* and *stock allocation*. The key attribute of each of these relationships is the planned amount of an item to be supplied to a certain market from the source involved in the relationship.

The other clarification necessary in order to allocate a sales forecast concerns transportation costs. Figure 7.11 includes a decomposition of the *transport* relationship of Figure 7.3 that provides this clarification. The *transport* relationship of Figure 7.3 has become a four-way relationship between supply location, market segment, commodity classification, and carrier service. This is the same relationship that was obtained in Figure 7.9 by decomposing the *transport* relationship of Figure 7.3.

Exactly how does the information structure of Figure 7.11 relate to the function of allocating a sales forecast? The first paragraph of this section summarizes the function. Each of the items of information described in that paragraph can be characterized as information about some entity type or relationship. To show a process of reasoning from that description to the information structure shown in Figure 7.11, the meaning of each item of information in the paragraph is described below in Figures 7.12 through 7.16. Two descriptions of the information are provided. One is a description in plain English and the other uses the terms of Figure 7.11.

The sales forecast allocation problem is a problem in planning that can be solved in several ways. It can be done using ad hoc strategies or using a formal resource allocation model (such as linear programming) and an algorithm devised for the model. Our concern in this discussion is not with the method of making the allocation but rather with the information structure.

ORDER RELEASE PLANNING

The information required to do the order release planning subfunction of MRP can be understood most easily from an example. Suppose one of the products (items) of our hard goods manufacturer is a toaster. The sales forecast calls for a specified number of toasters to be sold in each market area in each planning period. This projected demand has been allocated to warehouses where the toasters are stocked and to direct shipments from factories. Also, the sales forecast allocation process has determined required warehouse resupply quantities and these have been allocated to toaster factories.

The planning data for a particular warehouse from which toasters are shipped to customers might be as shown in Table 7.1. The difference between "projected on-hand before resupply" and "net requirement" in Table 7.1 is safety stock. A safety stock level of 4 is assumed in the table. When the on-hand balance is 3 and the safety stock level is 4, there is a net requirement for 1 unit.

The rule for determining the quantity of a planned order in Table 7.1 is very simple. Orders must be made in multiples of 30 units. (In general, any rule for determining order quantity can be implemented in MRP.)

The lead time used is 2 weeks. If MRP were scheduling production at the factories, the lead time might not be a fixed period, but would depend on when the planned order could be produced. It should be noted that the order quantity also might not be a fixed amount also if MRP is doing the production scheduling.

Order release scheduling is the process of recalculating the planned order releases in tables like Table 7.1 every time there is a change in gross requirements or a change in any other factors affecting the calculation, such as the lead time

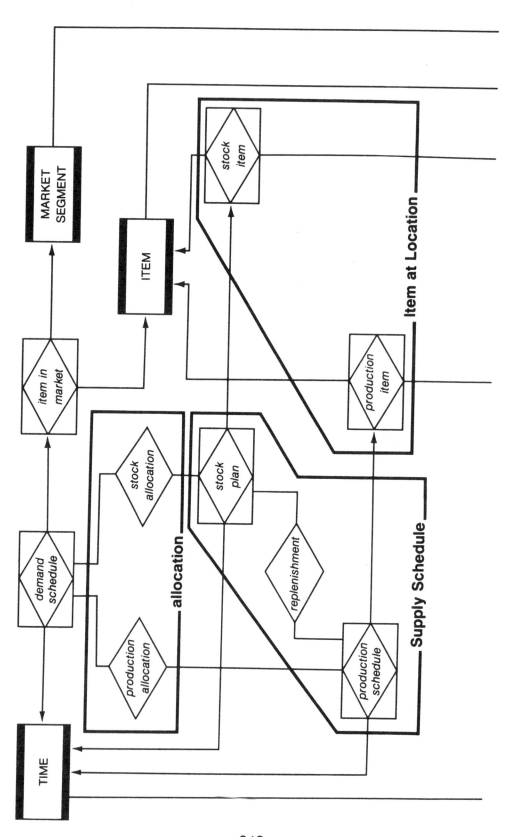

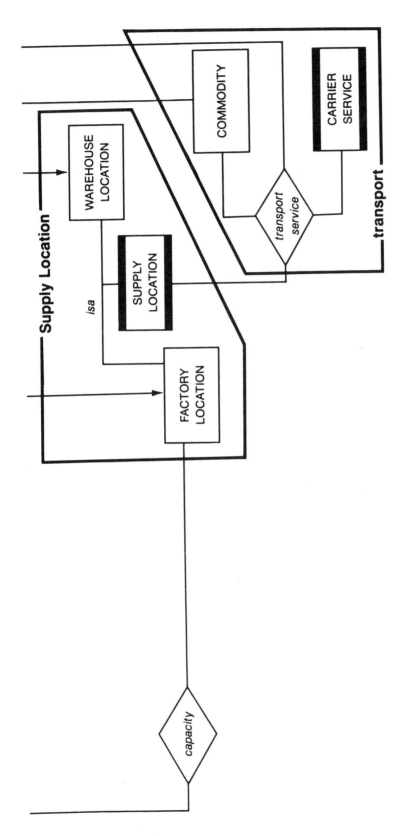

FIGURE 7.11. More detailed information structure for MRP.

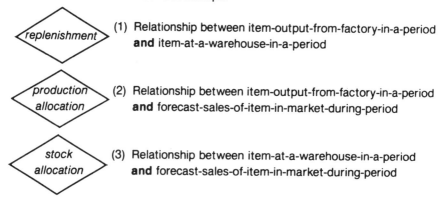

Best Plan

What It Means:

Amount of each product to ship

- From each factory to each market and warehouse and
- From each warehouse to each market area in a planning period

Information Structure Description:

- Attribute of either of three relationships:

replenishment   (1) Relationship between item-output-from-factory-in-a-period
and item-at-a-warehouse-in-a-period

production allocation   (2) Relationship between item-output-from-factory-in-a-period
and forecast-sales-of-item-in-market-during-period

stock allocation   (3) Relationship between item-at-a-warehouse-in-a-period
and forecast-sales-of-item-in-market-during-period

FIGURE 7.12. Attributes of Best Plan.

Transportation Costs

What It Means:

- The freight rate in $/lb. plus insurance and other transport charges

Information Structure Description:

- Attributes of relationship between:

supply location
market location
commodity type
carrier service

FIGURE 7.13. Attributes of Transport Service.

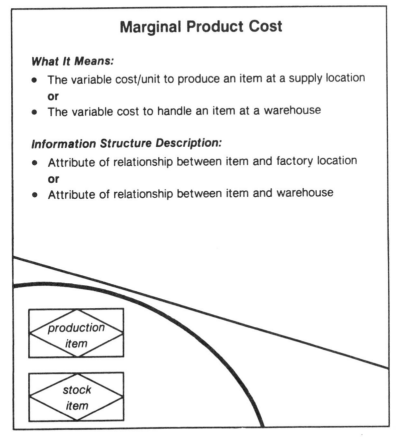

Supply Capacities

What It Means:
- Capacity of factory in terms of hours/time period and hours required/unit of item supplied

Information Structure Description:
- Hours of capacity is an attribute of relationship between time period and factory location;
- Production rate is an attribute of relationship between item and factory location

FIGURE 7.14. Attributes of Supply Capacities.

Marginal Product Cost

What It Means:
- The variable cost/unit to produce an item at a supply location
  or
- The variable cost to handle an item at a warehouse

Information Structure Description:
- Attribute of relationship between item and factory location
  or
- Attribute of relationship between item and warehouse

FIGURE 7.15. Attributes of Marginal Costs.

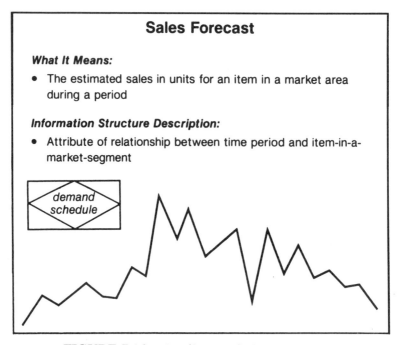

FIGURE 7.16.   Attributes of "Sales Forecast."

used. The information required for order release planning is therefore the type of information shown in Table 7.1, plus safety stock, order quantity, and lead time parameters.

This table illustrates the calculations of order release planning for a single item, a finished product stocked in a warehouse. But the database needs to contain a separate table of this type for each item stocked, for each item produced, and for

TABLE 7.1.   MRP data for a warehouse.

	Week 9	Week 10	Week 11	Week 12	Week 13	Month 4	Month 5	Month 6	Quarter 3
Gross requirements		6	2	8	23	20	23	25	60
Scheduled receipts			30						
Projected receipts					30		30	30	60
Projected on-hand before supply	12	6	4	26	3	13	−10	−5	−35
Net requirement					1		14	9	39
Planned orders	30		30				30	30	60
Projected on-hand after resupply	12	6	34	26	33	13	20	25	25

each raw material and semi-finished material involved in production. A supply plan is needed for each item at each location whether it is a warehouse or a factory.

Of which entity type or relationship in Figure 7.11 would the data in Table 7.1 be attributes? The data in any one column of Table 7.1 concerns an item at a location in a time period. This means that the data in a column is a set of attributes of a relationship between Time and any relationship of the type "item at a location." There are two such instances in Figure 7.11, *stock plan* and *production schedule*. There is a separate occurrence of each of these relationships for each item at a location and each time period. The safety stock, order quantity, and lead time parameters are attributes of *stock item* and *production item* in Figure 7.11.

EXPLOSION

The explosion process applies to manufactured items. It involves retrieving a list of the parts required to make the finished item and getting the order release planning process to plan the supply of parts. This list of parts is defined by a *product structure* relationship.

The *product structure* relationship is a recursive one. It relates one item to other items that are a component part of it. It can be derived from Figure 7.11 by decomposing "item." This decomposition is shown in Figure 7.17.

Product structure is a many-to-many relationship; a product can have many parts and any one part can be used in more than one product. The important attribute of the relationship for the explosion process is the number of units of the part required per unit of product produced.

REQUISITIONING

In general usage, a requisition is a request that one or more items be procured or produced. It is an internal request sent from any department to the purchasing department. A requisition in this sense is modeled in Figure 7.6.

The requisitioning function within MRP converts planned order releases into either purchase requisitions or work orders. Those converted into purchase requisitions are for items obtained from suppliers. Those converted into work orders are for items produced in-house.

The requisition entity type could be added to Figure 7.11 but it has not been for reasons of simplicity. As already mentioned, it is in Figure 7.6 which relates to

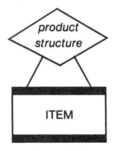

FIGURE 7.17.   Information structure of explosion subfunction.

purchased items. Chapter 8 describes production, and the work order that would be created by this requisitioning function is shown in Figure 8.2.

In a sense, requisitioning is the bridging function between MRP planning and transaction management. Figure 7.6 diagrams the database view that supports purchasing transaction management and Figure 8.2 does the same for work order processing. Requisitioning takes planned order releases defined in *stock plan* and *production schedule* relationships and converts them into item requisition occurrences when it is time to put the plan into action.

REPORTING

The attributes of the *demand schedule, production allocation, production schedule, stock allocation, stock plan,* and *replenishment* (in Figure 7.11) constitute a materials management plan. This plan can be compared with actual performance during each planning period. Actual demand and the way actual demand is supplied from warehouses and factories can be made *attributes of demand schedule* and the *production* and *stock allocation* relationships. Significant differences between planned and actual performance can be detected and reported for management review and action. The planned order releases and scheduled receipts in the production and stock plans can be compared with actual requisitions and the purchase orders, work orders, and deliveries to stock that have occurred. Again, significant differences can be reported as a guide to management.

Thus, the information required for the reporting function of MRP is defined by the information structures of Figures 7.6, 7.8, and 7.11, except for report definition information. The definition of reports is metadata which is discussed in Chapter 11.

SUMMARY

The conceptual database planning technique explained in Part 1 has been applied to the materials management function of a consumer hardgoods manufacturer. A breadth-first approach was taken. Two levels of the functional model and information structure have been developed, although the lower level of the information structure is incomplete. The lower level information requirements of only two of the three functions have been defined.

The proposition that the information requirements of a subfunction can be characterized as a decomposition of the information structure of the higher level function has proven viable. Three different decompositions of the information structure shown in Figure 7.1 were developed for the three first-level subfunctions of materials management. Then, for transaction management, decompositions of Figure 7.2 were developed to support four subfunctions (purchasing, receiving, order processing, and delivery). Finally, decompositions of Figure 7.3 that satisfy the needs of the MRP subfunctions were derived.

The methodology provides a systematic approach to defining the information requirements of materials management. The functional breakdown gives assurance that all materials management subfunctions are considered in the analysis. The decomposition method of deriving information structure leads to a modular concept of the structures in which certain sections of a given structure are seen as decompositions of higher level structures.

DISCUSSION QUESTIONS

1. What is the proper role of materials management in sales forecasting?

2. What planning activities does Materials Requirements Planning (MRP) include?

3. What are the penalties for failing to meet a commitment defined in a materials management plan? What are the penalties for failing to meet a commitment defined by a customer order that materials management accepts? What are the penalties of failing to meet a commitment made by materials management and defined by an order that materials management issues?

4. What does the *supply plan* relationship define?

5. Comment on the following opinion: the *plan* relationship of Figure 5.1 is concerned only with strategic planning and by nature is not very structured; it should be left out of consideration when defining the information requirements of materials management; it should be left to the Decision Support Systems (DSS) of the organization.

6. Should a sales order be considered a supply commitment or an instance of the *supply action* relationship as far as materials management is concerned?

7. Should negotiating a blanket purchase agreement (a long-term commitment to buy a range of products and services from a supplier within a certain volume range) be considered a part of the transaction processing or capacity planning subfunction?

8. What are the two different types of commitments made in materials management that create the need for the two specializations of the *supply action* relationship of Figure 7.1?

9. What could serve as key attributes of the *supply schedule* relationship in Figure 7.3 if it were implemented as a relation? What could serve as key attributes of the *allocation* relationship if it were implemented as a relation?

10. Which entities and relationships in Figure 7.3 would be affected if a piece of manufacturing equipment used in the production of a specific item requires a two-week overhaul before production of the item at the location can resume?

11. Compare and contrast the *capacity* relationship in Figure 7.3 with that relationship in Figure 7.4.

12. What is the rule of association for the relationship between Item and Operation shown in Figure 7.4?

13. Why should purchasing and receiving be treated as separate subfunctions of transaction processing rather than as a single subfunction, which could be called "procurement"?

14. How do the order release planning and explosion subfunctions of MRP interact?

15. Why is the *release line* relationship of Figure 7.5 between Shipment Release and *item of stock* rather than between Shipment Release and Item?

16. Define the rule of association for the many-to-many relationship between *requisition line* and *release line* in Figure 7.6.

17. How does the Purchase Requisition entity type of Figure 7.6 relate to the materials management information structure of Figure 7.1?

18. Why is the relationship between *shipment item* and *inspected item* one-to-many instead of one-to-one in Figure 7.6?

19. Suppose a portion of a shipment does not pass inspection and is sent back to the supplier. How would that be recorded in the database as defined in Figure 7.6?

20. What entity types and relationships do Figures 7.3 and 7.7 have in common?

21. Explain how the order processing subfunction can cause the MRP subfunction to make additional amounts of an item available (in a certain time period) from a supply location, if it is possible.

22. How would backorders be handled in the database defined in Figure 7.8?

23. What purpose is served by including both a Carrier Order entity type and a Delivery entity type in the database for the transport subfunction of the delivering customer orders subfunction?

24. Should the *invoice line* relationship in Figure 7.10 involve Item or *item at location*?

25. Figure 7.3 shows the structure of information requirements of MRP for the simple case of one type of supply location. Figure 7.11 shows the structure for the case of two types of supply locations (warehouses and factories). What is the structure of information requirements if there can be deliveries from suppliers to either factories, warehouses, or customers, and the suppliers have capacity limits?

26. How would the planned orders in Table 7.1 be changed if the gross requirements in Week 12 were 38 instead of 8?

27. How could the explosion subfunction trigger the order release planning subfunction?

28. Suppose the actual stock of an item in a warehouse is less than planned because some of the item has been stolen by an employee. Under what conditions would this cause an MRP exception report and which attributes of the entities and relationships of Figure 7.11 would be shown on that report?

29. Suppose the toaster of Table 7.1 is composed of 2 units of a subassembly, one unit each of 4 other parts and 4 units each of 3 other parts. The subassembly is composed of 4 units each of 2 parts and one unit each of 3 parts. How many stock schedule occurrences would the explosion process cause the order release planning process to re-plan for a single change in the gross requirements of Table 7.1?

30. In a large hospital, there are a number of organizational units, such as radiology, pharmacy, labor and delivery, and surgery. Some of these units have their own materials management system. In such cases, should the enterprise-wide functional model show materials management as a subfunction of the top-level function or as a subfunction of the various hospital departments?

8

Production Management

NATURE OF THE FUNCTION

A production process is viewed in economics as an input-output system. There are sets of resources such as raw materials, personnel, and machines that are called inputs. The materials are transformed through a series of operations into outputs that are the finished products that the system is designed to produce.

The purpose of the production function in a consumer hardgoods manufacturing enterprise is to carry out the necessary operations on raw materials and purchased parts in a way that accomplishes several objectives. One important objective is to produce products of consistently high quality. This at least means producing products that satisfy the design specifications prepared by engineering. In many situations, it means producing products that function reliably and eliminate customer complaints even if it requires doing more than simply meeting design specifications.

A second objective is to produce at the lowest possible cost. Accounting for costs and comparing them to the output is an important management information support service. If only one or a very few products are produced, it is relatively easy to determine cost but the information is not as useful as it is in the case of many products. If there are many different products produced, then assigning costs to products and evaluating how well costs are being controlled is difficult but it results in useful management information.

A third objective is to meet the production schedule. If outputs are delayed, then the commitments made to customers regarding product delivery are in jeopardy. This has a negative impact on future sales and in some industries results in penalties that must be paid to the customer. If the outputs are parts used by the customer in another product, the assembly schedule of the customer's production operations is likely to be upset if the production schedule slips. Failure to get finished goods out the door on time also delays customer payments which leads to an increase in the working capital requirements of the business.

Production management must also manage the components of production capacity on a continuing basis. Plans that either increase, improve, or reduce productive resources must be made and executed. The skills, experience, and motivation of the workforce can be substantially improved over time by various means. Optimizing worker safety is another way of protecting this vital productive resource and enhancing morale. The equipment, workplace layout, and methods of production must be improved and adapted to the product and delivery time requirements. In this regard, significant quality improvements and cost reductions can often be found by working with the product designers on product modifications that make the production process easier.

The relationship between materials management and production management is complex. The Material Requirement Planning (MRP) system used in materials management is capable of scheduling the use of productive resources. In effect, this means that materials management is setting one aspect of the goals of production management. In terms of input, the purchasing subfunction of materials management is responsible for assuring a supply of raw materials and parts appropriate for the production schedule. This creates the possibility that production management will fail to produce according to schedule because of a supply commitment obtained by materials management that was not fulfilled. Between input and output, there is a series of other subfunctions that serve both production management and materials management. Production planning and control are treated in this text as subfunctions of production management, but they are concerned with the flow of material through production processes, and they utilize the MRP system. Stockkeeping is another subfunction that serves both materials management and production management; it is assumed in this text that stockkeeping is a materials management function.

Product engineering sets another aspect of the goals of production management. The product specifications produced by engineering define quality goals for production. Production should use data about products developed by engineering. In many cases, the product specifications produced by design engineers are modified by manufacturing engineers to meet production requirements. This can lead to two (or more) versions of product specifications which can create misunderstanding between production and design engineering. Production management has a responsibility to turn these possible misunderstandings into cooperation with the engineering function in refining product designs and production processes in ways that promote the goals of production.

PRODUCTION INFORMATION STRUCTURE

The information requirements of production management certainly include information about the goals and resources of production. Information is required about how the resources should be, and are, used to achieve the goals. Also, production management needs to know that the goals that are set can be achieved with the available resources. Thus, there is reason to think that the information requirements of production can be derived as a decomposition of the CEO information structure shown in Figure 5.1.

GOALS

The goals of production management were briefly reviewed in the previous section. Four types were identified:

1. Produce consistently high quality product
2. Produce at the lowest possible cost
3. Fulfill the production schedule
4. Maintain competitive production capabilities.

These four goals are shown in Figure 8.1 as specializations of the Goal entity type of Figure 5.1. The goal of producing consistently high quality products is defined in terms of product specification data because it is concerned with producing a product that satisfies those specifications. The objective of producing at low cost is defined by the budget for production activities that is contained in a series of accounts. The goal of satisfying a planned production output schedule is defined by that production schedule. The goal of maintaining a competitive production capability is represented by the Capacity Change entity type in Figure 8.1.

The Capacity Change entity type includes a wide range of changes. It includes everything from upgrading worker skills to building an automated factory. It even includes moves to build strategic relations with subcontractors which may be an alternative to building a production capability internally.

It may seem incongruous that Product Specification is treated as a goal in this chapter whereas information about products was considered a resource in previous chapters on marketing and materials management. The fact that the same information can define a goal for one function and a resource for another is a result of the fact that the different functions use the information for different purposes. Manufacturing uses the information to define what is to be produced. Marketing uses it to prepare messages to broadcast to market segments.

RESOURCES

The Resource entity type of Figure 5.1 is decomposed into a series of five entity types in Figure 8.1. They represent the types of resources with which production management works in achieving its goals. There are various relationships between these entity types as indicated by the many-to-many relationships shown in the diagram, but it should be understood that further analysis may identify other relationships than those shown. An explanation of the relationships is best left until we consider these entity types at a more detailed level.

The Labor entity type represents both direct and indirect labor. It includes everyone in the production organization. Information about the way the production labor force is organized is considered information about labor.

The Facilities entity type includes items of equipment used in production, the buildings in which the equipment is housed, and the materials handling and computer-communication systems that link and coordinate the equipment. It also includes tools, dies, jigs, and fixtures used in production.

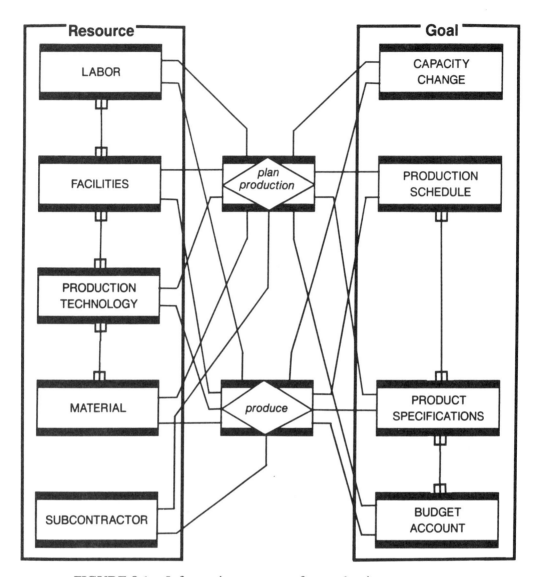

FIGURE 8.1.   Information structure for production management.

The Production Technology entity type refers to the codified knowledge used in production. This includes general instructions for using the facilities and specific instructions for using certain facilities to perform an operation on a specific part or assembly. To the extent that production is automated, the instructions executed by computers are also included in this entity type.

The Material entity type represents all materials used in production. This includes operating materials and office supplies as well as raw materials, semi-finished parts, and subassemblies. It should be noted, however, that some information about material requirements and material usage depends on the product specifications or the production job in which the material is used and therefore cannot be modeled as a simple attribute of Material.

The Subcontractor entity type refers to additional external production resources. It represents another producer who will accept a purchase order to perform one or more operations on material supplied by the purchaser.

THE MANAGE RELATIONSHIP

The *manage* relationship of Figure 5.1 is specialized to the *produce* relationship in Figure 8.1. It refers to the orders and actions whereby production resources are used to achieve production goals. It is conceivable that any of the five types of resources could be used in achieving each of the four goals shown in Figure 8.1. Therefore, the relationship is shown between all resources and all goals.

THE PLAN RELATIONSHIP

The *plan* relationship of Figure 5.1 is specialized to the *plan production* relationship in Figure 8.1. It refers to the ways in which the production resources are taken into account in setting production goals. As far as product quality is concerned, it refers to modifying product designs to solve production problems. In the case of costs, it refers to setting budgets based on the current costs of production resources and realistic resource usage rates. With respect to the production schedule, planning requires data on available capacities in future time periods and the existing supplies of materials and work-in-process.

In the case of the goal of keeping production capabilities competitive, analysis is required of the existing resources to identify "bottlenecks" in the production system and production operations that are too costly. Once these are clear, ways of improving the configuration can be defined and evaluated so that the best alternative is selected for implementation. The scope of production capacity planning opportunities can vary greatly and their data requirements vary correspondingly.

SUBFUNCTIONS

Each subfunction of production is concerned with managing a type of production resource. One subfunction manages the use of labor. Another subfunction develops and applies production technology. A third subfunction cares for the facilities. Then, there is a series of specialized services that are treated as a fourth subfunction because they are provided to more than one of the other three subfunctions.

The four subfunctions of production are shown in Figure 8.2 as the first-level breakdown of the production function. The figure also shows the breakdown of each of the four subfunctions in order to clarify their nature. The subfunction called operations is concerned with the management of labor.

OPERATIONS

The operations function applies the workforce to produce product. However, it is the workforce that uses the production facilities and technology to transform

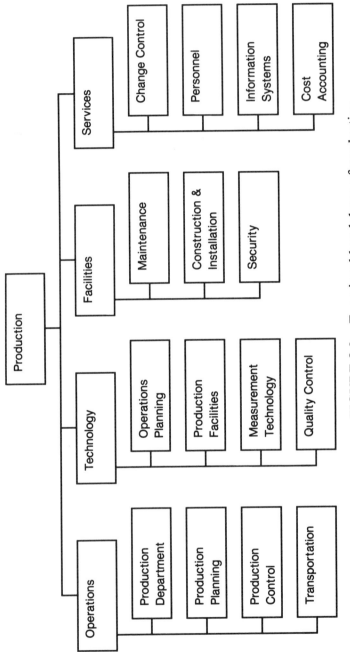

FIGURE 8.2. Functional breakdown of production.

materials into finished products. So the operations subfunctions must include production planning and control which determine the work to be done on a daily basis. The production department's subfunction is to carry out the production and inspection (testing) operations assigned by the production control subfunction. The transportation subfunction moves work-in-process and materials to the location where an operation is performed. A transportation service can be treated as another operation.

Production planning and control are essential subfunctions of operations, because when one resource needed to produce a product is missing, a whole order can be delayed. To cite an extreme case, if the order is for a jet plane and one screw is missing, the entire multimillion dollar order is delayed until the screw is added to the product.

To deal with the requirement that all resources be available, a subfunction of production planning is commonly recognized. It is often called work order preparation. Its role is to make sure all the resources necessary to produce an order are available before the order is released to production. The material, parts, and subassemblies needed for an order may be reserved in inventory or they may be scheduled for delivery from a just-in-time supplier. Special tools, fixtures, and machines required for certain operations may be scheduled for use. The drawings, computer programs for automatic machine tools, test instructions, and other engineering information are checked for availability. It may also be necessary to review skilled labor requirements; plans are made for having skilled labor available at the appropriate times. The more automated the production facilities, the more important it becomes that work order preparation be complete and accurate.

A subfunction of operations that is not shown in Figure 8.2 is configuration control. This subfunction has the responsibility for ensuring that an appropriate version of each subsystem is installed in a complex product and for recording the identity (and source) of every part put into each finished product. This subfunction is not normally required for a consumer hardgoods manufacturer but is important in the production of complex capital goods.

TECHNOLOGY

The technology function applies available production technology to the on-going production operations and to the development of production facilities. The operation planning subfunction develops the techniques that will be used to produce each part and product. It defines a series of operations that can be performed to produce a finished part or product. Each operation requires that certain facilities be used by workers, with appropriate qualifications, to transform certain materials. If the operation is automated, the information about the operation includes computer instructions.

The production facilities subfunction of technology plans and develops the production facilities. It deals with broader scope problems than does the operations planning subfunction. It applies group technology to identify groups of products for which a production line should be established and then works on the design and development of the line.

The measurement technology subfunction applies methods of sensing and measuring to production automation projects, and inspection and testing problems. The more production is automated, the more important this subfunction becomes.

The quality control subfunction is concerned with detecting the causes of defects. It monitors inspection and testing results and customer complaints and seeks to find and eliminate deficiencies in the production process (or in the product design).

FACILITIES

The facilities subfunctions deal with developing and maintaining production facilities and controlling who has access to them. The management of a tool and die storeroom, for example, is a security function, as is the control of access to areas in the plant.

SERVICES

The services subfunction of production management provides specialized professional services to the other production subfunctions. Four types of services are shown in Figure 8.2 as subfunctions of services. The change control service manages the introduction of changes in either the product design or the production process. The timing of a change is managed so that parts inventories are not obsoleted unnecessarily and so that necessary changes in instructions and worker training are completed before the change takes place. Change control also manages the announcement of changes and the requests for changes in records as a result of the change.

The personnel service in production is a subfunction of both production management and personnel management. It can include employment, labor relations, training, and benefit administration services.

The information systems subfunction develops and operates a factory data collection system for the operations function. It also works with the technology function in the development of factory automation applications and quality control information systems.

The cost accounting subfunction develops the production budgeting and cost reporting system and analyzes variances in production costs. Cost and investment analyses in support of the technology function may also be provided by this service subfunction.

SECOND-LEVEL PRODUCTION FUNCTION
INFORMATION REQUIREMENTS

The information requirements of the four second-level functions shown in Figure 8.2 can be derived by decomposing the entities and relationships shown in Figure 8.1. If this were done, it would turn out that the information structure for the operations function includes almost all of the entity types required by the other three functions. For this reason, only the development of the information structure for the operations function is described in detail in this section. The information needs of the other three functions are discussed only in general terms.

OPERATIONS INFORMATION REQUIREMENTS

The information structure that defines the requirements for all aspects of the operations function except for capacity change is shown in Figure 8.3. The planning and achievement of capacity change goals, particularly those that concern the labor force, is a part of the operations management function. But it involves longer term considerations than does the rest of the operations function. We simplify matters by ignoring this aspect of production management as far as information requirements are concerned.

Figure 8.3 was developed by taking each of the entities and relationships in Figure 8.1 and describing the information about that entity or relationship required to conduct production operations. In the following subsections, this process of analysis is described.

Production Schedule

The production schedule defines how much of each product must be produced in each time period. This information is clearly an attribute of a relationship between time period and product that is based on the fact that a product is planned to be produced in a given time period.

The development and maintenance of the production schedule is a material requirements planning (MRP) function that is briefly described in Chapter 7. It requires information on expected sales in future periods as well as the planning information shown in Figure 8.3 (available labor, available equipment, and inventory plan).

In addition to finished products, the MRP system plans for purchased materials and parts as well as parts and subassemblies produced in-house. To do this, it uses the information about part requirements which is an attribute of the recursive relationship on Item that is shown in Figure 8.3. Only plans for the products, parts, and subassemblies produced in-house are relevant to the goals of the operations function.

Plan Production

The information required in order to take production resources into account in preparing the production schedule has already been discussed in conjunction with consideration of the information structure for the production schedule. It can be treated as attributes of the three relationships shown in the plan production area of Figure 8.3.

What about information required to plan the other goals: product specifications and budgets? The technology subfunction of production, and not the operations subfunction, interacts with engineering design in modifying designs to accommodate production capabilities. So, operations requires no planning data in order to set product specifications.

As far as budgeting is concerned, there may be some types of planning information that could have been included in Figure 8.3 but were not. Three costs for which operations management usually must take responsibility are labor costs, scrap and spoilage, and overhead expenses. Assuming a variable budgeting system is used, the budget for direct labor costs will automatically be adjusted for

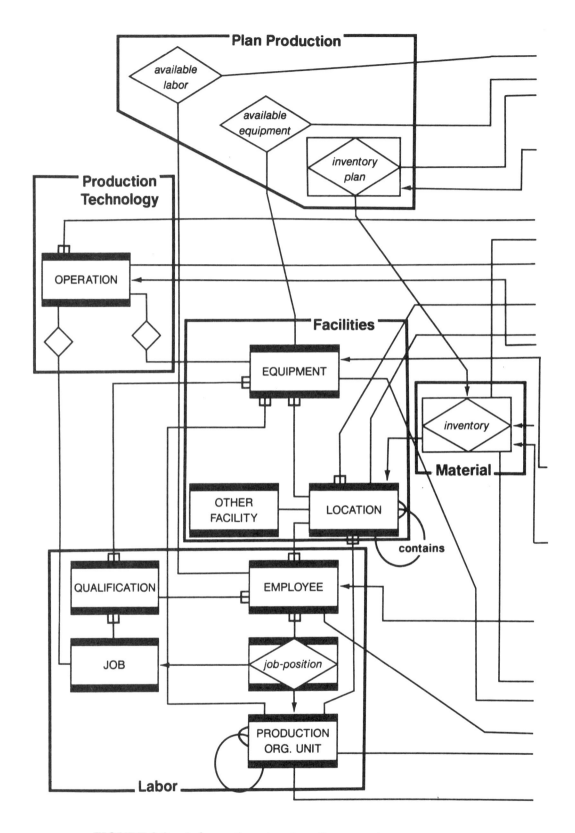

FIGURE 8.3. Information structure for operations management.

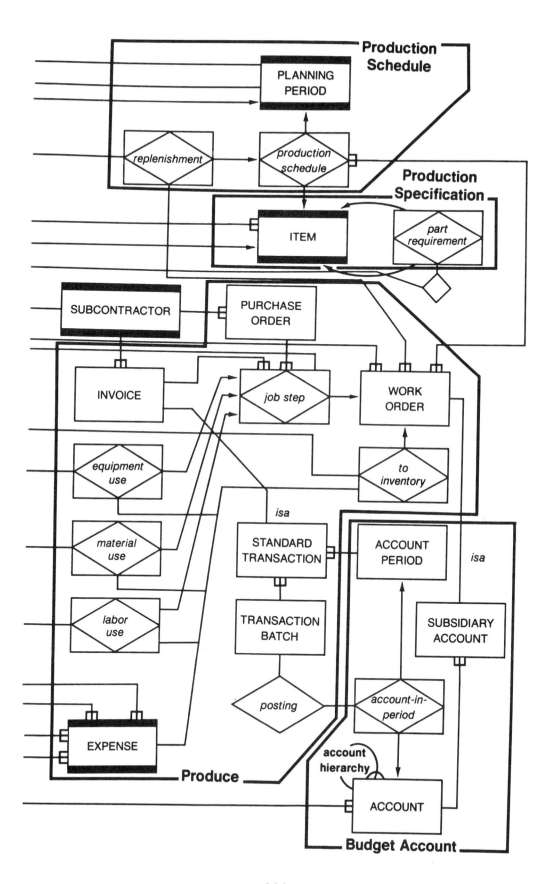

labor rate changes and productivity improvements made possible by better
equipment and production methods. It may be possible to divide the scrap and
spoilage expense into two categories, expense caused by worker error and expense caused by defective materials. The information structure could be further
decomposed to provide additional information on past and projected future
material usage. The overhead expense category covers a wide range of activities,
and information on some of those activities may be helpful in budget planning.
The entity type called Expense in Figure 8.3 refers to information about past
expenses; it could be considered planning information as well.

Product Specification

The Product Specification entity type is decomposed to Item and a recursive
relationship called *part requirement* in Figure 8.3. The term Item is used to represent either a finished product, a part, or a raw material. Thus, the construct
shown in Figure 8.3 for Product Specification provides for information about a
finished product and all of its parts.

The reason for linking a product to its parts is to provide for the information
required to manufacture and assemble the parts. Also, the parts and subassemblies must pass inspections and meet quality standards in order for the finished
product to satisfy its quality requirements.

Budget Account

The Budget Account of Figure 8.1 is decomposed in Figure 8.3 so that a budget
can be calculated for each accounting period. The budget for an account in a time
period is an attribute of the *account-in-period* relationship. Actual cost and expense totals are also attributes of this relationship. Thus, both the goal and the
measure of performance with respect to the goal are attributes of *account-in-
period*. A more complete explanation of the information structure for accounting
is given in the chapter on financial management.

Produce

The *produce* relationship of Figure 8.1 is decomposed in Figure 8.3 into a Work
Order entity type and a series of other relationships and entity types that identify details concerning the order and actions taken to complete it. Work orders
are generated by the MRP system; they implement plans defined in the *production schedule*. The relationship between Work Order and *production schedule* in
Figure 8.3 links a work order to two production schedule "entries": the one in
which the release of the work order is planned and the one in which the comple-
tion of the work ordered is expected. A work order is an order to produce a
certain quantity of one product or part (one item).

If all, or a portion, of the output resulting from a work order is planned to be
an inventory replenishment, then the Work Order occurrence is linked to the
appropriate *replenishment* relationship between *production schedule* and *inventory plan*. This link can be used to find the status of planned replenishment
actions for any inventory item. When the work order is completed (and the

items are delivered to the inventory location) then one or more *to-inventory* relationship occurrences are created. These occurrences are also linked to a Standard Transaction occurrence which is linked to a transaction and a series of *posting* relationship occurrences which record the transfer of material from the work-in-process account to the appropriate inventory account. Thus, the output of the production process is measured in terms of total cost and the quantity produced.

The relationship between Location and Work Order identifies the physical location of a given job (work order) at any time. This is important in a job shop where the job travels from one department to another, and operations are performed on it in each department. (To the extent that group technology has established a cellular organization of production, it is less important.) The *isa* relationship between Subsidiary Account and Work Order defines the work orders whose costs are totaled in a single work-in-process account. If there is more than one work-in-process account, then the event of moving a work order from an area covered by one account to an area covered by another needs to be recorded in the database and treated as an accounting transaction. This is not provided for in Figure 8.3.

The many-to-many relationship between Work Order and Operation is called *job step* in Figure 8.3. It represents the execution of an operation on a work order. Such facts as the times the operation was started and completed can be considered attributes of *job step*. But the resources used in performing the step (operation) must be modeled as attributes of relationships between Job Step and the appropriate resource entity type. In Figure 8.3, three examples of this type of relationship are shown; they are *labor use, equipment use,* and *material use.* In each case, the details about an instance of resource usage can be treated as attributes of the relationship. Resource usage is an important accounting event, and for this reason each of these relationships is linked by an *isa* relationship to a Standard Transaction occurrence. It can be set up so that there is an occurrence of *posting* for each instance of resource usage, and this correspondence can be mapped either by unique serial numbers or by one-to-one relationships (not shown in Figure 8.3).

It is possible that a work order is sent to a subcontractor in order for certain job steps to be performed. This constitutes a purchase of services from a supplier and requires a purchase order. When the work is completed, the subcontractor usually sends an invoice at the same time as the work is returned. For this reason, Purchase Order and Invoice entity types are shown in the *produce* shaded area of Figure 8.3.

The Standard Transaction and Transaction entity types represent accounting journal entries. Transaction identifies a batch of standard production transactions that occurred during a specified accounting period. The amounts posted to the cost, expense, and asset accounts are attributes of the *posting* relationship between Transaction and *account-in-period.*

The Expense entity type represents charges to production overhead accounts. Presumably, these are charges unrelated to any particular work order. However, to the extent that they can be allocated to work orders on some logical basis, such as labor hours or machine hours, they are debited to a specified account, and the total in the account is periodically allocated to work orders. The information structure required for the journal entries that allocate expenses to work orders is not shown in Figure 8.3. This structure is discussed in the chapter on financial management.

Labor

The Labor entity type of Figure 8.1 is decomposed in Figure 8.3 to show how the labor force is organized into job-positions, the qualification requirements of each job, and the individual workers. The Organizational Unit entity type (production department) is important because responsibility for achieving a goal is often assigned to a work center in production. The Job entity type identifies a certain type of position that has certain skill, education, and experience requirements. The Qualification entity type stands for any type of qualification that a job or operation or piece of equipment requires. It also can be used to define the qualifications that an employee has. It is important because certain operations should be performed only by workers with specific skills and experience.

The Employee entity is important for several reasons. It is important to record the work that each employee performs as a measure of productivity. For cost accounting purposes, the actual wage rate of the individual can be used to calculate the cost of a job step if the employee who performed the step is recorded. In Figure 8.3, the *labor use* relationship provides this link. For purposes of planning skills development (a type of Capacity Change) it is also necessary to work with information about individual employee skills and experience.

Facilities

The Facilities entity of Figure 8.1 is decomposed in Figure 8.3 to distinguish between equipment used to perform operations and the locations of that equipment. Location in this context should be interpreted to mean either an area in a building occupied by a department, a building, or a subcontractor site. A recursive relationship called *contains* is shown in Figure 8.3 to indicate that one location may be contained in another. The Other Facility entity refers to any other fixed asset used in operations; steam and power generating equipment and various nonproductive assets would fall into this category.

The relationship between Operation and Equipment defines the machines, tooling, and fixtures required to perform the operation. An important attribute of this relationship is the amount of time required to set up the equipment for the operation and the time per unit required to perform the operation.

Production Technology

The Production Technology entity type specializes to the Operation entity type in Figure 8.3. The techniques used to make an item are summarized as a series of operations by the operations planning subfunction of the technology function shown in Figure 8.2. It is the task of the operations function to execute this series of operations each time a work order for the item is received. The series of operations for a given item is defined by the many-to-many relationship in Figure 8.3 between Operation and Item.

The instructions for performing an operation are attributes of the entity type, but information about the equipment, labor, and materials required to carry out the operation is contained in relationships between the Operation entity type and Equipment, Job, and Part Requirement entity types, respectively. The relationship with Equipment can be used to define the time required to perform the operation. The relationship with Job can be used to define the labor hours it should take to set up the equipment for the operation and the equipment operator labor hours per unit of the item produced. The relationship with Part Requirement can be used to determine the quantity of a part that is added to the item by the operation.

The information about an operation provides the basis for calculating a labor and materials cost budget for the operation. All that is required is to multiply the Work Order quantity by the factors described in the previous paragraph. By adding these budget quantities for all operations for an item, the direct cost budget for the work order is obtained.

Material

The Material entity type of Figure 8.1 becomes the *inventory* relationship in Figure 8.3. This is a relationship between Location and Item. The quantity and value of the item at a location are two important attributes of this relationship.

The fact that an entity type decomposes into a relationship should not be surprising. The fact that the two entities are in different areas of Figure 8.3 may be confusing. The fact is that Figure 8.3 shows the final result and fails to indicate an intermediate step of the analysis in which Item and Location were each replicated in two places in the diagram. The appearance of Item and Location in the Material area of the diagram was eliminated in the interests of simplifying the drawing.

It should be noted that *inventory* is involved in relationships that define the planned and actual additions and withdrawals from the inventory of an item. The planned additions and withdrawals are attributes of the *inventory plan* relationship. The actual additions from production output is an attribute of the *to-inventory* relationship. (There may be other additions from outside suppliers.) Actual withdrawal is an attribute of the *material use* relationship.

TECHNOLOGY INFORMATION REQUIREMENTS

The technology function requires more information about some of the entities and relationships in Figure 8.3 than does the operations function. It is responsible for planning the operations and facilities used by the operations function, and this requires data on the alternatives to consider in planning as well as data on the performance of the production system as it exists.

Operations Planning

The operations planning subfunction requires more data about the items to be produced and the capabilities of the available equipment than does the operations function. Drawings of each part and assembly drawings are needed to plan each operation. Three dimensional views of parts and subassemblies make it easier to plan operations and to specify tolerances accurately.

Production Facilities Planning

The production facilities planning subfunction requires the capability to categorize occurrences of the Item entity type based on factors that relate to the operations required for its manufacture. This is needed to solve a basic problem of group technology (the technology of planning production facilities). The problem is how to define the items that should be produced on the same production "line" or cell. (A "line" can be described as the sequence of machines and other equipment required to perform the sequence of operations necessary to produce a category of items.) Interestingly, an article in *The Journal of Manufacturing Systems*[1] points out that the techniques commonly advocated to solve this planning problem are the same as the generalization and aggregation techniques used in database modeling. First, an organizing principle is postulated in group technology, then a hierarchical structure of subcategories based on that principle is developed. An example of a portion of a set of categories is shown in Figure 8.4. It is based on the Opitz Classification System.[2] (Opitz is the name of the person who developed the system.)

The percent (%) symbol in front of the top level breakdown in Figure 8.4 means that a decomposition of an aggregation is being defined. The part is viewed as an aggregation and Part Class 1, dimensions, material, initial form, and accuracy are defined to be aspects or components of the aggregation.

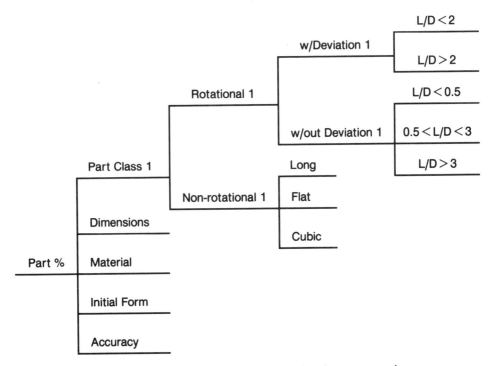

FIGURE 8.4. Example of group technology categories.

The breakdown of Part Class 1, on the other hand, does not have a % sign in front, which means that a specialization of a generalization is described. Rotational, and non-rotational, constitute an *isa* cluster linked to the Part Class I generalization.

Measurement Technology

The measurement technology subfunction requires information on the sensing and measuring devices used by the existing production equipment. Records on the calibration of these devices would be useful. There is also a need for a document retrieval capability so that tests and technical literature on any given measurement topic can be accessed when information on the topic is needed.

Quality Control

The quality control subfunction requires information on resource usage in order to trace defects back to their cause. The information structure of Figure 8.3 already records the equipment used in each operation and the employee who performed the operation. For quality control purposes, attributes should be added to the *material use* relationship in Figure 8.3 to identify the part numbers, or batch number, of each part or raw material used in a job step. Also, a Test Result entity type should be added to the database and linked to *job step* occurrences that are testing operations.

FACILITIES INFORMATION REQUIREMENTS

The facilities function requires information about the maintenance of equipment and other facilities. Information is required about the maintenance work that should be done, the work that is actually done, and the relationship between these two. The maintenance work that should be done can be derived as a decomposition of the Capacity Change entity type of Figure 8.1. The actual maintenance work is a specialization of the *produce* relationship.

The construction and installation subfunction plans and executes projects. It therefore requires a database than can store the goals of the projects, a plan for achieving them, and the resources devoted to the work of the project. The parts of the information structure of Figure 8.3 that are relevant to this project activity are the labor and facilities areas of the structure. For projects that modify or move an existing facility, many additional details would be required.

The security subfunction requires additional information about the facilities being protected and the equipment and staff available for protection purposes. An analysis of these requirements could lead to a significant decomposition of the Location and Equipment entity types shown in Figure 8.3.

SERVICES INFORMATION REQUIREMENTS

Each of the service subfunctions uses portions of the information described in Figure 8.3 and also has some additional information requirements of its own. The service function, as a whole, does not appear to have any general information requirements.

Change Control

The concept of a change in a product specification, or in production methodology, is an important new entity type that is required for this subfunction. The Change entity type needs to be related to the item or equipment or operation that is being changed. It also needs to be related to a plan that defines the things to be done to manage the change and who is responsible for doing them. Finally, provision should be made in the database design to record the status of the execution of the plan, what has been done, what remains, and is the change on schedule?

Personnel

The production personnel subfunction will require much of the same information structure as was described in Chapter 5 for any corporate personnel function. The information structure shown in Figure 5.4 is a reasonable starting point for modeling the information needs of this function. It should be noted that the decomposition of the Labor entity type shown in Figure 8.3 can be found in Figure 5.5 which is derived from Figure 5.4. Figure 5.5 gives further additions that could be made to the structure of Figure 8.3 for the production personnel subfunction.

One aspect of employee training that is particularly important in production should be noted. It involves rotating employees into different jobs so that each employee is capable of filling several different positions. Employee cross-training gives flexibility to the production system and makes it less susceptible to failures caused by the unexpected absence of individual employees. Management of the rotation process has information structure implications. The Employee entity type must be decomposed to show the experience and skills of each employee. Also, the Job entity type can be decomposed to show experience and skill requirements. The Qualification entity type in Figure 8.3 serves this purpose to a degree; Figure 5.5 shows how it could be further decomposed. From this data, position back-up analysis can be made that will show which positions are vulnerable, because only a few employees are qualified to fill the position.

Information Systems

The production information systems subfunction has extensive information requirements of its own, in much the same fashion as personnel. These are described in Chapter 11 and need not be reiterated here. But there are special characteristics of the system for capturing shop transaction data that should be described at this point.

The system for gathering work order status data as well as cost accounting and quality control data is an important information system subfunction. The operations data collection subfunction records the use of resources and the status of work orders. To capture the data in a timely manner requires specially designed terminals on the shop floor that are connected to micro- or minicomputers. The captured transaction data is processed daily to provide production reports showing orders completed, work-in-process, job costs, percent of machine and labor time used in direct production, absenteeism, spoilage, and other indicators of performance.

Operations data collection captures information about events and interprets it in terms of certain types of transactions. Four basic transaction types are labor, work order, material, and tooling transactions. In the case of labor, the system records when work on an operation is begun, when it is interrupted, when it ends, and the employee(s) involved. This data is then interpreted to define one or more labor transactions which become the basis for an occurrence of *labor usage* (Figure 8.3). This collection system requires a Labor Event entity type at the shop computer level; two or more labor events are then analyzed to determine that a labor usage transaction has occurred and that an occurrence of this entity type should be created in the main production database.

A work order transaction is the transfer of a job from one department to another. The departure of the work from one location and its arrival at another are recorded. The final transfer of the work to an inventory or shipping area can also be interpreted as a work order transaction. This is another example of an entity type required by the data collection system in order to track progress in the factory and in order to make appropriate updates to Work Order occurrences in the database.

A material transaction is the withdrawal of material from stock for use in making what has been ordered. In some cases, extra material may be returned to stock after an operation is completed, and this would be considered another material transaction. To make the *material usage* occurrences of Figure 8.3 more meaningful, the data collection system should consolidate the material usage reports it gets for any one item of material used in an operation into one *material usage* occurrence.

When an expensive tool is used in an operation, the fact of its withdrawal from tool storage and return to storage must be captured. If the life of the tool depends on the number of times it is used, the number of pieces (or impressions) made with the tool in a given operation may also be recorded. To handle this special information, it may be desirable to decompose the Equipment entity type of Figure 8.3 to identify a Tooling entity type.

Cost Accounting

Figure 8.3 represents the basic information structure required to account for direct costs. Resource usage is measured at the lowest possible level (the amount of a specific resource used in a job step on a work order) and can be aggregated for reporting purposes either by work order or by cost center (production organizational unit). By adding the *account hierarchy* recursive relationship to the Account entity type, the capability is provided to maintain these aggregations for the different levels in the organizational hierarchy. The relationship between Account and Organizational Unit allows a set of accounts to be set up for each cost center. This structuring of accounting information is further explained in Chapter 10.

In accounting for indirect costs and expenses, they are commonly first allocated to organization units (work centers) and then allocated to work orders. To record these allocations in a database, the bases for the allocations need to be defined as well as the individual allocations. The amount of an allocation base (labor hours, machine hours, or other base) for a given expense account and work order would be an attribute of a many-to-many relationship between Subsidiary

Account and *account-in-period*. The subsidiary account identifies the work order and the *account-in-period* occurrence identifies the expense account and accounting period.

INFORMATION REQUIREMENTS OF
JOB SHOP PRODUCTION CONTROL

In a functionally organized factory, individual work orders are moved from one work center to another as specified by a routing sheet. The complex flow of work-in-process that results requires a "job shop production control subfunction" to focus work on the most urgent orders. Job shop production control is a subfunction of the operations function that has some information requirements which are related to those of Figure 8.3. The purpose of this section is to explain the additional attributes and relationships required for the subfunction.

Once an order has been released and production operations begin, it is the responsibility of production control to monitor the progress of the order. In a production line arrangement this is easy because any delay in work on an order will quickly stop the whole line. A basic strategy of group technology is to organize as much work as possible as line production in order to provide automatic detection of delays. But it is not always economically reasonable to use line production, and when all work on an order cannot be done on one production line, the need arises for the production control subfunction to carefully control what is done.

Two basic techniques for controlling what is worked on are *flow control* and *priority sequencing*. The flow control method limits the work orders released to a production unit (department or work group) so that the total amount of work in the unit (measured in either labor or machine hours) does not exceed a target level. The target level is set so that some idle time (unused labor or machine time) will begin to occur when unanticipated problems arise with operations on one or more orders. This causes the management of the unit to take whatever action is necessary to solve the problems in order to eliminate the idle time charges.

To implement a flow control system requires that the database have certain features. One is the capability to store a flow control target level for each production department. Another is the capability to identify work orders that are being delayed until the next production department reduces its backlog of work below the target level.

The priority sequencing method puts the orders released to a production unit in the sequence on which they should be worked. Priority is usually based on three factors. One is the importance of delivering the finished work on time. Another is how far behind (or ahead of) schedule the work is. The third is the amount of production time required to complete the work (small orders often go before large orders). Exactly how these factors are combined to determine the relative priority given to an order at a point in time varies from one shop to another. In any case, the priority number becomes an attribute of the work order.

To evaluate whether a given order is on schedule, behind schedule, or ahead of schedule, data is needed about the operations that have already been performed on the order and the ones that remain. This information should be simple to obtain from the *job step* relationship of Figure 8.3. For each operation required to make the item, there will be one *job step* occurrence linked to the work order. As has already been noted, there can be various types of operations including machining, inspection, transport, assembly, packaging, and erection operations.

Information is needed about which orders are behind schedule and which are ahead. One way to structure this information is as attributes of the *job step* relationship. One attribute is the time by which the operation should be completed if the work order is to be completed on time. Another attribute is the earliest time by which the operation could be completed given its present status. Operations that should have been completed but have not been are late. Taking the first late operation on each late order and comparing the current time to the earliest time by which the operation could be completed provides a way of ranking orders in terms of lateness.

SUMMARY

In this chapter, the information structure of the requirements for production management is first developed. The CEO information structure of Figure 5.1 is decomposed to show the goals, resources, and the relationships between them that are of concern to the production function.

Next, the production function is divided into four subfunctions. The breakdown is based on the resources with which each subfunction is concerned. At least, the first three subfunctions reflect a responsibility for certain resources. The fourth subfunction represents a collection of special services provided to the other subfunctions.

The information structure for the operations subfunction of production is obtained by decomposing each of the entity types and relationships in the information structure for production as a whole. The decomposition of each of the entities and relationships of Figure 8.1 is designed to fit the specific kinds of data required to manage production on a day-to-day basis.

The impact of the information requirements of the other three production subfunctions on the structure of Figure 8.3 is discussed in general terms. It is shown that the technology, facilities and services subfunctions each have information requirements that partially overlap those of operations. The net effect of integrating the requirements of these three subfunctions with those of operations would be to clearly create a more complex structure than that shown in Figure 8.3.

Finally, it is noted that the operation function may include a production control subfunction that requires information about the priority of individual work orders, and about subgroups of work orders, that was not noted when the needs of operations as a whole were considered. The nature of this additional information structure is described in general terms.

REFERENCES

1. Billo, Richard E., Rob Rucker, and Dan L. Shunk, "Enhancing Group Technology Modeling with Database Abstractions," *Journal of Manufacturing Systems*, Society of Manufacturing Engineers, Vol. 7, No. 2, 1988.

2. Appleton, Daniel S., *Introducing the New CASA CIM Wheel*, Computer and Automated Systems Association of the Society of Manufacturing Engineers.

3. Gallagher, C. C. and W. A. Knight, *Group Technology Production Methods in Manufacture*, (New York: Halsted Press (a division of John Wiley & Sons)).

4. Tersine, Richard J., *Production/Operations Management*, (New York: Elsevier North Holland).

DISCUSSION QUESTIONS

1. What are the goals of production and how should they be represented in terms of entities and relationships?

2. What are the resources used in the production function and how should they be represented in terms of entity types and relationships in the information structure that describes the information requirements for production as a whole?

3. Compare and contrast the Item entity type about which the materials management function needs information and the Production Specification and Material entity types about which the production function needs information.

4. How should the *manage* relationship of Figure 5.1 be specialized for the production function?

5. How should the *plan* relationship be defined for the production subfunction?

6. Distinguish between the production planning and operations planning subfunctions.

7. Distinguish between the operations planning and production facilities subfunctions.

8. Distinguish between the change control and configuration control subfunctions.

9. Should production scheduling be considered a materials management or production subfunction?

10. Describe how the entity types and relationships of Figure 8.3 would be involved in recording the budgeted and actual direct labor costs for a work order and for a production department.

11. Where does information about scheduled maintenance of equipment and the consequent equipment down time belong in Figure 8.3?

12. How would information about who is qualified to operate each type of equipment be recorded in the information structure of Figure 8.3?

13. Does Figure 8.3 provide for planning the use of subcontractors to complete job steps? If not, how should the information structure be modified to allow for this?

14. Should the *material used* relationship involve *inventory plan* instead of *inventory*?

15. Should the Transaction Batch, Transaction, and *posting* relationship of Figure 8.3 be considered part of the decomposition of the *produce* relationship or part of the decomposition of the Budget Account entity type?

16. What is the problem addressed by group technology?

17. Can the production facilities planning subfunction use a DBMS that does not allow schema definition changes to be made as a routine operation (performed by users)? If not, why?

18. What does the quality control function need information about in addition to the entity types and relationships shown in Figure 8.3?

19. What augmentations and deletions does Figure 8.3 require to define the information requirements of the change control subfunction?

20. What changes are needed in Figure 8.3 to support the development of a production work force in which all employees are capable of performing many tasks?

21. For which entity types and relationships in Figure 8.3 are occurrences likely to be added or changed by the operations data collection subfunction?

22. Define the information required to implement the "flow control" method of production control and identify the entity (and relationship) attributes required to model this information.

23. What attributes does the *job step* relationship need for purposes of determining the lateness of a work order?

24. What changes in Figure 8.3 are needed to adapt it to the delivery of services rather than physical product?

9

Engineering

THE ENGINEERING FUNCTION

Engineering is the application of knowledge to the design of systems that meet human needs. The knowledge comes from the sciences and past engineering experience. The systems developed may be products, services, structures, or infrastructure such as roads and telephone systems. The human need may be manifested as a market opportunity or as a government requirement or program.

For the most part, engineering is evolutionary. Systems are refined as technology advances. A higher quality system displaces cruder versions of the system in most markets, unless the additional features of the new system are superfluous. But occasionally a new system concept emerges that develops sufficient demand to survive and evolve as a system type. The Video Cassette Recorder (VCR) is a relatively recent example of this.

Engineering is project-oriented. The system is first envisioned in terms of what it will do and the human need it will meet. The initial idea may come either from an engineer or from someone who is particularly aware of the human need. In any case, a sponsor for the development effort, who will fund the engineering work, must be found before the development project can proceed. The work is then performed as a project.

An engineering project may be undertaken by an individual, but it often is performed by a group with each member contributing an expertise required to design the system. There is a budget and schedule for the project. If the project is performed by a group, then there is likely to be a project leader, specific assignments for each member of the project team, and some means of group communication. The project organization is more elaborate for larger projects. Projects vary greatly in size.

One project can lead to another. A project to prepare a bid for a custom-designed system can lead to another project to design the system. A project to investigate a customer complaint can lead to a project to change the system design so as to eliminate the cause of the complaint. A project to design a better mouse trap may start with a project that studies all existing mouse traps and defines performance specifications for the new, improved mouse trap.

Engineering design must consider the economic viability of systems. The system must satisfy performance expectations of customers at a competitive price. This means that engineering includes consideration of market size and the problems of producing and distributing the system. Existing parts and subassemblies should be used, unless the cost savings of a new part will offset the cost of its development, production, and storage.

Testing and experimentation are important aspects of engineering. Most systems are too complex for their design to be based solely on theoretical knowledge. The performance of parts, the interactions between parts, and the interactions between the system and the environment can be only *approximately estimated* by theoretical models. To debug a conceptual design, a prototype is built and exercised to measure its performance under realistic conditions. The findings from these tests are used to refine the design.

INFORMATION STRUCTURE FOR ENGINEERING

In Chapter 4, the functional breakdown of the top-level function of Chief Executive Officer (CEO) includes engineering as one of the subfunctions for manufacturers of engineered products. So, it is appropriate to derive the information structure for engineering by decomposing the information structure for the CEO function shown in Figure 5.1.

A decomposition of Figure 5.1 that suits the information requirements of engineering is shown in Figure 9.1. The Goal entity type of Figure 5.1 is decomposed into three basic entity types (Performance Specification, Project Plan, and System Definition) and two generalizations (Proposed Objective and Project Objective). The Resource entity type is specialized into three basic types of resources (Market Segment, Financial Resource, and Technological Resource) and one generalization (Available Resource). The *manage* relationship of Figure 5.1 is specialized to a *project activity* relationship between Project Objective and both Technological Resource and Financial Resource. The *plan* relationship is specialized to a *develop system proposal* relationship between Proposed Objective and Available Resource.

The entity types and relationships shown in Figure 9.1 are intended to be general, yet specific enough to serve as guidelines for the design of engineering databases. The following comments about each entity in the figure should clarify their nature and scope.

PROPOSED OBJECTIVE

One objective of a development proposal is to define the objective of a development project. Another is to estimate what it will take to achieve project objectives. Accordingly, the Proposed Objective entity type is a generalization with two specializations. One is a description of the system that the project will design in terms of its performance characteristics. This is the Performance Specification entity

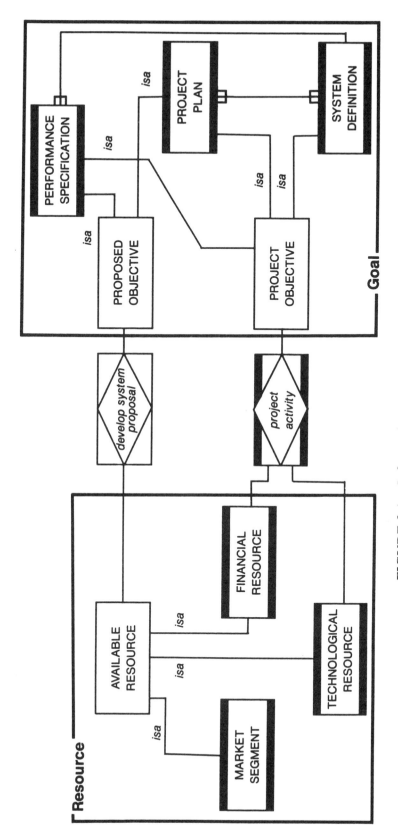

FIGURE 9.1. Information structure for engineering.

type. The other is a Project Plan that indicates the resources required to complete the project and the time required to complete it.

PERFORMANCE SPECIFICATION

The Performance Specification entity type is based on a distinction between a definition of what a system does and how it does it. A performance specification describes what a system does, not how it does it. This is in contrast to a system definition that describes the components of a system and how they interact.

A performance specification defines the nature of a system as a whole. It describes the functional capabilities of the system and how it appears to the user of the system. If the system is a truck, for example, the performance specification might include the dimensions and weight of the vehicle, its maximum load carrying capacity, its maximum acceleration rate and speed, and whether it has an automatic or manual transmission.

The performance specification may also define the economic performance of the system, including its price range, operating costs, and expected life. The total cost to produce and deliver the system might also be a part of the performance specification.

PROJECT PLAN

The Project Plan is the principal means of managerial control of the engineering function. It has two aspects, the schedule and the budget. The budget may be simply in terms of a dollar amount for each type of resource used on the project, or it may include cost targets for each category in a work breakdown structure. A work breakdown structure is a functional model of the project. In any case, the schedule and budget represent an important part of the objective for project managers.

SYSTEM DEFINITION

The System Definition entity type is a specification of the parts of a system and how they relate to one another. It is the system design. It describes how the system is made and how it functions. The electrical and thermodynamic characteristics of parts are specified as well as the material used in each part.

Geometric, electrical, and temperature tolerances may be specified on parts and subassemblies as necessary to achieve conditions described in the performance specifications for the system as a whole. Material specifications may include tolerances for the impurities or other characteristics of the material.

Various types of drawings may be used to define the system. Two-dimensional front, top, and side views, solid geometric drawings, cross sectional drawings, wiring diagrams, and assembly drawings are examples of ways to specify a part, subassembly, or complete system. Physical models may also be used to define the system.

Specification lists are another means of defining a system. A parts list identifies all of the parts in a system in terms of a part number, brief description, and the quantity of the part per system unit. A specification sheet can define important parameters of the system, such as its power consumption, weight, and environmental requirements.

PROJECT OBJECTIVE

The objectives of a development project can be of three types. One is the system definition that the project is chartered to create. A second is the project plan that defines the project budget and schedule for completing the system definition. A third is the system performance specifications that the system design should satisfy.

MARKET SEGMENT

A Market Segment is a group of potential users of a system (product or service). There are many points of information about a market segment that are relevant to the engineering subfunction of conceptual system planning. The size of the group is one basic attribute. The amount the users can justify paying for the system is another piece of information needed to calculate the price range within which the system must fit. Competitive products available to the group and their characteristics constitute another relevant aspect of market segment.

A market segment can be defined in any one of several ways, or in a combination of them. A market segment can include the customers reached through a certain distribution channel, such as a distributor and the retailer he serves. It can include the customers in a geographical region. Or, it can include the customers that have specified socioeconomic characteristics.

FINANCIAL RESOURCES

The financial resources available for an engineering project are an important consideration when planning engineering work. They place a limit on the project budget. For a major system development effort, it is often necessary to structure the development as a series of projects in which one project demonstrates the feasibility of the next. As feasibility is proven, financial resources become available for subsequent development efforts.

TECHNOLOGICAL RESOURCE

The Technological Resource entity is a generalization that includes many specializations. It includes the engineers and scientists who create the system concepts and designs. They may be employees of the enterprise or consultants, or they may belong to an independent organization that provides engineering services for the enterprise.

The existing system and part designs constitute a second type of technological resource. This means that the System Definition entity type shown in Figure 9.1 as part of the decomposition of Goal can also be considered a resource. Existing system definitions are a resource; the system definition that a project is developing is an objective.

Computers and engineering software available to the engineers and their computing staff can be treated as a technological resource. They are productivity tools for the system designers and testers.

The testing facilities and laboratories are a technological resource for the engineering function. The instances of this resource included in the database should be based on what is available to the project teams of the enterprise: Ownership of the facilities should not be a prerequisite to their being included in the database.

Test reports are another form of technological resource. Over a series of projects, an engineering organization can build an impressive collection of observations about the behavior of a certain class of systems under specified test conditions. If these observations are indexed and maintained in a form that makes it easier to find the previous results than to run the test again, then significant time and expense can be saved by the use of this resource.

Technological literature is an important resource for engineers. The published books and articles constitute an important part of this literature, but there are also project reports and unpublished articles that are useful. Finding the relevant material when it is needed may be a problem. Bibliographic databases can help. In many cases, however, a more specialized set of subject categories is required to locate the relevant material.

AVAILABLE RESOURCE

An Available Resource is an entity that can be used to either design, finance, or pay for an engineered system. A technological resource is one that is available to design the system. A financial resource is one that is available to finance the development project. A market segment is a resource that is available to ultimately pay for the newly created system.

PROJECT ACTIVITY

The relationship between Technological Resource and Project Objective in Figure 9.1 provides information about how resources are used to achieve the objectives of a project. The basic objective of a project is to create a system definition that satisfies a set of performance specifications. A secondary objective is to produce it according to a project plan. All information about project status, the resources used, and the intermediate results obtained, is considered information about the project activity.

Further decomposition is likely to reveal some one-to-many relationships between Project Objective (or one of its specializations) and Technological Resource.

DEVELOP SYSTEM PROPOSAL

The *develop system proposal* relationship provides for information about the process of showing how and why available resources should be used to develop a new or improved system. It is a relationship between available resources and a plan for a design and development project. Information about the investigations that are made to prepare such plans, and evaluations of such plans, is information about *develop system proposals*. Decomposition may reveal some one-to-many relationships between Proposed Objective (or one of its specializations) and Available Resource (or one of its specializations).

FIRST-LEVEL BREAKDOWN OF THE ENGINEERING FUNCTION

One functional breakdown principle that should be used is a breakdown by engineering discipline. The application of knowledge to the design of systems naturally breaks down by the body of knowledge being applied. Thus, mechanical engineering builds mechanical systems; electrical engineering builds electrical systems, and so forth. Knowledge is developed by concentrating attention on one system concept. The application of knowledge requires the same concentration.

This breakdown holds true not only for the conceptual design but for most prototype construction and testing activities as well. The purpose of physical models and computer simulations is to determine that a conceptual design, which is based on theory, functions as predicted by the theory. It is appropriate then that, because building the prototypes and testing them requires a knowledge of the theory being tested, model construction and testing should be broken down by discipline.

Many engineered products and services, however, represent integrated systems. Some, such as an electric motor, have electrical, mechanical, chemical, and acoustical aspects. Others, such as an electric water pump, are combinations of two systems, a motor and a pump.

Assuming that we are interested in the functional breakdown of engineering within the context of an enterprise that supplies products and services that are integrated systems, the breakdown should reflect both the need to function by discipline and the need to integrate different systems into a single product or service. This leads to the breakdown shown in Figure 9.2. In this breakdown, there are three subfunctions: discipline engineering, systems integration, and engineering administration.

DISCIPLINE ENGINEERING

This subfunction designs and tests single-discipline systems. Consider a radio, for example. It consists of four single-discipline systems: an electronic system, a power supply system, a speaker system, and a mechanical system. The electronic system detects the radio signal, amplifies it, and outputs it to the speaker system.

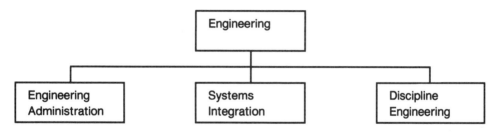

FIGURE 9.2.   First-level breakdown of engineering.

The power supply system provides electric power to the other systems. The speaker system converts the output of the electronic system to sound. The mechanical system houses the other systems and allows the user to select a radio signal and to adjust the sound volume.

SYSTEMS INTEGRATION

The systems integration subfunction is twofold. First, it provides leadership for development proposal efforts which result in system performance specifications and project plans. Second, it defines the interfaces between single discipline systems and coordinates the single discipline design activities within the framework of a development project.

The systems integration subfunction is required at every level in a hierarchy of systems except for the lowest level, which is the single-discipline system. There is a systems integration function in the design of a radio. There is another systems integration function in the design of a car which may contain a radio.

Systems integration work is performed in close cooperation with the marketing function in many organizations. Interaction with customers helps systems integrators understand the opportunities for new systems, and it can also give prospective customers confidence in the capabilities of the supplier.

ENGINEERING ADMINISTRATION

An engineering function requires a number of support services. Personnel, accounting, facilities management, purchasing, and information systems services are major examples of this subfunction. The purpose of this subfunction is to facilitate the execution of the other two subfunctions.

Engineering administration is not a pure engineering subfunction. It consists of a series of functions that have a subfunction relationship to two different functions. Engineering personnel, for example, is a subfunction of both personnel and engineering. Most of these dual subfunctions are discussed in other chapters of this text and need no further explanation in this chapter.

INFORMATION STRUCTURES FOR SECOND-LEVEL ENGINEERING FUNCTIONS

The information structures for the two pure engineering subfunctions can be derived by decomposition of the entities and relationships of Figure 9.1. The information requirements of engineering administration can be developed most easily by using both an engineering information structure and the information structure for the other function involved. In this section, the engineering information structure appropriate for engineering administration subfunctions is described.

AN INFORMATION STRUCTURE FOR DISCIPLINE ENGINEERING

A decomposition of the information structure for the engineering function, shown in Figure 9.2, that is designed for the requirements of a single engineering

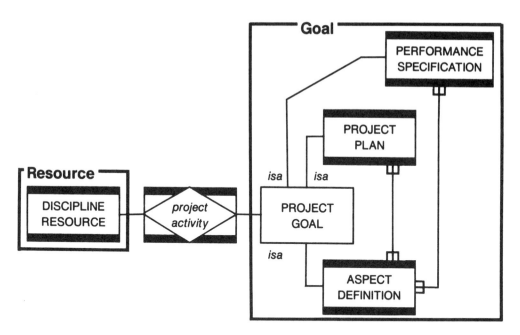

FIGURE 9.3.   Information structure for discipline engineering.

discipline is shown in Figure 9.3. The entity types and relationships could be specialized easily to any engineering discipline, such as mechanical engineering, electrical engineering, or chemical engineering.

The only resource type of entity shown is Discipline Resource. This is a specialization of Technological Resource in Figure 9.1. Discipline resource includes all of the kinds of resources that Technological Resource includes, but in each case, the resource is discipline specific. Thus, discipline resource includes the engineers and scientists of a specific discipline, and it includes the existing system designs produced by that discipline.

The goal information structure in Figure 9.3 differs from that of Figure 9.1 in only two respects. One is the specialization of System Definition to a series of Aspect Definitions. The other is the elimination of the Proposed Objective entity type which is not required because the development of system proposals are not a responsibility of the discipline engineering function.

An aspect definition is a description of the system from a single discipline viewpoint. Examples of occurrences of this entity type for an automobile design would be a description of the electrical system, a description of the mechanical aspects of the body, a description of the dynamics of the suspension system, and so forth.

The only relationship between the goal and resource information structures in 9.3 is *project activity*. This entity type must eventually be decomposed to show all project labor and materials expenses, meetings, and design decisions. The *development system proposal* relationship is not considered relevant to the discipline engineering role.

AN INFORMATION STRUCTURE FOR SYSTEMS INTEGRATION

The information structure of Figure 9.1 is appropriate for the systems integration function. The systems integration function does not require as much technological detail as the discipline engineering function, but it does require consultation with many types of discipline engineers, and it could require access to the other kinds of technological resources already described.

AN INFORMATION STRUCTURE FOR ENGINEERING ADMINISTRATION

Engineering administration, particularly with regard to the accounting and personnel subfunctions, is concerned with the use of technological resources according to the project plan. This means that engineering administration needs a more detailed information structure for these two entity types and their relationships.

A decomposition of Project Plan is shown in Figure 9.4. It is appropriate for both project cost accounting and project scheduling. It involves two entity types, Planned Task and Milestone. A planned task is any node in a work breakdown structure. A milestone is a planned project status condition in which certain planned tasks have been completed and work on other planned tasks can begin.

An example of a work breakdown structure is shown in Figure 9.5. The work breakdown structure describes a radio design project which has already been used as an example in our discussion of discipline engineering. A work breakdown structure is similar to a functional model as described in Chapter 4, but it is not the same. A work breakdown structure is a strict hierarchy. It shows every occurrence of every function, whereas in a functional model a given function is shown only once, although it may be a subfunction of several functions in the model. In Figure 9.4, this hierarchical relationship between planned tasks is indicated by the one-to-many recursive relationship labeled *work breakdown structure.*

Two relationships between Planned Task and Milestone are shown in Figure 9.4. One defines the planned tasks that must be completed before a milestone is reached; this is labeled *prerequisites* in the figure. The other defines the planned tasks that can begin once the milestone has been reached and is labeled *next* in

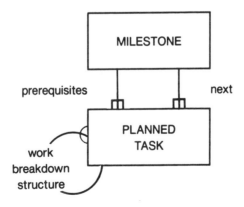

FIGURE 9.4.   Decomposition of project plan.

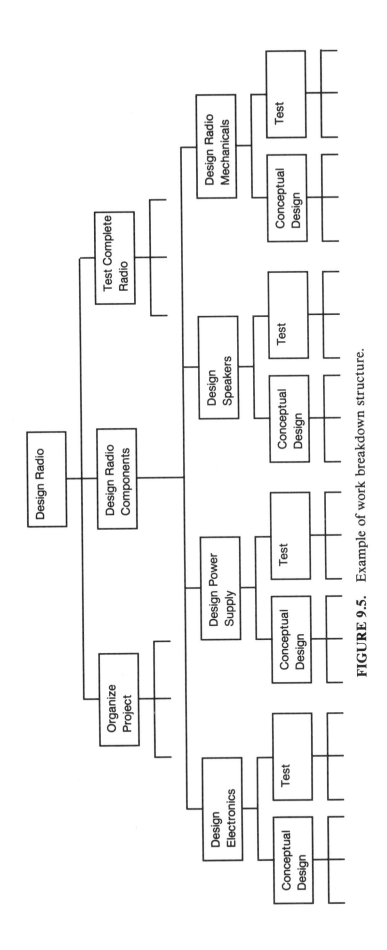

FIGURE 9.5. Example of work breakdown structure.

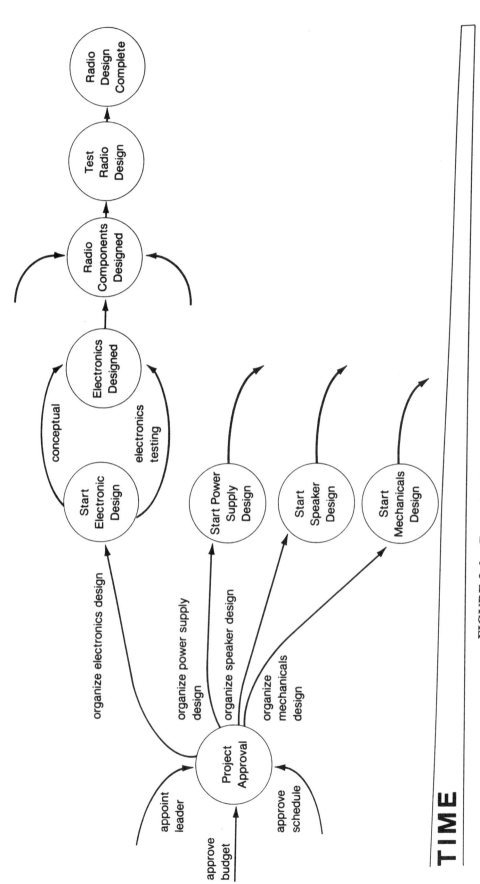

FIGURE 9.6. Example of production schedule chart.

the figure. An example of these two relationships is shown in Figure 9.6 which is a partial view of a PERT diagram of the radio design project. Milestones are shown in circles and planned tasks are represented by arrows.

The information structure for engineering administration is obtained by decomposing certain entity types in Figure 9.1 and omitting others. The Project Plan is decomposed as shown in Figure 9.4. The Technological Resource entity type is decomposed as shown in Figure 9.7, which shows the entire information structure for engineering administration. The Document specialization of Technological Resource in Figure 9.7 is intended to include both test reports and all other relevant technological literature. From the viewpoint of administration, the significance of the Document entity type is that it is the unit maintained in a document library which is an engineering administration responsibility.

In Figure 9.7, *project activity* is specialized to *resource requirement* and a relationship between Financial Resource and Planned Task. The relationships are shown as generalizations because eventually, for accounting purposes, a distinction must be made between the planned resource requirement, orders (or reservations) for the resource, the receipt or use of the resource, and charges for the resources used.

SECOND-LEVEL BREAKDOWN OF ENGINEERING FUNCTION

Each of the three subfunctions of engineering already identified can be further subdivided. This is done in Figure 9.8. Systems integration is shown with two subfunctions, discipline engineering with three, and engineering administration with six.

One important facet that Figure 9.8 does not depict is function replication. Some of the subfunctions in this breakdown are replicated for each project and others are not. The discipline subfunction (and all of its subfunctions) is replicated for each discipline (electrical, electronic, optical, mechanical, acoustical, thermal, civil, chemical, biological, and software engineering). As far as information structure definition is concerned, this is only a problem when the information requirements are different for different replications, which is the case for discipline replications.

SYSTEMS INTEGRATION SUBFUNCTIONS

Two system integration subfunctions were identified in our definition of this function. Identifying system development (or improvement) opportunities, analyzing their potential, and preparing project plans is one subfunction which is called system proposal in Figure 9.8. The other involves systems integration work on engineering projects.

The development of system proposals is a subfunction that involves marketing considerations. The functional breakdown of the marketing function shown in Figure 6.6 includes product planning as one of the subfunctions of internal marketing. That marketing subfunction and the engineering subfunction of developing system proposals are closely related. Ideally, the marketing and engineering functions collaborate in the development of a system proposal, with marketing defining system performance requirements and an estimate of market

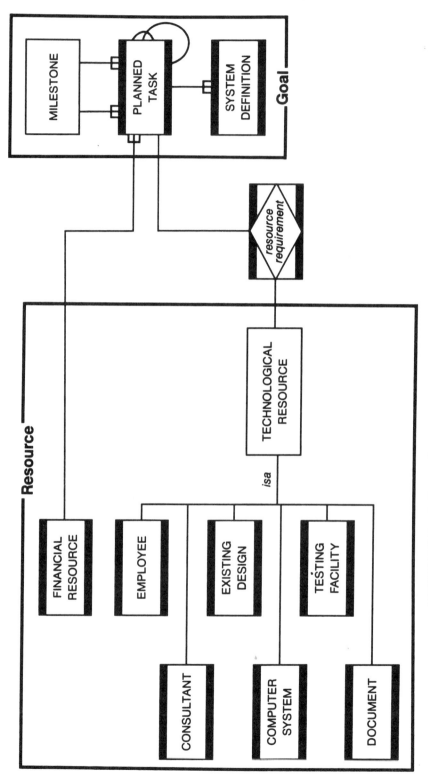

FIGURE 9.7. Information structure for engineering administration.

260

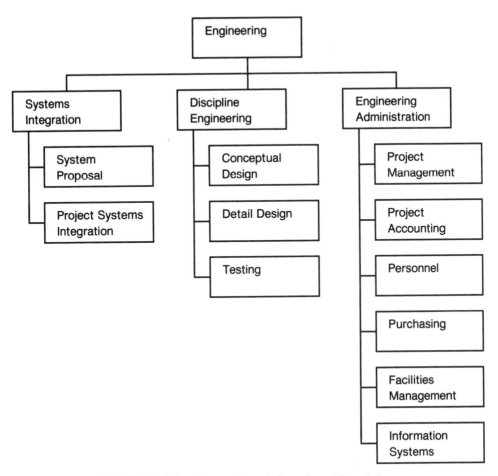

FIGURE 9.8. Second-level functional breakdown.

potential and engineering determining technical feasibility, providing proto-types, and proposing a development project plan.

The project systems integration subfunction theoretically requires a "super-engineer" who understands all of the engineering disciplines involved in a proj-ect. In practice, there are two mitigating factors. One is the fact that for most projects one engineering discipline is of prime importance. Other disciplines are necessary but they do not provide the basic conceptual model for the system. In the case of the radio, for example, electronics was certainly of central importance to the first designs in each era of radio designs. However, given a certain state-of-the-art in radio electronics, there certainly could be design improvement projects in which size reduction or better sound was the main objective, in which case, a mechanical engineer or an audio system engineer would probably be given the systems integration responsibility.

The other mitigating factor is the importance of communication and teamwork to the integration of systems on an engineering project. The best method for integrating systems takes into account the essential requirements imposed on the system by each engineering discipline. A good communicator can identify these essential requirements and perform the system integration work through team-work rather than through individual brilliance.

Another facet of project systems integration is adapting a system design to the conditions of production. With the growing importance of automation, the design of production processes for a product is becoming as important as designing the product itself.

Producibility Analysis

Manufacturing engineers plan the production operations required to produce each part and to assemble each subassembly and the final system. Machines, tools, jigs, fixtures, and software needed to efficiently perform each operation are specified. Testing, inspection, and transporting activities as well as production operations are planned. Additional drawings and instructions may be prepared to clarify how to make and assemble the parts and subassemblies.

If a group technology approach is taken, each part and subassembly will be classified as a member of an existing group if possible. All members of a group are produced by the same production unit using a fixed sequence of operations.

Producibility analyses may result in suggestions for change in the design to facilitate production. A change in the definition of subassemblies may be proposed to solve assembly or testing problems. Recommendations may be made to redesign a part so that it fits into a production pattern or so that the need for a certain type of machine is avoided.

DISCIPLINE ENGINEERING SUBFUNCTIONS

In this discussion about the subfunctions of a single discipline of engineering, two important issues are (1) the difference between conceptual design and detailed design and (2) the interactions between the two subfunctions, and with project systems integration.

Conceptual Design

A conceptual design describes the parts of the system to the extent necessary to determine system capabilities, but it does not define them in the detail that is necessary for production and assembly. Conceptual design is the first step in the system design process. It is planning oriented. In addition to a system description per se, it should include the analysis of how effectively the proposed system concept meets system performance specifications.

The original conceptual design may have to be altered if detailed design, testing, producibility analysis, or systems integration detects problems that can best be solved by changes in the overall system design. Thus, conceptual design is a subfunction that must be performed at an early stage in an engineering project, and then revised as necessary during the remainder of the project.

Detailed Design

The parts and subassemblies of a system eventually must be defined in complete detail. This is done in two stages. First, design engineers define subassemblies and consider each subassembly and each part in it. Subassemblies and parts that are commercially available (or should be procured with a custom-manufacturing contract) are identified and specified in terms that are sufficient for procurement purposes.

The other subassemblies and parts are specified in the detail necessary for manufacturing planning. The "rigged position"* of each subassembly and part must be shown, in addition to the complete description of each part or subassembly.

Second, buyers and manufacturing engineers study the specifications prepared by design engineers and raise questions about any ambiguities, contradictions, or difficulties they find. Subassembly and part definitions are revised as necessary to resolve problems.

In specifying parts, the design of new parts should be avoided. Aside from the expense of design time, the design of a new part implies additional testing, production planning, tooling, inventory, and spare parts cataloging expenses. Providing an information system that makes it easy for the design engineer to find information about existing parts so that designing new parts is not necessary is one important contribution that engineering information systems can make to the engineering function.

Testing

The plans formulated in conceptual and detail design are tested at many stages in their development. Models of the system can be tested in various ways. Prototypes can be used for more realistic testing of system performance. They can be tested by customers or they can be tested in a laboratory setting.

Production plans and equipment should be tested. Such tests identify additional tools or instructions that are needed. They may reveal missing operations that must be performed. They may provide additional information on the cost of an operation.

Testing often results in changes in design. Managing the process of evaluating test results, deciding whether additional tests are necessary, making design change decisions, and implementing design changes and their ramifications is a critical aspect of new product innovation. If it is not well managed, inconsistencies occur in the systems produced, obsolete inventory develops, and the reputations of the system and those associated with it are impaired.

ENGINEERING ADMINISTRATION SUBFUNCTIONS

The six subfunctions of engineering administration shown in Figure 9.8 will not be discussed in detail here. All, except for project management and facilities management, are described in other chapters.

Project management as a subfunction differs from project systems integration, although both functions may be performed by the same person. Project management is responsible for completing the project on time and within budget. It requires information about the Goal (Figure 9.7) and the *resource requirement* relationship. On the other hand, project systems integration is concerned with

---

* The "rigged position" is the position of the part in the system or subassembly.

the technical problem of integrating a series of separate system definitions. It requires information about System Definition (Figure 9.1) and Performance Specifications.

THIRD-LEVEL ENGINEERING INFORMATION STRUCTURES

The information structures required for the systems integration and discipline engineering subfunctions are discussed in this section. Derivation of the structures for the systems integration subfunctions is relatively straightforward. The information structure for the discipline engineering subfunctions is more difficult to describe. So, in this case, the discussion is concentrated on the most difficult part of the problem, namely decomposing the Aspect Definition entity type.

The information requirements of the engineering administration subfunctions involve the structure of Figure 9.7 in combination with structures from other chapters where the administrative function is considered in detail. The adaptation of the appropriate structure in the other chapters (Chapters 5, 7, 10, and 11) to the needs of engineering is left to the reader.

INFORMATION STRUCTURE FOR THE SYSTEM PROPOSAL FUNCTION

The information structure for the system proposal subfunction can be seen in Figure 9.1. It is the *develop system proposal* relationship. This means that it includes the Available Resource entity type and its specializations and the Proposed Objective entity type and its specializations.

A more detailed depiction of this structure would certainly include a decomposition of Technological Resource, Financial Resource, and Market Segment. The decomposition of Technological Resource would include Engineer, Consultant, Existing Design, and Testing Facility as entity types. The reason for identifying Test Facility is that it might be used to build a prototype of the new system concept as an aid in evaluating its market potential.

INFORMATION STRUCTURE FOR THE
PROJECT SYSTEMS INTEGRATION FUNCTION

The information structure for the project systems integration subfunction is shown in Figure 9.9. It appears to be similar to Figure 9.7 which is for engineering administration. There are some differences, however, in the two structures, and a more detailed consideration of the information about the entity types and relationships (in other words, the attributes) used by the two subfunctions would show that they have very little in common. Project systems integration deals with technical design issues, whereas engineering administration deals with issues in accounting, staffing, and facilities management.

The *used* relationship in Figure 9.9 is for design documentation purposes. It links the system definition specifications to test reports and any other technical documentation used in arriving at the design decisions.

The most important entity type for project system integration purposes is System Definition. Systems integration issues and decisions are facets of

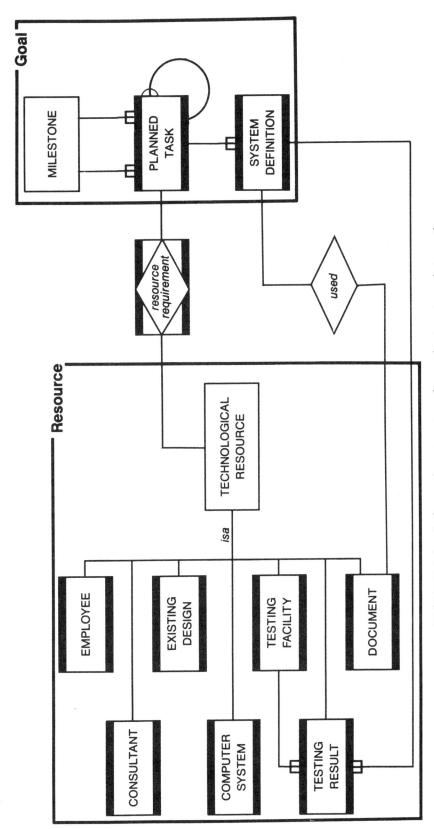

FIGURE 9.9. Information structure for project systems integration.

system definition. As is explained in the next subsection, this entity type is often considered a database itself. It is the database of what is commonly called a Computer-Aided-Design (CAD) system. Figures 9.1 and 9.9 indicate how this CAD database should eventually be integrated with other aspects of an engineering database.

THE DECOMPOSITION OF SYSTEM DEFINITION

The subfunctions of discipline engineering in Figure 9.8 are conceptual design, detail design, and testing. The relationship between conceptual design and detail design is similar to the relationship between a function and its subfunctions or an entity type and its decomposition. Detail design fills in the details in a conceptual design.

This design work may create new entity types. In the same way that a decomposition identifies new entity types (new sets of attributes), a design effort may create a product that has attributes not possessed by any of the existing product designs. The system defined by a design project can be viewed as an occurrence of some entity type and that entity type may be a new one.

Unlike all of the other functions and subfunctions that have been considered to this point, this design work defines the attributes of one or more entity types. It cannot be assumed that design work simply creates occurrences of previously defined entity types. It must be presumed that it creates new entity types, although it may simply create another occurrence of an existing entity type.

To accommodate this information requirement, the decomposition of System Definition must include an information structure that defines the entities and relationships required to define a system (product or service). Each system designed potentially requires a different database (in the traditional sense). However, an object-oriented database may allow data structures that permit each occurrence of a system definition to be composed of different entities and relationships. The database definition information structure must allow the designer to define the entity types and relationships of a system.

Metasystem Information Structure

The entity types of the information structures that define a system are: (1) the entity types of the system, (2) their attributes, and (3) the relationships between the entity types. Therefore, the information structure that will allow a system designer to define system attributes is one that consists of these three entity types and their relationships (Figure 9.10).

One attribute that each of the three entity types in Figure 9.10 should have is name. The Entity entity type might also have a rule for locating instances of the entity in storage as another attribute. The Attribute entity type should have a data type specification and an attribute definition as additional attributes. Possible additional attributes of the Relationship entity type are the cardinality of the relationship and the rule of association among the entity types involved in the relationship.

The two relationships labeled *key-1* and *key-2* are used to define the attributes of entities and the sort key of relationships, respectively. In both cases, an important attribute of the two keys is one that identifies the occurrences of Attribute that are to be set up as access keys for the entity or relationship.

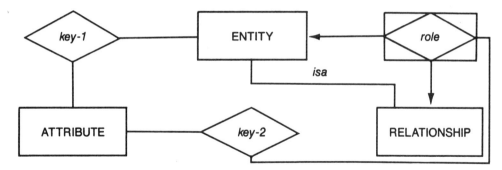

FIGURE 9.10. Meta-system information structure.

The *role* relationship between Entity and Relationship in Figure 9.10 has an occurrence for each entity occurrence that is involved in a relationship. Attributes of the *role* relationship would include whether participation in the relationship is mandatory or optional and the cardinality of the entity type's participation in the relationship.

The *isa* relationship in Figure 9.10 is for many-to-many relationships. Relationship is considered a specialization of Entity in this case.

As an example, consider the leg of a table (Figure 9.11). Viewed as a system to be designed, the leg involves several entity types and relationships. One instance of the Entity entity type is the leg itself without any holes for fasteners to attach

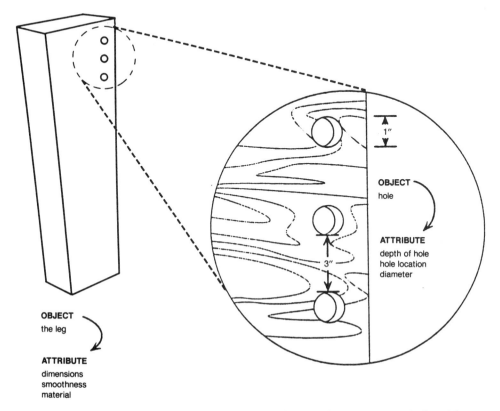

FIGURE 9.11. Example of table leg entities, attributes, and relationships.

it to the table, or to attach a glider to it. Some plausible attributes of this entity type are the type of wood of which the leg is made, its top and bottom end diameters (assuming it is round) and the smoothness of the surface. Another instance of the Entity entity type is a drill hole. Attributes of this entity type would be the depth and diameter of the hole. An instance of the Relationship entity type would be a relationship between leg and drill hole. If this is a many-to-many relationship, one of its attributes would be the location of the hole in the leg. This attribute would be defined as an Attribute occurrence in the structure of Figure 9.10 and this occurrence would be connected to a third entity type occurrence that is the "hole in leg" generalization linked to the relationship by the *isa* relationship.

There is no special need for the *key-2* relationship in this example. It could be used, however, to specify the sequence in which the holes in a given leg are listed, and the sequence in which the legs that have the same hole are listed.

Template

The metasystem information structure of Figure 9.10 can be used to define any number of what are called *templates*. A template can be defined as a set of Entity occurrences that apply to a single product or system. All product designs based on a given template have the same attributes organized into the same set of entity types and relationships.

To apply this metasystem information structure to the needs of engineering design, it has to be embedded in a larger information structure. In this larger information structure, it is important to have a template defined in terms of the entity types it involves and their relationships. To do this, we define Template to be an entity type and link it to the Entity entity type, as shown in Figure 9.12. For any given instance of Template, the structure in Figure 9.12 defines the attributes involved in a system concept and how they are organized into entity types and relationships.

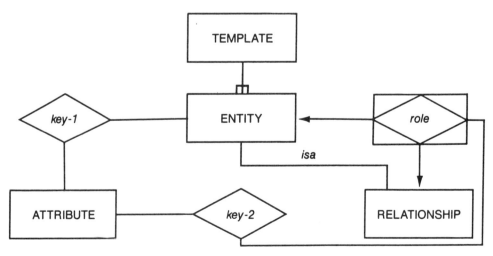

FIGURE 9.12.   Information structure for a template.

Concept Refinement

A template is not necessarily complete. Particularly, at the conceptual design stage in a project, there may be one or more templates, none of which is complete. The design of a system progresses through a series of design refinements, some of which are tentative and will be discarded later.

In a design team environment, it is particularly important to maintain the identity of concept refinements for a specified period until the refinement has either been accepted as a basic part of a template or modified or rejected in favor of an alternative refinement. To permit this, we create a Concept Refinement entity and link it to the Template occurrence it refines and to the metasystem information structure, as shown in Figure 9.13.

The management of concept refinements involves some complexities. Two occurrences of Concept Refinement can be independent, dependent, or incompatible. The system that manages the integration of concepts refinements into a template must be able to distinguish between these three cases and integrate them in an appropriate manner. If two refinements are independent, they can be integrated into the template independently. If they are dependent, they must be integrated in a certain order because one of the refinements is a refinement of the other refinement. If the two are incompatible, then a choice must be made; both refinements are not possible. A refinement algebra is developed which can be used to handle any number of refinements in a systematic manner.[1]

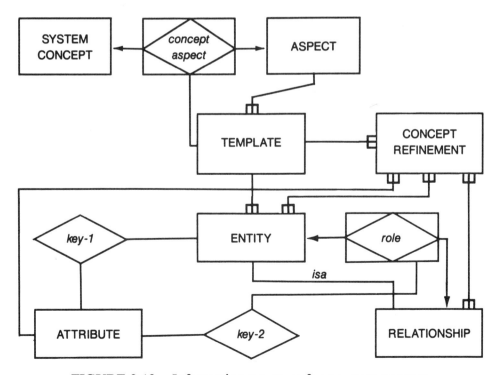

FIGURE 9.13. Information structure for a system concept.

Aspect

It is often important to analyze and describe a system in more than one way. For example, a bridge design must be described in one way to analyze its load-bearing capacity and in another way to calculate the amount of steel required for construction. For this reason, the System Definition decomposition must provide for multiple descriptions.

An aspect of a system or product concept is a certain way of defining the system. This implies that certain entity types and relationships are used in defining an aspect of a system. A Template occurrence will normally reflect a single aspect of a system. Therefore, in Figure 9.13, aspect is modeled as an entity type and linked to Template by a one-to-many relationship. The different Template occurrences linked to a single Aspect are the design concept alternatives, viewed from the single aspect, that are being considered by the design team.

This concept of system definition aspects is broad enough to include the System Performance Specification entity type shown in Figure 9.3. Defining a system in terms of its performance requirements involves considering the system from another aspect. This means that the decomposition of System Definition can be considered a decomposition of System Performance Specification as well. It is desirable that both the performance capabilities and the performance requirements of a system be defined by one information structure.

System Concept

The purpose of the System Concept entity type is to define a single design concept alternative for a single system. In Figure 9.13, it is shown in a many-to-many relationship with Aspect, called *concept aspect*. The *concept aspect* relationship has a one-to-one relationship with Template. This implies that an occurrence of System Concept will be associated with a Template alternative for each aspect that must be taken into account when describing the system concept.

It should be understood, however, that a System Concept is not a single, well-defined design. It represents all of the designs that can be defined using the entity types, relationships, and attributes of the Template occurrences linked to the System Concept via the *concept aspect* relationship.

Version

A version of a system concept is a single, well-defined design. The version is defined in terms of a series of Version-Aspect occurrences, one for each aspect that is linked to the system concept. Each Version-Aspect occurrence is a complete definition of one aspect of the system in terms of the entity types and relationships of the appropriate template.

Using the example of the table leg cited earlier, a Version occurrence would define specific values for all of the attributes of the Leg entity type, and for the attributes of the occurrences of the Drill Hole entity type. It would also use the two occurrences of the relationship between the leg and hole entity types to define where the holes are to be located in the leg.

Figure 9.14 depicts the Version-Aspect "entity type" and its relationships to the other entity types of the System Definition decomposition. It is important

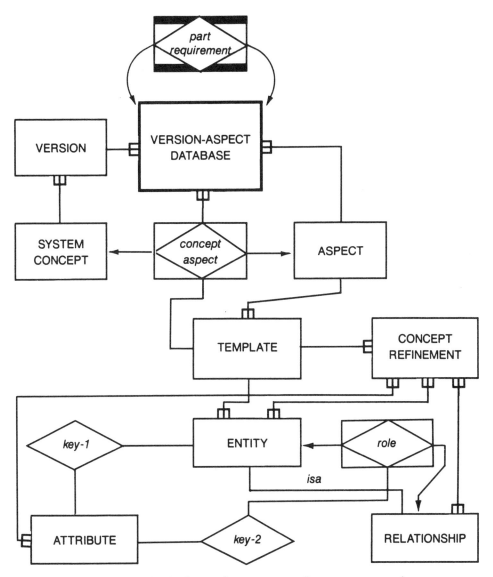

FIGURE 9.14. Information structure for a system version.

to understand the meaning of the generalization symbol on the Version-Aspect entity type in Figure 9.14. It means that this entity type is really the database required to define an aspect of the system being designed.

But Version-Aspect cannot be decomposed because its decomposition is variable. It varies with each aspect of each system concept that may be defined during an engineering design project. Each decomposition is defined by the system designer as he defines the design on a CAD system.

The nature of Version-Aspect implies that the database described by Figure 9.14 cannot be implemented using a traditional Database Management System (DBMS). It requires a DBMS that can treat the database schema as a variable (an "object" in the object-oriented approach).

There is another entity type, sometimes recommended as a part of this type of database, which is not shown in Figure 9.14. It is a Version Refinement entity type. Its purpose is to identify version alternatives that are studied in the process of defining a version. Because of the exploratory nature of most system design work, the capability to keep track of several design alternatives seems desirable. Version refinement is not shown in Figure 9.14, but not because we don't recommend it, but rather because it is not possible to show the relationship between Version Refinement and Version-Aspect easily. Version Refinement must link to the specific attributes in a decomposed Version-Aspect occurrence that are changed by the refinement.

Assembly

We have referred to the system being designed as though it were an atomic object, not composed of parts. This was to maintain simplicity while other basic facets of the way the design function must work with information were being described.

Most designed objects, and certainly all designed systems, are assemblies of parts and subassemblies. The word *system* implies parts. A table consists of a top and some legs, at least. A car consists of thousands of parts.

The recursive relationship in Figure 9.14 labeled *part requirement* enables the database to define systems that consist of parts. In this treatment, a part is simply another system. One system is linked to all of the parts and subassemblies of which it is composed. A system that has no parts (a raw material or purchased part) does not participate in this recursive relationship as an owner of a list of parts. It will participate, however, as a part going into a higher level system.

Part requirement is shown as a generalization in Figure 9.14 because it is the determinant of information about exactly how the part is attached to, or otherwise related to, the higher level assembly of which it is a part. The information about how two parts fit together (the "rigged position" of the part) has all the complexity of an assembly drawing. On assembly drawings, the points on two objects that should be together are usually shown by connecting them with dashed lines. This type of association between geometric points can be recorded in a database either by one-to-one relationships or by an "association record" set up to define two related points.

SUMMARY

The information structures for the engineering function developed in this chapter rest on the information structure postulated for the chief executive officer in Chapter 5. This structure contains the two entity types and two relationships shown in Figure 5.1. It is possible to trace all of the structures defined in this chapter to the components of the structure for the CEO information requirements. Thus, the chapter describes an engineering database design that is well-integrated with the information needs of top management.

The first-level breakdown of engineering identified three subfunctions: systems integration, discipline engineering, and engineering administration. The fact that the design of most products requires the application of multiple engineering disciplines is the basis for treating systems integration as a separate subfunction.

Information structures for two of the three first-level subfunctions are derived from the information structure for engineering as a whole which is shown in Figure 9.1. The third subfunction, systems integration, requires the full scope of information defined in Figure 9.1. To obtain the structure for engineering administration, the Project Plan entity type of Figure 9.1 is decomposed so that information about the budget and schedule for a design project is provided.

A breakdown of the three first-level subfunctions is developed and summarized in Figure 9.8. Eleven subfunctions are identified at this level. Most of these subfunctions support functions whose information requirements are described in other chapters.

The third-lev1l information structures are derived for the subfunctions of systems integration and discipline engineering. The information structure required for discipline engineering (and for some facets of systems integration) is shown to be different from the other information structures that have been considered. It is different because a part of the structure must be treated as variable; that is, it cannot be defined as a constant structure that is appropriate for all system design work.

REFERENCES

1. Ketabchi, M. A., and V. Berzins, *The Theory and Practice of Representing and Managing the Refinements, Alternatives, and Versions of Composite Objects*, Computer Science Dept., University of Minn., TR 85-40, October 1985.

DISCUSSION QUESTIONS

1. What specialization or disaggregation of the *plan* relationship of Figure 5.1 is appropriate for the engineering function?

2. What is the difference between Proposed Objective and Project Objective entity types in Figure 9.1?

3. In what sense is a performance specification a project objective?

4. Which of the three subfunctions of engineering shown in Figure 9.2 contains system testing and experimentation as a subfunction?

5. Why does the Discipline Resource entity type in Figure 9.3 not include market segment or financial resource information?

6. Would it be better to treat systems integration as a subfunction of engineering administration or discipline engineering rather than as a separate first-level engineering subfunction?

7. What is the appropriate characterization of the information requirements for the systems integration subfunction of engineering?

8. Which parts of Figure 9.4 relate to budgeting and which parts concern project scheduling?

9. Why is every occurrence of a subfunction (planned task) shown as a separate subfunction in a work breakdown structure, whereas in a functional model multiple occurrences of the same subfunction are linked together?

10. Should the product planning subfunction of Figure 6.6 and the system proposal subfunction of Figure 9.7 be considered as two separate subfunctions or as one subfunction?

11. What are the differences between the conceptual design and detailed design subfunctions?

12. The testing of the system, and subsystems, with respect to particular engineering aspects (disciplines) is provided for in Figure 9.8, but what about integrated systems testing? Where does this fit in Figure 9.8?

13. Consider a system that has already been designed that has a microcomputer embedded in it as a subsystem. There is a computer program designed to be executed by the microcomputer and an executable version of the program is fed into each microcomputer in each copy of the system that is produced. Where would the source code, object code, and executable code for the program be stored in the conceptual database as defined in Figure 9.9? Where would information about who wrote the program and how many manhours it took be stored?

14. In what way are the information requirements of design work more difficult to satisfy than are those of marketing, materials management, production, and financial management?

15. Which types of DBMS allow new entity types, relationships, and attributes to be routinely added to a database?

16. How would the E-R diagram of Figure 9.4 be stored in the database defined by Figure 9.10?

17. When would a Relationship occurrence in Figure 9.12 have an *isa* relationship with an Entity occurrence?

18. What interactions between "concept refinements" must an engineering design information system be prepared to handle?

19. Graphical information about a system can be stored either as a digitized version of a pixel pattern or as vectors that define the location of objects in a coordinate-space. Which way of storing graphical information is the database of Figure 9.14 designed to handle?

20. What does an occurrence of the System Concept entity type of Figure 9.13 represent?

21. Suppose we want to define a system that includes a microcomputer and some software. How could the software be defined in the database of Figure 9.14?

10

Financial Management

FUNCTION DEFINITION

The financial stakeholders in an enterprise are those who provide financial support. Those who buy an ownership interest in the business (common stockholders in a corporation) are the only required type of financial stakeholder. Long-term lenders to the business (bond holders) constitute another type of financial stakeholder. A lender has a more limited stake in the business than does an owner; the lender is more likely to have the enterprise fulfill its commitments with respect to the loan. Short-term creditors and factoring services take the least risk that the enterprise will not honor its commitments but they nevertheless depend on the firm to follow through on its commitments.

Financial management concerns the making and fulfilling of commitments to financial stakeholders. It includes arranging for the sale of common stock or partnerships. It involves contracting for long-term loans and bank credits. It also includes managing the use of short-term credit and working capital supply alternatives and contracting for other financial services, such as insurance, exchange rate protection, and securities transactions.

Financial management also includes providing the accounting information that financial stakeholders require. Payments to these stakeholders are often contingent on the financial performance of the business. Therefore, providing historical information about financial performance is basic to managing relations with the financial stakeholders. In some cases, projections of future financial performance as well as other information about the plans of the organization are needed to secure financing.

The integrity of the financial information provided by management must be certified by an auditor. Arranging for an independent auditor to audit the accounting records and to provide certification is another financial management responsibility. To ensure that the external audit will result in certification, an internal auditing staff is employed in larger organizations to identify deficiencies in the accounting system.

275

Finally, the basic commitment to the owners is usually to maximize long-term earnings. To fulfill this obligation, the management of the firm requires cost accounting data and budgeting plans and controls. This information must be consistent with the financial information provided to financial stakeholders. Thus, financial management has the responsibility to install and operate cost accounting and budgeting systems that give managers the detailed information necessary to make operating and investment decisions that are consistent with the goal of maximizing long-term earnings.

FINANCIAL MANAGEMENT INFORMATION STRUCTURE

The information structure shown in Figure 5.1 for the information requirements of the chief executive officer can be decomposed to characterize the requirements of financial management by simply specializing each of the two entity types and relationships. The result is shown in Figure 10.1.

Resource is specialized to Financial Asset in Figure 10.1. These are the resources that the owners of the business own and to which the lenders to the enterprise have first claim if the business goes bankrupt. They are the assets whose total value by type is shown on financial accounting statements. The value is actually an estimate based on the historical cost of the assets.

The Goal entity type of Figure 5.1 is specialized to Financial Commitment. This is a commitment made to an owner, lender, or short-term creditor. It may be a commitment to pay interest on a loan and to repay the loan according to a specified schedule. It may be a commitment to pay the government taxes withheld from payments due employees. Or it may be a commitment to give the owners of the business the net profits of the enterprise.

The *manage* relationship of Figure 5.1 is specialized to a *transaction* relationship in Figure 10.1. The *transaction* relationship defines the ways in which financial assets are used to satisfy financial commitments. Income is considered part of the financial commitment to owners, and any transaction that affects income will also relate to the assets that are used to generate that income. In theory,

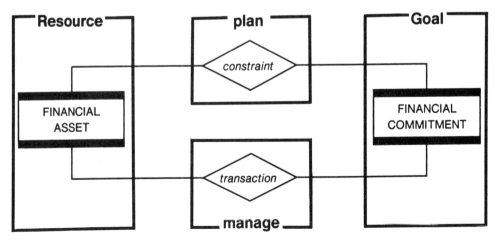

FIGURE 10.1. Information structure for financial management.

every accounting transaction is an instance of this relationship. In practice, batches of transactions will be treated as an instance of the transaction relationship at the top level of the information structure.

The *plan* relationship of Figure 5.1 specializes to the *constraint* relationship of Figure 10.1. A constraint on the way a financial asset can be used to fulfill financial commitments is modeled as a link between a commitment and certain assets. A loan in which assets are cited as collateral is one example of this relationship. A leased asset is another example. A more complex example is a budget that sets limits on assets, costs, and expenses in order to fulfill a net income commitment to the owners. This last example does not fit the structure of Figure 10.1 nicely but does involve a relationship between financial assets and the earnings performance commitment to owners.

SUBFUNCTIONS OF FINANCIAL MANAGEMENT

Commonly, financial management is divided into three major subfunctions: finance, accounting, and auditing. For some businesses, a subfunction of one of these three may be sufficiently important to rank as a first-level subfunction. Cost accounting, for example, is sometimes considered a separate subfunction. But, in this discussion, no purpose is served by making that distinction; cost accounting works with the transaction data of financial accounting plus some additional measures of output. The subfunctions shown in Figure 10.2 will be considered in this text.

The finance subfunction is responsible for planning and negotiating the financial commitments of the firm and managing relationships with financial institutions. This includes providing financial information to prospective stockholders and creditors but not the development of that information which is an accounting subfunction. It includes planning and making arrangements for financial services, such as insurance and factoring, but it does not include arranging for clerical or data processing services (which may be offered by financial institutions), such as processing of customer payments to lockboxes or the processing of payroll data.

The accounting subfunction is responsible for the preparation of financial statements, tax returns, and other government required reports regarding financial matters. It is also responsible for the processing of accounting transactions and for the general and subsidiary journals and ledgers that record those transactions, and on which the financial reports are based. Furthermore, it is responsible

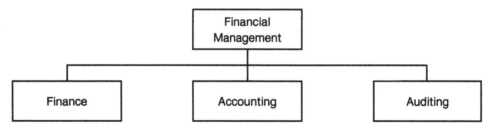

FIGURE 10.2. Subfunctions of financial management.

for managerial accounting services, including cost accounting, budgeting, and economic analysis of capital investment opportunities.

The auditing subfunction cannot be considered part of the accounting sub-function because its purpose is to assess the integrity of the financial statements produced by the accounting subfunction. Organizationally, external auditing should not report to the CEO. It should report to an audit subcommittee of the board of directors in the case of a corporation.

Because auditing has the responsibility of checking the accounting results, it must work with the information used by the accounting function. But, auditing must also consider the systems used to process transactions and look for defi-ciencies in those systems and the ways in which they could be used fraudulently. The successful auditor is an interesting cross between a detective and a systems analyst.

INFORMATION STRUCTURES FOR FIRST-LEVEL SUBFUNCTIONS

The three first-level subfunctions deal with financial information, but each re-quires that different aspects of this body of information be developed. The finance function requires information about external financial institutions and economic affairs that are not required by the accounting subfunction. On the other hand, accounting works with transaction details that are of no concern to the finance subfunction. Perhaps, it is the systemic information required for auditing (the information about how transactions processing is done) that derives least natu-rally from the information structure of Figure 10.1. In this case, the derivation must depend on the proposition that information about how transactions are pro-cessed constitutes information about the transactions.

INFORMATION STRUCTURE FOR FINANCE

The finance subfunction requires the results of financial accounting plus addi-tional information about financial commitments and their relationships to the assets of the organization. The structure of financial accounting information requirements is explained in the next subsection. In this subsection, we concen-trate on the additional information about financial commitments.

In general terms, financial management requires information about financial institutions and the arrangements that have been made or can be made with them. Information about the arrangements that can be made for financial serv-ices constitutes a vast and dynamic literature to which entire institutions are dedicated. There are publicly available databases covering financial services, institutions, and activity. The individual enterprise need not consider replicating information on possible financial service arrangements in an internally main-tained database.

Figure 10.3 shows a structuring of information that concerns financial ar-rangements that have been made by an enterprise. The Financial Commitment entity type of Figure 10.1 is decomposed into a Financial Institution entity type and a series of four financial services entity types—Receivables Sale, Lease, Loan, and Stock Issue. Withholding Tax is also shown as a financial service because it has the effect of providing some cash temporarily, although it is certainly not intended to be a financial service.

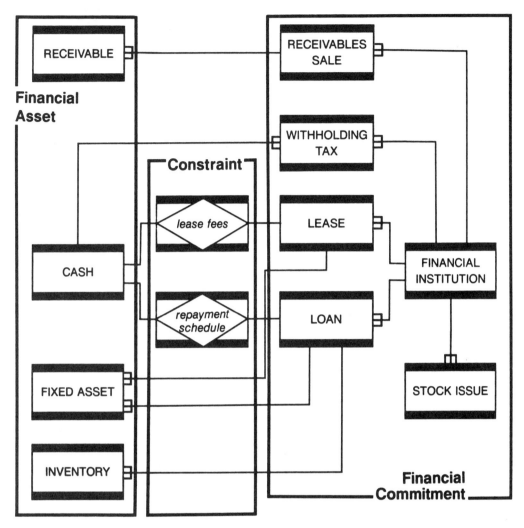

FIGURE 10.3. Information structure for finance.

The Financial Institution entity type is treated as a detail of Financial Commitment in Figure 10.3. It represents a bank, an investor, or any other institution to which the firm makes financial commitments.

The Financial Asset entity type is decomposed in Figure 10.3 into four types of assets: Cash, Receivable, Inventory, and Fixed Asset. These are not the only possible asset types, but they are certainly the major types for most nonfinancial enterprises. The Receivable entity type represents a payment due from a customer for product or services rendered to the customer. The Inventory entity type represents product that the business owns at a location that is for sale to customers. The Fixed Asset entity type includes equipment or facilities used to conduct business but are not being held for sale to a customer.

All of the relationships shown in Figure 10.3 are specializations of the *constraint* relationship of Figure 10.1. The asset linked by one of these relationships to a financial commitment is to some degree committed to satisfying the financial obligation. Stock issue is not involved in a commitment type relationship with any assets only because all ownership rights to assets not specifically dedicated to satisfying the claims of other financial services belong to the owners of the stock.

There are two reasons for not showing the *transaction* relationships between the assets and commitments in Figure 10.3 which certainly exist. The first is that it would greatly complicate the diagram because there is at least one stream of payments for each type of financial commitment shown. The other reason is that the model of transactions described in the next subsection includes the transactions caused by the financial commitments shown in Figure 10.3, and it has already been noted that the finance subfunction requires the information produced by the financial accounting subfunction.

INFORMATION STRUCTURE FOR ACCOUNTING

A primary accounting subfunction responsibility is to measure financial status and performance in quantitative terms. Financial status is summarized on a balance sheet which shows the value of the assets of the enterprise at a point in time as well as the claims on those resources that government agencies, creditors, lenders, and owners have as a result of existing financial commitments. Financial performance is summarized in quantitative terms by the income statement which shows the change in the total value of the assets during an accounting period. This change in value is the net effect of the transactions recorded for the accounting period. The transactions also record changes in individual assets and claims on those assets.

In addition to accounting for the effects of transactions on financial status, the accounting subfunction provides managerial accounting information. This information can be used to predict (and influence) future financial performance and to estimate the financial effects of possible management actions. Managerial accounting information is based on cost accounting and responsibility accounting. Cost accounting requires added details about transactions processed in order to relate costs incurred to the product or service obtained. Responsibility accounting records the effects of transactions in a way that allows each manager to see the actual versus planned effects of his or her actions on the financial performance of the organization.

Thus, the effect of managerial accounting responsibilities is not to divert attention from accounting transactions but rather to require more transaction details and to categorize the financial effects of transactions in a more complex way. This points to the decomposition of the *transaction* relationship of Figure 10.1 as the key to the information structure required for the accounting subfunction.

In developing this decomposition, two basic facts about transactions are important. One concerns the assignment of transactions to time periods. The other concerns the nature of the relationship between a transaction and the assets and financial commitments it involves.

The measurement of financial performance is a matter of accounting for changes during a period of time. These changes are composed of a series of individual changes each of which is defined as a transaction (or adjusting journal entry). This implies that the accounting time period should be treated as an entity type in the decomposition of the *transaction* relationship if only to facilitate access of transaction, asset and commitment data by accounting period.

The effects of an accounting transaction on asset and financial commitment values can be many. A given transaction can affect many asset occurrences as well as many commitment occurrences. This means that the transaction itself must be modeled as an entity type with many-to-many relationships with both the Asset and Financial Commitment entity types of Figure 10.1.

The result of these considerations is the decomposition of Figure 10.1 that is shown in Figure 10.4. In this structure, the *transaction* relationship is decomposed into two entity types (Transaction and Accounting Period) and four relationships.

The Transaction entity type in Figure 10.4 represents an accounting transaction, or journal entry, in the traditional sense. Its attributes are date and time of the transaction, transaction description, source document, and perhaps sum of the debits.

The Accounting Period entity type is shown in a one-to-many relationship with Transaction. This serves to identify in which period each transaction has occurred. The attributes of Accounting Period include fiscal year, period number, number of working days, and starting and ending dates.

The *asset-in-period* and *commitment-in-period* relationships are needed to measure the change in Assets and Commitments during each accounting period. The value of each asset and commitment at the beginning of each accounting period can be recorded so that the difference in value from one period to the next is available. The budget amount (or factors for calculating it) for each asset and commitment is also an appropriate attribute for these relationships. For cost accounting purposes, there may be measures of activity that are natural attributes of these relationships which can be used to assign costs to outputs of the enterprise.

The two relationships labeled *posting-1* and *posting-2* in Figure 10.4 are used to define how a transaction occurrence affects the values of assets and commitments. Because a transaction occurs in a certain time period, its effect on an asset

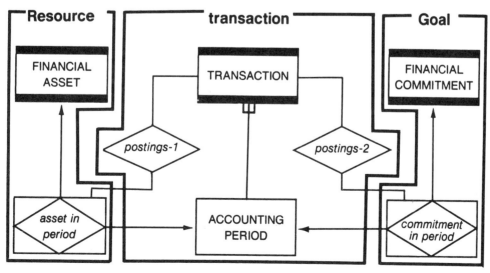

FIGURE 10.4. Decomposition of transaction relationship.

can be related to the value of that asset in the accounting period in which the transaction occurred. This is the reason *posting-1* is a relationship between transaction and *asset-in-period* rather than between transaction and asset. The key attribute of these posting relationships is the amount by which the value of the asset or commitment is changed by the transaction. Each change is either a debit or a credit and the sum of the debits must equal the sum of the credits for each transaction.

Simplification

The information structure of Figure 10.4 is unnecessarily complex for accounting purposes. The fact that the purpose of the accounting subfunction is to track and report the quantitative value of assets and commitments and their changes in value means that the significant attributes of these two entity types are virtually the same as far as accounting is concerned. For both assets and commitments, the accounting function needs to know type, name, description, and value (actually, value as a function of accounting period).

To simplify Figure 10.4, we substitute a generalization for the Financial Asset and Financial Commitment entity types. This generalization is the Account entity type. The core attributes of this generalization are the type, name, and description of the account. The domain of the type attribute is asset, liability, equity, income, revenue, cost, and expense. If the type value of an Account occurrence is "asset," then it is a generalization of an Asset entity type; otherwise an Account occurrence is a generalization of a Financial Commitment entity type.

Figure 10.5 shows the information structure of Figure 10.4 with the Account generalization substitution made. The layout of the diagram is changed, but the only real difference between Figures 10.4 and 10.5 is the substitution of Account for the Financial Asset and Financial Commitment entity types. This simplified accounting information structure should be adequate for developing a more detailed structure to serve all accounting purposes, except for accounting personnel and facilities management purposes which should be analyzed separately.

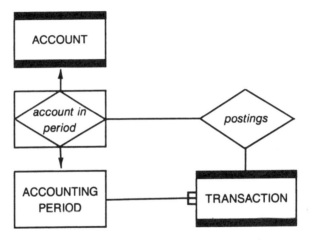

FIGURE 10.5. Simplified accounting information structure.

The next step in developing the detailed information structure adequate for financial, responsibility, and cost accounting purposes is shown in Figure 10.6. It has several refinements that are obtained by decomposing the Account and Transaction entity types of Figure 10.5. These refinements are explained in the following subsections.

Account Hierarchy

For both financial and managerial accounting purposes, there are reasons for Account occurrences that have a summary-detail relationship between them. For example, for financial reporting purposes, it is sufficient to have a single account for cash, a type of financial asset. However, for auditing and management purposes it is useful to have a separate account (a separate occurrence of Account) for each bank account, money market account, and other cash equivalent asset of the enterprise.

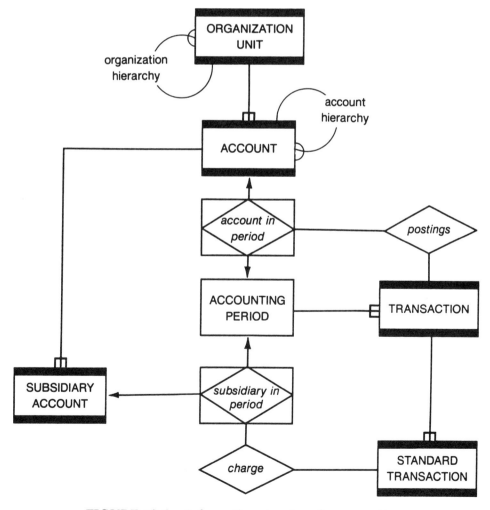

FIGURE 10.6. Information structure for accounting.

The recursive relationship in Figure 10.6 labeled *account hierarchy* provides for the *summary-detail* relationship between accounts. Suppose, for example, that the portion of the chart of accounts of an enterprise had the cash accounts shown in Figure 10.7. One occurrence of the *account hierarchy* relationship would link the cash account to the Citibank, Bank of America, and Dean Witter Sears Liquid Asset accounts. Another occurrence would link the Citibank account to the A/C No. 3325363 and A/C No. 4726867 accounts. A third occurrence would link the Bank of America account to its accounts and a fourth would link the Dean Witter Sears Liquid Asset account to its accounts.

This recursive relationship eliminates the need for block-coded account numbers. Instead of the account number defining the account type, subtype, organizational unit, and reporting sequence, the recursive relationship defines them. Any type of name or acronym can serve as a unique account identifier.

Responsibility Accounting Requirement

In responsibility accounting, each manager is given financial reports showing the status (and changes) in the assets, liabilities, revenues, costs, and expenses over which he has some control. The reports can be similar in format to the basic financial statements (balance sheet and income statement); however, they should only show things for which the manager is responsible.

To produce this data, it is necessary to have Account occurrences for each asset or commitment over which each manager exercises control. It is also useful to be able to access all of the accounts that relate to a given manager. The Organization Unit entity type in Figure 10.6 and its relationship to the Account entity type serve this purpose. All of the account occurrences for a given manager are linked to the organization unit of the manager by this relationship.

The *organization hierarchy* relationship defines management reporting relationships. In order to describe the financial performance of managers, upper level managers need to see financial statements that summarize the statements of all of the managers that report to them.

Chart of Accounts for XYZ Company

```
Cash
        Citibank
                A/C No. 3325363
                A/C No. 4726867
        Bank of America
                A/C No. 987-5543
                A/C No. 223-4421
        Dean Witter Sears Liquid Asset
                A/C No. 7764-F-3324
                A/C No. S-3345-445
                . . . .
```

FIGURE 10.7. Example of a chart of accounts.

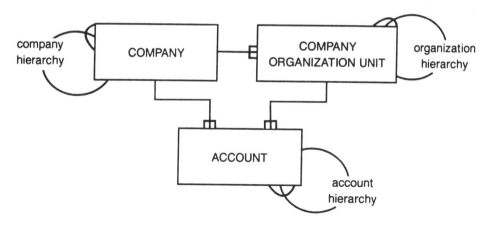

FIGURE 10.8. Possible decomposition of organization unit.

Organization Unit is shown in Figure 10.6 as a generalized entity type, because it can be specialized to units within one corporation, separate corporations, or both. In Figure 10.8, a possible decomposition is shown for Organization Unit. It describes an organization that consists of a set of subsidiary companies and an organizational structure within each.

Subsidiary Accounting Systems

The automatic processing of common, high-volume transactions requires more flexibility in the Account and Transaction record structures than Figure 10.5 provides. Additional information for the Account occurrences can be useful and descriptions of individual transactions are not needed if all transactions in a batch have the same explanation. The Subsidiary Account and Standard Transaction entity types in Figure 10.6 provide this flexibility.

To explain the Subsidiary Account and Standard Transaction entity types, we will use the example of customer invoices. In a subsequent section on the information requirements of second level subfunctions, other examples of standard transaction processing are discussed.

A customer invoice is a definition of some products and services that have been provided to a customer in response to a customer order. The invoice shows the charges for each product and service provided and requests that the customer pay the total of the charges according to certain terms of payment.

An invoice describes a standard accounting transaction. Thus, it can be treated as a specialization of the Standard Transaction entity type. In Figure 10.9, an *isa* relationship is shown between Standard Transaction and Customer Invoice. This means that for each invoice sent to any customer, there is an occurrence of Standard Transaction, and, of course, an occurrence of Customer Invoice.

Figure 10.9 has all the entities and relationships of Figure 10.6, except for Organization Unit which is not shown to simplify. In addition, Figure 10.9 shows the entities and relationships involved in customer invoice processing. To clarify where data are stored in the structure of Figure 10.9, lists of the basic attributes of each ledger entity type and relationship from Figure 10.9 are given in Table 10.1. These entity types and relationships apply to all kinds of standard accounting transactions.

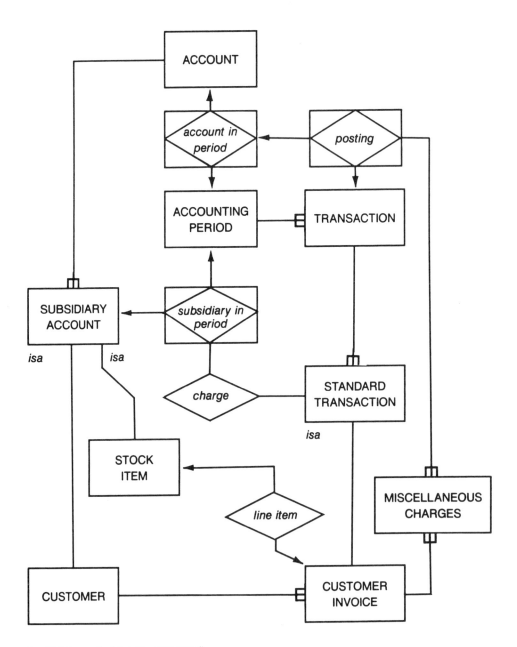

1. Debit receivables (invoice total)
2. Credit sales account (invoice total)
3. Credit inventory
4. Credit sales expense
5. Debit cost of sales (sum of 3 and 4)
6. Debit sales tax expense
7. Credit sales tax payable

FIGURE 10.9. Information structure for receivables function.

TABLE 10.1. Basic attributes of accounting entities and relationships.

Account type Name Definition	ACCOUNT	SUBSIDIARY ACCOUNT	Subsidiary type Subsidiary ID Description
Posting date Posting time Description Source ID Sum of debits	TRANSACTION	STANDARD TRANSACTION	Date Time Transaction type Source ID Sum of debits
Balance Fixed budget Budget rate Budget volume Actual volume	account in period	subsidiary in period	Balance Fixed budget Budget rate Budget volume Actual volume
Description Amount	postings	ACCOUNTING PERIOD	Period number Start date End date Working days
Description Amount	charge		

The basic attributes for entities and relationships in Figure 10.9 that pertain only to customer invoicing are listed in Table 10.2. The lists in this table are not necessarily complete. Only the attributes used in the accounting transaction are shown.

The *isa* relationship between Subsidiary Account and Customer in Figure 10.9 indicates that Subsidiary Account is a generalization of Customer. Notice how general the attributes of Subsidiary Account are in Table 10.1. Any kind of asset (or commitment) can qualify for a subsidiary account occurrence. In the case at hand, it is not really the customer that is the special case but rather the obligation of the customer to pay. The customer has a commitment to pay the enterprise for the products and services received. Where is the amount owed stored? It is not an attribute of either Customer or Subsidiary Ledger, according to Tables 10.1 and 10.2. Instead, it is an attribute of *subsidiary-in-period*. This treatment allows the processing of customer invoices chargeable to more than one accounting period to go on simultaneously.

Another example of an *isa* relationship between subsidiary account and a specialization of it is the one involving Stock Item in Figure 10.9. In this case, the Subsidiary Account occurrence would be linked to the Account occurrence that

TABLE 10.2. Attributes of entities involved in invoicing.

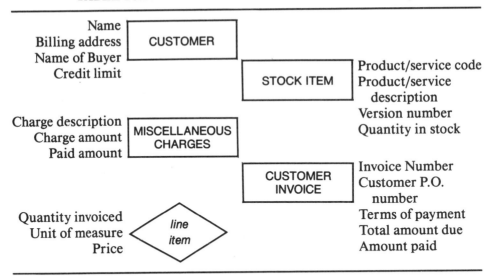

measures the total value of certain stock items. The balances for a particular stock item are kept in the appropriate *subsidiary-in-period* occurrences.

The one-to-many relationship between Transaction and Standard Transaction is a mandatory relationship for Standard Transaction and is based on a rule of association that is not evident from Figure 10.9. The standard transactions linked to an occurrence of Transaction by this relationship are all assumed to be for the same specialization of Standard Transaction. In the example being considered that specialization is Customer Invoice. Thus, all Customer Invoice occurrences that are entered into the database during a certain time period (often a shift, or a day) are linked to Standard Transaction occurrences that are all linked to the same Transaction occurrence. The Transaction occurrence is essentially a batch control record for a batch of customer invoices, in this case. The time period covered by the batch can be entered as part of the description attribute of Transaction.

The one-to-many relationship between Account and Subsidiary Account is a mandatory relationship for the Subsidiary Account entity type. An occurrence of this relationship contains all the Subsidiary Account occurrences that refer to assets (or liabilities or ownership) included in the Account occurrence. In other words, the Account occurrence on the "one side" of this relationship is a "control account" relative to the Subsidiary Account occurrences in the set on the "many side." The balances in the *subsidiary-in-period* occurrences linked to subsidiary accounts in the set must sum to the balance in the *account-in-period* occurrence linked to the "control account," for a given period.

Subsidiary accounts are normally only set up for some of the accounts that appear on the balance sheet type of financial statement. This includes asset, liability and equity type accounts. If subsidiary accounts were allowed for revenue, cost, expense, or income type accounts then it would be possible that the same entity type would be a specialization of both Subsidiary Account and Standard Transaction. Customer Invoice, for example, could be a specialization of both types of generalizations. It can be said that the only significant differences between an Account and a Subsidiary Account occurrence are:

1. An account refers to groups of assets or financial commitments whereas a subsidiary account refers to an individual asset or commitment.

2. A subsidiary account usually refers to asset, liability, or equity type accounts, not revenue, cost, or expense accounts.

The *charge* relationship between *subsidiary-in-period* and Standard Transaction is optional. It links standard transactions to the subsidiary ledger whose balance is affected by the transaction. In the case of customer invoicing, it links all the invoices sent to a given customer in an accounting period to the *subsidiary-in-period* occurrence whose balance (for that customer) is increased by the invoices. In the case of other standard transactions which are discussed in a subsequent section, they are linked to whichever *subsidiary-in-period* occurrences have balances changed by the transaction. This *charge* relationship is analogous to the *posting* relationship. It operates at the level of individual transactions and only for standard transactions.

Seven basic postings that an invoice transaction can generate are listed in Figure 10.9. The first and second record the amount receivable and the sale. The third, fourth, and fifth postings record the cost of the sale. In terms of the E-R diagram, posting 4 refers to a miscellaneous charge, such as a prepaid freight charge on a shipment to the customer. Postings 6 and 7 record the sales tax collected. Each of these postings for a customer invoice results in either a change in the amount of a *posting* occurrence or the creation of a new *posting* occurrence for the transaction batch if a posting to the account involved does not already exist for the Transaction occurrence. In the case of postings 1 and 3, new occurrences of the *charge* relationship will also be created.

The one-to-many relationship between Miscellaneous Charge and *posting* is an example of a way to store more detail about individual postings to an account. The credit posting to an "outgoing freight expense" account, for example, for a batch of customer invoices is a total amount for all the shipping expenses invoiced to customers in the batch of invoices. The relationship between Posting and Miscellaneous Expense provides a way to obtain a list of the individual shipping charges that are included in that particular credit posting.

The information structure required for accounting is summarized in Figure 10.6. However, as the example of the customer invoicing system shows, the two generalized entity types at the bottom of Figure 10.6 will be decomposed to very different entity types for each type of transaction that requires a processing system. Later in this chapter, these subfunctions of accounting are identified and their information structure requirements are described. Then the full information structure required for accounting should be evident.

It should also be noted that the information structure of Figure 10.6 is not sufficient for some additional features that are common in accounting software packages. Additional entity types and relationships must be added to provide for recurring transactions and the more complex expense allocations of cost accounting. However, these can be obtained by further decomposition and are not vital to demonstrating that the appropriate information structure for accounting can be derived from Figure 10.1.

INFORMATION STRUCTURE FOR AUDITING

The audit subfunction checks the financial reports produced by the accounting subfunction. As has already been noted, this implies that the audit subfunction requires access to the same information as the accounting subfunction. So, the information structure of Figure 10.6 applies to financial auditing as well as to accounting.

The audit subfunction looks for mistakes and fraud as summarized in the table shown in Figure 10.10. Random mistakes and random fraud are very difficult to detect unless they make a significant difference in the financial statements. So, a comparative examination of certain account balances is used to determine whether significant inconsistencies exist that may be the result of random errors. If so, then the nature of the inconsistency guides further investigation of the accounting figures.

On the other hand, to detect systematic errors and fraud, auditors review the internal accounting control environment. This includes management policies, manual procedures and computer systems that relate to the accounting information. Computer systems are often checked by processing a set of transactions that have a predetermined effect on the account balances. If the test transactions do not produce that effect, there is a systematic error (or fraudulent feature) in the computer system.

Beyond the accounting information structure, auditing requires information about the internal accounting control environment of the enterprise. Documentation of this environment can, of course, be computerized and stored in a database. However, unless evidence is also stored that the policies and procedures are followed, this documentation is only a starting point for the auditor who must determine the controls that really exist in day-to-day practice.

The structure of information about the internal accounting control environment fits the pattern developed in Chapter 11 about information systems management better than it does that of Figure 10.1 and its derivatives. Therefore, further consideration of this aspect of the audit subfunction information requirements is deferred to that chapter.

SECOND-LEVEL FUNCTIONAL BREAKDOWN

Each of the three first-level subfunctions of financial management has a number of subfunctions. Further development of the information structures shown in

	Mistake	Fraud
Systematic	System error	Fraudulent system feature
Random	Human error	System weakness

FIGURE 10.10.   Types of errors in accounting.

Figures 10.3 and 10.6 is possible by analyzing the requirements of these subfunctions. In this section the subfunctions are defined and in the next section the information requirements of the accounting subfunctions are explained.

FINANCE

The subfunctions of finance are by no means standard across all types of organizations. A capital intensive business, such as an airline, will have more finance subfunctions than one that is not, such as a law firm. Most firms must give periodic attention to short term financing issues (cash management). If the business requires significant capital investments, then capital budgeting is an important subfunction which leads to issues concerning the capital structure of the business (equity versus debt). The management of the long-term capital structure of the enterprise is an important finance subfunction. Another subfunction which may be closely related is managing a portfolio of securities. This is an important subfunction if the capital requirements of the business fluctuate or if there are special funds, such as pension funds, to be managed.

Four subfunctions of finance are shown in Figure 10.11. The short-term financing function includes cash budgeting, bank account management, customer credit management, use of supplier credit, short term borrowing and lending, and foreign exchange management. The capital budgeting function includes the evaluation of capital investments and leasing alternatives, the allocation of capital to investments, and the management of capital investments after the initial investment decision. The capital structuring subfunction includes dividend policy management, debt policy and the evaluation of various forms of debt, coordination of investment and financing decisions, financial planning, and the evaluation of merger opportunities. Portfolio management refers to the management of assets other than fixed assets and the working capital required for receivables and inventories.

ACCOUNTING

The subfunctions of accounting, except for budgeting, concern the management of certain kinds of transactions. In Figure 10.11, six subfunctions are shown that deal with specific types of transactions, and the seventh subfunction is budgeting. The budgeting subfunction concerns developing financial performance objectives and then evaluating actual performance against the objectives.

Receivables

The receivables subfunction produces the invoice sent to a customer when goods are delivered. It also processes payments received from the customer and periodically produces reports on what customers still owe. If collecting amounts owed requires attention, the receivables function can include the activities performed in order to collect amounts owed by customers. Furthermore, the subfunction includes implementing credit policies set by the short term financing subfunction (and internal marketing), which involves setting terms of payment extended to customers and placing limits on the credit granted to each customer.

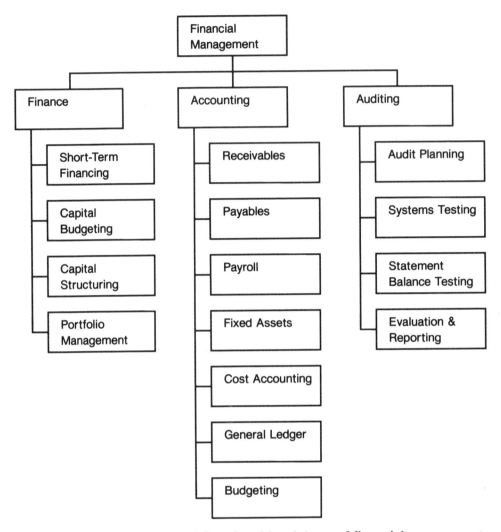

FIGURE 10.11. Second-level functional breakdown of financial management.

Payables

The payables subfunction evaluates invoices received from suppliers and determines whether they should be paid. If so, the timing of the payment is planned. The subfunction also includes making the payments at the appropriate time. This must be coordinated with the short-term financing subfunctions of cash budgeting and bank account management so that payments are made from an account that has sufficient funds.

Payroll

The payroll subfunction pays employees. Specified amounts must be withheld from what the employee has earned and paid to tax agencies and providers of employee services. The function may also include the allocation of wage and salary costs to cost and expense accounts.

Fixed Assets

This subfunction handles transactions that involve equipment and facilities used in the business. It records the acquisition, location, depreciation, and retirement of such assets. The differences and similarities between this subfunction and cost accounting can be confusing. Depreciation and maintenance transactions can have implications for both fixed assets valuation and cost accounting. In the case of depreciation, the amount of a depreciation charge is usually considered a fixed asset valuation problem, but the way the charge is allocated to the goods produced is a cost accounting problem. In the case of maintenance, routine maintenance is a cost accounting transaction, but major equipment or facility renovation projects should be treated as fixed asset transactions.

Cost Accounting

The cost accounting subfunction has the problem of relating the costs of a business to the outputs of that business. Flexible production facilities and automation are making the problem increasingly difficult. They cause direct labor cost to decline as a percent of the total cost of a product. When a large percentage of the cost of a product is indirect labor, operating expenses, and fixed asset charges, the allocation of these costs makes a big difference in the apparent profitability of the product.

The cost accounting subfunction includes the definition of cost and expense accounts, the processing of inventory and work-in-process transactions (including labor cost distribution), the allocation of overhead, and the determination of the cost of goods sold. If a standard costing system is used, it sets standard costs and evaluates and disposes of variances.

General Ledger

The general ledger subfunction manages the creation of the financial statements produced by accounting. This function reviews account balances and makes adjusting entries and non-standard transaction entries, so that the final statements properly reflect the financial performance and status of the enterprise.

Budgeting

The budgeting subfunction prepares an account balance plan for future accounting periods and then checks performance against the plan. This is particularly useful in controlling expenses and indirect labor costs.

From a theoretical viewpoint, budgeting should be a finance subfunction, instead of a subfunction of accounting. The decisions on expenditure levels and expected revenues concern the financial commitments of the enterprise. Only the process of comparing actual expenditures and revenues to the budgeted levels involves accounting.

Nevertheless, budgeting is commonly considered a part of the accounting function. More importantly, the information required for budgeting fits the structure developed for accounting. Therefore, budgeting is treated here as a subfunction of accounting.

AUDITING

The auditing subfunctions shown in Figure 10.11 apply mainly to external auditing. They are project-oriented. The first step is to become acquainted with the business and evaluate the internal accounting control environment. Based on these findings, a plan is established for the audit. The second subfunction, or project phase, tests the accounting subsystems to determine whether they process transactions correctly. The third subfunction verifies statement balances. All of the transaction types that affect a balance must be considered and those types that the subsystem test results indicate are suspect must be checked. The final subfunction makes an evaluation of the audit findings and issues a report.

INFORMATION STRUCTURES FOR SELECTED SECOND-LEVEL SUBFUNCTIONS

In Figure 10.6, there are two generalized entity types that must be specialized in different ways to satisfy the needs of the second-level subfunctions that have just been described. One is the subsidiary account and the other is the standard transaction. A major objective of this section is to show these decompositions.

The subfunctions that require decomposed versions of these two entity types include the short term financing subfunction of finance and the first five accounting subfunctions discussed in the previous section. Accordingly, the information requirements of these six subfunctions are described in the following subsections.

To emphasize the fact that the information structure requirements for the six subfunctions considered in this section are all decompositions of the structure in Figure 10.6, all six decompositions are shown in one diagram. This is the diagram depicted in Figure 10.12. The column of entity types shown on the left that are linked to the Subsidiary Account entity type are all specializations of that entity type, from the accounting viewpoint. From some other viewpoint they are entity types involved in another function, such as marketing, materials management, or production.

The column of entity types on the right in Figure 10.12, each of which is linked to the Standard Transaction entity type, are all specializations of that entity type. Again, from the viewpoint of another subfunction, they are each an entity type involved in that other function and are derived by decomposing the generalized entity types of that function.

SHORT-TERM FINANCING

One of the subfunctions of short-term financing is cash budgeting. It involves forecasting the inflows and outflows from each bank account based on current commitments and then planning fund transfers that will provide necessary cash where it is needed at minimum cost.

The information useful in cash budgeting is:

1. Bank balances by account

2. Compensating balance requirements

3. Interest payments on account balances

4. A forecast of cash receipts from customers

5. A payment plan for payables

6. Projected payroll cash requirements

7. Loan repayment requirements.

The first three items on this list concern bank account information. Except for float effects, the current balance is an attribute of the *account-in-period* relationship in Figure 10.12 for the appropriate cash account and accounting period. But, for compensating balance requirements and future interest payments, as well as float effect estimates, a decomposition of the Subsidiary Account entity type must be defined that consists of two related entity types. One is a Bank entity type and the other is a Bank Account entity type. The attributes of the Bank entity type include the name and address of the financial institution, the contact person, and other data that applies to all accounts opened with the institution. The attributes of the Bank Account entity type would include compensating balance requirements, interest rate, and timing of interest payments. These two entity types and their relationships are depicted in Figure 10.12.

A relationship between Bank Account and Accounting Period (*period bank account* in Figure 10.12) can be used to store time-dependent bank account information needed for cash budgeting. To plan cash flows on a daily basis, the Accounting Period entity type could be specialized to Day. The information that can be modeled as attributes of this relationship includes the remaining items in the above list (now allocated to the specific account they will affect) and the projected net account balance for each week.

The remaining items in the above list, starting with a forecast of cash receipts and excepting the last one, can be considered attributes of other entities obtained by other decompositions of Subsidiary Account and Standard Transaction. These other decompositions are explained in later subsections. At this point, we take these other decompositions for granted and simply refer to entity types in Figure 10.12 that can have attributes useful to cash budgeting.

The cash receipts forecast can be based on attributes of Age Interval in Figure 10.12. Each customer invoice is linked to the Age Interval occurrence that measures how long it has not been paid. The attributes of Age Interval are the length of the interval, the probability of payment for the interval, and the total amount of the invoices linked to the interval.

The plan for paying supplier invoices can be obtained from the one-to-many relationship between *period bank account* and Supplier Invoice. This relationship links an invoice to the bank account from which it will be paid. The planned date of payment is an attribute of Supplier Invoice. Summing the amounts to be paid

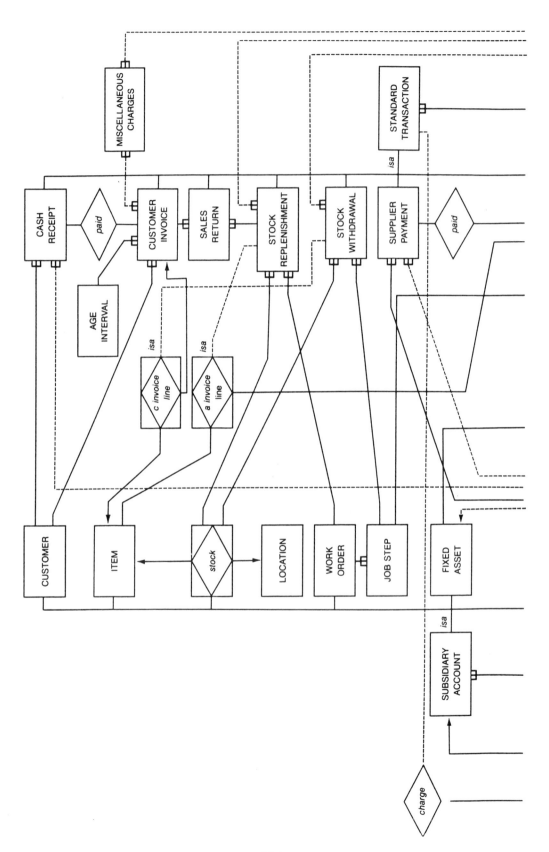

296

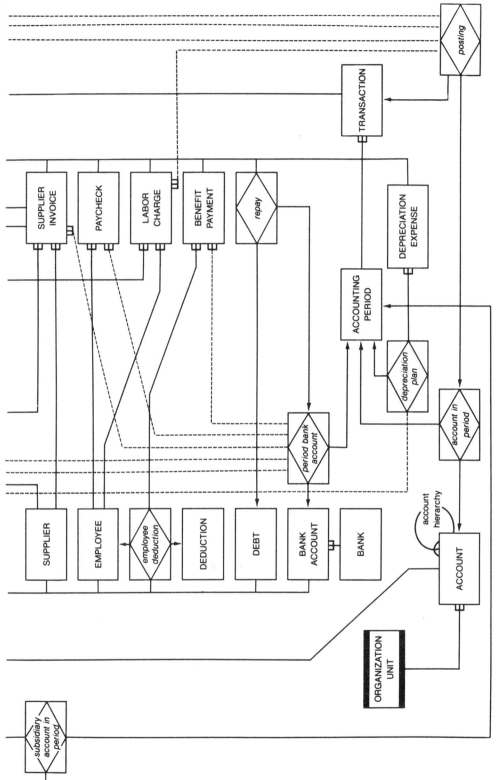

FIGURE 10.12. Integrated information structure for accounting.

by date of payment, as defined on the Supplier Invoice, can give the total expected cash outflow by day for each bank account.

The near term payroll requirements for cash can be obtained from accrued salary and wage accounts, and the withholding accounts in the general ledger. However, these balances only show amounts already owed. To project future payroll system cash outflows, the expected payment per period is needed. Data for this can be made attributes of the Employee entity type. Totals for future payroll expenditures can be calculated based on these expected values.

Debt Payment Requirements

Managing debt liabilities requires information about each debt of the enterprise. This information includes interest rates, the schedule of interest and principal repayments (and any flexibility therein), collateral, lender data, and possibilities for refinancing or conversion to equity.

Some of this information can be characterized as attributes of Debt, which is considered an entity type that is a specialization of the Subsidiary Account entity type. The interest rates, collateral, lender data, and refinancing possibilities can be treated as attributes of debt.

The schedule of repayments can be stored in a relationship between Debt and *period bank account*. In Figure 10.12, this relationship is labeled *repay*. Repayment obligation is an attribute of this relationship. The date and amount of each repayment are other possible attributes.

Each repayment is a general ledger entry. The *isa* relationship between Standard Transaction and the *repay* relationship is a way of providing the supplemental information about the journal entry normally associated with a set of standard transactions.

Bank Account Reconciliation

Reconciling a bank account to its account balance can be considered a subfunction of cash budgeting. For this reason we note the information structure requirements for this subfunction.

The subfunction requires all payments from each account and all deposits to each account. To obtain this, a series of one-to-many relationships are needed between the *period bank account* relationship and various standard transaction specializations. Four are shown in Figure 10.12. The specializations of Standard Transaction called Cash Receipt, Supplier Payment, Paycheck, and Benefit Payment are each linked to *period bank account* by a one-to-many relationship.

A Miscellaneous Payment entity type could be added to record any other checks written on an account or special deposits made. It should be linked to *period bank account* by a one-to-many relationship as well.

RECEIVABLES

The management of receivables involves credit granting, invoicing for products delivered (or services rendered or resources used), depositing payments received, collecting amounts owed, processing sales returns, and recognizing bad debts.[1] Each of these processes requires certain types of data if it is to be done effectively.

For making credit granting decisions, information about past payment performance and current financial condition of the credit applicant (and potential customer) is commonly used. Some of this information can be structured as Customer attributes. The specialization of Subsidiary Account to Customer in Figure 10.12 serves this purpose.

The information required for invoicing has already been discussed and is summarized in Figure 10.9. This structure is embedded in Figure 10.12 with one exception. The exception is the relationship called *line item* in Figure 10.9. In Figure 10.12, a *c invoice line* relationship is used instead. *C invoice line* is a relationship between Customer Invoice and Item, in contrast to *line item* which is a relationship between Customer Invoice and Stock Item. The reason for this is to allow for the invoicing of services which are not stock items. In cases where a product is being invoiced, the *isa* relationship between *c invoice line* and Stock Withdrawal can be used to record the inventory effects of invoicing.

To manage the receipt of payments from customers, a Cash Receipt entity type is appropriate. This entity type is involved in four relationships in Figure 10.12. The link with Customer identifies the customer from whom the payment was received. The link with *period bank account* identifies the bank account and accounting period in which the payment was deposited. The *paid* relationship between Cash Receipt and Customer Invoice allows for open item accounting in which a payment can be allocated to certain invoices. The *isa* relationship between Cash Receipt and Standard Transaction recognizes that a cash receipt is treated as a standard transaction.

Collecting amounts owed depends on information about the customer and the invoices and payments in question. The information structure already described for credit granting partially meets this information need. In addition, a relationship between Customer Invoice and Age Interval in Figure 10.12 is helpful in collections management. The amount owed by a customer that is past due by a certain number of days is an attribute of the relationship.

Sales returns are atypical transactions (hopefully). A Sales Return entity type is recognized as part of the same decomposition of Standard Transaction as are Customer Invoice and Cash Receipt. It has a relationship with Customer Invoice and serves to explain an adjustment made on a specific invoice.

However, a sales return also has inventory implications. It involves the return of product to inventory and should therefore be related to the information structure for cost accounting transaction processing. A relationship is shown in Figure 10.12 between Sales Return and Stock Replenishment. The derivation of this relationship from a cost accounting requirement standpoint is explained in the subsection on cost accounting.

PAYABLES

The payables subfunction is part of a purchase-payment cycle that has five steps or activities:

1. Create internal requisition

2. Place purchase order

3. Receive product/service

4. Receive supplier invoice

5. Pay supplier.

The first three of these steps are the responsibility of the materials management function; their information requirements are described in Chapter 7. At this point, the information requirements of the last two steps are considered.

In steps 4 and 5, we are dealing with supplier payment demands. Assuming that we do business on a continuing basis with many of these suppliers, each will present a series of payment requests over time. Thus, it is appropriate to structure the information as being about two separate entities. One is the supplier and the other is the payment request, or supplier invoice. We can view the Supplier entity type as a specialization of the Subsidiary Account entity type because we consider the supplier an entity to whom we make financial commitments on a continuing basis. The Supplier Invoice is a specialization of the Standard Transaction entity type. The one-to-many relationship between them in Figure 10.12 defines the Subsidiary Account occurrence affected by the Transaction occurrence.

A liability should be recognized when a legitimate supplier invoice is received. To be legitimate, an invoice must be a payment request for products or services that have been ordered, have been received, and have not already been paid for. This means that information about orders, receipts, and payments is needed to determine invoice legitimacy.

The need to determine that an invoice is legitimate points to a requirement for more detail about the transaction than the single entity type called Supplier Invoice can provide. The decomposition of Standard Transaction for payables transactions must be reconsidered. Instead of simply specializing it to Supplier Invoice, it should be decomposed to a structure that identifies the purchase order, shipment receipts, and payments involved in the transaction. The part of this structure that involves purchase orders and shipment receipts is shown in Figure 7.5. The payments part is shown in Figure 10.12.

To correlate Figures 7.5 and 10.12, two differences in terminology must be noted. First, the relationship called *item of stock* in Figure 7.5 is simply called *stock* in Figure 10.12. Second, the entity type in Figure 10.12 called Stock Replenishment is equivalent to the relationship called *shipment item* in Figure 7.5.

In Figure 10.12, a *paid* relationship is shown between Supplier Invoice and Supplier Payment. It is used to record the amount of a payment that applies to a particular invoice sent by the supplier. It is analogous to the other *paid* relationship in Figure 10.12 between Cash Receipt and Customer Invoice.

PAYROLL

The payroll subfunction manages wage payments to employees and deductions for various employee benefit plans and government mandated tax withholding requirements. It may also handle employer payments to employee benefit plans and employer payroll taxes. In many organizations, it also takes responsibility for entering and maintaining all information required about employees for personnel administration purposes. The reason for this latter responsibility is probably psychological: Employees will make sure any data required by the payroll office is correctly provided and updated because their wages might not be processed on time otherwise. The data required for personnel administration has already been described in Chapter 5.

The liabilities affected by payroll processing are labor payment liabilities to employees, employee payment obligations to benefit plans and government withholding taxation, employer payment obligations to benefit programs and government taxation, and benefit plan payment obligations to employees (or their beneficiaries). Therefore, the decomposition of Subsidiary Account must provide for employees, benefit plans, government withholding taxes, and government payroll taxes.

Employee needs to be recognized as a specialization of Subsidiary Account. Important attributes of Employee needed for processing payroll transactions include social security number, number of withholding deductions, and accrued salary or wage obligations. Employee provides access to a subsidiary ledger for the accrued salary and wage liability accounts in the general ledger.

In the case of benefit plans, withholding requirements and employer payroll taxes, an analysis of the attributes required for payroll processing shows that they are virtually the same for the three candidate entity types. In each case, the amount to be deducted or paid by the employer is determined by a fixed fee and/or a percentage which may apply only to a certain portion of total wages. For this reason (and for the sake of simplicity) one entity type, labeled Deduction in Figure 10.12, can be used for all three.

The Deduction entity type, however, is not sufficient to serve as a subsidiary ledger, because details about the deductions for individual employees are required for payroll processing. In the case of benefit plans, withholding obligations, and payroll taxes, the subsidiary ledger must also show the situation with respect to the individual employee. Normally, there is an account in the general ledger for each benefit plan, withholding obligation, and payroll tax. The question is, how does that liability account total relate to individual employee obligations? To model this detail, a relationship between employee and each plan or withholding tax requirement or employer tax is needed. The *employee deduction* relationship between Employee and Deduction serves this purpose.

There are a number of payments made in connection with payroll. Two that often warrant standard transaction treatment are employee pay checks and employee benefit checks. In Figure 10.12 both are shown. Pay Check has a one-to-many relationship with Employee and *period bank account,* and an *isa* relationship with Standard Transaction. The relationship with *period bank account* is for purposes of bank reconciliation, as was previously explained. Benefit Payment has one-to-many relationships with *employee deduction* and *period bank account,* and an *isa* relationship with Standard Transaction.

Other payments that might be described by Standard Transaction specializations and might be related to the Deduction entity type (and *period bank account*) are employer payroll tax and withholding payments to government. Employer contributions to benefit plans also can be handled this way.

Labor cost distribution is the allocation of wage and salary costs to products and services and expense budget categories. It serves cost accounting and budgeting purposes. Direct labor is debited to work orders and credited to accrued wages according to the time spent on an operation as measured by the timekeeping system. Indirect labor and overhead labor are charged to expense accounts and then allocated to products by the cost accounting system.

The timekeeping system, which is briefly described in the chapter on production, generates labor time allocations which become labor charges when an appropriate rate is applied. These labor charges can be categorized as an entity type that is a specialization of the Standard Transaction generalization. This entity type has a one-to-many relationship with both the Employee and Job Step entity types, which can be considered two specializations of the Subsidiary Account generalization. As shown in Figure 10.12, Labor Charge also has relationships with Standard Transaction and *posting*. The Transaction entity type serves as a batch control record. The relationship with *posting* ties a labor charge posting to the set of labor charges being recorded in the ledger.

No relationship is shown in Figure 10.12 between Labor Charge and Organization Unit. The labor charges to the Account occurrences of an organization unit can be obtained, however, through the Account relationship to *account-in-period* and its relationship to *posting*. In a process-oriented cost accounting system, there could be a relationship between Job Step and Organization Unit which would more directly link labor charges to the organization unit responsible for controlling them.

FIXED ASSETS

The fixed assets of a business are items of property used in the business over a period of years that were acquired at a significant cost. They become resources of the business that generate benefits over the years of their useful life. Plant and equipment are common examples of fixed assets.

The management of fixed assets concerns the acquisition, control, depreciation, maintenance, and disposal of such assets. To perform these activities, information about individual fixed assets, or groups of similar assets, is needed beyond information available from the attributes of the Account entity type. In addition to the current book value of the asset and current depreciation charge, the first cost of the asset and its estimated useful life are needed to calculate depreciation charges.

A specialization of the Subsidiary Account entity type of Figure 10.6 can be used to identify individual fixed assets (or groups of similar assets). The attributes of this Fixed Asset entity type include asset identification, first cost, useful life, depreciation method, estimated salvage value, and depreciated value.

The acquisition of a fixed asset begins with a capital budgeting decision. This decision is commonly based on a projection of cash flow effects over the useful life of the asset. These cash flow effect estimates can be characterized as attributes of a relationship between Fixed Asset and Accounting Period. This relationship is labeled *depreciation plan* in Figure 10.12. Another attribute of this relationship is the portion of the first cost allocated to each accounting period as a depreciation expense. The recording of depreciation expense should also be treated as a separate event, shown in Figure 10.12 as a Standard Transaction specialization.

The event of acquiring a fixed asset may involve a purchase or a construction project or a trade. In the case of purchase, the fact that a fixed asset is involved could be recorded in the database as a relationship between the Fixed Asset and Supplier Invoice entity types as shown in Figure 10.12. In the case of a construction project, a Work Order could be used to accumulate the costs involved. In such a case, Work Order should be considered a generalized entity type that could be expanded into a work breakdown structure and scheduling information structure as described in the chapter on the engineering function.

The control aspect of fixed asset management concerns the location of each fixed asset and which organizational unit has responsibility for it. This information could be treated as an attribute of Fixed Asset, or it could be stored as a relationship between Organizational Unit and Fixed Asset. The second approach would facilitate access of fixed asset information by organizational unit; the relationship alternative is not shown in Figure 10.12 only for reasons of diagram simplicity.

The relationship between the Subsidiary Account occurrence for a fixed asset and Account is more complex than indicated in Figure 10.12. The Subsidiary Account occurrence can be linked to the fixed asset account or the cumulative depreciation account for the fixed asset, but not both. First cost and cumulative depreciation for individual fixed asset can be attributes of Fixed Asset.

The information useful in managing maintenance of fixed assets can be treated as attributes of fixed assets and of maintenance work orders related to the fixed asset repaired. The disposal of a fixed asset is an event that should be treated as a conversion of a resource to cash, outside of the normal working capital cycle; it should not be treated as a sale. In most cases it is reasonable to record such events directly as Transaction occurrences.

COST ACCOUNTING

The management of inventories has two aspects. One is physical and the other evaluative. The objective of physical management is to have adequate quantities of product, parts, and supplies on hand to meet production and customer demand but at the same time not to have excess quantities or obsolete items. The objective of evaluative management is to set a value on inventories that is the lesser of market value or cost. This value determines the cost of goods sold. The information needed for physical management of inventories is not considered here. It is discussed in the chapter on materials management.

To determine the market value of inventories it is necessary to be specific about what the inventories include. They must be segregated into separate stocks of specific items for which a market price exists or can be estimated. Thus, the evaluation function needs information about the specific items held in stock. Two attributes of the *stock* relationship needed to establish the market value of inventories are quantity and market price.

Stock, viewed as an entity type, is a specialization of the Subsidiary Account entity type shown in Figure 10.6. The *stock* entity type in Figure 10.12 is depicted as a relationship between Item and Location, two entity types that are of basic importance in materials management. Since the market value of an item may depend on its location, this interpretation of *stock* is not inappropriate for setting inventory values as well.

Inventories also must be defined at the "item held in stock" level for cost determination purposes. The cost of an item consists of two parts, direct and indirect costs. The direct cost per unit varies depending on the item and therefore the quantity of each item is important for costing purposes.

There are various methods for calculating the inventory cost for a given item in stock. The most commonly used methods are the first in, first out (FIFO) and last in, first out (LIFO) methods with specific allocations of cost to stock replenishments and withdrawals. These methods require that each addition to a stock be recognized as an entity type. The attributes of this entity type include quantity added to inventory, direct cost, indirect cost allocation basis (or bases), and indirect charge per base unit. Commonly used bases for allocation of indirect costs are direct labor hours, or cost, machining hours and direct materials cost.

Stock withdrawal is another essential entity type for inventory costing purposes. The cost of the stock withdrawn is the key attribute, as well as the quantity. In the FIFO and LIFO methods, this cost is determined from the cost of stock replenishments.

These two event entity types, Stock Replenishment and Stock Withdrawal, should be viewed as specializations of the Standard Transaction entity type in Figure 10.6. In Figure 10.12 they are each linked in a one-to-many relationship with the *stock* relationship. However, they are also linked to another subsidiary ledger, called Work Order.

The Work Order entity type has attributes that describe the total cost incurred in the process of making a product. However, for more detail, a cost accounting system should account for costs by the production operation in which they were incurred. To obtain this additional detail, a Job Step entity type is decomposed from Work Order (or, as described in Chapter 8, a relationship between Work Order and Operation can be set up). As raw material and semi-finished parts are withdrawn from stock to make the product, those costs are added to the Work Order materials cost attribute and linked to Job Step. As direct labor is expended in carrying out the work, that cost is also added to the Work Order total and linked to Job Step. When the work is completed, the total cost of the product becomes a stock replenishment debit to a finished product (or semi-finished item) inventory account. For more information on the information structure required for production cost accounting, see Figure 8.3 and the discussion of that figure.

BUDGETING

Planning the amounts to be spent in future accounting periods for various types of expenses, and indirect costs, is the first half of expense budgeting. Comparing actual expenses to budget and analyzing the reasons for discrepancies is the other half.

Both budgeted and actual expenses can be viewed as attributes of the *account-in-period* (and *subsidiary-in-period*) relationship of Figure 10.12. To the extent that this planning and control activity requires only historical actual and budgeted account balance figures, the database design as already defined in Table 10.1 should be sufficient.

The budget volume and actual volume attributes in Table 10.1 are for variable budgeting systems. In some cases, actual and forecast measures of activity (for example, sales volume, number of orders, lines of advertising) can be used to calculate a budget. In such cases, the budget and actual volume attributes are appropriate.

SUMMARY

This chapter assessed the effectiveness for financial database planning of what could be called a progressive specialization approach. This approach, as described in Part 1, involves first creating a generalized information structure, based only on the objectives of top management. The very general information structure is then specialized to the needs of a particular business function, such as financial management. Next, the more specific processes of performing the function are defined as subfunctions and the information usage requirements (and supplemental data) of each subfunction are identified. This information is structured as decompositions of the information structure defined for the more general function, or as attributes of an entity type in the decomposition.

Three subfunctions of financial management are defined: finance, accounting and auditing. The general information structure of Figure 10.1 is decomposed to suit the needs of each of these three subfunctions. The information structure for finance is shown in Figure 10.3. The structure for accounting is shown in Figure 10.6. For auditing, two types of information structures are needed; one is the accounting structure and the other is structures defined in the next chapter that describe the accounting information systems and their operation.

The subfunctions of the finance, accounting and auditing functions are identified and summarized in Figure 10.11. Four subfunctions are defined for finance and four for auditing. Seven subfunctions of accounting are described.

The information requirements of the seven subfunctions of accounting are described in the last section of the chapter. Their combined requirements are summarized in Figure 10.12. In this figure, common specializations of Subsidiary Account and Standard Transaction are shown. The most useful relationships between these specializations are also depicted. The discussion of each subfunction explains which parts of the Figure 10.12 structure are required and the general logic of the subfunction.

REFERENCES

1. Burton, John C., Russell E. Palmer, and Robert S. Kay, *Handbook of Accounting and Auditing* (Boston: Warren, Gorham & Lamont, 1981).

DISCUSSION QUESTIONS

1. Compare and contrast the objectives of financial management with the goals of the enterprise.

2. How do the objectives of obtaining financial support and fulfilling financial commitments relate to one another? Should the goal in Figure 10.1 be specialized to financial support instead of financial commitment?

3. What should the entity type called Financial Asset in Figure 10.1 include?

4. For which types of enterprises is the functional breakdown shown in Figure 10.2 appropriate? A privately held company? A bank? A government agency, such as the federal Housing and Urban Development (HUD) Department?

5. In what sense is the sale of receivables to a factoring service a commitment made by the financial management subfunction?

6. Why is the *transaction* relationship of Figure 10.1 shown as two entity types (Transaction and Accounting Period), a one-to-many relationship between them, and two many-to-many relationships (*postings-1* and *postings-2*) in Figure 10.4?

7. Is the single one-to-many *account hierarchy* relationship shown in Figure 10.6 sufficient for managerial accounting purposes?

8. Should the account for income be a top level account in a separate hierarchy created by occurrences of the *account hierarchy*, or should it be at the top of a sub-hierarchy for which a total equity account is the top level account?

9. Compare and contrast the Account and Subsidiary Account entity types shown in Figure 10.6.

10. Compare and contrast the Transaction and Standard Transaction entity types.

11. Referring to Figure 10.9, how many occurrences of the *charge* relationship and the Standard Transaction entity type are there for each occurrence of Customer Invoice?

12. How can the E-R diagram of Figure 10.6 be modified to accommodate the data required to automatically initiate recurring transactions, such as payment of a monthly insurance premium?

13. What type of information is needed to detect systematic accounting errors and fraud?

14. Should budgeting be a subfunction of accounting, as shown in Figure 10.11?

15. What does the cost accounting subfunction include and why is it becoming more difficult to accomplish?

16. Which audit subfunction includes verifying that the physical inventory is the same as the book inventory?

17. How has the emergence of computerized accounting systems affected the audit subfunction?

18. Describe a report needed for the cash budgeting subfunction.

19. For bank balance reconciliation purposes, should Cash Receipts be linked by a one-to-many relationship with Bank Account or with a many-to-many relationship between Bank Account and Accounting Period?

20. Customer X phones our salesman to say that the shipment of Product 122 that he received two months ago is the wrong color and he will be returning

it for a refund. The invoice has already been paid. Is the database of Figure 10.12 sufficient to handle this sales return transaction? What entities and relationships would be affected or used in processing the return?

21. What information is required for the payables subfunction?

22. Employers in most states must pay a state unemployment insurance tax. It is calculated as a fixed percentage of wage and salary payments for payments up to a certain maximum annual total. For which entity or relationship in Figure 10.12 could the fixed percentage be an attribute?

23. Under what conditions would it be worthwhile to link Job Step to Organizational Unit?

24. How should the accounting for a fixed asset be handled in the database of Figure 10.12 (and Figure 8.3) if the asset is purchased from a vendor and then customized as part of an in-house construction project?

25. Traditional charts of accounts have both fixed asset accounts and control accounts for cumulative depreciation of the fixed assets. How can both a fixed asset control account and its cumulative depreciation account be linked to the details about each fixed asset included in the control account?

26. Under what circumstances would a single instance of Stock Withdrawal in Figure 10.12 be involved in relationships with both Job Step and *stock*?

27. Does Figure 10.12 provide for charging the cost of machine tools to production jobs? If not, how can such charges be accommodated?

28. Does budgeting require only data that can be modeled as attributes of the *account-in-period* relationship of Figure 10.12?

11

Information Systems Management

NATURE OF THE FUNCTION

The computer-communication systems that are used to encode, transmit, store, process, display, and print data are the concern of the information systems function. Computers and digital communication links are merely a new way of executing a very old function, namely to record and transmit the agreements, observations, thoughts, and laws of mankind.

This new way of performing an old function has advantages and disadvantages. Consider some of the advantages: Printed results are of excellent quality; the integration of graphics and text makes for an effective presentation of ideas; a high level of accuracy and completeness in record keeping is possible; the exact required data can be quickly retrieved from a vast store of data; access to data can be controlled; and data can be easily broadcast to a select few or to many thousands.

To provide these benefits, however, the information systems function requires investments. It requires systems planning which is an investment of professional time. It requires investments in hardware and software. It requires training and documentation. It requires an investment in a technical support staff.

Information systems management is a form of investment management. It is a matter of identifying an opportunity to make an organization more effective and efficient by providing better information systems and then marshalling the resources needed to take advantage of the opportunity. As with all investment opportunities, there are risks. Judging the improvement in the performance of an organization that will result from its having better data and communications capabilities is difficult. It requires an awareness of the current mistakes and waste and a realistic assessment of the impact that better data management can have on the performance of the people involved. The risk lies in misjudging the opportunity or what it will take to succeed.

An investment in information systems is an investment in education. Those who will use the system (the users or customers) must thoroughly educate those who will plan, design, and implement the system (or system improvement) in the nature of their functions and the information requirements of the functions. Those who plan the system must educate the customer in the costs and limitations of the information systems that can be obtained. Those who build and maintain an information system must educate users how to make the system do what they want done and what precautions must be taken to avoid system failures and loss of data.

All investments require trust and good will in order to be successful. But investments in information systems require an especially high level of these spiritual qualities. If the customer thinks of an information system as a product that can be separated from its designer and supplier, the result is disappointment and failure because of changing information requirements and inadequate technical support. If the system supplier (designer and supplier) thinks of the customer as someone to be misled until the system has been sold and paid for (or, in the case of an in-house supplier, as someone to be told what he can have), the result again is disappointment and failure because the customer's needs are not adequately addressed. Everyone involved in an information system must realize that the others involved are real people not objects to be manipulated, and that all roles are long term. There are no "you lose, I win" outcomes possible. It is either "you win, I win" or "you lose, I lose."

A future time can be anticipated in which computer-communications technology will have stabilized and the information systems used by organizations will be standardized, at least compared to the present. The educational processes will also, eventually, be built into the educational systems of society. At that point, the information system management function may well become part of the facilities management function that already exists in every organization. At this time, however, the systems in place are far from satisfactory, and it appears that it will be at least another generation before new application systems begin to reach a point of diminishing returns.

INFORMATION REQUIREMENTS

Managing the information systems used by an organization is one of the subfunctions of managing an organization identified in Lists 4.1, 4.2, and 4.3. Accordingly, it should be possible to derive the information requirements of this subfunction by decomposing the general management information requirement defined in Chapter 5 and illustrated in Figure 5.1.

The information required to manage information systems and their development fits the structure of Figure 5.1 quite easily. Information systems management has goals and resources. It also has the two types of relationships between goal and resource information depicted in Figure 5.1.

The decomposition of Figure 5.1 to apply to the information systems management subfunction is shown in Figure 11.1. The Goal entity type is decomposed to four entity types (and relationships between them): Information Requirement, System Requirement, Development Plan, and Information. The Resource entity type is decomposed to two entity types, Customer and Technical Resource. The *plan* relationship is decomposed into two relationships, *information planning* and

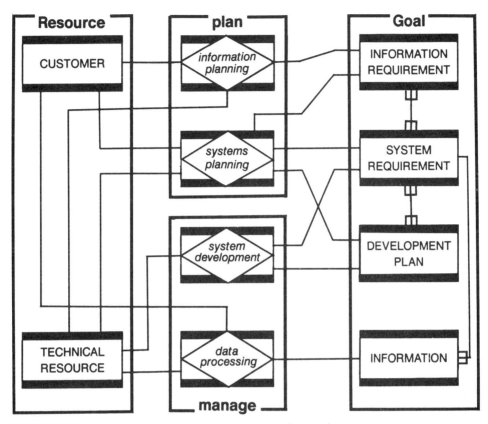

FIGURE 11.1. Information structure for information systems management.

systems planning. The *manage* relationship also has two specializations, one is *system development* and the other is *data processing.*

The following subsections describe the entities and relationships of Figure 11.1. Because this information structure provides the basis for all of the more detailed structures developed in this chapter, it is important to understand the meaning of each entity type and relationship. The lack of standard terms and concepts in this new and dynamic field makes it easy to misunderstand how a familiar word or phrase is being used.

INFORMATION REQUIREMENT

An information requirement is a type of data that someone in an organization needs for decision making, for communicating, or for documenting an event. It is not usually considered a specific fact but rather a type of fact, such as the sales to a customer last month or the price of certain products.

An information requirement can be described in varying degrees of specificity. It can be in terms of an unlimited group of facts about an entity type or relationship. Or it can be described in detail as a datum, specifying not only its symbolic representation but also its availability, update frequency, location, ownership, and archival requirements. The information structures discussed in previous chapters are relatively general descriptions of information requirements.

The more specific requirement descriptions can become complex. For example, the availability of the data can be an important aspect of a requirement. It has two facets. One is the form and timing of data availability. The other is control over access; who has access and who does not? Both are important and can become quite complex to specify.

SYSTEM REQUIREMENT

A system requirement is a description of a data processing system that a customer wants. It describes a capability or procedure that the system should have, including the reports and forms it will produce, the types of transactions it will process, the kinds of queries it can answer, its modes of interaction with users, and the hardware and system software with which it is compatible. If there are security or data validity controls required, they are specified as well.

The relationship between Information Requirement and System Requirement defines the database requirements of each system. Through this relationship, the data required for each report and query is identified. If the system captures data, the items in the database that are populated and managed by this system are defined.

One person's data requirement can be another person's data capture responsibility. If one person executes a transaction that others need to know about, the facts about the transaction can become a data capture responsibility for the person executing the transaction.

The system requirement is the goal of the *systems planning* relationship in the sense that it is the result of that planning effort. It is the goal of the *system development* relationship in the sense that it defines the objective of the development project.

DEVELOPMENT PLAN

A system development plan is a project plan for the development effort. It is similar to the project plan discussed in Chapter 9 on engineering information, and shown in Figure 9.4. It includes cost and schedule plans for the development project. In the case of application software to be developed as part of the project, it contains the structured breakdown of the system which identifies program modules and programming and testing tasks to be performed.

INFORMATION

The term information is used to describe data that is provided to someone. It is the output of the data processing operations. The attributes of information that are required for the management of information systems include to whom the data was provided, when it was provided, feedback on its utility, and the cost of providing it.

CUSTOMER

A customer is an individual or a group for whom an information system is developed. When the system is functioning, the customer either uses the system or uses the data derived from the system. The customer may be the one who pays for the system or the one who uses the system, if there is a difference.

Customer also includes the notion of the owner of data stored in the system. Different customers may have ownership rights to different types of data in a system. These rights may include the right to control access to the data and the right to create or destroy the data.

The concept of a customer as a resource is based on the same reasoning as was used in the chapter on marketing for the Market Segment entity type. The customer is a key factor, if not the source, of the information and system requirements goals.

TECHNICAL RESOURCE

The Technical Resource entity type refers to all of the resources commonly considered part of the information systems or data processing department of the enterprise. Computers, communication networks, computer and communication experts, system software, development software, applications software, databases, programmers, system analysts and designers, and database administrators are all included in this entity type.

Technical Resource should also include technology that is available in the marketplace as well as that which exists within the organization. For systems planning and development purposes particularly, the new technology available and information on technological trends is an important part of the resource base.

INFORMATION PLANNING

The *information planning* relationship is shown as a three-way relationship in Figure 11.1. The relationship links customers to their information requirements and technological resources that are available (or required) to satisfy those requirements. Both requirements to retrieve the information and requirements to capture the information for later use are identified.

The *information planning* relationship can define the data sharing opportunities in the organization. It can identify the customers who require the same information. The location of these customers for a given type of information determines to some extent the technological resources required to supply the needed information.

SYSTEMS PLANNING

Systems planning is a joint effort by the customer and systems analysts (part of the technical resource) to define processing systems that will meet the needs of the customer and the business. The outcome of this effort, if successful, is a set of system requirements. The analysis process should include a determination that all of the data processed by the system is defined as an information requirement. Thus, the Information Requirement entity type is included in the relationship.

Systems planning includes evaluating systems design alternatives from economic, technological, and operational standpoints. It must take into account the economics of the investment opportunities and weigh the adequacy of the technical resources to successfully develop a system that will exploit the opportunity. This means that the *systems planning* relationship may include an evaluation of a system requirement in terms of its economic, technical, and operational feasibility.

The formulation of a project development plan for individual systems is also part of systems planning. The estimates of cost and a development schedule for the system are based on this project development plan. The plan identifies the staffing, computer system, and software development methodology that will be required. Thus, the *systems planning* relationship involves the Development Plan entity type in Figure 11.1.

SYSTEM DEVELOPMENT

System development is executing the system development plan. The objective of the project is set by one or more system requirements. The development plan describes how to build the system and proposes the staffing, facilities, budget, and schedule requirements of the project.

The distinction between systems planning and system development is one of scope as well as of planning versus doing. The scope of systems planning is business-wide. It is concerned with coordinating systems development. The scope of systems development is limited to the system being developed. Anything outside of the requirements placed on that system is beyond the scope of a system development effort.

In Figure 11.1, system development is shown as a specialization of the *manage* relationship of Figure 5.1, because it is mainly concerned with applying resources to achieve a result, namely an improved information system. The improved system is the goal of system development. This goal is shaped by the systems planning process. Therefore, systems planning is considered a specialization of the *plan* relationship of Figure 5.1. Nevertheless, the distinction is not as clear as it may seem because of the refinement of goals that often occurs as part of the system development process.

DATA PROCESSING OPERATIONS

The *data processing* relationship of Figure 11.1 is based on the routine use of technical resources to produce information for customers. It is a relationship based on a type of event, the event of providing useable data to a customer. To some extent, this event is manageable, and it is a responsibility of the information systems management function to make sure that the benefits to the organization exceed the cost of the technical resources used to create them. A system of charging for technical resources is one means of managing the responsibility, but it is not an easy system to manage.

FIRST-LEVEL BREAKDOWN OF INFORMATION
SYSTEMS MANAGEMENT

The management of information systems includes both management of existing systems and management of the development of information systems. As explained in the first chapter, management of development involves managing the environment in which individual system development initiatives take place. The initiative for a system usually comes from a customer who sees an opportunity for a profitable investment in systems. If the environment has been properly managed, a system can be proposed to the customer that takes advantage of, and enhances, the existing information systems of the business.

There are three basic subfunctions of information systems management. One is to manage customer relationships. A second provides the technical leadership and support that customers of the information systems function and the business as a whole need. The third subfunction manages the day-to-day functioning of existing information systems. In addition, there are subfunctions that provide services to these three subfunctions. These are grouped under the title of administrative services. This breakdown is depicted in Figure 11.2.

Remember that this is a functional breakdown, not an organizational structure for the information systems function. A functional breakdown does not need to consider locational factors or the ways in which sub-subfunctions may interact in practice. These are considerations which should certainly influence the organizational arrangement, however.

Each of the four subfunctions is explained in a following subsection. The descriptions focus on the subfunction as a whole. Further details concerning the subfunction are given at the next breakdown level.

SERVICE MANAGEMENT

The service management subfunction performs a vital part of the investment management function for which information systems management is responsible. That part identifies profitable investment opportunities and marshals the resources needed to seize them. Many of the opportunities are relatively small and require only a small investment. In handling these small investment opportunities well, however, an account representative (who performs this subfunction) builds a trust relationship with the customer for whom the system improvement is made, which can lead to larger opportunities.

The service management function provides coordination between the customer and the other two subfunctions which provide the technical support and operations. The customer looks to the account representative for leadership in obtaining appropriate technical support for maintenance and system development. The technical services and operations staffs, on the other hand, look to the account representative as a salesman for their services. He must understand the

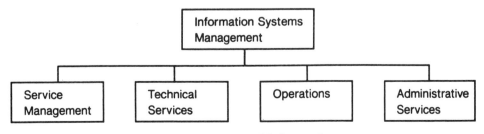

FIGURE 11.2. First-level breakdown of information systems management.

systems, software, and expertise they have to offer and show the customer how they can benefit his function and the business. This education of the customer can take the form of seminars and workshops at which the capabilities of computers are discussed and potential applications are considered.

Organizationally, the account representative may be a part of the information services department or he may belong to the customer's department. He may be a programmer/analyst or staff analyst in the customer's department, for example, who solves the day-to-day problems of using microcomputers and accessing computer databases. Or, he may be someone in the information systems department who has gained the confidence of a customer. Someone who can marshal the necessary technical resources and manage their application must also have a trust relationship with the customer before significant information services can be successfully delivered.

This service management subfunction has a role to play at all levels in the organization. In particular, there are some information management services that must be provided to the business as a whole. In this case, top management is the customer. If there is no account representative that has the confidence of top management, then these business-wide information services will not be provided. Unfortunately, this is all too common. The result is uncoordinated systems and a lack of executive information systems.

TECHNICAL SERVICES

This subfunction provides the expertise required to adapt computers and communication systems to the needs of the business. It includes the planning, guidance in acquisition, and testing of hardware and system software. It includes the planning of databases and application systems. It includes the programming, testing of software, documentation of applications, and training of users. In an object-oriented environment, it includes the definition, development and management of object software.

OPERATIONS

This subfunction operates the computers and communication networks of the enterprise. It takes care of the archival libraries of software and data maintained by the enterprise. It provides a quality control service for data entered into the system and for reports produced by computer. It performs routine tests on the system and performs routine maintenance tasks. It operates and monitors security systems that protect the physical resources and control access to the system.

There is a certain amount of interaction between the programming and testing facets of the technical services subfunction and the operations subfunction. From the viewpoint of operations, however, the programming and testing activity is simply processing the data of another customer.

ADMINISTRATIVE SERVICE

The breakdown in Figure 11.2 includes a subfunction that is really a collection of subfunctions that can be viewed as subfunctions of either information systems management or another function, such as personnel, accounting, or facilities management. The information systems function is very labor intensive which makes the personnel services of training, counseling, benefits administration, and compensation management critically important. Cost accounting and billing for both project costs and computer operations costs can be as complex for information services as for any function in the business. Also, facilities management can involve special air conditioning and power supply requirements.

INFORMATION STRUCTURES FOR SECOND-LEVEL FUNCTIONS

In this section, information requirements should be defined for each of the four subfunctions just described, in terms of entity-relationship diagrams that define the structure of required information. However, three of the four subfunctions are too general to exclude any of the entities or relationships shown in Figure 11.1. Service management can require information about any of the entities or relationships of Figure 11.1. The same is true for Technical Services and Administrative Services.

The operations subfunction, on the other hand, is not concerned with the information planning, systems planning, or system development relationships. Nor is it concerned with occurrences of the Information Requirement or Development Plan entity type (except for information about when new systems will be implemented). The information requirements of this subfunction can be clarified by a decomposition of Figure 11.1.

OPERATIONS INFORMATION STRUCTURE

Managers of the operation of information systems need data about the programs executed and to be executed. A program is either an application program, utility program, or test run on a computer system or network. A program may require access to a certain tape or disk drive. It may require a certain type of printer or a preprinted form in the printer. When the program is run, it produces certain results. A record of these results is a measure of the output of the operations subfunction.

Management also needs data on the utilization of resources. It needs to be able to identify the bottleneck in the system of computers and network links and peripheral equipment that is the hardware aspect of the system being operated. It also needs information about the percentage of time the technical staff is spending on operational problems, as opposed to system development and planning problems.

The information structure that describes the data needs of operations management is shown in Figure 11.3. In this structure, the *data processing* relationship of Figure 11.1 is specialized to a Program Execution entity type, and the Information, System Requirement, Customer and Technical Resource entity types are each decomposed to identify the entities and relationships of importance to the operations subfunction.

The decompositions in Figure 11.3 are explained in the following subsections. The subsection headings refer to the entity type in Figure 11.1 that is decomposed.

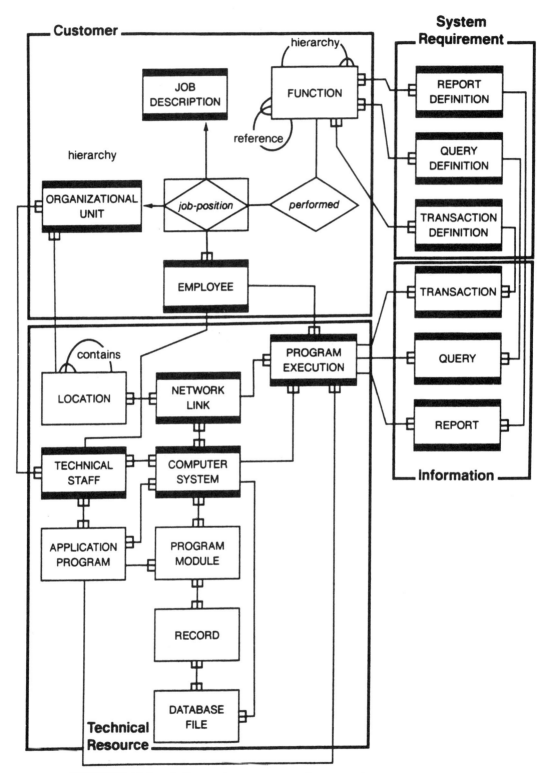

FIGURE 11.3. Information structure for operations management.

Information

The Information entity is decomposed to three entity types, Report, Query, and Transaction. These are the three possible types of program outputs. There is a Report occurrence for each report produced by an application program or system test or utility program. Similarly, for each query submitted, there is a Query occurrence that records the query and response. A Transaction occurrence is entered into the database for each transaction processed by an application program. In this case, the term transaction refers to the execution of an application program that involves some data entry and perhaps calculation.

System Requirement

The System Requirement entity is decomposed to three entity types that define the three types of system outputs. In the case of Report Definition, the data about this entity type must be adequate for a utility program that produces reports to use in formatting the report and retrieving the data contained in the report. The generalization symbol in Figure 11.3 indicates that it is anticipated that more than a single entity type will be required for this detail.

The Query Definition entity type defines the types of queries required for a certain customer function. The database query processor should refer to this information to determine whether the user who makes the query has a "need to know" and should therefore be given the data requested. The person who makes the query is assumed to be an employee in Figure 11.3 who is filling a certain job-position that is responsible for performing the functions linked to it via the *performed* relationship.

The Transaction Definition entity type defines the transactions entered by each function and can serve the same kind of security and integrity control purposes as does Query Definition. A transaction definition, like a report definition, must eventually include the specification of each input field on each input screen involved in capturing the transaction.

Customer

The Customer entity type is decomposed in Figure 11.3 to the same Organization Unit to Job Description relationship that we have seen in Figure 5.3 and in a number of other figures. This *job-position* relationship is involved as an entity type in two other relationships, one with Employee and the other with Function. The *performed* relationship is the same as that shown in Figure 4.11. It is explained in Chapter 4, where there is also an explanation of the Function entity type.

Operations requires information about the customer's organizational context in order to effectively manage the execution of data processing jobs in a secure and responsible manner. Employees requesting the execution of programs must be identifiable in terms of the job-position held and the organization unit that will be charged for the processing.

Technical Resource

The decomposition of Technical Resource is intended to show the kinds of resources involved in operations management. Three of the entity types, however, still appear as generalizations that will probably require further decomposition at a later stage. These three are Network Link, Computer System, and Technical Staff.

The Location entity type is the same as that shown in Figure 4.11 and is explained in Chapter 4. The linkage of Location to Organization Unit rather than to the *performed* relationship (as in Figure 4.11) requires that all the functions performed by the job-positions of an organization unit be done at one location. This is a more restrictive model than that of Figure 4.11 and may not be appropriate in all organizations. It is used in Figure 11.3 to provide an easy way to pull together all of the information that operations management needs about any location where there are data processing operations.

The Network Link entity type represents what operations needs to know about the data communications network that links computer systems and that links users to computers. A link implies a node at each end. In the diagram, the nodes are assumed to be computer systems. Closer investigation, however, would reveal switching computers and other gear at each end. The main function of the link is to connect computers. Operations management needs to know the links that are available, their capacities, access procedures, and costs.

The Computer System entity type represents a computer and the peripheral equipment to which it is connected at a site. It also represents the operating system and utility software used to manage, test, and monitor the hardware. The term computer is intended to be vague and to include everything from simple personal computers to mainframe supercomputers. Important attributes of this entity type as far as operations management is concerned include percentage utilization, percentage down time, the organization unit that has control of it, the system software loaded into it, and its processing and storage capacities.

The Technical Staff entity type includes both hardware and software specialists. It includes both system software and applications software experts. Networking specialists would also be considered part of the technical staff. A many-to-many relationship is shown linking Technical Staff to Organization Unit. This indicates that the technical staff could be distributed in the organization. Depending on how technical staff is decomposed, this relationship might be one-to-many or one-to-one.

The Application Program entity type represents a suite of program modules customized to the requirements of a particular computer application. The application program when executed displays a menu of options, and depending on the option chosen, a certain sequence of program modules is executed. The application programs and modules exist in the disk storage of various computer systems where they can be executed.*

Program modules are computer programs that perform a certain function which may involve accessing a database either to retrieve or to add data. The records accessed by the module are defined by the relationship between Record and Program Module.

Records exist in physical files on computer systems. A file containing data records is referred to as a database file in Figure 11.3. If a Record occurrence exists in more than one physical file then the record is replicated in the databases of the business. It is possible, however, for a record type to exist in more than one

---

* This breakdown is for the traditional method of software organization. It would be different if an object-oriented approach is taken.

database file without having any replication of occurrences of that record type. In Figure 11.3, Record represents a record type, not a record occurrence.

SECOND-LEVEL BREAKDOWN OF INFORMATION SYSTEMS MANAGEMENT

The four subfunctions of information systems management each have important subfunctions. For example, the service management function can be analyzed to distinguish the types of services provided to customers. Technical services breaks down along technical discipline lines. The operations function has some support functions in addition to the operating functions of the computer systems.

A second-level breakdown of the four subfunctions is shown in Figure 11.4. It shows three service management subfunctions, four technical service subfunctions, four operations subfunctions, and four administrative service subfunctions. These 15 subfunctions are briefly described next.

SERVICE MANAGEMENT

Customer Service

The general management of the delivery of information system services is the essence of the service management function. The customer service subfunction

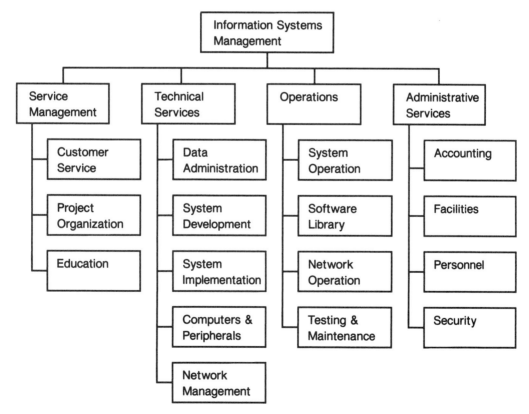

FIGURE 11.4. Second-level breakdown of information systems management.

makes the customer the focus of this function. It requires that someone be responsible for communicating to a customer the ways in which information systems and related services could be applied to the business functions of the customer. As the customer requests that these applications be developed (and related services provided), this subfunction is responsible for coordinating their delivery.

Explicit recognition of this subfunction may not be common at this time as far as the way information systems departments are organized. However, many data processing departments have long had quality control sections to deal with customer problems and concerns. Leaders of system development projects are commonly selected as much for their ability to work with the customers as for their technical abilities. There is also a growing use of formal customer service agreements as a way of clarifying the quality and quantity of service the customer can expect from their information systems department (see reference 1, for example).

Project Organization

The project organization subfunction is distinguished from the customer service subfunction only in the scope and focus of the activity. Whereas, customer service cultivates relations between a customer and the information systems function, generally project organization works with technicians and customer personnel to investigate, define, and evaluate a specific system application possibility or policy issue. The subfunction does not conduct the planning project but it sees that others are assigned to the project and makes sure the project team understands the issues and is able to carry out the assignment.

Education

The purpose of this subfunction is to educate customers in the use of computers and communication systems so that they can perform business functions more effectively and efficiently. New ideas and developments in information technology are presented to potential users in a way that they can understand.

The education subfunction should not be confused with the function of training employees in how to operate a new system. Training users to work with a new system is a part of the system implementation function described below. This education function is oriented toward introducing managers to new system development possibilities or system management issues and their solutions.

TECHNICAL SERVICE

Data Administration

This subfunction coordinates the way data are defined, stored, and accessed across all information systems of the organization so that unplanned data redundancy is eliminated and duplicate data entry is minimized. It is often referred to as managing the information resources of the organization.

As explained in the first chapter, the strategy of data administration is to create an environment in which a plan already exists for organizing the data in the business for sharing. Then, as system development projects get funded, that part of the data plan that relates to the funded system can be implemented. The data administration subfunction ensures that this strategy is implemented.

Computers and Network Management

In terms of the steps of Table 1.1, this subfunction is responsible for Step 5. It continually reviews the options as far as computing and communication hardware and system software is concerned and recommends the best system for each situation.

The selection of database management system (DBMS) software and CASE tool sets is made in cooperation with experts in systems development. The CASE and DBMS software should be selected to be compatible with the computing platform and to best meet the requirements of the applications of the organization.

Management of the installation and testing of computing and communication hardware, system software, DBMS, and CASE tools is also a part of this function. In the case of distributed systems, the execution of this part of the function may also be distributed. This depends on the way information systems management is organized.

System Development

The system development subfunction provides the technical expertise required for application software acquisition or customized development. It may also provide the leadership for application development projects. In terms of the steps of Table 1.1, it is concerned with Steps 6 and 8. It can include application feasibility studies, systems analysis, system design, code generation, and system testing.

The system development subfunction also includes modifying, upgrading, and debugging existing software, which is often called software maintenance. These are smaller projects but they are often a part of systems development.

System Implementation

The system implementation function begins with the testing of new systems using realistic data. It includes preparation of user documentation of the new system and the user training on the new system. As the system is put into use, the system implementation staff identifies problems and obtains the necessary technical support to fix them as quickly as possible.

OPERATIONS

Four subfunctions of operations are shown in Figure 11.4. The first, systems operation, refers to the execution of the application programs designed to run on each computer. This may be done by the information systems staff or by the staff of the customer depending on where the equipment is located.

The second subfunction concerns the management of software stored on tapes, removeable disks, and diskettes. It includes responsibility for periodically backing up critical files and for archiving transaction data for which on-line access is no longer needed.

The network operation subfunction monitors the functioning of the communication network and takes appropriate action when a switch or link is malfunctioning. It is also responsible for making changes in the network as people and computers are moved or changed and as new equipment is obtained.

Routine testing of computers and peripheral equipment and the repair of defective units is another subfunction of operations. This subfunction can also include the development of procurement guidelines for items commonly purchased by many units in the organization.

ADMINISTRATIVE SERVICE

The four subfunctions of administrative services shown in Figure 11.4 are self-explanatory. The accounting subfunction can include the billing of customers for system usage as well as project cost accounting and expense budgeting. Facilities management refers to the buildings, furnishings, and equipment other than the computer and communication systems.

INFORMATION STRUCTURES FOR THIRD-LEVEL SUBFUNCTIONS

The information requirements of the subfunctions of Figure 11.4 can be derived from the information structure shown in Figure 11.1. In the case of the subfunctions of operations, Figure 11.3 provides an even better guideline because it concerns only the information involved in operations.

For the subfunctions of service management, the information requirements include details about the customer, technical resources, and the formulation of system requirements and development plans. In cases of service failures, the customer service function also will require details concerning Information entity type occurrences. The decomposition of the structure in Figure 11.1 to explicitly identify the information needs of the subfunctions of service management is straightforward, but it will not be developed in this discussion. To some extent it depends on how the subfunctions are viewed by those performing them and on the use they want to make of information systems to support their work.

The information requirements of the subfunctions of technical services vary considerably. The data administration subfunction is primarily concerned with the Information Requirement entity type and its relationships. The computers and network management subfunction requires a decomposition of Technical Resources that identifies the components of the hardware and communications equipment used by the business or that can be obtained by the business. The systems development subfunction focuses on systems planning and systems development and the entity types to which they relate, which include almost all of the entities in Figure 11.1. The systems implementation subfunction is particularly concerned with system development and the software to be tested and documented, which is a part of Technical Resource.

In this section, the information requirements of two of the subfunctions of technical services are considered in some detail. They are the data administration and system development subfunctions. Detailed treatment of all of the subfunctions of Figure 11.4 is not practical, so some selectivity must be exercised. Data administration is a central concern of this text and therefore should be discussed. System development is the subfunction with which data administration has much interaction.

DATA ADMINISTRATION

Managing the development, evolution, and implementation of a plan for the data of a business requires information about the plan and how it is being implemented. For the plan to be implemented it must satisfy two conditions. First, it must be based on a careful assessment of the data required to perform the functions of the business. Second, the definitions of data must be explicit so that the data will be defined in the same way by different system development teams, and therefore, the data captured by the different systems can be shared.

The information about the implementation of the plan must relate the plan to the database files that are implemented and considered part of the technical resources managed by the information systems function. It should be possible to show that every database file on the computer systems of the business is an implementation of some subset of the conceptual database plan.

The decomposition of Figure 11.1 that provides for this kind of information about a plan for data and its implementation is shown in Figure 11.5. It consists of a decomposition of three entity types in Figure 11.1. They are the Customer, Information Requirement, and Technical Resources entity types. These are the three entity types involved in the *information planning* relationship and, of course, that relationship is also reflected in some of the relationships shown in Figure 11.5.

Customer Decomposition

The decomposition of the Customer entity type is the same as is shown in Figure 11.3. As explained in Chapter 4, the Function entity type in this decomposition is any function identified in a functional breakdown of the business. The recursive relationship labeled *functional hierarchy* in Figure 11.5 links a function at one level in the hierarchy to the subfunctions into which the function is divided at the next lower level. So, for example, in an information resource dictionary system (or repository system) that included the Function entity type with this recursive relationship, the information management function would be linked to the service management, technical services, operations, and administrative services functions if the breakdown discussed in this chapter were used.

Information Requirement Decomposition

Information requirements need to be defined in two ways. They need to be defined the way system users see them, in terms of reports, transactions, and queries. (This is called the "logical view" of data requirements.) They also need to be defined in terms of the entity types, relationships and attributes that are required to produce the outputs required by users. (This is called the conceptual view of data requirements.) The decomposition of Information Requirement shown in Figure 11.5 provides for both views.

The Transaction, Report, and Query entity types are for descriptions of the transactions, reports and query capabilities required by a particular function.

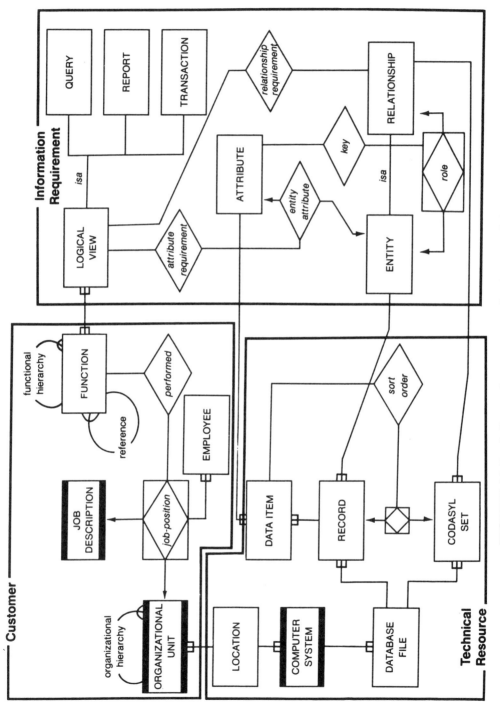

FIGURE 11.5. Information structure for data administration.

Facts such as output frequency and who can have access to the output would be common to all three entity types and thus would be attributes of Logical View. Maximum response time and validation requirements are possible attributes of Transaction. A description of the output and a title are attributes of Report. The query format and variable factors in the query form are attributes of Query.

The conceptual view is represented by the Entity, Relationship, and Attribute entity types in Figure 11.5. Entity means entity type in this context. The attributes of a given entity are defined by the *entity-attribute* relationship. There is an occurrence of Attribute of each attribute in any entity type included in this meta-database.

The links between the logical and conceptual views of the data of value to the organization are the *attribute requirement* and *relationship requirement* relationships. They define the data requirements of each query, report and transaction in terms of the entity types, attributes, and relationships involved.

The *role* relationship identifies the entity types involved in each relationship. The attributes of *role* include the cardinality of the entity type in the relationship and whether it is mandatory or optional for an entity type to participate in the relationship.

The *isa* relationship between relationship and entity identifies many-to-many relationships, which can also serve as entity types in other relationships. The *key* relationship defines the attributes of each entity in a relationship that are sort keys of the relationship.

It should be clear that we are describing "metadata" here. In other words, data about data are being defined. If this is confusing, consider the following example. The small information structure in Figure 9.4 is a decomposition of Project Plan. This information structure can be described using only the Entity and Relationship entity types of Figure 11.5. It requires two occurrences of Entity, one for the Milestone entity type and one for the Planned Task entity type. It requires three occurrences of the Relationship entity type, one for the *prerequisites* relationship, one for the *next* relationship, and one for the *work breakdown structure* relationship. Five occurrences of the *role* relationship between Entity and Relationship are needed to define the Entity occurrences involved in each of the three Relationship occurrences. In the case of the *work breakdown structure* relationship there is only one occurrence of the *role* relationship because there is only one Entity occurrence involved.

In this example, the Attribute entity type was not used because no attributes are defined in Figure 9.4. To illustrate the use of the Attribute entity type, suppose that Milestone has two attributes: (1) date milestone achieved and (2) definition of milestone. To store this information in the metadatabase of Figure 11.5, two occurrences of the Attribute entity type would be required, one for each of the two attributes of Milestone just mentioned. Each of these Attribute occurrences is linked to the Entity occurrence for Milestone by the *entity-attribute* relationship between Attribute and Entity shown in Figure 11.5.

Technical Resource Decomposition

The decomposition of the Technical Resource entity type is shown in the lower right side of Figure 11.5. It provides for a definition of the Record, Data Item, and Set occurrences in a database file that is stored in a computer system. The location of the computer system can also be defined and Figure 11.5 indicates that the Location entity type can be linked to both the organization units at the location and the computer systems at that same location.

Information Planning Decomposition

The *information planning* relationship of Figure 11.1 is decomposed into two groups of relationships in Figure 11.5. One is the many-to-many relationship between Function and Logical View.

The other group of relationships that are a decomposition of *information planning* is the three relationships between the Information Requirement and Technical Resource decompositions. Data Item has a one-to-many relationship with Attribute; Record has one with Entity; and Set has one with Relationship.

These three relationships show the implementation of the conceptual database plan. In other words, they show how the information resource that the organization believes it should have is being developed as a technical resource. Notice that information about an entity type can be stored in different physical records in different computer systems that are in different locations. Thus, the conceptual database (represented by the Information Requirement portion of Figure 11.5) can serve as a directory to the physical databases of the business.

It should be clear that all of the information requirements, defined in terms of information structures, in Chapters 5 through 11 of this text can be defined in terms of the structure used in Figure 11.5. The functional breakdowns have the structure represented by the Function entity type and its two recursive relationships. The information requirements of each subfunction have the structure represented by the Entity, Relationship, and Attribute entity types and their relationships. The *attribute requirement* and *relationship requirement* relationships define the Entity attributes and relationships that are relevant to each function.

Both the generalized entity types and relationships and the final atomic entity types and relationships obtained by decomposition can be described by this structure. To distinguish between generalizations and nongeneralizations (from the viewpoint of the database designer), an attribute can be assigned to the Entity and Relationship entity types that identify each occurrence as a generalization or a nongeneralization. To define decomposition relationships between a generalization and the entities and relationships in a decomposition of it, additional relationships would have to be added to the structure of Figure 11.5.

SYSTEM DEVELOPMENT

The information requirements for the system development subfunction are a superset of those for data administration. In addition to knowing the information requirements of each function at the atomic level of entity types and relationships, the way in which that information is to be obtained, processed, and presented must be defined. The definitions of inputs, processing, and outputs become the performance specifications for a system of application programs and software modules that will cause the computers to handle data as required by each function. The computer systems and networks also need to be planned and developed as part of the system development function.

The information structure for the system development function is a superset of that shown in Figure 11.5. This superset is shown in Figure 11.6. The decompositions of Customer and Information Requirements are virtually the same in both figures. The decomposition of Technical Resource is more complex in Figure 11.6 than in Figure 11.5 because information about application programs, the technical staff, and communication system possibilities must be added. In addition, Figure 11.6 contains decompositions of two Figure 11.1 entity types that Figure 11.5 does not show. These are the System Requirement and Development Plan entity types.

Technical Resource Decomposition

The decomposition of Technical Resource includes two entity types that concern application software. One is an Application Program entity type. Examples of this entity type are a general ledger program, a sales analysis report program, and a CAD program. The other entity type is Program Module. This is a module within an application program that performs a certain task, such as finding a record in a database or checking that a number entered at a terminal is within a certain range.

In an object-oriented approach to systems design, the Application Program entity type would not be needed. As explained in Chapter 14, entity types can be treated as objects and program modules can be defined as object operations if a BWIS exists. The database described in Figure 11.6 allows for a Program Module occurrence to be linked to one entity occurrence via the Program Specification entity type. For this approach, the relationships involving Application Program should be changed to involve Program Module instead.

The relationships between Program Module on the one hand and Data Item, Record, and Set on the other identify the data that each program module accesses in the database files. This is useful when planning any changes in a database schema; it identifies the modules that must either be revised or interfaced to the database via a subschema. In an object-oriented approach, one would expect a program module to link to only one occurrence of Record.

The Technical Staff entity type in the decomposition includes systems analysts, programmers, computer engineers, networking specialists, software testers, documentation specialists, and trainers. It is shown as a generalization because different information is needed for these different specialists. This will become evident as the system development function is broken down further.

System Requirement Decomposition

In the previous discussion of the *systems planning* relationship of Figure 11.1 it is noted that a system requirement is the result of a systems planning activity. In Figure 11.6, the content of a system requirement is characterized as information about six entity types. Three of these are types of processing that the system is required to perform: reporting, transaction processing, and query processing. A fourth is a description of an application program module (or set of modules) that does one or more of the three types of processing. This is the Program Specification entity type. It is a customer-oriented description that users can understand and approve before the programming work is done. An example of a program specification is shown in Exhibit A at the end of Chapter 14.

The one-to-many relationship between Entity and Program Specification is for the object-oriented approach to system design. In this approach, the programs

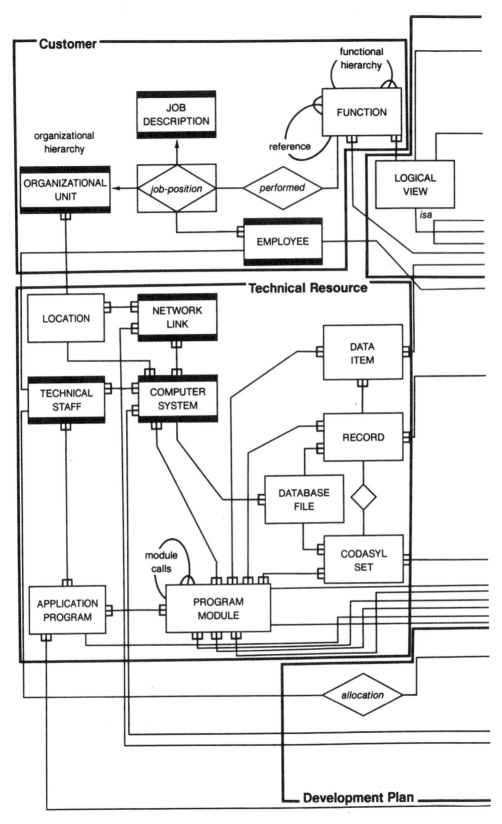

FIGURE 11.6. Information structure for systems development.

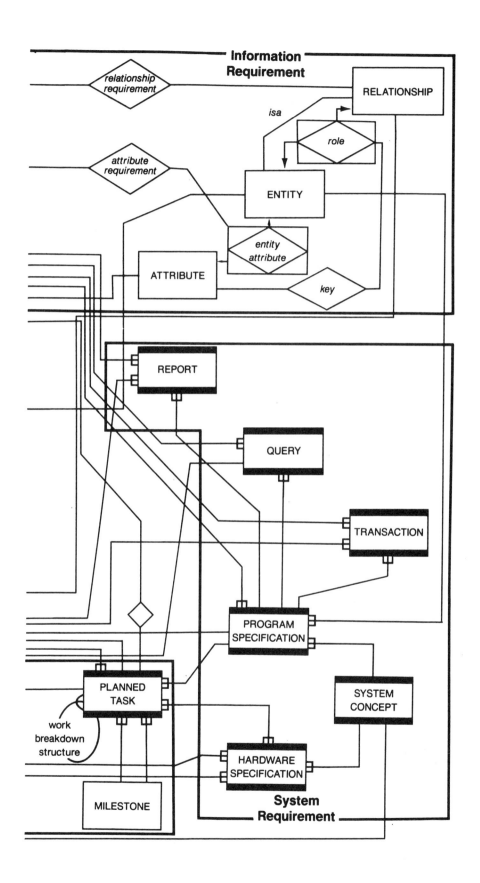

needed to manage each entity type are defined as separate program modules. This is explained more fully in Chapter 14.

The Hardware Specification entity type represents specifications in the system requirement regarding the computer systems and network links (and system software) that will be part of the planned system. They may refer to existing equipment and software or to new equipment that must be acquired.

The sixth entity type in the System Requirement decomposition is the System Concept entity type. This entity includes information about the system as a whole, its scope and purpose, and its economic and operational feasibility. As indicated by the two relationships in which it is involved, it serves to link all components of the system in a unified definition.

The components of the System Requirement decomposition are involved in relationships with each of the other decomposed generalizations shown in Figure 11.6. The definitions of the three types of processing (Report, Transaction, and Query) have relationships with Function, *entity attribute* and Relationship through Logical View. They are also linked to Program Module.

The program specification is related to the functions for which it describes support systems and the program modules that satisfy the specifications. It is also linked to planned tasks that must be performed to satisfy the specification. The hardware specification is linked to the computer system and network link occurrences that constitute part of the specification, and to the planned tasks that develop the required computing environment.

Development Plan Decomposition

The decomposition of Development Plan should look familiar. It is the same as was presented in Figure 9.4 for engineering projects. As explained in Chapter 9, this structure provides for both cost and scheduling information.

For software development tasks, the *work breakdown structure* relationship can be used to define the results of a structured analysis of the system to be developed. The planned tasks are the steps to be taken in developing each program module and then the steps taken in testing the modules separately and together.

The relationships between Planned Task and Technical Staff and Employee define the manpower resources planned for each task. It is conceivable that another relationship is required between Computer System and Planned Task to define needed computing time for a task.

The other relationships involving Planned Task and the entity types of other decompositions further define the objective of the task. The relationship with Program Module defines the module that a programming task will create. The relationship with Program Specification defines the application program specification used in carrying out a programming assignment. The relationship with Application Program defines the result of a high-level programming task. The relationship with Hardware Specification defines the guideline for a hardware procurement or development task.

THE INFORMATION RESOURCE DICTIONARY STANDARD

The National Bureau of Standards (U.S. Department of Commerce) is leading the development of a standard for Information Resource Dictionary Systems (IRDS).

IRDS is an acronym for the database appropriate to the needs of the information management function—the subject of this chapter.

The standard[2] leaves room for all sorts of database designs including the one described in this chapter. It is a standard based on the entity-relationship model and requires that all data be identified in terms of entity types, attributes, and relationships. The standard is more concerned with defining essential characteristics of the software that manages an IRDS than the contents of the IRDS. Thus, it defines naming conventions, functional capabilities, and security measures that must be incorporated in the software.

The standard does require that the database schema include certain entity types, attributes, and relationships that are needed for security purposes. For example, it requires the following three entity types:

```
IRDS-USER          (DUSER)
IRD-VIEW           (DVIEW)
IRD-SCHEMA-VIEW    (SVIEW)
```

With these entity types in the database, the system can check that anyone wanting access to the dictionary is an approved user (has a DUSER record occurrence). The DUSER entity type is linked to the DVIEW entity type that is linked to the occurrence to which the user has access. The SVIEW entity type plays a similar role with respect to accessing the schema itself.

REFERENCES

1. Singleton, John P., Ephraim R. McLean, and Edward N. Altman, "Measuring Information Systems Performance: Experience with Management by Results at Security Pacific Bank," *MIS Quarterly*, University of Minnesota, June, 1988.
2. Goldfine, Alan, and Patricia Konig, *A Technical Overview of the Information Resource Dictionary System*, 2nd ed. (Washington, DC: National Bureau of Standards, NBSIR 88-3700, January, 1988).

DISCUSSION QUESTIONS

1. Compare and contrast managing an investment in commercial real estate with managing an investment in corporate information systems.

2. Why are trust and goodwill especially important to the successful management of information systems?

3. What is the difference between the Information Requirement and System Requirement entity types in Figure 11.1?

4. What is the difference between the *systems planning* and *system development* relationships?

5. Can the organizational concepts of an "information center" be reconciled with the functional breakdown shown in Figure 11.2?

6. Suppose a "virus" has penetrated your organization's computing facility. This virus is a block of code that has attached itself to multiple unidentified

program modules. Each time a contaminated module is executed it further propagates the virus. As the security auditor of the organization, it is your task to identify the contaminated modules. What possible attributes of the entity types and relationships of Figure 11.3 would help to identify the contaminated modules?

7. Distinguish the system development subfunction from the system implementation subfunction of technical services (in Figure 11.4).

8. Is there any data that the subfunctions of the technical services function all have a need for? If so, describe it in terms of entity types and relationships.

9. The IS department often seems to be the "bad guy" in an organization, unable to fulfill user needs on-time and within budget. What can IS do about this?

10. What are the difficulties in using account representatives to execute the service management function?

11. What are the necessary attributes of the *entity-attribute* and *key* relationships in Figure 11.5? Are both relationships absolutely necessary?

12. Suppose occurrences of an entity type in a relationship need to be accessed in the order of the values of an attribute of the entity type (for example, in transaction date order). How could this requirement be stored in the database of Figure 11.5?

13. Could the database of Figure 11.5 be used to describe an ANSI/SPARC Three Schema Architecture?

14. The Program Specification entity type in Figure 11.6 is shown as a generalization. How should it be decomposed to accommodate the data shown in Exhibit A, at the end of Chapter 12?

15. What is an Application Program, a Program Module, and a Program Specification? What relationships among them need to be recognized?

16. What are the two one-to-many relationships between Milestone and Planned Task shown in Figure 11.6?

17. Why is Planned Task shown in Figure 11.6 in relationships with both Technical Staff and Employee?

IMPLICATIONS: PLANNING INTEGRATED SYSTEMS

In Part 1, a methodology for defining information requirements business-wide was justified and explained. In Part 2, the feasibility of the BWIS methodology was demonstrated. We now consider in Part 3 the benefits that can be derived from a business-wide description of functions and their information requirements.

Benefits in three areas are considered. In Chapter 12, the feasibility and advantages of integrating databases across traditional functional boundaries are explored. At least nine information structures (subject areas) have usage requirements that span more than one major functional area. Significantly, these nine structures include the largest files in most businesses, so that there are substantial benefits to be gained from integrating these structures.

In Chapter 13, the contribution that a functional model and BWIS can make to the planning of physical databases is discussed. A more realistic evaluation of database distribution alternatives is possible as compared to working with a conceptual model defined only in terms of relation fragments, as is commonly done.

Finally, in Chapter 14, the impact of a BWIS on the whole systems development process is considered. The functional model and BWIS make possible a true object-oriented approach to systems planning and design. The object-oriented paradigm has been successfully applied for years to programming, but its application to systems planning and design has been hindered by the lack of an object-oriented view of the business as a whole. The BWIS provides that view and thus opens up a whole new approach to application systems development.

12

View Integration

Our approach to information systems design rests on certain propositions asserted in Part 1. First, functions are activities undertaken to achieve goals, and second, goals give informational value to any data that makes it possible to perform the functions more effectively. In effect, the goals give managers and analysts a viewpoint that allows them to see the importance of functions necessary to achieve them and the value of the facilitating data. This is analogous to a football player who, having the goal of winning a game, sees the value of the information provided by a videotape of play by the opposing team before the game.

The functions required to achieve the goals adopted by an organization are broken down so that the people in the organization can work together to carry them out. This division of functions causes different individuals responsible for different subfunctions to view different data as valuable. A running back and a linebacker on a football team viewing the same videotape are likely to have some differences in the data they find valuable because they perform different functions. In the same way, individuals in a business who are performing different functions are likely to focus on somewhat different aspects of a subject. Consider, for example, a product offered for sale by a business. Marketing is interested in the price, style, and performance characteristics of the product. Materials management is interested in the packaging requirements, weight, volume, and cost of the product. The production function is interested in the components of the product and how it should be produced. The engineering function is interested in the efficiency, durability, and reliability of the product, as well as other aspects already mentioned.

Does this mean that every subfunction in an organization should have a separate database, one that contains only the information valuable to that subfunction? In one sense every individual not only *should* have a separate database but in fact *does* have one: his or her own memory. We each remember what we find worth noticing. To the extent that the information required by a subfunction is unique, it should be made available only to that subfunction. But much data are needed by more than one individual and more than one subfunction. Also, data needs to be placed in a context and this context, like the videotape of the football game, is needed by many subfunctions. Because there are significant costs incurred in capturing and storing data needed by many, an organization should, and will, utilize ways of sharing that data, if they are practical.

This chapter is about identifying the opportunities to share data. In Chapters 5 through 11, many views of valued data are defined as information structures. For every subfunction, there is an information structure that defines the data of value to those performing that subfunction. What do these structures have in common? Each instance of two information structures containing the same entity type or relationship may be an opportunity for data sharing, and there is a cost savings and an increased use of available data which accompany data sharing.

As a first step in identifying real opportunities to profit by sharing data, a distinction should be made between coordinating views and integrating views of data. At a minimum, coordinating views means recognizing that two or more descriptions of an entity type or information structure are different views of the same thing. At a maximum, coordinating means using the same definitions for attributes that the entity types have in common. Key-attribute standardization is an objective of the data administration function in many organizations.

Beyond coordinating views, there is view integration. Fully integrating two views creates a third view that combines the two views. All of the features of each view are included in the combined view. Several variations on the general idea of integrating views are explained in the next section.

View coordination and integration are central to accomplishing the basic purpose of information resource management. The information encoded by an organization should be made available to all people in the organization (and outside) who can use it to the benefit of the organization. The reason this ideal is not generally achieved is because each manager builds his own database and keeps it to himself. Officially recognizing that different managers are keeping their own data on the same subject is the first step toward realizing that the organization would benefit if everyone shared their data on the subjects in which they have a common interest. Major gains in effectiveness as well as efficiency can come from sharing. For example, if production management is able to share its data on producibility problems (including scrap and rework costs) with engineering management, engineering becomes more alert to the manufacturing problems that certain designs cause and can avoid them.

With this chapter, the focus moves from describing information requirements toward planning the systems that will satisfy those requirements. A first planning step is to identify coordination and integration opportunities. These can then be incorporated in a definition of conceptual databases (and views of those databases) and their geographic distribution. The analysis leading to this definition is the topic of Chapter 13.

TYPES OF INTEGRATION

Different views on the same subject can appear in several forms. In terms of entity-relationship analysis, the different views can appear as two (or more) entity types with different sets of attributes, and perhaps different names. This is the most widely understood case.[1] But there are other cases involving relationships. A generalization in one information structure may appear in another as a specialization. Or an aggregation in one structure can appear in another in its decomposed form. The most obvious case is the same information structure embedded in two or more larger structures.

In the top-down approach taken in this text, exhaustive lists of entity type attributes are not required at the business-wide database planning level. It is expected that the attribute lists will develop as the business-wide database is implemented via "bottom-up" system development projects. As explained in Chapter 1, the business-wide conceptual database is a plan that can be used by the data administrator and project database administrators to steer the organization toward a data sharing capability.

This means that the most widely understood form of view integration, namely, two versions of the same entity type, is not of major significance to business-wide database planning. As is explained next, the integration of two entity types with completely different attribute sets, except for keys, is not worthwhile. The other forms mentioned above are important to business-wide data planning, however.

Integration of Entity Types

Two entity types can be integrated if they are really two descriptions of the same entity type. As an example, suppose the buyer for an art dealer has a database with the Painting entity type in it. Suppose Painting has the attributes, painting number, title, artist, date purchased, and cost. The painting number is just a serial number to uniquely identify a painting. In relational terms, this entity type is represented as,

```
Painting = ({painting no., title, artist, date-purchased, cost},
{painting no.→title, artist, date-purchased, cost})
```

Now, suppose the gallery manager for the art dealer has a database with a Picture entity type in it. Suppose Picture has the following relational format:

```
Picture = ({picture no., price, title, location, put-up-date, take-
down-date}, {picture no.→price, title, location, put-up-date,
take-down-date})
```

The Painting and Picture entity types each have a key that is simply a serial number to uniquely identify a painting owned by the art dealer. They represent two views of the same basic entity type. To integrate these two views, we simply combine them and cancel out duplicate attributes (title occurs in both). The result is the following relation, P:

```
P = ({painting no., title, artist, date-purchased, cost, picture
no., price, location, put-up-date, take-down-date}, {painting
no.→title, artist, date-purchased, cost, picture no., price,
location, put-up-date, take-down-date; picture no.→painting no.,
title, artist, date-purchased, cost, price, location, put-up-date,
take-down date})
```

If the buyer and gallery manager can agree on a common serial numbering scheme, one of the serial numbers in P can be eliminated, but this coordination measure is not necessary for the integration of the two views. Notice that the P relation satisfies Boyce-Codd normal form (BCNF) conditions provided that the entity types being integrated are also BCNF, which is the case in the example.

There is a subtle difference between integrating two views of the same entity type and creating a generalization for two (or more) specializations. In the example just cited, it was assumed that the buyer and gallery manager were describing the same object. But suppose the buyer keeps information on unframed paintings while the gallery manager deals with framed paintings. In this case, there are really two different types of objects involved and an integration of their attributes does not necessarily create a relation that is appropriate for all occurrences of the generalization. In the (carefully chosen) example, the integration still works because there are no attributes that concern the frame of the painting. If there were such attributes, however, such as color of frame, then a relation integrated as described above would not satisfy the normal form requirement of no null-valued attributes. The frame attributes should be kept in a separate frame relation in this case.

Why is combining two different sets of attributes desirable? If the sets are indeed different, are they not descriptions of two different viewpoints on the same subject? Why combine them? It will be more efficient to store and retrieve them separately if they are used by different subfunctions. A one-to-one relationship between them is the most that is needed.

Integration of a Generalization and a Specialization

A generalization relates to its specializations via an *isa* relationship. If the information structure that describes the requirements of one subfunction contains an entity type (or many-to-many relationship) that is a generalization of an entity type (or relationship) in another information structure, then the two structures can be linked by an *isa* relationship.

Many examples of this are shown in Figure 10.12 where there are two *isa* relationships that connect a wide range of entity types to the Subsidiary Account and Standard Transaction generalizations.

Another example involves the *ad purchase* relationship shown in Figure 6.8. This is a specialization of the Purchase Order entity type shown in Figure 7.5. An *isa* relationship between these two is appropriate for several reasons. It makes it easier for the accounts payable function to verify receipt of the service purchased before paying the ad agency invoice, because the invoice contains the purchase order number. It also makes it easier for the advertising manager to track the actual costs of advertising services ordered, because the purchase order is linked to the payments made to the ad agency.

Integration of an Aggregation and Its Decomposition

If one function needs more detail and another function requires less detail about the same subject, then the information structures of the two functions are likely to have an aggregation-decomposition relation to one another. This can be the case for a planning function and a supervising function. Consider, for example, production capacity planning and the function of managing production operations (the operations subfunction of Figure 8.2). Both require information about the capacities of work centers (production departments). But the capacity planning function requires only the total capacity (by type of capacity) whereas production operations management needs to know daily availability by employee and piece of equipment.

The information about resource capacities required for production capacity planning is represented in Figure 12.1 by the Resource entity type, which is the same entity type shown in Figure 7.4 (this is the generalization). The information about the availability of employees and equipment required to supervise operations is represented in Figure 12.1 by the Employee and Equipment entity types, which are entity types taken from Figure 8.3. Two one-to-many relationships link Resource to the Employee and Equipment entity types in Figure 12.1. These two define the relationships between an aggregation (Resource) and its decomposition into Employee and Equipment entity types. Notice that for a given occurrence of Resource only one of the two relationships will be used, assuming that a Resource occurrence either represents a group of the same type of equipment items or a group of employees that have the same skills. For planning purposes, it is not helpful to have data on individual employees or pieces of equipment. All that is needed is the *total* capacity of a *group* of employees, or equipment items, with similar capabilities.

Integration of Portions of Information Structures

A portion of an information structure is itself an information structure. For example, Figure 12.2 shows the structure of information about the positions in an

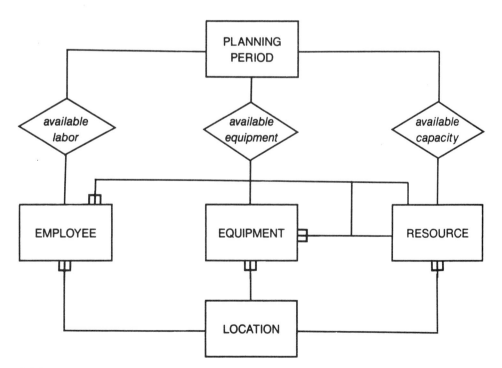

FIGURE 12.1. Relationship between an aggregation and its decomposition.

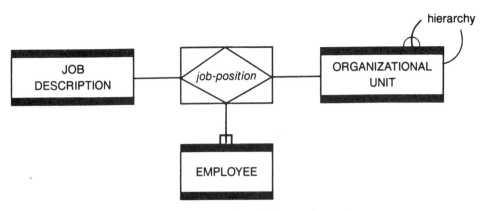

FIGURE 12.2. Example of an information substructure.

organization and the employees filling them. This structure can also be found as part of a larger structure in Figures 5.4, 8.3, and others.

The fact that the same information structure appears in two or more larger structures means that those larger structures have something in common, something that may be worth sharing. Each structure is a description of the information required to perform certain functions and subfunctions. Functions that need the same type of information can at least share some of the same software for managing that information, and if in fact the functions require the same data they can, at least, save data encoding and storage costs by sharing data.

If two information structures have portions in common, then they can be integrated by simply combining them. The portions that are common appear only once in the combined structure. All relationships that involve a common portion in either of the two structures appear in the combined structure linked to the common portion.

MAJOR VIEW INTEGRATION OPPORTUNITIES

Another fundamental proposition that the approach to systems design should take into account is that business-wide conceptual database planning should address the problem of coordinating the various information system development projects in different functional areas. Well-integrated databases are often designed for individual systems using E-R analysis and CASE tools. The major unexploited data sharing opportunities are between the databases of different systems.

In Chapters 5 through 11, the information requirements have been described for seven major functional areas of manufacturing type businesses—personnel administration, marketing, materials management, production, engineering, financial management, and information systems management. In the discussion of this chapter, the integration of the information structures for subfunction within the seven major functional areas is ignored. To some extent, it has already been dealt with in Chapters 5 through 11. In general, we can assume that the project Database Administrators (DBAs) will integrate the data used in a single system. Efforts to build databases that are integrated within the confines of the individual system do not conflict with the organizational hierarchy and the desire for managerial independence within each functional area.

Instead, attention in this chapter is focused on the view integration opportunities that involve information structures for subfunctions from different functional areas. Integrating information structures for marketing and production subfunctions, for example, is considered. To implement view integrations of this type, a business-wide conceptual database plan must exist before individual system development projects are undertaken. Then, as information system development projects are undertaken in functional areas, the integration opportunities can be pointed out and promoted by the data administration function.

For organizations that already use computers, the major unexploited opportunities for data sharing are interfunctional and interorganizational. We can assume that the significant opportunities within the purview of a single manager have been exploited, or will be exploited, as a result of natural, existing motivations. Redundancy in data capture operations and in storage as well as incompatibilities between related data items are mainly the result of separate system development projects undertaken for different managers.

How significant are the interfunctional and interorganizational opportunities? An analysis of information structures that occur in more than one of the seven functional areas described in Chapters 5 through 11 indicates that the interfunctional view integration opportunities are many and that they involve the largest files in a manufacturing business.

Evidence that interorganizational opportunities for data coordination (and in some cases integration) are compelling is seen in the rapid development of Electronic Data Interchange (EDI) Systems in recent years,[2] and in the imposition of the Computer-Aided Acquisition and Logistics Support (CALS) system by the U.S. Department of Defense (DOD) on all defense contractors. It has been estimated that approximately 30 percent of the cost of all weapons procured by DOD is spent on technical documentation;[3] CALS is aimed at significantly reducing that percentage.

The results of the analysis of interfunctional view integration opportunities is shown in Table 12.1. The seven functional areas are represented by the seven columns in the table. The portions of information structures that occur in more than one functional area's information structure are listed in the nine rows of the table. It should be noted that this list of information structures is not a complete list of all of the data requirements of the seven functional areas. It is not even a complete list of all of the multifunctional information structures that further decomposition of the information structures for the seven areas might reveal. Thus, Table 12.1 should not be confused with the subject area versus function table used in a Business Systems Planning (BSP) study.

The body of Table 12.1 references figures in previous chapters that show the information structure in question. Three of the structures have references for all seven functional areas. They are the structures for position, purchase, and account. The product/service structure has references in five of the seven columns. Four other structures are used in three of the seven functional areas and the metadata structure is used in both engineering and information systems.

Each of these nine integration (or coordination) opportunities is discussed in a following subsection. In some cases, the different functions use the same data and view integration makes sense. In other cases, the data are not the same, even

TABLE 12.1. Information structures required in multiple functional areas.

	Marketing	Materials Management	Production	Engineering	Accounting	Personnel	Information Systems
			Functional Areas				
Positions	Fig. 6.1 (decomp. of Market Resource)	Fig. 7.1 (decomp. of Supply Capability)	Fig. 8.3	Fig. 9.1 (decomp. of Technological Resource)	Fig. 10.6 (decomp. of Organizational Unit)	Fig. 5.4	Fig. 11.3, 11.5, 11.6
Market Segment	Fig. 6.1	Fig. 7.3		Fig. 9.1			
Product/ Service	Fig. 6.1	Fig. 7.3, 7.4, 7.5, 7.7	Fig. 8.1 (Material and Product Specification)	Fig. 9.1 (System Def. and decomp. of Tech. Resource)	Fig. 10.12		
Work Center		Fig. 7.4	Fig. 8.3 (Location)		(Not shown in Fig. 10.2, but could be)		
Sale	Fig. 6.3	Fig. 7.2, 7.7, 7.10			Fig. 10.12		
Purchase	Fig. 6.8 (and other decomps. of Marketing Re-source)	Fig. 7.2, 7.5, 7.6, 7.9	Fig. 8.3	Fig. 9.1 (decomp. of Technological Resource)	Fig. 10.12	Fig. 5.4 (Contract Service)	Fig. 11.1 (decomp. of Technical Resource)
Account	Fig. 6.1 (decomp. of Marketing Re-source)	Fig. 7.1 (decomp. of Supply Capability)	Fig. 8.3 (also expense accounts for other subfunc.)	Fig. 9.7	Fig. 10.6, 10.8	Implied in Fig. 5.4	Fig. 11.1 (decomp. of Resource)
Project			Fig. 8.1 (possible decomp. of Produce)	Fig. 9.4, 9.7			Fig. 11.6
Metadata				Fig. 9.10			Fig. 11.5

though its structure is the same, and only coordination is needed so that the same software can be used to access the structure.

POSITION INFORMATION

The position information structure is shown in Figure 12.2. It consists of a *job-position* relationship between Job Description and Organizational Unit and a one-to-many relationship between Employee and *job-position*. It represents all of the information about the employees (and certain contractors) of a business and how they are organized.

According to Table 12.1, the structure appears explicitly in Figures 5.4, 8.3, 11.3, 11.5, and 11.6 and implicitly in Figures 6.1, 7.1, 9.1 and 10.6. By an implicit appearance, we mean that further decomposition of the figure cited will identify the information structure in question.

The basis for the assertions about the implicit appearance of this structure is the fact that managers in each of the seven functional areas require data about their employees. This is true even for the personnel function. Although the information structures developed in Chapter 6 for marketing, for example, did not explicitly include this position structure, it is almost certain that the managers in marketing are going to require some information about their employees. This requirement can be expected to surface if the analysis of information requirements in this area is extensive enough.

Do the seven functions need the same data occurrences concerning position information? For the most part the answer is "No." Marketing requires data about marketing employees, materials management requires data about its employees, and so forth. This implies that view integration would lead to no significant savings. Only coordination is worthwhile; let each function manage its own position information, using the same software.

However, view integration of position information *is* profitable because three of the functions require data about employees of other functional areas. They are the accounting, personnel, and information systems functions. If the views are not integrated with respect to position information, we can estimate that four copies of the same data about each position and employee will exist in four databases: one in accounting, one in personnel, one in information systems, and one in the relevant functional area. This estimate is conservative; many additional files on employees are likely to sprout for miscellaneous purposes, such as parking space assignments, sales commissions, travel expenses, and so on.

The accounting function requires information about all positions and employees for several reasons. The most obvious is for the payroll subfunction. Closely related is the allocation of labor costs to cost and expense accounts for cost accounting and budgeting purposes. In addition, the budgeting subfunction needs data about the number of authorized job-positions in each organizational unit in order to develop budgets and project the effect of pay increases.

Personnel requires information about all positions and employees for many reasons. In addition to the use of this information in the employment subfunction, which is described in Chapter 5, it is required by the compensation, labor relations, benefit administration, and health and safety subfunctions.

In addition to the data processing benefits that are derived from integrating the accounting and personnel views of position and employee data, the quality of the data used for payroll purposes is much better than any data personnel can collect independently of the payroll system. Employees throughout an organization will make sure that the payroll data are correct.

The information systems management function requirement for data about positions and employees throughout an organization is based on the needs of three subfunctions. The operations subfunction needs the data to control access to computer systems and databases. Data administration needs position information in order to determine who is performing each subfunction. This is required to identify experts on each subfunction for which information and system requirements must be defined. Finally, information about employees participating in system development projects is required by project management for a number of reasons, such as estimating project costs, contacting project employees, and keeping track of assignments made.

MARKET SEGMENT INFORMATION

Marketing, materials management, and engineering are the three functions that require information about market segments. Marketing certainly requires the most information of this type. For direct sales management purposes, it requires information about the standing of the business with each direct customer as they relate to major competitors (Figure 6.7). For advertising and promotion purposes, it requires information about the effectiveness of advertising alternatives (Figure 6.8). For purposes of sales forecasting, it requires information about sales trends and their relationship to industry and macroeconomic variables (Figure 6.11).

Marketing and Materials Management View Integration

Presumably, materials management is mainly interested in the sales forecasting information of marketing. Thus, the materials management and marketing functions share a common interest in the structure shown in Figure 6.11, and in particular, they are both interested in the *sales* relationship in Figure 6.11. This sales relationship corresponds to the *demand schedule* relationship in the MRP information structure of Figure 7.11.

In addition to the common interest in sales data, marketing and materials management have a common interest in stocks of finished goods. The information structure (except for Formatted Message) in the product/service area of Figure 6.9, which is for the promotions function, is repeated in Figure 7.11. This indicates that both functions should share this information.

The information structure that marketing and materials management need to share is summarized in Figure 12.3. Because this includes a significant part of the MRP information structure, it has implications for a decision to buy a commercially available MRP software package. The purchased system should satisfy the needs of marketing for sales statistics as well as the needs of materials management.

Marketing and Engineering View Integration

The marketing data required by engineering must come from market research for the most part. The question is, how will consumers react to a new product or a

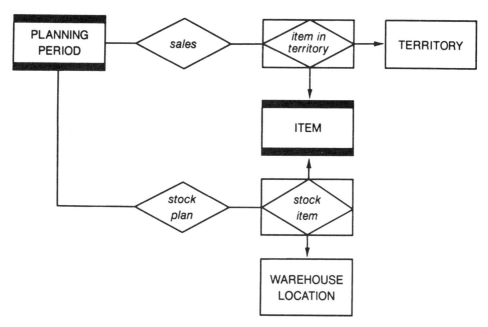

FIGURE 12.3. Integrated information structure for marketing and materials management.

new feature for an old product. The sales data used by marketing and materials management cannot answer such questions directly, although some of the industry and macroeconomic data used in sales forecasting may be useful in estimating the market potential of a new product.

Additional data for new product decisions can be gathered by the market research techniques of opinion surveys and marketing tests. Marketing test data are collected through the same system as is used to gather sales data, but opinion survey data must be processed separately, using software and a database designed for opinion survey data processing.

The potential of view integration in this case does not appear to be significant. The marketing function is usually involved in the evaluation of new product innovations and to the extent that internal marketing takes responsibility for estimating market potentials, engineering does not need to be concerned with marketing data. There may be some potential for integrating sales and opinion survey data; however, if both types of data are within the control of internal marketing, we can assume that the integration will take place naturally to the extent that it is worthwhile.

PRODUCT AND SERVICE INFORMATION

Table 12.1 shows five functions requiring information about the products and services provided by the business. These five functions take six different views of the Product/Service entity type. These six views are as follows:

1. *A system with multiple aspects.* This is the view taken by the designers in engineering. It is summarized in Figure 9.13.

2. *A product to be described.* This view is taken by the marketing function whose goal is to broadcast information about the product to all potential customers. It is summarized in Figure 6.4 by the relationship between Product Service and Formatted Message.

3. *A system of parts and operations.* This is one of the views taken by the engineering, production, and materials management functions. It is summarized in Figure 12.4, which shows a structure that is embedded in the information structures shown in Figures 7.4, 8.3, and 9.13.

4. *An item stocked.* This view applies only to products not services. It is taken by marketing, materials management, production, and accounting. Its E-R representation is shown in Figure 12.5. Portions of this structure are embedded in Figures 6.9, 6.10, 7.3, 7.4, 7.5, 7.6, 7.7, 7.8, 7.9, 7.10, 7.11, 8.3, and 10.12. In addition to showing stock of an item as a relationship between an item (product) and a location, Figure 12.5 shows the plan for the stock maintained by the MRP system and the orders and execution of orders for resupply of the stock and for deliveries from the stock. The resupply may come from either an outside supplier or from a production location; the deliveries may be either to an outside customer or to a production center where material and parts are used to make other items.

5. *That which is purchased and sold.* This view is taken in the marketing, materials management, and accounting functions. The Product/Service entity type in Figure 6.3 is an example of this view in marketing. The Item entity type in Figures 7.5 and 7.7 represents the same viewpoint for materials management, and Item in Figure 10.12 represents the same viewpoint in accounting.

   Identification of exactly what was sold or purchased is a primary concern. For goods of modest price, this need can be satisfied by a product model number or code attribute which can be used to access the engineering specifications of the model. For expensive items, a serial number which is an attribute of the transaction, not the product, is used to identify the exact instance of the model, and this can be linked to information about the parts that were used to assemble it and the results of tests performed during manufacture.

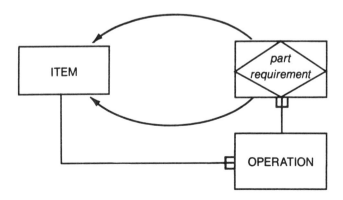

FIGURE 12.4. Product viewed as a system.

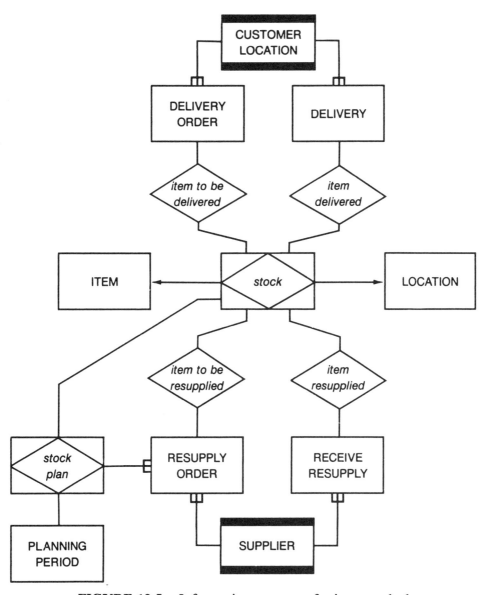

FIGURE 12.5. Information structure for item stocked.

Information about asking price, required margin, and sales commission rate is also important. The information about actual price paid is normally treated as an attribute of the transaction rather than of the product or service, and this is discussed further in the sections on sale and purchase. But the standard or minimum acceptable price is an attribute of the product and so are other policy variables, such as commission rate and margin requirement.

In this case, view integration at the business-wide database planning level is a matter of recognizing that Product/Service and Item refer to the same entity type. Integrating the marketing, materials management, and accounting databases with respect to this view of product information may be conceptually simple but it is difficult in practice because this Item (or Product/Service) entity type is involved in so many other information structures of importance to these functions.

6. *Items to be classified and compared.* This view is important to marketing, materials management, production, engineering, and accounting. One example of the marketing interest is shown in Figure 6.10 where there is a recursive relationship between Product/Service occurrences called *product group.* Materials management's need for grouping information is shown in Figure 7.9 where a Commodity entity type serves to identify groups of Items. The production requirement is in the use of group technology to plan production facilities which was briefly referred to in Figure 8.4 but not modeled as an E-R diagram. Engineering's need to categorize parts is implicit in the Existing Design entity type in Figure 9.9; being able to find existing part designs so that they can be reused in new products depends on an easily understood way of grouping and subgrouping existing part designs. The accounting requirement to group items is shown in the *isa* relationship in Figure 10.11 between Subsidiary Ledger and Item and the one-to-many relationship between Account and Subsidiary Account.

Integrating these different views of how Item occurrences need to be grouped is done by providing for all of these grouping capabilities in the integrated database. Each requires a relationship, either with another entity type or as a recursive relationship. There is no reason that all of these relationships cannot involve the same set of Item occurrences.

The integration of the six views of product and service information is shown in Figure 12.6. As far as the first view is concerned, only the Version entity type is shown. This links to the System Concept, Version-Aspect, and other entity types shown in Figure 9.13. A one-to-one relationship links Version to the Product/Service entity type. Thus, a Product/Service occurrence represents a version that has been (or will be) produced and sold commercially.

The second view is represented by the Formatted Message entity type in Figure 12.6. The third view is represented by the structure in Figure 12.4 which is repeated in Figure 12.6. The fourth view is represented by the structure in Figure 12.5 which is also repeated in Figure 12.6. The fifth view is represented by the Product/Service entity type, especially by the model identification. As has already been noted, this view actually involves all the relationships involving either Product/Service or Item in the chapters on marketing, materials management, and accounting. Figures 12.7 and 12.8, which will be discussed later, summarize these relationships.

All of the grouping relationships mentioned in the description of the sixth view are represented in Figure 12.6. A Group Technology Classification entity type (and recursive relationship) is shown that represents the view of the production function. Similarly, an Engineering Classification entity type is shown that represents the way product designers choose to classify parts for retrieval purposes.

The integrated view of product and service information in Figure 12.6 does not show all the relationships in which Product/Service is involved. The relationship called *item-in-territory* shown in Figure 12.3, for example,

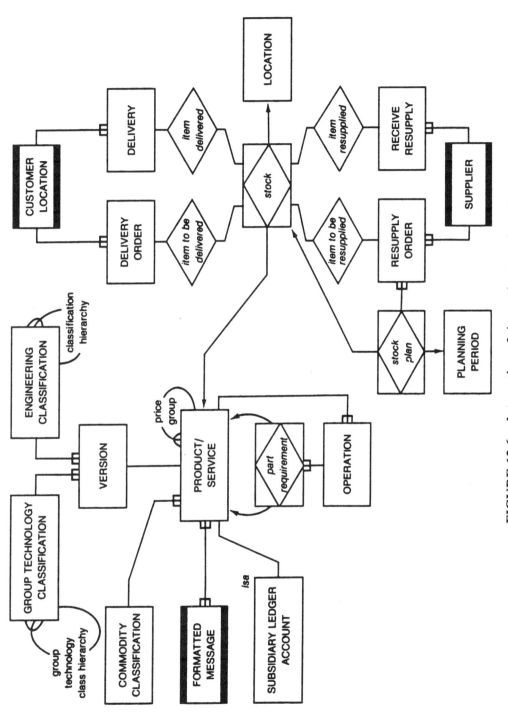

FIGURE 12.6. Integration of six product/service views.

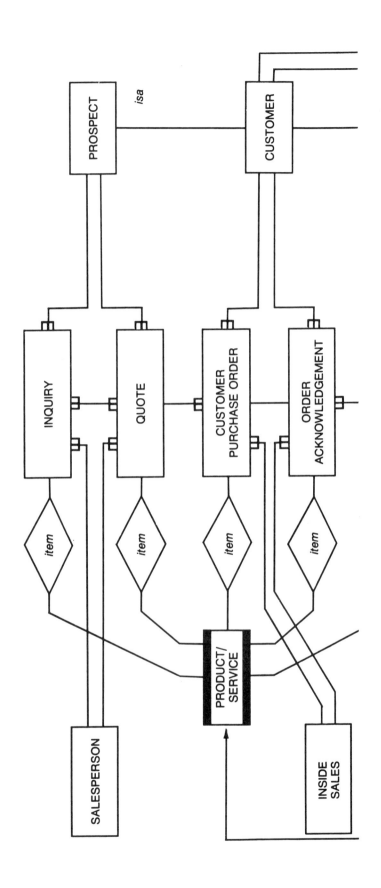

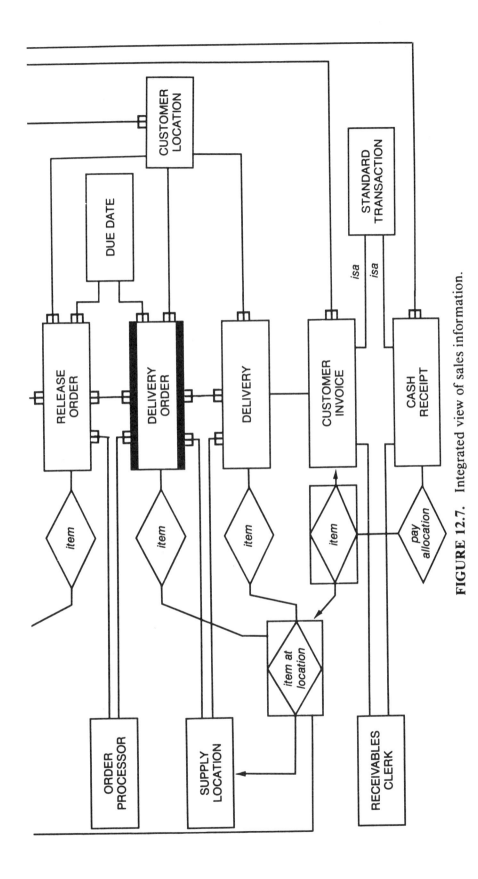

FIGURE 12.7. Integrated view of sales information.

is not included. Other relationships involving Product/Service are mentioned in subsequent subsections. Figure 12.6 only summarizes the six views of information about products and services described above.

WORK CENTER INFORMATION

Information about work centers concerns the work being done in a production unit and the resources used to do it. A work center is a production unit. It occupies building space; it consists of a group of employees, and it has the equipment and other facilities needed to perform certain types of operations.

Table 12.1 indicates that the materials management and production functions require work center information. Materials management needs it for capacity planning purposes. Production management requires it for the operations, technology, facilities, and services subfunctions. If a process costing system is used (as opposed to job costing), then the accounting subfunction also needs basic information about each work center.

The integration of the production and materials management views of work center information was discussed on page 346. The integrated view is shown in Figure 12.1. The Location entity type in this figure could also be called a Work Center entity type.

If the process accounting approach is taken, then Location entity type becomes a subsidiary ledger, which means that an *isa* relationship is required between Location and Subsidiary Ledger Account and certain cost factor attributes are added to the Location entity type.

SALE INFORMATION

Information about a sales transaction begins with an inquiry about a product or service from a prospective customer and ends when the customer pays for the product or service that was ordered and received. Parts of this information structure are shown in Figures 6.3, 7.7, 7.10, and 10.12. Table 12.1 indicates that the marketing, materials management, and accounting functions use this data.

An integrated view of sales information is depicted as an E-R diagram in Figure 12.7. This combines the structures shown in Figures 6.3, 7.7, 7.10, and 10.12. A distinction is made between a prospect and a customer; this is a refinement of Figure 6.3. An Order Processor entity type is also added to identify who (or which batch processing job) in materials management received a shipment release order and initiated a delivery order in response.

The Delivery Order entity type is shown as a generalization because it involves more than a simple order. It may include picking and packing instructions and purchasing a transportation carrier service to deliver product to the customer. This is discussed in Chapter 7 and a decomposition of Delivery Order is shown in Figure 7.9.

This integrated view contains much valuable management information. A comparison of inquiry and quote data can reveal opportunities to improve the way inquiries are handled. A comparison of quotes versus customer purchase orders may teach something about which quotes lead to orders and the average number of quotes per order received. A comparison of customer purchase order to order acknowledgment dates can show how well-organized the business appears to its customers. An analysis of release orders per blanket customer purchase order can provide a basis for projecting future sales and cash receipts. A comparison of release orders to delivery orders and delivery orders versus delivery can reveal the failures in logistics planning and the extra freight charges and late delivery performance that were the result of these failures. A comparison of delivery to customer invoice will identify delays in sending invoices which lead to delays in payments received from customers. A comparison of invoices to cash receipts results in the aged receivables report which is probably the only one of these comparisons that most business managers can obtain, because most business information systems do not provide for an integrated view of sales.

PURCHASE INFORMATION

Purchase information, like position information, is required by all seven functional areas shown in Table 12.1. Just as management in each area has a need for information about employees working in the area, so management (and each employee) has a need to buy the equipment, supplies, and services required to perform its functions.

As described in the previous chapters, the execution of purchase transactions only involves two functions, materials management and accounting. (This assumes that purchasing is a subfunction of materials management.) The planning of purchases is done in all functional areas, and the result of this planning is a decision to issue a purchase requisition to the purchasing subfunction. When purchasing receives a purchase requisition, it buys what is requested.

However, there are several types of purchases for which this is not a feasible way to buy. The purchases associated with business travel frequently must be made by the employee doing the traveling. The ordering of freight carrier services is often done by a shipping clerk rather than by someone in the purchasing department. The equivalent of a shipment release order (see Figure 7.5) for telephone service is implicitly given when an employee dials for long distance service.

Figure 12.8 is an integrated view of the purchasing activity in an organization. The terms and structure represent an integration of Figures 7.5, 7.6, and 10.12; however, some other entity types and relationships have been added to identify roles played by employees in the activity. For example, a Manager entity type is linked to the Account and Requisition entity types as shown in Figure 12.8. This shows how the authority to charge expenditures to an account can be related to the issuing of purchase requisitions.

The Authorized Agent entity type represents anyone authorized by the business to order the delivery of goods and services. The purchase order is linked to those who are authorized to issue shipment release orders under a Purchase Order occurrence. The Shipment Release entity type is meant to represent any order, explicit or implicit, to provide goods or services purchased under a blanket purchase agreement.

The Receiver entity type is another new one. It may or may not be the same entity as the Authorized Agent. In the case of a long distance telephone call, they would be the same. In the case of a clerk in purchasing who orders product to be delivered to the receiving dock of a warehouse, they would not be the same. In most cases of requisitions for product, there are actually two different occurrences of the Receiver entity type involved in a purchase. One is the clerk in the

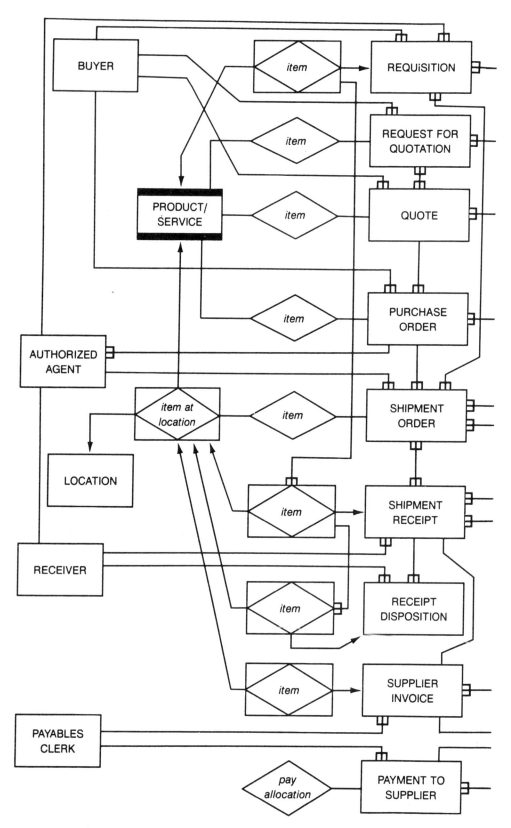

FIGURE 12.8. Integrated view of purchasing information.

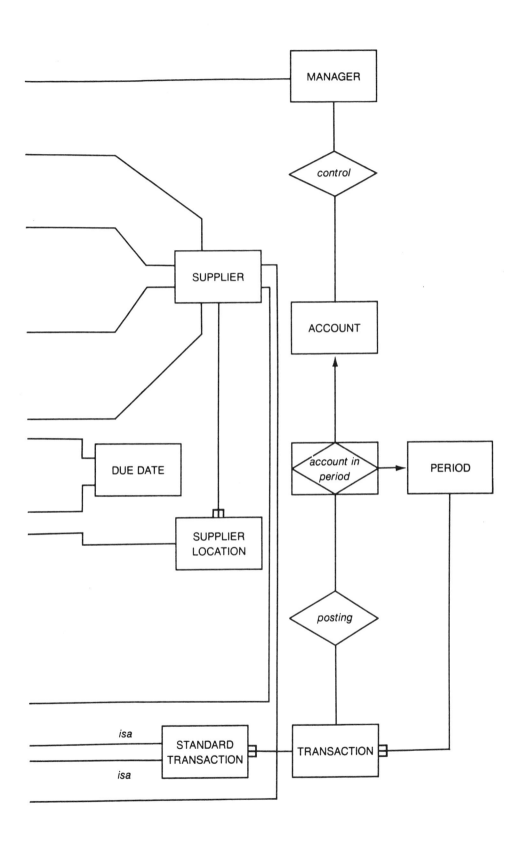

receiving department; the other is an employee in the department that issued the requisition for the product.

Other new entity types in Figure 12.8 are Payables Clerk and Request for Quotation. The payables clerk is the one who authorizes payment of supplier invoices. One control on embezzlement is to require that the receiver (particularly the final receiver of the goods or services) is not the same entity as the payables clerk. The request for quotation is useful in the case of capital goods purchases for which several quotes are obtained before a purchasing decision is made.

The information in Figure 12.8 is vital to executing virtually all decisions made in an organization, except for product design, personnel, financing, and some production decisions. Delays in obtaining equipment, materials, and services are often caused by the lack of an integrated view of purchasing and the consequent inability of management to identify and eliminate needless delays.

Part of the problem lies in the fact that management wants to both expedite and control purchasing actions. The lack of an integrated database means that the control measures must be cruder and more time consuming than would be the case if complete information on each requisition, and the status of actions required to fulfill it, were readily available.

ACCOUNT INFORMATION

The information about accounts is the information developed, maintained, and interpreted by the accounting subfunction of financial management. It is used by the managers of all of the seven functional areas, but it is provided by one function, accounting. As a result, the view of accounting described in Chapter 10 is an integrated view.

The accounting information database of Figure 10.12 provides an integrated view of the subject. The Account occurrences are related to a wide variety of other entity types via the Subsidiary Account entity type which serves as a universal interface for the Account entity type. The relationship between Account and Organizational Unit is particularly useful for expense budgeting and control. Each organizational unit can have its own set of accounts and monitor all charges to those accounts.

In Table 12.1, Figure 9.7 is cited as reference to the use of the Account entity type in engineering. The Financial Resource entity type in Figure 9.7 is the generalized entity type that can be decomposed to the Account entity type and, in fact, to all of Figure 10.12. The Planned Task entity type of Figure 9.7 is similar to the Organization Unit entity type of Figure 10.12. It can be viewed as a temporary extension of the organizational structure (for the duration of the project). An information structure based on this view is shown in Figure 12.9. Planned Task is linked to a set of accounts and to the organization unit responsible for performing the task. In Figure 12.9, Organization Unit is also linked to Account, but these are different accounts than Planned Task is linked to. Planned task is linked to a set of project accounts. Organization unit is linked to a set of permanent expense accounts, and possibly to other types of accounts, for which the unit is responsible. Figure 12.9 indicates how Figure 9.7 can be integrated with Figure 10.12. The structure of Figure 12.2 could also play a role in this integration by linking Organizational Unit to the Employee entity type of Figure 9.7.

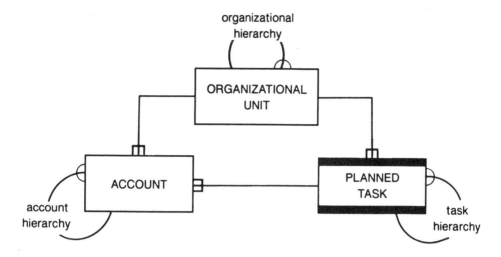

FIGURE 12.9. Integration of accounting and project management information requirements.

PROJECT INFORMATION

The structure of project information is discussed in Chapter 9, and Figure 9.4 summarizes the structure. It is also used to define the information requirements of information systems development function in Chapter 11 (see Figure 11.6). In Table 12.1, there is a comment about the possibility of needing this type of information in the production function (in ship building, for example).

The important point in this case is that the projects in engineering, information systems, and production are not related. They do not need the same data. The structure of the data are the same but not the data occurrences. The only data they may have in common is occurrences of time. As was just discussed, this is not a significant data sharing opportunity.

The conclusion, therefore, is that the information structures used in project databases should be coordinated but not integrated. They should be coordinated so that they can use the same software.

METADATA

Is the situation with respect to metadata the same as for project information? Engineering and information systems both need metadata structures but for separate classes of data. Engineering needs to describe entity types and relationships involved in product designs. On the other hand, information systems needs to define the entity types and relationships required in the databases of all functions of the business, including engineering.

The seeming overlap is an illusion. Information systems may require information about the entity types and relationships of Figure 9.13, but engineering takes these entity types and relationships for granted. Engineering requires information about the entities and relationship occurrences that they define. In other words, the engineering metadata is at a lower level than that of the data administration subfunction of information systems.

Consequently, there is no need to integrate the metadata structures. Coordinating these structures may be of some value; however, other requirements of CAD databases, especially the capability to store a repertoire of operations that an object can perform, make it unlikely that any significant sharing of software can occur.

SUMMARY

View integration identifies data requirements that two or more subfunctions have in common. If two subfunctions require different information about the same entity or the same information about different occurrences of the same entity type then coordination rather than integration is appropriate.

There are several guises that integration opportunities can take. They range from the straightforward detection of the same entity type, or information structure, in two larger structures to the recognition that the decomposition of an entity type is in one structure while the entity type is in another.

The most likely data sharing opportunities in organizations that already have computers involve the data that is used in different functional areas. A review of the information structures developed in Chapters 5 through 11 reveals seven types of data that should be shared across functional boundaries. They are data about:

1. Job-positions and employees

2. Market segments

3. Products and services

4. Work centers

5. Sales

6. Purchases

7. Accounting.

There are interrelationships between these seven types of data, which means that all of the information structures in the seven functional areas that include any of these seven types of data should be integrated into one structure. This does not, however, imply that there should be only one database. Several reasons for this conclusion are provided in Chapter 13.

REFERENCES

1. McFadden, Fred R., and Jeffery A. Hoffer, *Data Base Management* (Menlo Park, CA: Benjamin/Cummings, 1988), p. 276.

2. Seither, Mike, *EDI Reaches Critical Mass, Creates Opportunities for Integrators* (Boston: Mini-Micro Systems, July, 1988), pp. 17–19.

3. Blum, Ivan J., "The Impact of CALS—Integrating Enterprises for Enhanced Quality and Productivity," 1988, DACOM (D. Appleton Company, Inc.). These are published

notes on a speech given at the CALS Benefits Strategy and Implementation Conference held in Chicago, November 3, 1988.

DISCUSSION QUESTIONS

1. Under what conditions should two subfunctions that can benefit from data about the same entity type share the same physical database of information on that entity type?

2. What are the benefits of sharing data among subfunctions?

3. What is the difference between coordinating and integrating database views?

4. What is the difference between integrating two views of the same entity type and creating a generalization for two or more specializations?

5. Define how the purchasing information requirements of Figure 7.5 can be integrated with the accounting information requirements of Figure 10.6.

6. What type of relationships are likely to exist between an aggregation and its decomposition?

7. To what extent must the attributes of entity types and relationships be known in order to make view integration decisions? At what stage in the planning process must the attributes be specified?

8. Compare and contrast intrafunctional and interfunctional view integration opportunities.

9. Compare and contrast interfunctional and interorganizational view coordination and integration opportunities.

10. Compare the Information Resource Dictionary System (CALS IRDS) to view coordination.

11. Should the job-position information of an organization be integrated? If so, why?

12. Which views of market segment information should be integrated in a manufacturing organization?

13. In modeling information it is often necessary to distinguish between an abstract concept and specific examples of the concept. At some point in the specialization of concepts, we get to physical instances of the concept. To what extent are physical instances of products and services represented in Figure 12.6? How would Figure 12.6 have to be modified to record the serial number of physical items (and instances of services) that are purchased and sold?

14. Is the Location entity type of Figure 12.1 ambiguous? What type of location does it refer to?

15. Compare and contrast the way delivery order information is modeled in Figures 7.9 and 12.7.

16. Identify the information structure in Figure 12.8 that is common to both materials management and accounting.

17. Figures 7.5 and 7.7 have several entity types and relationships in common. Discuss which of these should be coordinated or integrated.

18. What are possible effects of not integrating the purchasing information?

19. Discuss how the accounting information required for the planned tasks on an engineering project should be modeled.

20. Should the time information structure of Figure 12.10 be included in a database or not?

21. Are there other uses for metadata in addition to those mentioned in engineering and information systems management? If so, do they create any integration opportunities?

13

Distributed Database Planning

Chapter 12 shows a pattern of complex interrelationships between subfunction information requirements. Virtually every information structure in Chapters 5 through 11 relates to every other structure in some way. The integrated information structures for sales and purchasing information (in Figures 12.7 and 12.8) can both be integrated with the structure in Figure 12.6 which is an integration of various views of information about products and services of the business. The materials management planning information shown in Figure 12.3 also has the stock item relationship in common with Figures 12.6, 12.7, and 12.8, and can therefore be added to it. The capacity planning information of 12.1 has Location and Planning Period in common with these others, so it can be integrated with them. Finally, the employee information of Figure 12.2 also appears in Figures 12.1, 12.7, and 12.8.

Conceptually, the information useful to an organization should be considered one resource. The goals of the organization create a view of data that finds value in the data that relates to those goals. Data that is unrelated to the goals is not identified as a requirement by any subfunction. The result is a definition of an information resource that, like the bits of iron attached to a magnet after it is drawn through a pile of dirt, only includes data that is relevant to the goals of that organization.

Charting the structure of this unitary view of information, however, is not the whole of database planning. The conceptual database must be made applicable to the database implementation actions of individual managers in the organization. If these actions can include the development of separate information systems on separate computer systems then the conceptual database plan needs to indicate a compatible version of the unitary database for each likely computer system location.

The objective of data administration should not be to establish a single physical database. Rather it should be to ensure that the databases established are coordinated with respect to data definitions and relationships. The databases may exist in separate computer systems located in different cities, but to the user they should function as if they were a unitary database.

The ability to access any meaningful, reasonable combination of data in a computer system, or network of computer systems, is the capability that makes computers useful for management purposes. A system capable only of producing the reports deemed vital at the time it was designed lacks this flexibility. To avoid this result, a database management system approach separates the capture and storage of data from its retrieval and presentation and provides general purpose programs for retrieval and presentation. This approach to system design and development is well understood by most professional systems designers.

What is not so well understood is the added value obtained by coordinating database designs across multiple systems so that the data in one system is available to users of the other systems. The previous chapter identified seven types of data required in three or more functional areas (see Table 12.1). According to Table 12.1, the organization that allows separate uncoordinated systems to be developed in each of the seven major functional areas (shown in the column headings) will have 28 instances (the 35 entries in the first seven rows less seven) of incompatible versions of data about the same basic entity types and relationships. Many of these incompatible versions involve the most voluminous files maintained by the organization, such as customer, product, and sales invoice files.

Integrating different files of data on the same subject yields gains in effectiveness as well as efficiency. When the marketing, materials management, and accounting functions all share the same customer data, for example, invoices are more likely to be sent to the right address, and additional shipments are less likely to be sent to customers on the verge of bankruptcy. In addition, salesmen can obtain a more complete picture of the state of existing business relationships with a customer, and marketing analysts can work with customer profitability figures that reflect the cost of financing the receivables and other sales expenses associated with a given customer.

If integrated databases are so great, why are there so few of them? The answer is that there is a lack of an effective planning method for data administration[1] and a lack of software capable of managing distributed databases. In the special case of one physical database at one location, the hardware and software are available and the only factor lacking is an effective way of coordinating system development projects. But many wonder if building a centralized information system is wise for the long term. The pace of developments in microcomputers in recent decades has been more rapid than has the development of mainframe computers. Is it better to wait for software capable of managing a distributed database?

CENTRALIZED VERSUS DECENTRALIZED SYSTEMS

What are the economic, organizational, and operational factors that will govern system architectures in the next decade or so? The factor that should, and does, predominate in the absence of strong countervailing forces is the distribution of the organization. If the organization is spread over multiple lines of business or over multiple geographical markets or over multiple production locations or over multiple technologies, then the information systems of the organization will tend to follow that organizational pattern. The whole reason for information systems is to support the organization in the pursuit of its goals. So, these systems naturally reflect the organizational arrangement, in the absence of strong reasons not to do so.

One strong reason in the past was the economies of scale of large computers. The cost per million instructions processed (cost per MIP) used to be significantly lower for large computers than for small computers. This is no longer the case.[2] A microcomputer is as cost effective as a mainframe and it has the advantage of being in small modules so that the capacity that must be purchased can more nearly equal the capacity required at any point in time.

There is another strong force, however, in favor of centralization. It is the advantage of local-area networks over wide-area networks. Centralization does not necessarily mean one large computer. A number of organizations have tried to implement an integrated database system on one large computer and failed. For an organization that is not small, even a supercomputer is unable to handle the transaction processing workload, plus management queries and reporting requirements. For business data processing, as opposed to scientific calculations, the hardware solution seems to lie in a network of small computers rather than in one larger computer. The parallel processing that a network of small computers can do seems better suited to the relatively simple calculations and many database accesses that are characteristic of business transaction processing.

If parallel processing is the answer then two interesting alternatives arise: should all the processors (computers) be located at one location or should they be geographically distributed. Thus, there are still centralized and decentralized alternatives. The difference is in the communication links connecting the processors. In the centralized alternative, a local-area network connects the processors. In the decentralized alternative, a wide-area network connects them. The difference in the transmission speeds of these two networks is typically about two or three orders of magnitude, which means a local-area network is at least 100 times as fast as a wide-area network. This can make a big difference in response times at the user's workstation, or terminal, and response time is of decisive importance in on-line systems.

An operational factor that favors centralization is the difficulty of communicating with, and coordinating, people who are at another location. A data processing system may fail to perform tasks as needed for a variety of reasons. If the effectiveness, and even survival, of the organization depends on getting the system running again as soon as possible, the logic of having the computer where it can be serviced most easily can seem very compelling. If the experts cannot be decentralized, then it may be risky to decentralize the hardware.

However, the high cost of expertise in using computers is a reason for centralization that is slowly being eroded. As more people become available who are able to make computers do what organizations need them to do, their cost will come down and each organizational unit will have its own technicians. This has already happened as far as operating computers is concerned and it seems likely to develop with respect to programming and hardware maintenance. It should also be noted that the standardization and simplification of these tasks contributes to the erosion of this reason for centralization, as much as the education of more people for these jobs erodes it.

What is the conclusion? The advantage of the local area over the wide-area network in linking parallel processors appears to be a very strong reason for not "doing what comes naturally," which is to build decentralized systems. Personal computers are fine for desk-top publishing, electronic mail, calculations, and small relational databases, but when it comes to sharing an integrated, organizational database, centralized systems have a distinct advantage.

Nevertheless, for organizations located in more than one place, the best solution most likely is to be found somewhere between the extremes of total centralization and total decentralization. In the 1960s and 1970s, giving those who used data control over encoding it very definitely improved the quality of that data; the same effect can be expected from giving users the responsibility for maintaining their database. There is some corporate data, such as engineering test data and MRP data, for which the usage is so highly concentrated in one organizational unit that physically locating it at the location of that unit is clearly justified. In such cases, enough is saved in communication costs to justify the slow response that this causes when someone at another location needs to retrieve it for some unusual purpose. In the case of image data, as opposed to alphanumeric data, local storage may be justified by the sheer volume of the data that would otherwise have to be sent over the wide-area network.

A Distributed System Planning Methodology

Planning databases for decentralized systems is the main concern of this chapter. The conceptual database that can be obtained by integrating the structures of Part 2 is a description of the database that would be implemented in the case of a centralized system. In the case of a decentralized implementation, on the other hand, a separate version of the integrated database is required for each location and provision must be made for keeping replications of data synchronized.

Implementing integrated databases in a decentralized environment is more difficult than doing so in the case of a centralized system. In a decentralized environment, the needs of the organizational unit at a location must be identified. The extent to which the data needs at the location are strictly local must be determined, as compared to the need for data that is also required in other locations. Data required at multiple locations has to be managed in a way that makes its location transparent to the local user. This can be a complex system design problem.

FUNCTIONS, DATA, PROGRAMS, AND COMPUTERS

Data is managed by one or more programs running on a computer at a location. Conceivably, a user can be at one location while the data the user needs is at another, and the program is run on a computer at a third location. Obviously, the more locations involved, the higher the communication costs and the longer the delays in performing the tasks defined by the user.

High communication costs and slow response times can be avoided by placing programs and the data they use at the same location, and by replicating data (and programs) at multiple locations. The penalty is additional computer, technical staff and data storage costs and the added complexity of keeping multiple copies up-to-date. So, there is a trade-off to be evaluated: large communication costs and slow response times versus large computer system site costs and added database management complexity.

Basically, the subject of this chapter is the evaluation of this trade-off. Where should the data and programs of a business be stored given the information requirements of the organization? It is treated as a planning problem to be solved by finding an arrangement of computer sites, databases and program libraries that provides adequate access to data at the least cost.

An important implication of this formulation of the planning problem is that database planning is inextricably linked to information systems planning. To plan the location of data within the constraints of a predefined configuration of computer/communications hardware and technical support sites is to suboptimize. The only distribution that should be accepted as a given is the information requirements at each location where the organization does business.

BASIC CONFIGURATION GUIDELINES

In theory, finding the best configuration, for a given distribution of information requirements is a complex combinatorial problem. At how many sites should computing systems be located? What hardware, software, and technical staff are justified at each computing site? What communication links should be established between sites?

In theory this combinatorial problem is made difficult by the nonlinearities involved. One nonlinear aspect is the fixed costs of establishing a processing node. If a decision is made to store even one piece of data at a location, this implies that all the costs of establishing an entire computing system, and support staff, at the location must be incurred. Another nonlinearity is the fact that an interactive program may have an unacceptably slow response time if even one item of data that it requires if not locally available. These nonlinearities place the problem in the mathematical class of large integer programming problems for which mathematicians have yet to find a feasible solution.

An alternative strategy for finding a reasonably cost-effective solution to this distributed design problem is to use a heuristic solution technique. In considering the possible alternative locational configurations of data, programs, computers, and communication links, there are some heuristics (common sense rules) that can serve to eliminate many distribution alternatives from consideration. Using such rules simplifies the design problem.

For example, consider the heuristic:

> H1. The data used by a program should be at the
> same location as the program.

This heuristic[5] is based on the difference in transmission speeds of local and wide-area networks previously mentioned. The factor that determines the speed of a business data processing program is almost always the time that it takes to get data from an external storage device, or to store new data. If the storage device is a disk at the same location, the delay is a matter of milliseconds. If it is a disk at another geographic location (linked by a typical wide-area network), it takes at least 100 times longer. Thus, this first heuristic is based on the importance of response times. It also tends to reduce communication costs.

One implication of the first heuristic is that database processing should not take place at the user's workstation unless the database is located there (on the same local area network). As already stated, response times are usually governed by the speed of interactions between processor and disk, not those between processor and the workstation screen, or keyboard. A full screen of characters is less than 2000 characters (25 × 80). A wide-area network transmission speed between processor and screen of 9,600 bits per second (approximately 1,000 characters per second) implies that it will take less than two seconds to transmit a screen of data. This transmission speed is quite common; thus, it should be clear that the processor-screen interaction is not what causes response times in excess of two seconds.

Now, consider another heuristic:

> H2. It is better to replicate programs than data.

This second heuristic is based on the empirical fact that programs do not change as often as data. A program changes only when it is modified by a programmer. Data changes as transactions are entered, which is done by many people every day. Thus, if there is a choice between replicating a program or replicating data, the replication of the program is always to be preferred.

Replicating a program does *not* ensure that all the data used by that program will be at the location at which the program is executing. A program may access many items of data and the two heuristics we have so far considered do not guarantee that all items of data required by one program will all be at one location. In other words, program replication does not obviate the need to replicate data in order to have all the data required by a program at the location of the executing copy of the program.

If we accept the proposition that programs should be where the data they used is located then the question becomes, Where should the data be located? There are two alternative heuristic approaches to answering this question. One starts with a decentralized solution; the other starts with a centralized solution.

The decentralized approach uses a heuristic that is described in detail in the literature.[3, 4] It can be stated as follows:

> H3. Place each fragment of each relation in the conceptual database
> at the location where it is most frequently accessed.
> Replicate the fragment at other locations if this reduces
> total communication costs.

As explained in Chapter 2, a relation is a two-dimensional table and each entity type and many-to-many relationship in the BWIS can be considered a relation. A fragment of a relation is a subset of the relation. A subset of the attributes of the relation and a subset of the tuples (occurrences) of the relation constitute a fragment.

Aside from providing no aid in solving the practical difficulty of defining fragments for a conceptual database consisting of hundreds of relations, this heuristic has the defect of ignoring the fixed site costs. The fixed costs of establishing a computing capability at a location are ignored. A fragment of data required at only one site is automatically placed at that site by H3, regardless of the cost of setting up and maintaining the computing system required to store it there.

The centralized approach uses the following heuristics:

> H4. Place all data at one location unless by establishing a
> satellite computer site, communication costs and response time
> penalties are reduced by more than the fixed costs
> of the additional computer site are increased.

In using H4 to search for the best system distribution, we start with a totally centralized system. All data, programs, hardware, and staff are at one location. Then we consider an alternative in which some data are placed at another location. The first and second heuristic lead to the conclusion that the programs that refer to the data at the other location should also be there. The H4 heuristic provides a way to evaluate the alternative. When a distribution of some data are found that leads to reduced total costs, this H4 heuristic approach concludes that it should be adopted.

The H4 heuristic does not provide a way to automatically identify the data distribution alternatives that should be considered. But, obviously, the fixed costs of a computing site are more likely to be offset by communication cost reductions if all data used only at that site are included in the set of data to be transferred to the site. Whether to include other pieces of data that are needed at multiple sites is more problematical.

Whereas, the H3 heuristic leads to a fragment by fragment allocation approach, the H4 heuristic leads to a site by site evaluation approach. All, or a subset, of the information requirements of the site are considered as a distribution possibility. The only reason for considering a subset is because the communication cost of maintaining multiple copies of data used at multiple sites may be too large. (This is explained in more detail in the following subsection.)

The site-by-site evaluation approach seems intuitively easier to understand than the fragment allocation approach. Because it is based on the H4 heuristic, it also avoids the mistake of ignoring the fixed site costs. For these reasons, it is the strategy explored in the remainder of this chapter.

GENERATING DISTRIBUTION ALTERNATIVES

To apply the H4 heuristic, a method is needed to identify the plausible distributions of data (and therefore programs and computers) that should be evaluated. The justification for any information system configuration rests on the simple fact that it efficiently and reliably provides the data that enables people at each location to effectively perform their functions. Therefore, the method should begin with an analysis of the locations at which there are functions that need to be supported. Once all of the functions that require support at each location are known, then the information they require needs to be defined. It can be assumed that the information that these functions require is derived as explained in Parts 1 and 2 of this text. Integrating the information structures required at each location, as described in the previous chapter then provides a basis for identifying plausible system distribution possibilities.

The approach then is to identify all of the entities and relationships that should be considered for distribution to a given location. Some of these possibilities can be excluded from consideration based on the fact that the frequency of their use at the location is low compared to the frequency of use at other locations. For other possibilities, it will be obvious that their distribution will pass the test of H4. The remainder of the possibilities are probably close calls that merit both a quantitative analysis as defined by the H4 and careful consideration of the risks and other intangible factors.

This approach is illustrated by example in the next section. In this example, generic types of locations are used, rather than the actual locations of the organizations. This simplifies and generalizes the logic used in assigning functions to locations, which is an advantage from an expository standpoint. The generic locations are described in the next subsection.

Also, before giving the example, it is necessary to distinguish between two types of database distributions. The concepts of replication and partitioning need to be discussed as they apply to this methodology. So, a subsection on this topic is included in this section.

KINDS OF LOCATIONS

The decentralization possibilities can be described in general terms by considering the kinds of locations organizations typically have and the data that it may be economical to place there. Most organizations have a headquarters location, for example, at which various administrative and planning functions are performed. If this location is centrally located, it may well be the location of the centralized information system proposed as a null hypothesis. Although, in some cases, much larger transaction volumes need to be processed by the organization elsewhere and communication costs would be lower if the data center were placed at one of these locations.

A second kind of location is the branch office, or sales office. This is a location set up to more effectively serve customers in an area. Data about customers is used and generated in branch offices. Data about the services and products that have been or could be provided to customers is also required.

Offices and testing laboratories for the engineering function is a third type of location. The data used at this location is summarized in Chapter 9, and one might be tempted to conclude that this data are of little use to other functions. However, it should be noted that the column in Table 12.1 for engineering shows a number of information structures that this function shares with other functions.

A fourth kind of location is the warehouse used by materials management to receive, store, and ship goods. Information about shipments received is captured here. Inventory data are used to store and locate product. Data are also used (and captured) that concern picking, packing, and delivering items from stock.

Processing plants and factories are a fifth kind of location that should be considered when planning an information system. Chapter 8 describes data that are required at production locations, and it is evident from Table 12.1 that important parts of this data are also used by other functions.

These five kinds of locations are taken into consideration in the next section where the location of functions is discussed. Obviously, these are not the only types of locations that are a part of organizations. Thus, the discussion in that section must be confined to manufacturing types of organizations which often have only these five kinds of locations. However, the method of analysis illustrated in that section should be applicable to other types of organizations.

REPLICATING AND PARTITIONING

In formulating plausible distributions of parts of the conceptual database to locations other than the central location, remember that two types of distributions are possible. One is to maintain copies of the data at both the central location and the other location(s). This is called *data replication*. It requires that a modification (or addition or deletion) to the data at one location must be made at the other location(s) as well. Thus, a distinction must be made in this case between merely retrieving a copy of the data and changing the data. Only for the latter type of access is it necessary to revise the comparable data at the other location(s).

Partitions

The alternative to replication is to keep different occurrences of a certain type of data (record type) at different locations. This is called data partitioning. In a distributed database system, we can assume that the system knows which occurrences are at which locations, so that it will refer any requests for a given occurrence to the appropriate location. In this case, the only additional cost of the distributed alternative is the cost of sending the request to the satellite location, plus any added cost of sending the requested data from the satellite location. An update of one or more attributes in a partitioned database does not have to be propagated to other copies.

It should be noted that partial replication or partitioning of a file is possible. That is, it is not necessary for all occurrences of an entity type to be replicated or partitioned. For example, the alternative of replicating only the Employee occurrences for employees at a factory location might be considered. In this alternative, the employee records for workers at the factory would be maintained at two locations while the employee records of all other employees would only exist at the central location.

Another alternative is a partial partitioning of the employee records. If the employee records for the factory worker are maintained only in the database at the factory and the employee records of all other employees are maintained only at the central location, this would be a partial partitioning of the database.

If more than two locations are involved in an alternative, then the partial versus full distinction may become meaningless. If all of the occurrences of the Employee entity type are partitioned to the location where the employee works, is that a full or partial partitioning? Some employees probably work at the location of the data center and their records would remain there by the stated rule of the partition.

Vertical and Horizontal Distributions

The data for a given entity type can be partitioned or replicated either vertically or horizontally. When data are partitioned or replicated vertically, only certain attributes of the entity type (columns of the relation) are distributed. When it is partitioned or replicated horizontally, only certain occurrences (tuples) are distributed. The examples given above for employee data are all examples of horizontal distributions.

Of course, it is possible to define a subset of the data for an entity type in terms of a combined horizontal and vertical segmentation. The name, address and years of service of all employees at a certain location is an example of a subset of the employee data defined in terms of both a vertical and horizontal segmentation. A subset of the data for an entity type is a portion of the relation for that entity type in a physical database. Such portions are sometimes referred to as fragments.

Evaluation of Replication and Partitioning Possibilities

Evaluating the alternative of placing data at a satellite location (rather than at the central site) that is only used at that satellite location is easy in the sense that it is certainly preferable if the costs of having the necessary computing capabilities at the satellite location can be justified. Such a partitioning usually implies a reduction in the cost of data communication between the central site and the satellite location equal to the cost of accessing the data involved.

The evaluation of replication possibilities is not as simple. Also, evaluating partitions that involve data used at multiple sites can be problematical. In this subsection, we discuss these more difficult evaluation problems.

Analysis of Replication Opportunities

Changes in replicated data made at one location must also be made at the other sites where the data are replicated. If the data are not replicated, no updating at other locations is required. So, distributing replicated data can result in a net increase in communication costs if the data values change frequently. The more volatile the replicated data, the more costly it is to maintain the replications of it.

A simple model is given in reference 5 that makes the trade-off clear. Suppose there are N locations at which the occurrences of a given entity type are needed and replication is being considered. For simplicity, let us assume that the two types of data accesses, namely retrievals and changes, are each at the same intensity at all of the N locations. Let:

```
R = the average retrievals per hour at a location, and
C = the average changes per hour at a location.
```

(This assumption is, of course, unrealistic, but it is necessary to keep the mathematics simple, so that we reach a result that clearly shows the basic trade-off.)

Furthermore, let us assume that the data communication capacity required to handle a retrieval or a change at a remote location is the same regardless of the locations involved and constitutes one "data traffic unit." This is not true to the extent that distances affect the data transmission capacities required but it can serve as a first approximation of the amount of traffic generated by data replication.

Then, using DC to represent the average data traffic units per hour per location for the centralized alternative (no replication), we can write the following:

```
DC = (R + C) * ((N - 1) / N).
```

Using DD to represent the average data traffic units per hour for the distributed (replication) alternative, we can write:

```
DD = C * (N - 1).
```

The basis for this expression is that in the case of replication, each change must be communicated to the N - 1 other locations where a replication of the data exists.

Now, the condition under which the centralized alternative results in more data communication activity (and therefore costs) than the distributed alternative can be stated as follows:

$$DC > DD$$

Or, by substitution

$$(R + C) * ((N - 1) / N) > C * (N - 1).$$

By some simple algebraic steps, this implies that the centralized alternative is less desirable than replication if:

$$R / C > N - 1.$$

The volatility of the data for the entity type is measured by the ratio of R to C in this formula. If this ratio is larger than the number of locations less one, then replication is the best alternative. If C is large, this ratio will tend to be small and so not larger then $N - 1$. Thus, the formula yields a positive recommendation for replication only if the rate of change in the data are sufficiently small. In other words, data volatility is the sole determinant of whether data should be replicated; it does not depend on the absolute values of the frequency of read or write accesses but on the ratio between them.

The amount of wide-area network data communications generated by the need to update copies of the same data at different locations can be reduced by batching the changes and by only sending them to the other locations periodically, say once every H hours. In this case:

$$DD = (N - 1) / H$$

and DC is the same as defined above because there is no batching in the centralized case. Substituting for $DC > DD$ in this case gives the following formula:

$$R + C > N / H.$$

This formula shows that if the sum of the retrieval and change rates is greater than the number of locations divided by the time interval between update messages, then the replication alternative is preferred. This is much more favorable for replication, because of the greater efficiency with which the changes are communicated to the other locations.

Analysis of Partition Opportunities

Consider the case in which the occurrences of an entity type are partitioned so that some of them are at one location and others are at another. What are the data communication implications of this alternative compared to the centralized alternative? If all of the retrievals and changes to the partitioned data are at the location where it is located, then the net advantage of the partition alternative is $R + C$, because this is the number of data communication messages on the wide-area network that are avoided per hour and no updating of copies at other locations is required. However, if some of the retrievals or changes must come from another location then the advantage of the partition alternative is only a fraction of R + C.

In the case of a partitioning, any retrievals or changes coming from another location would probably have to go through the central computer system. Thus, they would require two data communication messages instead of one. This implies that if more than half of the retrievals or changes come from other locations, then the partition alternative is inferior to the centralized alternative.

THE "CHUNKING PROBLEM" IN DISTRIBUTION PLANNING

The distribution of relation fragments is considered by some to be the essence of the distributed database planning problem. In reference 4 for example, two methods for allocating fragments to sites are given. Characterizing the database planning problem as one of planning the location of fragments, however, may be an oversimplification.

The fixed cost associated with establishing a satellite data storage and processing site is one factor that suggests that larger "chunks" than fragments of individual relations need to be the unit of distribution to be evaluated. If distributing some chunk of data (probably involving a number of relations) does not result in a larger communication cost saving than the fixed costs of the new site, the allocation of fragments to the site based on marginal communication cost savings is misleading.

Another factor to consider is the integral nature of the information requirements of a subfunction. The entry of sales orders, for example, requires data on both the products that may be ordered and customers that may place orders. If both of these types of data are not at the same location then the application program for order entry cannot be at the location where the data it requires is located (as stipulated by the second heuristic cited in a previous section). It must remotely access either the product data or the customer data. This would lead to intolerable response times for order entry.

One approach to searching for a satisfactory (satisficing) solution is to first consider all of the information required at a site as the chunk to be replicated/partitioned to the site. If distributing this chunk is not cost effective then consider a subset of it that does not contain some of the replications that have a large updating cost associated with their distribution.

If distributing the original chunk is cost effective, this does not mean that it is the best solution. It only means that there are distributed solutions that are better than the pure centralized solution. There is still a need to determine if some of the replication activity implied by distribution of the original chunk is too expensive.

A reliable and computationally feasible search algorithm for the general distributed database planning problem remains to be discovered.

In the absence of an algorithm that will automatically find the best distributed database design, it is important to really understand the nature of the problem so that a solution technique is not misapplied. Obtaining the right answer to the wrong problem has been the far too frequent outcome of past attempts to use computers to solve business planning problems.

ILLUSTRATION OF THE PLANNING METHOD

In this section, an illustration is given of the database planning methodology that has been described. The first step of the method defines the functions performed at each location. Then, the information requirements of these functions are identified. A third step integrates the information structures that define the requirements of individual functions into a view of the conceptual database appropriate for the location.

The fourth step identifies portions of the locational database requirement that either should clearly not be stored at the location or clearly should, using the fourth heuristic criterion previously defined. The fifth step evaluates the idea of distributing those portions of the locational database requirement remaining after the fourth step, again using the fourth heuristic.

LOCATION OF FUNCTIONS

To illustrate this step, we consider the six functions defined in Part 2 of the text and the personnel function discussed in Part 1. The locational aspects of each function are described in a following subsection. At the conclusion, the results are summarized by a list of the functions performed at each location other than the headquarters location, which is assumed to be the location of the centralized alternative.

The locations considered are the five previously defined. No assumptions are made about the geographical relationships between the locations. It could be argued that there is probably a warehouse at a factory location, and that locations house both a warehouse and a branch office. However, such assumptions are unnecessary for purposes of assigning functions to locations.

Personnel

The subfunctions of personnel are discussed in Chapter 4. That discussion identifies six subfunctions at the first breakdown. It then proceeds to further breakdown the employment subfunction in a depth-first manner. The result is the breakdown shown on the left in Table 13.1.

TABLE 13.1. Location of personnel functions.

	Headquarters	Branch Office	Engineering Laboratory	Warehouse	Factory
Employment	X	X	X	X	X
Selection					
Interviewing					
Compensation	X				
Labor relations	X				
Benefit					
administration	X				
Health and safety	X		X	X	X
Training	X		X	X	X

The employment subfunction is shown as one to be performed at all of the five types of locations. The health and safety and training subfunctions are shown as required at all locations except branch offices. The compensation, labor relations, and benefit administration functions are shown as headquarter functions only.

For this example, the Table 13.1 distribution of the personnel function is assumed to exist and is considered desirable for the future. Such distribution may not be appropriate for a given organization. For purposes of illustrating the method of analysis, however, this is not of vital importance.

Marketing

The locational distribution of the marketing function is shown in Table 13.2. The functional breakdown on the left is taken from Chapter 6. It is assumed that the outside and inside sales activities are performed entirely in the branch offices. The external marketing function, on the other hand, is split between the branch office and headquarters, with the direct selling subfunction treated as a branch office activity and advertising and promotion subfunctions treated as headquarters activities. For a large business, some advertising and promotion could be done at the branches, but for purposes of this example, this possibility is ignored.

The internal marketing functions are all assumed to occur at headquarters. Again, in a large firm some of these activities may also be performed at branches and the engineering lab but this possibility is ignored.

TABLE 13.2.   Location of marketing functions.

	Headquarters	Branch Office	Engineering Laboratory	Warehouse	Factory
Outside sales		X			
Determine customer needs					
Prepare quotation					
Negotiate sales agreements					
Resolve problems					
Inside sales		X			
Order entry					
Customer service					
External marketing					
Direct selling		X			
Advertising	X				
Promotion	X				
Internal marketing	X				
Pricing					
Credit					
Sales forecasting					
Market research					
Product planning					

Materials Management

The materials management subfunctions in Table 13.3 are taken from Chapter 7. Four subfunctions of transaction processing are shown. The purchasing function is shown as occurring at headquarters, at the engineering labs, and at factories. The centralization-decentralization issue with respect to purchasing is at least as contentious as it is with respect to computers, so the conclusion should not be drawn from the distribution shown in Table 13.3 that this is the only way to distribute purchasing; it is one plausible alternative.

The receiving function is one that is required at each location where goods and services are received, which is assumed to be all five types of locations. The entering of customer orders into the computer system (part of processing sales orders) is assumed in this example to be done by the inside sales function. Thus, processing sales orders only involves determining how to supply what has been ordered, as explained in Chapter 7. It is assumed this is done at the headquarters location.

The delivery function is shown in Table 13.3 as occurring at warehouse and factory locations. The delivery from a factory location could be to a warehouse or to a customer. It is assumed that the transportation subfunction within the operations subfunction of production operations in Figure 8.2 is limited to transportation services within a production facility and does not include transportation to other locations, although this will not always be the case.

The facilities and staff management subfunction is one mentioned in Chapter 7, and elsewhere. It would be at all locations if shown. It is omitted from this example because its information requirements are not described in Part 2.

The sales forecast allocation subfunction is assigned to the headquarters location because it concerns all factory and warehouse locations and is a planning

TABLE 13.3. Location of materials management functions.

	Headquarters	Branch Office	Engineering Laboratory	Warehouse	Factory
Transaction processing					
Purchasing	X		X		X
Receiving	X	X	X	X	X
Processing sales orders	X				
Delivering				X	X
Materials requirements planning					
Sales forecast allocation	X				
Order release planning				X	X
Explosion					X
Requisitioning				X	X
Reporting and analysis				X	X
Capacity planning					X

function that must be performed at the enterprise-wide level. The other subfunctions of MRP take place at the factory and warehouse locations, except for the explosion subfunction which only come into play when an assembly of parts must be planned.

Capacity planning is shown in Table 13.3 as a factory level activity. A simplified version might be needed at a warehouse, but this possibility is ignored for purposes of this example.

Production and Engineering

For these two functions, locational specification is easy. The production subfunctions all take place at factory locations, and only at those locations. The engineering subfunctions are assumed to be performed only at the engineering offices and laboratories.

Financial Management

The location of financial management functions is shown in Table 13.4. The finance subfunction is assumed to be a headquarters activity as are most of the accounting subfunctions. However, it is common to have some accounting services at a factory, particularly cost accounting. Also, branch offices may get involved in the collection of receivables from customers and therefore some of the receivables function is shown as occurring at branches.

TABLE 13.4. Location of financial management functions.

	Headquarters	Branch Office	Engineering Laboratory	Warehouse	Factory
Finance	X				
Short-term financing					
Capital budgeting					
Capital structuring					
Portfolio management					
Accounting					
Receivables	X	X			
Payables	X				
Payroll	X				X
Fixed assets	X				X
Cost accounting	X				X
General ledger	X				
Budgeting	X	X	X	X	X
Auditing					
Audit planning	X				
Systems testing	X	X	X	X	X
Statement balance testing	X				
Evaluation and reporting	X				

Budgeting is a subfunction that needs to be carried out at all locations where there are managers with authority to incur expenses. All five locations probably have such managers and therefore qualify for some budgeting activity. The auditing subfunctions are done at headquarters except for the testing of systems which can involve investigation of systems at all locations.

Information Systems Management

The service management subfunction is certainly one that could potentially require activity at any of the five location types, regardless of the information system configuration. There are input and reporting activities that involve functions performed at all types of locations. So, in Table 13.5, the service management subfunction is shown as taking place in all locations.

The other subfunctions will take place at the headquarters location, assuming that this is the location of the centralized system alternative. They may also take place at other locations and some of these possibilities are indicated by a question mark (?) in Table 13.5.

TABLE 13.5. Location of information management functions.

	Headquarters	Branch Office	Engineering Laboratory	Warehouse	Factory
Service management Customer service Project organization Education	X	X	X	X	X
Technical service Data administration	X				
System development	X				?
System implementation	X	?	?	?	?
Computers and peripherals	X				?
Network planning	X				
Operations System operation Software library Network operation Testing and maintenance	X	?	?	?	?
Administrative services Accounting Facilities Personnel Security	X				

Subfunctions per Location

The definition of locations at which a function is performed can be reshuffled to show all of the functions performed at a single location. This is illustrated in Table 13.6.

The functions performed at branch offices, engineering facilities, warehouses, and factories are shown in Table 13.6. The functions to be performed at the headquarters location are not shown in Table 13.6. However, they can easily be obtained from Tables 13.1 through 13.5 in the same way as are the summaries by location shown in Table 13.6. The headquarters location is assumed to be the location of the centralized computer system. It is the default location for all data that is not specifically distributed to another location. Even the data that is distributed to another location may also be at the centralized location if a replication type of distribution is selected.

ENVELOPE INFORMATION STRUCTURE FOR A LOCATION

The second step in the database planning procedure is to define the information required for each of the functions that is performed at a location. The functions performed at a certain type of location are shown in Table 13.6. The information requirements for each of these functions is defined, to some extent, in Chapters 5 through 11. Therefore, defining the information requirements for a location can be done by locating the relevant requirements in Chapters 5 through 11.

A third step is to integrate the information structures that define the requirements of individual functions into a view of the conceptual database appropriate for the location. The view integration techniques described in Chapter 12 can be applied to do this. The result is an information structure that shows all entity types and relationships that should be considered for distribution to the location. This is not the same as the information structure that should be established in a database at the location. It is an envelope structure that contains all of the possibilities that should be evaluated for distribution. Only after the evaluations of Steps 4 and 5 in the procedure have been completed is the appropriate conceptual database for the location clear.

Steps 2 and 3 are illustrated in this subsection. They are performed for the branch office location type. In a full-scale database planning project, the steps must also be performed for the other location types (engineering laboratories, warehouses, and factories). However, for the purpose of illustrating the method of analysis, it is sufficient to show the steps for one location.

Branch Office Envelope Information Structure

The information requirements for each of the functions executed in branch offices are defined in a figure in a previous chapter. The figures that are relevant are listed in Table 13.7.

The branch office as defined in Table 13.6 is a sales office. It has a sales staff performing sales and external marketing functions. There is a small administrative support staff. The question is whether there should be any information systems functions carried out at these branch sales offices.

TABLE 13.6. Functions at each type of satellite location.

FACTORY

Personnel	Employment
	Health and safety
	Training
Materials management	Receiving
	Delivery
	Purchasing
Materials requirements planning	Order release planning
	Explosion
	Requisitioning
	Reporting
Capacity planning, production	Operations
	Technology
	Facilities
	Services
Accounting	Payroll
	Fixed assets
	Cost accounting and control
	Budgeting
Auditing	Systems testing
Information systems management	Service management

WAREHOUSE

Personnel	Employment
	Health and safety
	Training
Materials management	Receiving
	Delivery
Materials requirements planning	Order release planning
	Requisitioning
	Reporting
Accounting	Budgeting
Auditing	Systems testing
Information management	Service management

ENGINEERING FACILITY

Personnel	Employment
	Health and safety
	Training
Materials management	Purchasing
	Receiving
Engineering	Systems integration
	Discipline
	Administration
Accounting	Budgeting
Information management	Service management

BRANCH OFFICE

Personnel	Employment
Marketing	Outside sales
	Inside sales
	Direct selling
Materials management	Receiving
Accounting	Receivables
	Budgeting
Auditing	System testing
Information management	Service management

TABLE 13.7. Location of information requirement diagrams.

Function		Information Required
Personnel	Employment	Figure 5.5
Marketing	Outside sales	Figure 6.3
	Inside sales	Figure 6.3
	Direct selling	Figure 6.7
Materials management	Receiving	Figure 7.6
Accounting	Receivables	Figure 10.12 (part)
	Budgeting	Figure 10.12 (part)
Auditing	System testing	Figure 10.12 (part)
Information management	Service management	Figure 11.1

Employment Subfunction

The information requirements for the employment subfunction are developed in Chapter 5 and are summarized in Figure 5.5. The structure shown in Figure 5.5 is reproduced in Figure 13.1. The reproduction is transposed (right side of Figure 5.5 is on the left in Figure 13.1) and the schedule relationship has been added to it. In Chapter 5, this schedule relationship is necessary for a subfunction of employment and is shown in Figure 5.8 which is for the interview subfunction.

Marketing and Receivables Subfunctions

The marketing subfunctions performed at branch sales offices have information requirements that have a number of entity types in common. Figures 6.3 and 6.7 have Prospect, Customer, Product/Service, and Salesperson in common. Both of these structures also have entity types in common with the employment requirement structure of Figure 5.5. Therefore, one structure needs to be used to summarize the requirements for the four subfunctions involved. This structure is shown in Figure 13.1.

The structures of Figures 6.3 and 6.7 have been rearranged in Figure 13.1 but all of the entity types and relationships in either of them appear somewhere in Figure 13.1. An *isa* relationship has been added between employee and salesperson in Figure 13.1. Also, the Inside Sales entity type of Figure 6.3 has been replaced by the Organization Unit entity type in Figure 13.1; this is based on the assumption that the inside sales function is performed by a certain organizational unit.

The part of Figure 10.12 that pertains to the accounts receivable function is also shown in Figure 13.1. It is not obvious but Figures 6.7 and 10.12 have sales data in common. The *sales* relationship of Figure 6.7 is decomposed to Customer Invoice and *line item* in Figure 13.1. The sales to a customer are normally measured in terms of the amount invoiced to the customer. The other items of information needed for accounts receivable are the payments made by the customer and the outstanding customer balance. The Cash Receipt entity type represents payment data, and the *subsidiary-in-period* relationship includes the outstanding customer balance. For collection work, it is useful to have the outstanding customer balance broken down by how long it has been owed. The Age Interval entity type in Figure 13.1 and its relationship to Customer Invoice provides that information.

Associated with each entity type and many-to-many relationship in Figure 13.1, there is the letter P or R (or both). P stands for a partitioned type of distribution and an R stands for a replication type of distribution. If the occurrences of an entity type or relationship are not "commonly required" at any location including headquarters, except a specific branch office, then the entity type is a candidate for a P type of distribution. On the other hand, entity types whose occurrences are needed at other locations are labeled R. This means that if these entity types are distributed to branch offices, they must be replicated at more than one location.

Consider a few examples of categorizing entity types as partitionable or replicatable. Company Policy is clearly an entity type whose occurrences should be the same at all locations; so, it is classified as an R entity type. An applicant for a job at a local branch office, on the other hand, might plausibly be classed as a P entity type. If the applicant is hired, then he becomes an employee and an employee occurrence is established; an Employee is clearly an R entity type because functions at a number of locations commonly require employee data.

The criterion for this classification is whether data about instances of the entity type (or relationship) is required by functions at many locations or only one location. Not one type of location but one location. If the data are required at only one location then the entity type is partitionable.

The phrase "commonly required" is used in describing the need of a function for certain data, because partitioning an entity type should not mean that the data for that entity type is not available at other locations. It should still be available if a true distributed database management system is controlling the data. To access partitioned data from another location, however, the wide-area network must be used. This means that the response time for a request for partitioned data at another location will be long. It may take 100 times as long. But it can be accessed remotely. So, for data that may be needed once in a while at other locations, the partition classification still is appropriate because the data are not "commonly required" at other locations.

In some places on Figure 13.1 there is both a P and an R. For example, Employment Agency has both letters. This means that there are some occurrences of this entity type that are replicated at other locations and other occurrences that are strictly local. It may be useful to replicate information about a national employment agency, whereas, information about a local employment agency is unlikely to be of use at any other location.

Receiving Subfunction

The receiving subfunction at a branch office is likely to deal mainly with office supplies and fixed assets. On occasion, something may be shipped to the branch office for delivery to a customer, however. So, there may be some overlap between Product/Service occurrences and the Items of Figure 7.6, which includes supplies and fixed assets. Item is a generalization of Product/Service. (The Product/Service entity type only encompasses items sold to customers.)

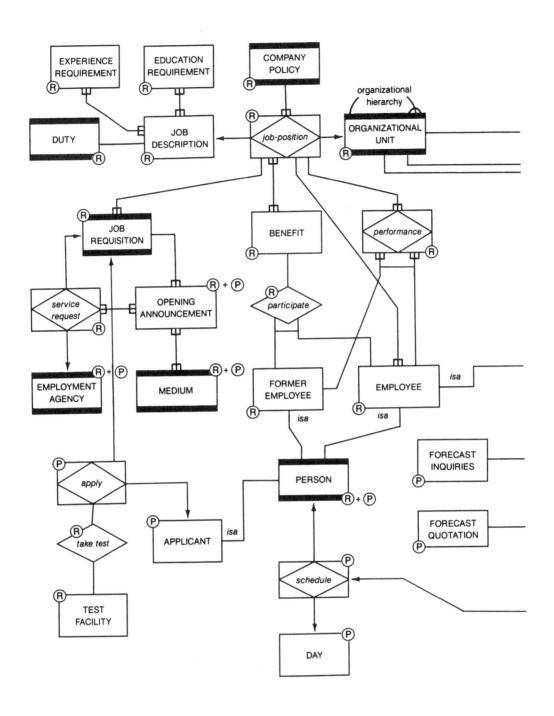

FIGURE 13.1. Integrated information structure for branch office marketing and personnel functions.

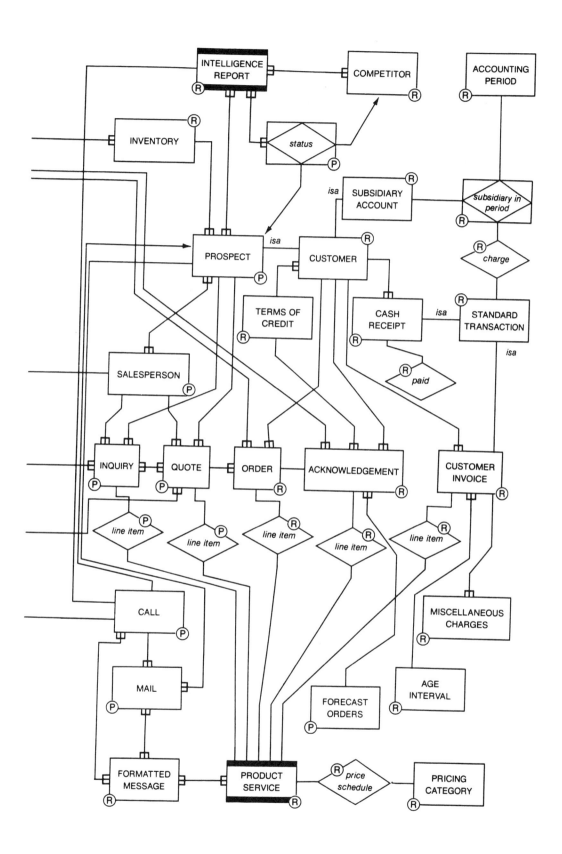

385

A copy of the information structure of Figure 7.6 is shown in Figure 13.2. The only difference is the R and P classifications shown in Figure 13.2. The other location involved in the replications referred to in Figure 13.2 is the headquarters location where the purchasing function for branch sales offices is assumed to take place.

There are two possible links between Figures 13.1 and 13.2. One is a potential *isa* relationship between Item and Product/Service. The other is a link between Receipt and Customer Invoice for the case in which the product to be delivered to the customer is sent to the branch office for personal delivery. Because this relationship may not be necessary, it is not shown in Figure 13.2.

Budgeting Subfunction

Budgeting for a branch sales office requires information about the expenses of the office, salaries and commissions, various marketing expenses, travel expenses, sales revenue and the gross margin on sales. All of the expense items in this list are modeled as Account entity occurrences in Chapter 10. The budget for these expenses is contained in attributes of the *account-in-period* relationship of Figure 10.9.

The sales revenue budget and gross margin on sales budget can involve the Customer (or Product/Service) Subsidiary Account occurrence as well as the Account occurrences for sales and gross margin. A sales budget broken down by customer and accounting period is commonly used for sales and marketing planning purposes.

Budgeting involves actual revenues and expenditures, as well as budgeted (planned) amounts. This means that the other entity types shown in Figure 10.9 are required for budgeting. For sales budgeting, the information on Customer Invoices and its relationship with Item are also needed to provide details about actual sales and actual gross margin on individual sales.

The information structure that summarizes the information required for sales office budgeting is shown in Figure 13.3. It is an integration of Figure 10.9 with the portion of Figure 13.1 that concerns the receivables function.

All of the entity types and relationships in Figure 13.3 are marked R because it is assumed that they must all be replicated for the accounting function at headquarters. The bulk of this replication would be for sales invoices and customer payments, which must be done not only for budgeting purposes, but also for use in direct selling, order entry, and receivables management work done at the branch.

System Testing

The system testing subfunction of auditing mainly concerns the expense recording systems of the branch. Nevertheless, verification that customers in fact owe the amounts indicated by the customer subsidiary ledger is also important.

Verifying that the expenses for the branch, as recorded by the payables system at headquarters, are for services and supplies actually provided can involve a variety of data. It includes evidence that branch employees worked as represented, which might be recorded as attributes of the Employee entity type. It also includes evidence that the supplies and fixed assets paid for were in fact received. The receiving information structure of Figure 13.2 can provide evidence of this type.

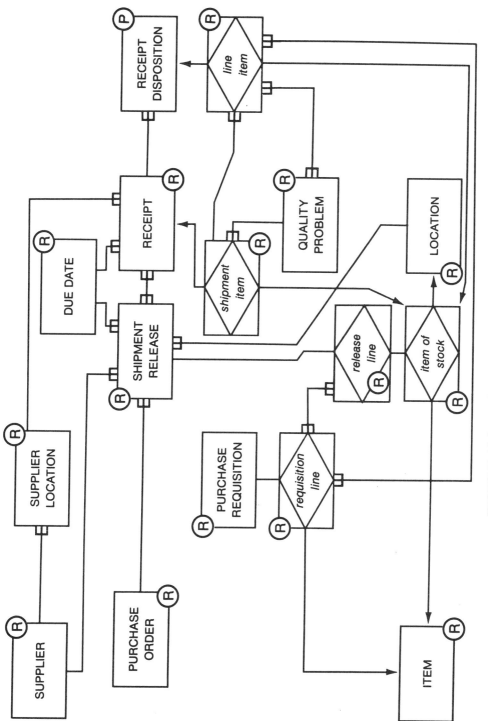

FIGURE 13.2. Information structure for receiving function.

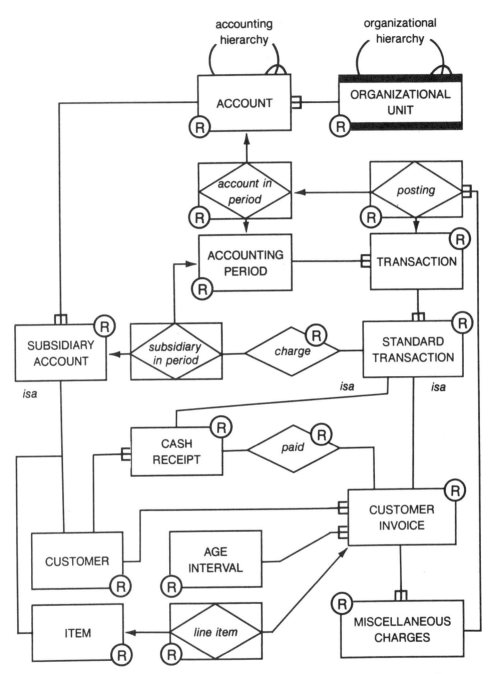

FIGURE 13.3. Information structure for branch office accounting.

As explained in Chapter 10, system testing also requires that the documentation and operation of any processing system be examined. Thus, system testing can benefit from the types of information structures described in Chapter 11 for information systems management. Specifically, the structure shown in Figure 11.3 for information systems operations management can store data about every transaction, query, and report processed by the computer systems of the enterprise. This provides a great deal of evidence about how the expense reporting system and other systems have been working.

It is not necessary that the structure defined in Figure 11.3 be stored at the branch, however, in order for this data to be available, unless there is a computer used for transaction processing at the branch. If all transactions are processed at headquarters, then the structure of Figure 11.3 can provide evidence of branch transaction processing at the headquarters location. If there is a computer at the branch doing transaction processing, then the Figure 11.3 structure should be maintained at the branch by heuristic rule 1 cited previously.

Service Management

The management of information system services provided to the users of the systems requires potentially all of the information discussed in Chapter 11. If there are computers at the branch office, then certainly some of that data should be stored at the branch, and storing all of it should be considered.

Given that there are computers at the branch, it is highly likely that a partitioned version of the information structure of Figure 11.3 would pass the test of the fourth heuristic for distributing systems. Maintaining the currency of data about the Program Execution, Transaction, Query, and Report entity types requires almost continuous accessing of these files as programs are executed.

The distribution of other structures described in Chapter 11 is more problematical. Depending on the frequency of access, distribution of the structures of Figures 11.5 and 11.6 may or may not be warranted.

DATA DISTRIBUTION DECISIONS

The data to be considered for distribution to branch sales offices should be derived from Figures 13.1, 13.2, 13.3, and the structures of Chapter 11, particularly Figure 11.3. If the data represented by these figures is not distributed, then we assume it exists at the central computer location and must be accessed remotely using a wide-area data communication network. By distributing the data to the branches, the amount of data communication activity between branch and central site can be reduced. It cannot be eliminated, however, because of the need to keep replicated versions of data consistent and because of remote accessing of partitioned data at a branch from other sites.

As far as the H4 heuristic is concerned, the trade-off is data communication and response time costs versus site computer system costs. To avoid accessing data at the central site, a branch must have the computer hardware, software, data, and staff to maintain the database locally. The questions are, what is the net increase in computer system costs (at the two sites), and what is the decrease in communication costs that will occur if a satellite computing system is established at the branch?

The only qualification on this statement of the decision problem concerns the cost of maintaining replicated data. It has been stated that the information structures in Figures 13.1, 13.2, and 13.3 represent envelopes that contain all of the data that should be considered for distribution to branches. It may not be best to choose the alternative of distributing all of this data. Some of the replicated data may be too volatile. The formulas for evaluating whether data that must be replicated if it is to be at the branch sales offices have already been discussed. The branch sales office satellite data center concept is an appropriate application for them.

The basis for rationally making the decision as to whether branch sales offices should be computer system sites should be clear at this point. A subset of the branch sales office data requirements is first identified that includes the partitioned and replicated data that should be distributed based on a marginal cost analysis. (Are communication costs, plus response time penalties, minimized by the distribution?) The costs of a branch office computer system are then compared with the communication and response time cost reductions of the distributed alternative. If the branch office computer system costs are larger then the branch offices should not have computer systems; otherwise, they should.

SUMMARY

Database planning is more complex for a distributed system than for a centralized system. For the centralized case, database planning requires only the view integration methods described in Chapter 12.

Integrated centralized databases exist, but they are not appropriate in many cases because the organization is distributed and different units use specific data at very different levels of intensity. Also, it has been difficult to implement centralized databases because of a lack of an effective database planning method and because of hardware limitations. The development of a distributed database that exists at many locations yet is based on one integrated design has also been made difficult by a lack of database management system (DBMS) software capable of managing a distributed database.

Distributed database planning is a very complex problem if it is formulated as an optimization problem in mathematics. There are many possible combinations to consider and key variables are nonlinear. A strategy of searching for a good solution based on some heuristic rules seems to be the appropriate approach.

Four heuristic rules are considered. They eliminate from consideration the possibilities in which a program at one location routinely accesses data at another location. The possibility that a program may occasionally access data at a remote location is not ruled out but the data distribution should be planned so that the data required at a location is either at that location or at a central location, and the program will be where the data are located.

It is explained that the heuristic approach can lead to either of two methods of analysis. One allocates fragments of relations to locations based on a marginal cost analysis. The other identifies satellite computing sites based on the total information requirements at the site. This later method is recommended and further explained by example.

In the example, the null hypothesis is that all data and programs are located at one location. The distribution of programs and data to other locations is made if total costs are reduced by doing so. This reduces the planning problem to a series of trade-off analyses in which the fixed costs of a satellite computer facility are compared to the data communication cost reduction that it makes possible.

The trade-offs to be considered are identified by analyzing where functions are performed and the data required at that location in order to perform the functions of the location. Each entity type and relationship required at the location is evaluated for either a replication or partition type of distribution to the location. Those for which the trade-off analysis favors distribution are identified and their total saving in data communication costs is calculated. This is then compared to the increase in fixed operating costs that the additional site would cause. If the increase in fixed cost is less, then setting up the satellite computer center and distributing the data are justified.

REFERENCES

1. Lederer, Albert L., and Vijay Sethi, "The Implementation of Strategic Information Systems Planning Methodologies," *MIS Quarterly*, September, 1988, pp. 445–461.
2. Mendelson, Haim, "Economies of Scale in Computing: Grosch's Law Revisited," *Communications of the ACM*, 30, 12, December, 1987, pp. 1066–1072.
3. Ceri, Stefano, and Giuseppe Pelagatti, *Distributed Databases, Principles and Systems* (New York: McGraw-Hill Book Co., 1984).
4. Teorey, Toby J., Jarir Chaar, Kunle Olukotun, and Amjed Umar, "Allocation Methods for Distributed Databases," *Database Programming and Design* (San Francisco: Miller Freeman Publications, Vol. 2 No. 4 (April 1989)) pp. 34–42.
5. Martin, James, *Strategic Data-Planning Methodologies* (Englewood Cliffs, NJ: Prentice-Hall, 1982) p. 197.

DISCUSSION QUESTIONS

1. How can we avoid creating a system that is only capable of producing the reports defined and provided for at the time of system development?

2. In a world of insignificant communication costs, wide-area networks that move data as fast as do local area networks, and insignificant computer system economies of scale, would you choose a distributed or centralized database architecture? Why?

3. How much control should a user organization have over the information systems that it uses and why?

4. Assuming the bottleneck in a centralized physical database architecture is the number of database file accesses that can be completed per second, what can be done to relieve the bottleneck?

5. Summarize the reasons for allowing distributed physical databases.

6. Are reduced computer, communication and data center site costs the main reason for developing distributed database systems?

7. Characterize the distributed database planning problem as a two stage decision problem in which the hardware decisions are made in the first stage. Does this simplify the planning problem?

8. Suppose an object-oriented approach is taken to software. Reformulate the four heuristics given in the chapter in object-oriented terms.

9. What factors could make a distributed database plan that is based on the four heuristic less than optimal?

10. System security is a multifaceted subject. Do control over access to data and minimizing the effects of a system operating failure both benefit from database centralization?

11. Give an example of an entity type, or relationship, that should certainly be distributed according to the fourth heuristic, in a hard goods manufacturing enterprise in which the headquarters and factory locations are not the same.

12. Why should candidate locations for data storage be distinguished by type for distributed database planning purposes?

13. Give an example of a vertical partition of a relation. Is it possible to have a partition that is not horizontal?

14. Give an example of a replication of a relation that is both vertical and horizontal.

15. Why is it misleading to characterize the distributed database planning problem as one of finding all partitions and replications of relation fragments that reduce the sum of data storage and communication costs?

16. Define the envelope information structure for an engineering facility using the list of functions at an engineering location shown in Figure 13.6. The information requirements for the health and safety and training subfunctions can be either ignored or derived from the information structure for personnel shown in Figure 5.4.

17. Define the envelope information structure for a warehouse location using the list of functions at a warehouse location shown in Figure 13.6. The information requirements for the health and safety and training subfunctions can be either ignored or derived from the information structure for personnel shown in Figure 5.4.

18. What is the relation between Steps 4 and 5 of the distributed database planning methodology and the alternatives of partitioning versus replicating?

19. Fiber optics technology promises to reduce the cost of wide-area data communications services in the future. How will this cost reduction affect the storage-communication cost trade-off between replicating data at multiple locations and not doing so? Does it depend on the volatility of the data?

20. According to Figure 13.1, Former Employee is a candidate for replication at branch sales offices. What information is required to analyze whether this data should in fact be replicated and how should the analysis be made?

14

Effects on System Development

Information systems traditionally have been planned and developed in an environment that does not include a business-wide conceptual database. Where a business-wide database plan does exist, it is often too vague to be of any real use to the systems analyst. So the traditional system development methodology is not based on utilizing the information contained in a functional model and what we have called a Business-Wide Information Structure (BWIS).

The System Development Life Cycle (SDLC) describes the traditional system development process. There are many versions of it. Different versions have different numbers of steps. There can be as few as three steps and some versions define more than 9 steps. A commonly used seven-step version is shown in Figure 14.1. The cycle begins with an investigation and planning of an application system that is instigated by one or more managers of organizational units that will use the system. It continues with an analysis of the existing way of conducting affected functions and the requirements that the new system should satisfy. The result is a definition of system performance requirements that is presented to the managers along with an estimate of the resources and time required to develop the system. If management elects to proceed with development then the system is designed and the design specifications become the basis for creating the application programs and computing system as specified. After the system has been created *and tested*, the training and initial data entry required for implementation is performed. The inevitable further refinement and training in use of the system is done in the maintenance phase.

The SDLC does not contain a BWIS development step nor does it give any indication that a business-wide conceptual database should be taken into account. The fact that it makes no reference to the establishment of a business-wide conceptual database is evidence that most systems have been developed without reference to such information.

What effect should the existence of a functional model and BWIS have on the system development process? In Chapter 1, the discussion of reconciling the balkanizing forces with the coordinating and integrating forces implicitly touched on

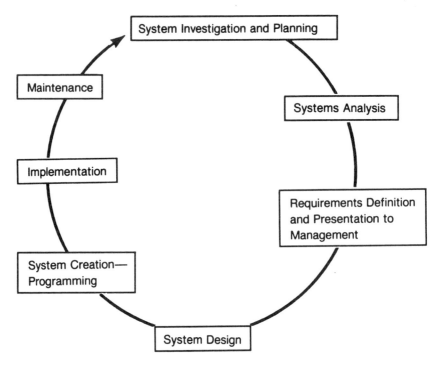

FIGURE 14.1. The system development life cycle.

the answer to this question. It was suggested that the BWIS act as part of the environment within which systems are developed. In this chapter, we explore what it can and should mean to build systems in this environment.

The potential effects of the functional model and BWIS infrastructure on systems development are profound. The way an application can be defined changes. Instead of asking the prospective system users, "What do you want the computer to do for the business?" we can ask, "What do you need to know to function effectively?" BWIS makes it possible to design at this higher level of abstraction. The system can be defined as a set of objects to be simulated. With this object-oriented view, a way to modularize the application programming by object class opens up. This makes it possible to divide large development projects into a series of small projects.

It is not possible in a single chapter to consider all of the implications of this profound change in approach to application system development. Only an overview of the implications can be given. In the following section, a modification of the SDLC to incorporate business-wide information requirements planning is proposed. This is followed by a section on basic changes in the way an application is delineated and its application programs defined. This is followed by sections on the way phases of the SDLC can benefit from the functional model and BWIS.

AN OBJECT-ORIENTED DEVELOPMENT LIFE CYCLE

The traditional SDLC is based on what any engineer would call common sense. Of course, a system must be envisioned and its development requirements assessed before it can be built. And, designing it in detail before starting construction is worthwhile because it avoids costly changes in a system after it has already been partially or fully constructed.

So, incorporating the development and maintenance of a functional model and BWIS into a development methodology is not a matter of abandoning the traditional SDLC. It is a matter of relating an infrastructure development effort to application development projects. A proposed articulation of these two types of development activities is summarized in Figure 14.2.

The first step in this Business-Wide System Development Methodology (BWSDM) is to conduct the business-wide data modeling project as described in Part 1 of this book. The result is a functional model and BWIS in an Information Resource Dictionary (IRDS). The existing computer-communication systems and data files may also be documented by the project as well. In this case, the IRDS at this first stage essentially contains the database defined in Figure 11.5 (except for the physical databases).

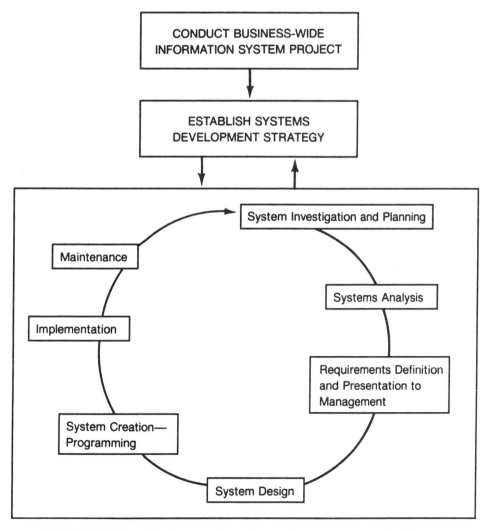

FIGURE 14.2. Business-wide systems development methodology.

The second step shown in Figure 14.2 (called Establish Systems Development Strategy) includes the following actions:

1. Decide whether to use the application software provided by a vendor or to develop custom-designed software.

2. If developing custom-designed software, establish software development tools and standards.

3. Identify the application systems needed that have a high priority and organize project teams to develop them.

4. Establish a data administration organization to coordinate the work of project database administrators.

An organization may conduct a BWIS project and then discover that a software vendor has a complete set of application software that, in essence, implements the conceptual database defined by the BWIS. In this case, the organization is likely to decide to develop its systems by obtaining the application software from that vender, and installing it on whatever hardware is required.

If appropriate application software cannot be found then an object-oriented approach can be taken to developing it. The first step in this approach is to establish a set of object-oriented software development tools. An IRDS (repository system) should be one of the basic tools in this set. Other important tools, which should be compatible with the IRDS and with each other, include an operating system and compiler, a DBMS, a screen design and prototyping system, and a code generator. The latter three items on this list may come as a set of CASE tools designed to interact with a specific IRDS.

Step 3 is partially political in the sense that it is driven by the system development priorities of the organization. If these priorities are rational then they will tend to focus system development efforts on systems that are likely to significantly improve organizational performance. However, it is often the case that other applications must be in place before the most profitable application is viable. Thus, defining system development priorities involves some logical prerequisites as well as the political imperatives of the business.

An object-oriented approach to Step 3 requires that application systems be defined in terms of the entity types and relationships involved in the application, rather than in terms of business functions or procedures. This is an important departure from the traditional approach to systems definition. In the object-oriented approach, programs are defined for each object in a system. This means that the application system should be viewed as a set of objects (entity types, relationships, and other objects), with each object having a repertoire of operations (programs).

The organizational unit established in Step 4 is key to obtaining a payoff from the BWIS development effort. Without the coordination of project database administration activities, neither coordinated nor integrated databases will be developed. Each project will create its own database.

In this coordination, work the IRDS plays a vital role. The two arrows in Figure 14.2 between the traditional SDLC box and the "Establish Systems Development Strategy" box represent the interaction between the Data Administrator (DA) and the project DataBase Administrators (DBAs). The arrow pointing down to the

SDLC box represents data definitions obtained by DBAs (and programmers) from the BWIS in the IRDS. The arrow pointing up to the "Establish Systems Development Strategy" box represents up-dates and additional details (attribute definitions, for example) that are generated by DBAs. The DBAs must adapt the BWIS to user requirement details that are detected only during the detailed design and programming phases of a system development project.

The traditional SDLC of Figure 14.1 is shown in Figure 14.2 as the third step in the system development process. The arrow from the "Establish Systems Development Strategy" box to the SDLC box represents the influence of the IRDS infrastructure on individual system development projects. It should be understood that the cycle of traditional SDLC steps is repeated for each application developed.

The nature of this influence of the IRDS infrastructure on individual application developments can be fully understood only after the object-oriented approach to developing individual applications is clear. This is explained in the next section. At this point, we can think of the IRDS as providing a common set of data definitions and relationships for all applications. The applications that use these definitions are able to share data, either the same copy or by accessing data kept in the database of another application.

OBJECT-ORIENTED SYSTEM DEVELOPMENT

The existence of a BWIS, a functional model and a set of relationships between the two, as defined in Figure 11.5, makes it possible to take a purely object-oriented approach to systems planning and development. The entity types and many-to-many relationships of the BWIS become candidate object classes for inclusion in an application system. Instead of defining an application in terms of the business procedures that it automates, we can define the application in terms of objects to be simulated and the operations each object needs to be capable of performing.

Since the relationships between the BWIS and the functional model define a "sub-BWIS" for each subfunction, the identification of the entity types and relationships that may need to be included in an application for a given subfunction (at any level in the functional model) is directly available from the repository containing the data of Figure 11.5. All of the entity types and relationships of the sub-BWIS will be required in the application unless the decision is made to develop support for the subfunction as a series of applications, rather than as a single application. If a series of applications are preferred, they can be defined in terms of subsets of the entity types and relationships of the sub-BWIS, as well as in terms of other types of object classes, such as input screen and report objects.

A system defined in terms of objects, and object classes, has its programming defined in terms of object operations (also called methods). An object operation is a program that:

1. has access to the data that defines the simulated state of the object

2. is able to send certain messages to other objects

3. is able to receive and act on certain messages received from other objects.

The planning and development of a system so defined revolves around these object operations. Identifying, defining, and developing the programs that give the objects of the system their operational capabilities is of central importance. It is therefore important to understand that the operational requirements of the objects that represent entities and relationships in the BWIS depend on certain entity-relationship characteristics, which are explained in the next subsection. Thus, the BWIS can be of substantial assistance in identifying the programming requirements of an application.

DATA OBJECT TYPES

The object classes defined by the entity types and relationships of a sub-BWIS can be called data object classes. A data object is a simulation of an entity (or many-to-many relationship) by the system. This terminology distinguishes data objects from other types of objects in the system, such as report objects, window objects, printer objects, and so forth. The distinction is made because data objects have some unique characteristics in common.

Data objects are *persistent objects*. This refers to the need to store the state of these objects on a secondary storage device when the objects are not being simulated. This is not to say they are the only persistent objects, however. Report objects and printer objects, for example, would also be persistent objects.

The unique feature of data objects is that they all must possess the same types of operations (methods) in their class (or super-class) repertoire of operations. Basically, the common operations are:

1. Retrieve an object in the stored database

2. Add an object to the stored database

3. Modify the stored state of an existing object

4. Retrieve a list of stored objects in a class

5. Delete an object in the stored database.

For certain types of data objects a straightforward version of these five operations is all that is required. For other types, more complex versions of the operations are needed. Data objects that are *permanent* tend to have a relatively straightforward version of the five operations; data objects that represent *event* entity types have a more complex version of the operations.

The distinction between permanent and event data objects is based on a parallel distinction between entity types (or many-to-many relationships). It is analogous to the distinction between a noun and a verb. A noun can either serve as a subject or object of a simple sentence. A verb denotes the action (or existence) described by the sentence. For example, in the sentence, "The product is delivered to the customer," there are two nouns and one verbal phrase.

Entity types that either take actions or are affected by actions are permanent entity types. Customer is a permanent entity type that requests quotations, gives orders, and makes payments, for example. Product/Service is a permanent entity type that is quoted, sold, shipped, and invoiced.

Entity types that represent events or actions are event entity types. Quote (or "quotation") is an event entity type. Purchase Order and Customer Order are different names for the same event. Day, Year, and Time Period are event entity types because they refer to something that happens.

On the other hand, Age Interval is a permanent entity type. It does not refer to a specific time that comes to pass but rather to a measure of time. If the entity type Day is used to refer to a unit of time rather than to a specific day then it also should be classified as permanent.

The concept of an event as applied to business includes more than raw action. Orders and decisions are events. Four types of events can be distinguished which have a sequential relationship to one another with respect to the duration of their impact:

1. Actions

2. Orders to take actions

3. Decisions on plans for future orders

4. Strategic decisions on goals.

In the case of order events, it is the order and not the action ordered that is the event entity type. Similarly, we must distinguish between the decision on a plan and the plan itself. The decision to adopt a plan is an event entity type; the plan itself is likely to involve one or more permanent entity types.

Some writers refer to permanent entity types as 'objects' and they use the term 'event' for event entity types.[1] The term 'object' is not used for this purpose in this text because it does not conform with its meaning in object-oriented programming. The term 'event' is very appropriate, but 'event entity type' has the advantage of reminding the reader that an entity type (data object) is being discussed.

OPERATIONS FOR EXISTENTIALLY DEPENDENT DATA OBJECTS

The main reason for distinguishing between permanent and event entity types (and data objects) is because the operations (programs) of certain types of permanent data objects are the same, and the operations required for event data objects have a similarity in their structure. In the following subsections, these patterns are described for three categories of data objects.

Simple Permanent Data Objects

The operations (programs) required for permanent entity types with no dependent entity types can be easily identified and standardized. An operation is required for each of the five procedures listed earlier. These programs can be standardized to apply to any data object by parameterizing all references to the permanent data. They can thus be applied to any data object that belongs to the 'simple permanent data object class.'

Sets of Existentially Dependent Permanent Data Objects

By definition, if one entity type is existentially dependent on another, then the dependent one only can have occurrences if a corresponding occurrence of the other entity type exists. If the entity type that has other entity types depend-ent on it is a permanent entity type then the operations for that entity type and its dependent entity types will be somewhat more complex than those for the "simple permanent data object class." The program that adds the non-dependent permanent data object should, in most cases, make calls to the programs that add dependent data objects. Thus, for the permanent data objects that have other existentially dependent data objects, the required operations should include calls to the dependent data objects. The operations for the dependent data objects will be similar to the fives standard operations for permanent data objects but they may also need to send replies back to the calling program.

An example of two permanent data object classes that should be managed as a set of "existentially-related permanent data objects" is Customer and Customer Location. The Customer Location entity type is existentially dependent on Cus-tomer because occurrences of Customer Location are relevant only if there is a corresponding Customer occurrence in the database. The program that adds a customer to the database should call the program that can add locations for that customer.

Sets of Existentially Dependent Event Data Objects

Operations for event data objects are not as easily defined as are those for permanent data objects. In addition to the five procedures listed above, proces-sing can involve combinations of adding an occurrence of one event data object and changing other permanent (and event) data objects. Programs that do archival updating may work with many event data objects, removing them from disk storage and placing them in some form of less accessible and lower cost storage.

Identifying the processing programs for event data object, however, is still not too difficult. Most applications will involve less than a half-dozen sets of existen-tially dependent event entity types. The "processing programs" of major event data objects will tend to be larger and more complex than the programs for permanent data objects, but they are not usually as numerous. In general, a set of five processing programs is required for each event entity type and each depend-ent event entity type involved in the application. That is to say, add, change, delete, and list programs are usually required for each entity in a set of event entity types composed of an independent event entity type and all entity types that are existentially dependent upon it.

Existential dependencies tend to be more complex for event entity types than for permanent entity types. For example, in Figure 12.7, there is a series of nine event entity types shown in the middle column of entity types starting with Inquiry and ending with cash receipt. In each case, there is a many-to-many relationship to the left of the event entity type that is existentially dependent on both the event entity type and either Product/Service of *item at location*. In the cases of Customer Invoice and Cash Receipt, the Standard Transaction occur-rence is also existentially dependent on them.

It could be argued that any many-to-many relationship occurrence is existen-tially dependent on all of the entity types participating in the relationship. This may be true in theory but it appears, from Figure 12.7 and other examples, that when a permanent and event entity type are involved in a many-to-many relationship, it is the event entity type that should be viewed as controlling the existence of the many-to-many relationship occurrence.

There is obviously much more to be said about defining the programs required for event data objects. The subject is discussed further in the section on system design where an example is given of how to analyze the programming requirements of a set of existentially dependent event entity types. However, there are many open questions regarding this subject and further research is needed.

SYSTEM INVESTIGATION AND PLANNING

We turn now to the first of the seven steps of the SDLC as depicted in Figure 14.1. Can this investigation and planning step be simplified by taking advantage of an available BWIS and functional model?

This first step in the SDLC is a survey of a computer application possibility in which one or more managers in an organization are interested. It is the initial phase of a dialogue that should take place between those who will use the computer system and those who will develop it. The users of the potential system describe the computer tool capabilities they could profitably use and the system developer estimates the cost and time to develop.

Educating the developer in the intricacies of the functions to which the users want to apply the computer may not be a trivial task. In most organizations, these functions are not defined and documented in a way that makes it possible to give the developer a definition of the relevant subfunctions which can be studied prior to giving an estimate of cost and time. Rather, a time-consuming sequence of meetings, memos, and observations are commonly required to convey the system application requirements from user to developer.

USE OF THE FUNCTIONAL MODEL

If a business-wide conceptual database has been developed as described in the previous chapters, then a functional model of the business is available and can be used by the developer to quickly get a fix on the scope and details of the subfunctions involved in the application. Consider, for example, supporting the selection subfunction of the personnel function. Suppose the manager of the employment subfunction has asked information systems developers to investigate the possibility of supporting with a computer system the selection of an applicant to fill a position. If the developers look at the functional model of the business shown in Figure 4.5, they would immediately see the four subfunctions involved. If they could then go down in the functional hierarchy for each of these four subfunctions to lists of steps at the lowest subfunction level, they would have a clear description of the functions to be supported down to the flow diagram level. (A flow diagram could be drawn from the information at the bottom of Figure 4.5.)

A reduction in the time required for the system planners to learn about the business functions to be supported by an application is one important impact that a business-wide approach to database planning can have. However, there are other impacts that are equally or more important. One is the ability to quickly count and categorize the computer programs needed for the application.

TYPES OF COMPUTER PROGRAMS

In the traditional SDLC, the definition of computer programs required by the system is not considered until Step 4 or 5. The existence of a BWIS makes it possible to identify the computer programs required at Step 1. The way in which this can be done is outlined in the previous section.

Being able to count the number of programs of each type required by the application makes a more accurate estimate of development cost and time possible. This is a major objective of the first step of the SDLC. Thus, the BWIS infrastructure has very important implications for this first step. It makes it possible to execute it in a far more effective and efficient manner.

SYSTEM PLANNING

The third impact of a business-wide conceptual database on the first step of the SDLC is a different approach to envisioning the system. Instead of relying upon only a brief investigation of how the relevant subfunctions are now carried out, the planners can think in terms of how the database can most efficiently be populated and accessed to serve the purposes of the functional managers involved. This tends to free thought from the pattern of the present way of performing the subfunctions. For example, the fact that there is one database, which has already been defined in terms of the entities and relationships involved, and this one database can be shared simultaneously by all who carry out the subfunctions, makes it easier to detect parallel processing opportunities, where before a serial processing approach was necessary because of a limitation in the availability of data. This can lead to the detection of important opportunities to use systems to gain an additional competitive advantage because parallel human processing is one important way to respond more quickly to customer inquiries and orders.

It is not expected that in this initial step a final system design will be developed. Nevertheless, the fact that the programs required by the application can be identified (if a BWIS exists) means that the initial vision of the system is more concrete and detailed than is the case if the planners have only the process-oriented description of the application that a user description of the functions to be supported tends to create. This concreteness about the software also makes possible better estimates of the computer-communication system requirements of the application and of the time it will take to obtain need components.

STAGES OF DEVELOPMENT

The fourth impact of the business-wide database plan on the first step of the SDLC is not really dependent on the plan so much as it is on an understanding of the sequential relation between the four types of event entity types. An order entity type occurrence is related to a series of action entity type occurrences which are results of the order. Similarly, a planning decision entity type occurrence is related to a series of order entity type occurrences, namely, the orders that were issued under the plan.

These relations lead to an advantage in, if not a requirement for, developing systems in a certain sequence. Systems that manage action and certain routine order event entity types in the conceptual database should be developed and implemented before systems that manage planning decision entity types. For example, a purchasing system should be implemented before an MRP system is developed. The purchasing system populates the database with basic facts about products, suppliers, purchase orders, and inventory balances, which the MRP system needs in order to plan future procurement actions.

In general, the procedures for creating new occurrences of a higher level event entity type call for information about the lower level event entity type occurrences that are the result of the existing occurrences of the higher level entity type. This is a cybernetic requirement that holds true for materials planning, manpower planning, fleet operations planning, and new equipment planning.

This first step in the SDLC is the place to check the existence and adequacy of the transaction processing systems that must be in place if an operations planning system is being contemplated. If they are not in place, or are not suitable for use with the new system, then they should be developed before the system under investigation is developed.

SYSTEMS ANALYSIS

The analysis of the existing systems that will be affected if a new computer system is developed is much more detailed in the systems analysis step than in the system investigation and planning step. The existing forms and reports must be scrutinized. Timing requirements in performing various subfunctions must be defined. The use of existing data needs to be assessed. If there are data not currently available that would improve performance, the cost and utility of making them available should be estimated. The sequence of events in the current systems, and current and projected transaction volumes are defined and documented.

The existence of a business-wide conceptual database and the program analysis described above should have the effect of making systems analysis more focused and less laborious. In this environment, systems analysis should really have only three objectives. One is to identify all of the attributes that each entity type in the conceptual database must have for this application. The second is to glean all of the insights that the existing system can reveal about the capabilities and features that the processing programs should have. The third is to identify new capabilities and features required for the new system because its scope, objectives, or logic is different than that of the old system.

Exhaustive flow diagramming of the existing systems, particularly if they are manual systems, is a questionable use of resources. An analysis of those parts of the systems concerned with transaction processing and a careful analysis of all items on each form and report in the existing systems is a better use of staff resources. The purpose in both of these analyses is to sift what the new system should incorporate of the old from all that should be left behind by the new system.

ATTRIBUTES REQUIRED

Many, but not all, of the attributes that each entity type and relationship must have can be detected by analyzing the reports and forms of the existing systems. A single report or form can easily have attributes of a half-dozen or more entity

types and relationships. Thus, one analysis skill needed in a database environment is the ability to assign each datum on a report or form to a conceptual entity
type or relationship.

The attributes detected by this analysis that may be relevant to the new system
should either already exist in the IRDS, which is depicted in Figures 11.5 and
11.6, or be added as Attribute occurrences. In any case, this analysis should
result in one or more attribute requirement relationship occurrences being added
to the IRDS.

It should be noted that this IRDS is independent of any particular application
development project. It contains the business-wide conceptual database as well
as information about individual application programs. This is in contradistinc-
tion to those CASE tools which limit the data dictionary to the scope of one
project.

PROCESSING PROCEDURES

If the first step in the SDLC is carried out as previously described, then the
systems analyst begins Step 2 with certain processing procedures already identified. The task is to investigate what those procedures must include so that, in the
next step, they can be made part of the system performance requirements.

As previously noted, there are four types of events to be recorded in terms of
event entity types. They are actions, orders, plan decisions, and strategic decisions. By recognizing with which of these four types of events a given processing
procedure is dealing, a systems analyst is better able to formulate the questions
that the analysis should answer. This in turn should lead to a more concise and
complete set of findings upon which Step 3 can build.

In this brief discussion, it is not possible to describe exactly how the analysis
can be conducted in each of the four cases, however, by considering the questions that should govern the investigation in each case, the scope, and focus of
the analysis is indicated.

Action Events

For processing procedures that are concerned with recording actions, the following questions may be appropriate:

1. What facts about the action need to be captured? In addition to a date,
there are usually certain parties involved in the action and there may be reaction
alternatives to be selected.

2. Are there order or planning decisions that should be initiated by the action
recorded? If the actions are emergency calls to a police station, for example, then
there is a series of possible reactions that need to be defined and provided for in
the system design.

3. Is the action in response to a previously issued order? If so, should the
system determine that it conforms to the order and if not notify someone or take
certain actions?

4. What validity checks are needed to make sure that the actions recorded
really occurred?

Order Events

An order is a resource commitment. It is a decision at a point in time to authorize actions that will occur in the future, and the result will be a use of the organization's resources. In analyzing a type of ordering decision for which a processing system is to be designed, the following questions may be relevant:

1. What information may the decision maker want to consider before issuing the order? Information about the status of stocks, for example, is often needed before a stock replenishment order is issued.

2. What information about the order needs to be recorded?

3. What provision needs to be made to rescind or modify an order?

4. What security measures are warranted to ensure that orders cannot be issued without proper authority?

Planning Decisions

The decision to adopt a plan is intimately connected with the planning activity. President Eisenhower once said, "Plans are nothing. Planning is everything." This view strongly suggests that a processing system dealing with planning decisions should not be separated from the planning system.

Some questions that a systems analysis of a planning system should seek to answer are as follows:

1. What are the objectives the plan seeks to achieve?

2. What factors need to be taken into account by the plan? Are the systems in place to collect data on these factors?

3. What are the timing constraints on the planning activity? Must plans be revised on short notice? How important is it to evaluate many alternative plans before a decision is made?

Strategic Decisions

The systems analysis for strategic decision making must encompass the whole strategic planning process in the same way that the analysis for planning decisions must consider the whole planning process. In the case of strategic decisions, however, people play the main role and computer systems can only provide support. The ways in which this support can be provided are so many and varied that no short list of questions can adequately suggest the range of issues to be investigated.

Some ways in which strategic decision making can be supported are the following:[2]

Library information retrieval system

Intelligence gathering and retrieval system

Long-range planning information system

Special analyses of internal transaction data

Gaming and simulation systems

Group decision support system

Business communication systems.

Each of these ways of supporting strategic decision making requires major system development efforts that normally warrant separate system development projects.

Augmenting the Conceptual Database

From the brief review of the analysis of processing procedures for each of the four types of events, it is clear that new entity types and relationships can be detected by the analysis. Particularly, in the cases of strategic and planning decisions, required additions to the conceptual database are likely to come to the attention of the analysts.

REQUIREMENTS DEFINITION AND PRESENTATION TO MANAGEMENT

The third step, requirements definition and presentation to management, is a key milestone in the development of a system. It is the point at which a definition of what the system will and will not do is formulated and a project to develop the system is proposed. The project proposal normally defines the resources required for the development and sets a schedule for the work.

The system capabilities should be based on the findings of the systems analysis step. They will be more or less specific depending on the level of trust that exists between the users and the developers. The really finite details of the system can be left to the next step, system design, unless either party insists on having them settled before commitments are made.

The existence of a business-wide conceptual database makes it easier for the two parties to communicate and understand one another at this stage. The functional model can be used to state more clearly exactly which subfunctions will be supported by the proposed system and in what ways. The entity types and relationships in the database that will be populated and/or used by the proposed system can be specified to clarify the data that must be entered by the users of the system and the data that they can obtain from the system.

Since achieving a meeting of minds on the system to be developed is the fundamental purpose of this third step, the business-wide database plan can be of vital importance in successfully completing it. The time invested in developing the functional model of the business can pay a big dividend if the model is used to clarify what the proposed system will do.

SYSTEM DESIGN

This fourth step in the SDLC is the one in which the application programs are defined in detail. It is the one in which structured system design techniques are used. The result of this step should be software specifications that can be given to a programmer (or fed into a code generator) who performs the next step in the process. To serve this purpose, the specifications need to be quite detailed.

In addition to producing clear directions for the programmer, however, the system designer also must involve the users in the system design process. Failure to do so will result in dissatisfaction with the system after it is implemented. The general description of the system to which the parties agreed in Step 3 does not provide sufficient guidance for the designer without user involvement. It is the details of the design that make the difference between a system that really fits the need and one that is more trouble than it is worth.

In working with users on the details of a design, one important guideline is to minimize the level of abstraction used. Prototyping is recommended by many experts as the best way to present alternatives to users in a way that they can understand.[3, 4]

The existence of a BWIS and functional model can benefit the system design process in a number of ways. Four are described in the following subsections.

DESIGN DECISIONS

One major impact of the existence of a BWIS relates to the way the design issues are formulated. Rather than approaching the design task as an unconstrained procedures modeling exercise, the object-oriented approach can start with the query and data object programs identified in Step 1 as given. The only open design questions concern the screen designs and processing logic for these programs.

The programs to be designed have been discussed in general terms in the third section of this chapter. A somewhat more detailed breakdown of programs for event data types is shown in Table 14.1. For a single system development project, it can be assumed that only one of the four event entity subtype categories will be involved. That is, a given project will either be concerned with actions and orders, or orders and plans, or plans, or strategic plans. As explained previously, an application dealing with orders and plans needs to use data about actions and orders that are already in the database.

The design decisions are different for each of these types of programs. They are discussed in the following subsections.

TABLE 14.1. Types of programs required.

Data Object Type	Programs
All	Query and report
Permanent types (add, modify, delete, list)	Master file
Event types	Processing
Actions and orders	Transaction processing
	Archival processing
Orders and plans	Order processing
Plans	Operations planning
Strategic plans	Strategic planning

Query and Reporting Programs

In the design stage, the standard queries to be selected from a menu need to be defined. This is best done by prototyping. A query can be formulated using SQL or a similar language in a matter of minutes by an experienced database administrator. Queries suggested by users can be run using sample data so that the user can confirm that the result is useful and in an appropriate format.

The output reports that require special formats, such as checks and purchase orders, need to be designed. This is a matter of agreeing on the exact data to be shown on the report and preparing a pro forma version of the report. The definitions of data in the conceptual database can be used in this work to clearly define the data that will be in the report and to quickly determine the number of character spaces that need to be allowed for each data item.

Permanent Data Object Programs

The main issues in the design of these programs concern formats, list capabilities, and the extent of the help screens to be provided. The procedures to be executed by these programs are simple enough to be predefined (add, modify, delete, and list occurrences of a permanent entity type). As explained previously, these programs should be automatically generated, with the programmer supplying only the parameters that vary from one program to another. (One exception is special validity checks that must sometimes be added.)

Prototyping is an effective way to agree on the style of screen formats, including the location of titles, prompt lines, the program status line, and menu options. The main objective is to standardize these aspects of the screen so that users can take the layout for granted. Ideally, this should be done at the business level (or national level), not at the system development project level. (Microsoft's Windows system has set a standard that is being adapted by many.)

The list capabilities of these programs refers to the extent to which the user can simply ask for a list of alternatives whenever data must be entered and the user does not know what to enter. When a user wants to modify or delete an occurrence of the permanent entity type, for example, can he obtain a list of all occurrences and choose the one to be deleted? One answer to this question should be given for all permanent data object programs. Again, the reason for standardizing is to minimize what users must know in order to operate the system.

A help screen policy should be defined in a way that can be applied to all programs, or at least to all permanent data object programs. Are there to be any help screens? Is there to be one help screen for each screen or for each data input field on a screen? These are questions that should be answered during the design step of the SDLC.

Processing Programs

The logic of the design of a processing program is made easier to develop and communicate if the event entity type that the program manages (and its dependent entity types) is made the focus of attention. In Table 14.1, five variations on the processing program concept are listed. It is easier to identify a single event entity type in the case of transaction processing and order processing than it is in the case of archival or operations planning. Nevertheless, if the logic is based on the theme of recording the effects of an event, it is easier to understand and follow than is the case if the processing of several events is intermingled in the logical analysis.

This approach to the analysis problem is not inconsistent with the concept of structured software design. It provides a criterion for dividing the processing into a hierarchical structure. Consider, for example, the analysis of an accounts receivable system. The part of a conceptual database relevant to receivables processing is shown in Figure 13.3. A structured breakdown based on the event entities involved in this E-R diagram is shown in Figure 14.3. Two of the three programs at the first level breakdown correspond to two event entity types involved in the system. Invoicing corresponds to the Customer Invoice entity type. Cash receipts corresponds to the Cash Receipt entity type. The third program at the top level is a menu of query and special report program options which is another kind of program design problem that has been discussed in a previous subsection of this chapter.

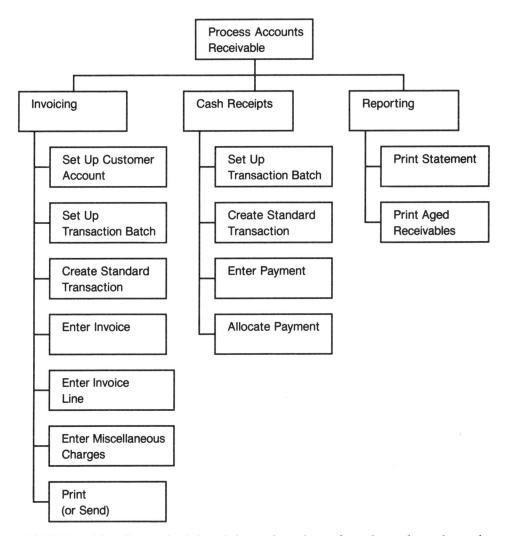

FIGURE 14.3. Structured breakdown based on interdependent dynamic entity types.

The second level breakdown of the programs also follows the logic of the event entity types involved (and the one permanent entity type involved). The event entity types involved in invoicing are Transaction, Standard Transaction Customer Invoice, Customer Invoice Line, and Miscellaneous Charge; the breakdown of invoicing in Figure 14.3 shows one subprogram for each of these entity types, plus a subprogram for managing the Customer entity type, which is a permanent entity type, plus another subprogram for printing the invoice. The event entity types involved in cash receipts processing are Transaction, Standard Transaction Customer Payment, and Payment Allocation; again, there is one subprogram for each.

The "Set Up Transaction Batch" program occurs in both the invoicing and cash receipts breakdowns. The same data object, Transaction, is the subject of both operations. Thus, only one transaction object operation (program) is really required for both types of processing. The program will be called by both the invoicing and cash receipts processing programs. The same can be true for Standard Transaction.

A detailed analysis of the programs at this second level would reveal that they are at about the same level of complexity as a permanent data object program. In fact the main difference is that they are called by the program of another data object (invoicing or cash receipts) rather than from a menu of user options. Each program obtains the data for a certain event entity type occurrence and manages the storage and accessing of that type of occurrence in the database (in the same way as a permanent data object program).

One complexity omitted from this example is the handling of debit memos received from the customers. If the analysis were to include this, however, the conclusion would be the same because Accounting Memo is an event entity type required in the database to handle this type of transaction. The processing of the memos would be another program at the top level and it would divide into two subprograms.

The analysis of the processing for a planning decision is not as simple as in the receivables example. It is likely to involve one or more algorithms to locate desirable solutions to the planning problem. Nevertheless, the results will be stored as attributes of one or more event entity types because they are merely plans designed to control the generation of orders, which are other event entity types. Therefore, the approach of breaking down the processing according to the event entity type involved is workable, even in this most difficult case.

The analysis of strategic planning procedures is usually simpler than in the case of planning procedures. Strategic planning support systems are either database processing systems with their own event entity types (such as the "entry" of an intelligence system) or logical modeling systems that use relatively small amounts of data; or they are communications support oriented systems which require little, if any, database management.

PROTOTYPING

If a prototyping approach is taken, the business-wide conceptual database can be used to obtain the descriptions of relations used in the relational database of the prototyping system. Most prototyping systems are built on a relational database management system and include the capability to easily create screen layouts by referencing attributes of the relations in the database. Thus, the BWIS can play the role of an important resource used to facilitate prototyping.

In the process of prototyping, details about specific data items, such as the maximum number of characters required for the item on the screen, are often detected that reveal a need to change the conceptual database. If the prototyping system has a good interface with the IRDS, a change made in the prototype can be reflected in a proposed change in the conceptual database as defined in the IRDS. There should be adequate DBA control over these changes.

ACCESS CONTROL POLICY

Access controls are a system aspect that is not efficiently reviewed with users by referring to a prototype. The access to data that various classes of users should have is more efficiently reviewed with management by referring to a table of user types versus data types. Table 14.2 is an example.

In this example, the data types are described in terms of subject areas. But, for each of the five subject areas shown, a list of specific entity types and relationships in the conceptual database can exist. These lists can be the link between the general access policy shown in the table and its implementation for a physical database.

It should also be noted that the existence of a business-wide database design makes it possible to coordinate access policy across all physical databases. The access policy can be defined at the conceptual database level. That policy can then be applied to all physical implementations of each conceptual attribute, entity type, and relationship via a link between the physical implementation and its conceptual counterpart. Figure 11.5 shows three of these links between entity types in the information requirements section and those in the technical resource section of the figure.

USER-ORIENTED PROGRAM SCENARIOS

Two other facets of system design for which prototyping is not well-suited are validity check specification and transaction update action specification. Input

TABLE 14.2. Database access control policy.

Data Types	Sales Staff	Inside Sales	Marketing Manager	Materials Staff	Materials Manager	Accounting & Controls Staff	General Management
						User Types	
Accounting		S:R/U	S:R	S:R/U	S:R	R/U	R
Travel expenses	S:R		S:R		S:R	R/U	R
Sales orders	S:R	R/U	R	S:R/U	R	R	R
Purchasing and inventory	S:R	S:R	S:R	R/U	R	S:R/U	R
Products	S:R/U	R/U	R	S:R/U	R	S:R	R

S = selected occurences; R = retrieval access to data; U = ability to update and add data.

data validity checks are more easily defined by explicit discussion with the users than they are by prototyping. Leaving it entirely to users to discover needed validity checks by entering invalid data are not the best use of their time. Also, the more complex types of validity checks are not easily implemented on most prototyping systems.

After a transaction has been defined on one or more screens by a user, there is a series of changes that must be made to the database to record all of the effects and implications of the transaction. The prototype is of little value in reviewing these changes in the database with users because they are often difficult to detect at the screen display level. A simple list of the changes is often a more useful means for obtaining user viewpoints on the impacts that the transaction should have.

One approach that works well for terminal (or workstation) based systems is to prepare a document that describes how a program will function from the user's perspective. The description should include screen layouts starting with the first options menu screen and describing the screens that follow for each option on the first screen. The cursor movement and options on each screen can be discussed in detail so that the users (and later the programmer) have a clear picture of how it is proposed that the system function. Validity checks and transaction update actions can be listed in this document at the point in the program execution where they should take place.

Users can be asked to review and approve these program descriptions. In the process of reviewing these documents with the system designer, the availability of an E-R diagram of the conceptual database can help to identify validity checks that should be made and transaction update actions that are needed.

The program specifications in this user-oriented program description should be stored as attributes of the program specification entity shown in Figure 11.6. The IRDS should include the database shown in this figure, and thus these descriptions.

A simple example of such a description is given in Exhibit A at the end of this chapter. It is for a permanent entity type, Sales Tax, whose principle attribute is the tax rate of a specific sales taxing authority. In the conceptual database, Sales Tax has a many-to-many relationship with each location to which the company may ship taxable goods, of which there are three types (Customer Location, Supplier Location, and Company Warehouse Location).

SYSTEM CREATIONS PROGRAMMING

The fifth step in the SDLC is the one in which the application programs are generated (or written) and debugged if custom applications are required. This traditionally has been the step in which the budget and time schedules are endlessly revised. Getting the programs written, compiled, and linked usually is the easy part. Finding and correcting the subtle bugs that appear as the program is being tested and put into use is what generally upsets budgets and schedules.

To bring this step under control, many attempts have been made, and are being made to automate it. Fourth and fifth generation programming languages are aimed at dealing with the problem. Packaged application software that can be customized by the selection of parameter values, by calls to external programs, and by importing and exporting data are other proposed solutions.

A satisfactory solution must provide flexibility so that a business can be run in the most effective way, not the way an application software package assumes it will be run. Yet the solution should not require the programmer to write code at a lower level than necessary. The method of software design described in the previous section suggests an approach to coding that has both this flexibility and power. It is based on the use of a program generator that produces a standardized program module designed to manage one entity type in the database.

In the analysis of the design problem in the previous section, it is shown by example that processing procedures can be structured so that the lowest level program modules each manage one entity type (or many-to-many relationship) in the database. This means that these lowest level modules require virtually the same logic as a permanent data object program. The steps in this logic, in its simplest form, are those described in Exhibit A. This description is in terms of a particular entity type (sales tax); however, they are easily generalized to apply to any entity type.

The idea is that customized application programs for permanent data object and processing programs be constructed by generating low level modules to manage each entity type in the database. These low-level modules can then be linked by control modules that only call other programs based on passed parameter values. The result is a set of program modules that exactly mirrors the customized structured design for the application software, yet a large percentage of the code is produced by a program generator that produces bug-free standard programs.

The goal is design-level control of coding. All of the coding should be automatically generated for the system design specifications. Changes in code should be made only by changing design specifications. Much remains to be explored and developed with respect to this approach to programming for event type objects. We know that it works for permanent data object programs of the type described in Exhibit A. But for processing programs further development of the methodology is needed.

IMPLEMENTATION

Training and documentation is the main activity of implementation on which the business-wide conceptual database can have an impact. Training people to use and control a new system is of critical importance to a successful implementation. If an individual does not receive a sufficiently complete and accurate introduction to a new system, misconceptions about what the system can and cannot do can linger on for years. And it will only do what the user understands it can do.

It takes time for anyone to become familiar with a system. The time can be reduced if the system uses terms for data and functions that users already understand. If the users have been involved in developing a business-wide conceptual database, then the terms they used in developing that plan can be used when the new system is implemented. This happens naturally if the system is analyzed and designed as described in previous sections.

The Information Resource Dictionary System (IRDS) can be very useful in training users. It can be the source of "help information" about available data, the meaning of data labels, available reports, and program descriptions. It can also record information on system usage and performance that the system administrator can use to fine tune the system and detect operational problems.

MAINTENANCE

Traditionally, the most challenging step in any software maintenance job has been coming to an understanding of the existing code. Making the changes and recreating an executable production version is the easy part.

Use of a program generator to produce 100% of the code is the best way to standardize the terms and logic of programs and thereby reduce the time required to understand a given instance of the code produced by the generator. This method of creating code results in program modules that have the same logic. Only the names and attributes of the data change from one module to the next.

Ironically, the achievement of standardized code structures through the use of code generators makes it possible, and advisable, to stop all maintenance coding. Instead of patching existing code, the code generator should be used to generate completely new code whenever a change needs to be made. Available CASE tools for re-engineering existing software make this approach to maintenance feasible even for existing application software.

SUMMARY

The traditional SDLC does not take into consideration the existence of an IRDS that contains a functional model of the business and a Business-Wide Information Structure (BWIS). To adapt it to this infrastructure it needs to be embedded in a more comprehensive methodology as shown in Figure 14.2.

The existence of a BWIS makes a purely object-oriented approach to systems development possible. In this approach, application systems are defined in terms of objects instead of processes. The BWIS provides the source of one important type of object, namely, the data object.

The programming required for an object-oriented business system corresponds to the permanent and event data objects in the system. Thus, once the system has been defined in terms of these types of objects, the application programs required to implement it can be defined.

The existence of a functional model and BWIS can simplify and improve the quality of all steps in the system development process. There are four advantages for the first step, system investigation and planning. A more focused approach to systems analysis is possible. Communication is facilitated in the third step, requirements definition and presentation to management. There are four improvements in system design methodology.

The use of CASE tools in the programming step is facilitated by the IRDS with its BWIS and definition of physical databases. The IRDS also has benefits for the Implementation Step in system development. Finally, the very significant benefits of the standardized coding produced by CASE tools for system maintenance work are described.

REFERENCES

1. Sweet, Frank, "Objects and Events," *Datamation*, June, 1987, p. 152.
2. Gessford, John E., *Modern Information Systems: Designed for Decision Support* (Reading, MA: Addison-Wesley, 1980), Chapter 11.
3. Jenkins, Milton A., "Prototyping: A Methodology for the Design and Development of Application Systems," *Spectrum*, Society for Information Management, Chicago, Ill., April, 1985.
4. Cerveny, Robert P., et al., "Why Software Prototyping Works," *Datamation*, August 15, 1987, pp. 97–103.

DISCUSSION QUESTIONS

1. The System Development Life Cycle (SDLC) has been characterized in different ways by different authors. The seven steps shown in Figure 14.1 can be consolidated to a four-step process or expanded to nine or more steps. Describe your favorite version of the SDLC.

2. What does the first step in the SDLC, system investigation and planning, accomplish and how can a functional model of the business aid in executing the step?

3. How do the three types of programs that can be identified in the first step of the SDLC (if an enterprise-wide data model exists) relate to objects in an object-oriented approach to programming?

4. Discuss the reasons for distinguishing between permanent and event entity types.

5. Categorize the entity types and many-to-many relationships in Figure 5.8 as either permanent or event entity types.

6. Identify the dependent permanent entity types and count the number of master file programs required to implement the order processing database shown in Figure 5.8.

7. Identify the dependent event entity types and count the number of processing programs required to implement the order processing database shown in Figure 5.8.

8. Give three examples of each of the four types of events that can be represented by event entity types.

9. How does the existence of an business-wide information structure, and functional model, affect the way a new or revised computer application is envisioned?

10. How are the four kinds of event entity types (actions, orders, planning decisions, and strategic decisions) related to the sequence in which application systems should be developed?

11. What should be the objectives of the systems analysis step if an business-wide information structure and functional model exist and are stored in an IRDS?

12. Categorize each of the event entity types (and relationships) in Figure 5.8 as being one of four types of events (action, order, planning decision, strategic decision).

13. Analyze the events of (1) receiving purchase orders from customers (distributors) by a consumer hard goods manufacturer, (2) deciding whether to accept the order, (3) sending an order acknowledgement or rejection, and (4) issuing supply orders to fulfill accepted customer shipment release orders. How can the a processing system be designed that will maximize customer satisfaction with the way purchase orders are handled? What questions should the systems analyst ask about these events in order to identify important system requirements?

14. The systems analysis step can be expected to detect new attributes that need to be added to the business-wide conceptual database. New entity types and relationships may also be identified. When should these database definition changes be incorporated into the database and by whom should the adoption decisions be made?

15. In what ways can the existence of an business-wide information structure and functional model facilitate Step 3, requirements definition and presentation to management?

16. At what level should menu, data entry, and display screens be prototyped and designed? Or, in other words, how much of the screen design and user interaction at terminals should be done in Step 4 and how much should be set by business-wide standards?

17. What information that should be provided by user experts during the system design step is not easily conveyed by the prototyping process? Can the business-wide information structure facilitate the communication of any of this information?

18. What should be the main impact of business-wide data plan on system design?

19. In defining the methods (master file programs) required for "permanent objects," the text asserts that list capabilities are one of three main design issues. Consider the listing capabilities that could be warranted for a program to add occurrences of a customer entity type to a database. If customer has the following attributes (or relationships), what listing capabilities would you want the customer addition program to have?

Attributes of Customer

Customer code (up to five alphanumeric characters)

Customer name for reporting purposes (up to 15 characters)

Customer full name

Customer billing address

Customer's accounts payable manager name

Customer's buyers (names and phones)

Customer credit limit

Terms of payment code for customer

Default sales tax status of sales to customer

Identification of primary salesman on the account.

20. Apply the method of defining processing programs that is described in the text to the definition of the programs required to handle customer quotes and sales orders. Assume the relevant database is that given in Figure 5.8. To simplify the problem, exclude the issuing of supply orders from your analysis. Assume that a "program" executes one of the four basic operations on a data object (namely, add, change, delete, list) or performs a retrieval and display/print operation.

21. What benefits can be gained in Step 5 (system creation–programming) from the existence of an BWIS stored in an IRDS?

22. In the implementation step, Step 6 of the SDLC, what are the advantages and disadvantages of introducing a customized application system as opposed to a standard purchased application package?

23. There are (at least) two possible effects of the BWIS approach and the use of program generators on the maintenance step of the SDLC. One is that it will make it easier for the programmer to understand existing source code and change it. The other is that it will eliminate the practice of changing source code; instead, the change will be made at the design level and the program generator will be used to generate new code. Which scenario seems more likely?

24. What effect is the BWIS approach likely to have on CASE tools?

APPENDIX A
PROGRAM DESCRIPTION FOR A SALES TAX RECORD

This is a description of a program to manage the sales tax records in the database. Each of these records contains the tax rate for a specific taxing authority. For example, in California, there is a basic sales tax levied by the Board of Equalization. There is also a county sales tax in Los Angeles and most other counties. In addition, there are various special districts that levy a sales tax on sales consummated (delivered) within certain areas, for example, the Bay Area Transit district and the Los Angeles transit district.

Managing these records means allowing sales tax records to be added to the database. It also means being able to change or delete existing records (under certain conditions) and being able to see a list of sales tax records.

DETAILED PROGRAM DESCRIPTION

Program: Add, change, list, or erase sales tax records (called SALESTAX records in database).

Step 1: User is asked: Add, change, list, erase, or return to Main Menu. (Note: there are very specific standards for this menu screen. See the pro forma Main Menu in the file STDMNU.PNL.)

Step 2: If the "change" or "erase" option is selected, a prompt for values for the two keys of the SALESTAX record is given. The key values of the record occurrence to be changed/erased is awaited. Either key values or (CR) can be entered. If keys are entered and the corresponding sales tax record is found then the system proceeds to Step 4. If a (CR) is entered (or a SALETAX record with the key values entered cannot be found) then a list of SALESTAX records is displayed and one may be selected from the list before proceeding to Step 4.

If the "list" option is selected then a prompt is given to enter a starting code at which the list will begin. If one is given, this is where the list starts; otherwise, the list starts at the beginning, if a (CR) is entered.

Step 3: If a listing of sales tax records is requested, an opportunity is provided to enter the keys of the first sales tax that will appear on the list. Either a pair of key values or only the Enter Key can be given as a response. If only the Enter key is pressed then the list begins with the first sales tax in the SYSSTAX set (set of all sales tax records).

The listing has the following columns:

1. Name of nation and state (NATNSTAT)

2. Name of taxing authority (AUTHRITY)

3. Total Locations Linked (count members of STAXCLOC, STAXSC and STAXWLOC, which are the customer locations, supplier locations, and company warehouse locations, respectively).

The listing displays 19 rows at a time. To move from one set of 19 rows to the next, press the "Pg Dn" key.

An inverse video bar can be moved up or down the list using the arrow or page keys and when Enter Key is pressed that record is displayed on the screen as defined in Step 4.

Step 4: The form shown below is displayed on the screen (with values filled in unless user wants to "add").

SALES TAX RECORD
Nation/State: _____
Tax Authority: _____
Tax Rate(%):   _____ . _____

The user fills in, or revises, the data in the above screen. Then the system creates, or changes, a sales tax record in the database to correspond to the data on the screen.

Step 5: If user wants to erase a sales tax record, the program should first check to see if there are any members of any of the sets STAXCLOC, STAXSC or STAXWLOC. If there are not, the program deletes the SALESTAX record as requested. If there are, the user is informed of the number of each type and asked if he wishes to delete the SALESTAX record anyway. The program then does or does not delete the record as requested.

Step 6: Return to Step 1.

Index